**DECISION BY DEBATE**

# DECISION BY DEBATE

Douglas Ehninger & Wayne Brockriede

⌘⌘

international debate education association

New York • Amsterdam • Brussels

Published by:
International Debate Education Association
400 West 59th Street
New York, NY 10019

Introduction © 2008 International Debate Education Association
All rights reserved. No part of this publication may be reproduced or transmitted in any form or by any means, electronic or mechanical, including photocopy, or any information storage and retrieval system, without permission from the publisher.

Library of Congress Control Number: 2008934128

ISBN: 978-1-932716-47-4

Printed in the USA

**IDEBATE PRESS**

KEY TITLES IN RHETORIC, ARGUMENTATION, AND DEBATE makes available important texts and monographs that have long been unavailable. Revised or reissued with new prefaces, the books in this series are significant texts that offer teachers valuable resources long missing from their classrooms.

Books in the series include:
- *Logical Self-Defense* by Ralph H. Johnson and J. Anthony Blair
- *Perspectives on Argumentation: Essays in Honor of Wayne Brockriede* by Robert Trapp and Janice Schuetz
- *Elements of Logic* by Richard Whately
- *Decision by Debate* by Douglas Ehninger and Wayne Brockriede

IDEBATE Press is actively soliciting other volumes for this series. If you know of a valuable text that we should reissue, please send us your suggestions. If you are the author of an out-of-print text you think might be appropriate, please contact us. You can reach us at: IDEA@willamette.edu.

For books from IDEBATE Press, go to:
http://www.idebate.org/main/books.asp

# Preface to the IDEBATE Press reissue of *Decision by Debate*

In his introduction to the first edition of *Decision by Debate*, Karl Wallace situates Ehninger and Brockriede's volume within "the great tradition of public address," arguing that its fusion of a "self-critical and self-regulative method" with a perspective on reasoning "appropriate to action and its values" makes the text far more than "merely another book on argumentation and debate." As a consequence, he predicts that its significance could approach that of a "book like Richard Whateley's *Elements of Rhetoric*."[1] Wallace thus implicitly contrasts the work with more rationalistic approaches to the study of argumentation, debate, and rhetoric embodied in textbooks by Austin J. Freeley, Arthur N. Kruger, and James Howard McBurney, Glen Earl Mills, and James O'Neil, or Lester Thonssen and Albert Craig Baird's well-known *Speech Criticism*.[2]

Wallace's assessment synthesizes the way *Decision by Debate* positions debate within a theory of argumentation that integrates the methodological and the rhetorical. Its methodological or epistemological dimensions stem from its treatment of debate as cooperative inquiry because such activity is both reflective and self-regulative. This placement counters criticisms of the early 1960s that characterized debating as an uncritical, combative activity aimed at subduing competing positions. That characterization stemmed from the juxtaposition of debate with the cooperative method of inquiry labeled discussion, a perspective inspired by the work of John Dewey.[3]

Rather than embracing a cooperative–competitive dichotomy, Ehninger and Brockriede detail two approaches to decision making: the "internal" method of dialectic and discussion and the "external" method of debate. Internal modes, which result in capitulation, compromise, or consensus, feature decision making by the participants involved in discourse—through either dialectic's question–answer or discussion's exchange and evaluation of information and ideas by small groups. Debate, however, is an external method in which restrained partisans take the risk of testing their ideas within a system

---

1 "Editor's Introduction,"(New York: Dodd, Mead, 1963), v–vi.
2 Austin J. Freeley, *Argumentation and Debate: Rational Decision Making* (San Francisco: Wadsworth, 1961); Arthur N. Kruger, *Modern Debate: Its Logic and Strategy* (New York: McGraw-Hill, 1960); James Howard McBurney, Glen Earl Mills, and James O'Neil, *Argumentation and Debate: Techniques of a Free Society* (New York: Macmillan, 1951); Lester Thonssen and Albert Craig Baird, *Speech Criticism: The Development of Standards for Rhetorical Appraisal* (New York: The Ronald Press, 1948).
3 *Decision by Debate*, 16.

governed by rules that (1) give each position an equal opportunity to be heard and (2) cede decision-making power to an informed outside agent who renders a decision only after hearing the entire debate.[4]

Such an interaction is reflective because it probes the strengths and weaknesses of contending positions and defers judgment until both cases are heard; it is self-regulative because it subscribes to rules fostering fairness. Debate tests ideas and renders decisions at the public level when other methods fail to generate a decision. Interestingly, the authors compare debating a proposition to a scientist's testing of a hypothesis, arguing that to enter into debate is to agree to abide by social constraints governing an investigative process, constraints that create conditions placing decision makers in position to make an informed decision. Rather than being mere advocacy, then, debate is a reflective, self-regulative method of decision making that serves an epistemological as well as a pragmatic function.[5]

The rhetorical dimensions of *Decision by Debate* stem from the authors' adaptation of ideas drawn from Stephen Toulmin's *The Uses of Argument*.[6] Ehninger and Brockriede merge his model, a jurisprudential alternative to systems derived from formal logic, with the distinction between field dependence and field invariance to create a foundation for analyzing arguments, propositions, and controversies. They argue that Toulmin's model involves a dynamic rather than static description of arguments as moving from believed data/evidence to a problematic claim/conclusion authorized by the reasoning implied in a warrant. Hence, argumentation is a process of making inferences. Supplementing this basic structure are three additional elements: backing stipulates the principles grounding warrants; rebuttals limit the scope of a claim by specifying conditions under which it will not hold; a qualifier indicates its force by articulating the degree of confidence attributed to it.

The authors use this structure to create a typology of arguments centered around kinds of claims and propositions (designative or fact; definitive or definition; evaluative or value; advocative or policy), patterns/kinds of reasoning (substantive or *logos*; motivational or *pathos*; authoritative or *ethos*), and possible weaknesses associated with each of the elements of the model.[7] Thus, they create an approach to public argumentation that advances pedagogy but

---

4 Ibid., 7–11.
5 Ibid., Chapters 1 and 2. The book's first two chapters are an extension of Douglas Ehninger, "Decision by Debate: A Re-Examination," *Quarterly Journal of Speech* 45 (1959): 282–288.
6 Stephen Edleston Toulmin. *The Uses of Argument* (Cambridge: Cambridge University Press, 1958).
7 Chapters 8–13; these chapters expand earlier work contained in Wayne Brockriede and Douglas Ehninger, "Toulmin on Argument: An Interpretation and Application," *Quarterly Journal of Speech* 46 (1960): 44–53.

also proffers a critical analysis of argumentative practice as based in the material reality of arguers.

The rhetorical properties of the analysis embedded in *Decision by Debate* flow from Ehninger and Brockriede's interpretation of the distinction between field invariance and field dependence. Field invariant factors are those that transcend situations, whereas field dependent ones are unique to a particular venue/situation/context. In other words, depending on the context—legal, religious, personal, or political, for example—different rules/standards and patterns of reasoning apply.[8] The distinction highlights the rhetorical nature of arguments as being made by and directed toward persons who participate in decision making in concrete situations. The definition of data or evidence as that which people believe[9] implies a person-centered argumentation, as does the idea that claims are conclusions that need support by credible data and warrants to be plausible. The idea that warrants have backing drawn from the specific discipline or context validating them depicts argumentation by individuals positioned in a material reality in which standards for drawing inferences vary situationally. Rebuttals and qualifiers that delimit an argument's scope and force imply that such discourse is both person- and context-centered. Hence, the movement from data through the inference implicit in a warrant to a claim is not a matter of manipulating relationships among facts using abstract logical principles. Rather, it is a rhetorical activity in which people make and justify choices relevant to themselves and the conditions in which they live.[10]

The era that spawned *Decision by Debate* was a time in which rhetorical studies were expanding exponentially and the discipline of speech was morphing into speech communication on its eventual way to being simply communication. In his keynote address to the first Alta Conference on Argumentation in 1979, Bruce E. Gronbeck identified the shift in the study of argument and debate as one in which argument became argumentation.[11] Ehninger and Brockriede's work established a foundation for this transformation through its unique grounding of debate as method in material rhetorical action. Scholarship in succeeding decades followed two interrelated trajectories, ones reflecting the concepts set forth in *Decision by Debate*.

8 *Decision by Debate*, 6.
9 The authors devote Chapter 13 to a discussion of the nature of belief.
10 Brockriede extends these ideas in a later essay, "Where Is Argument?" *Journal of the American Forensic Association* 11 (1975): 179–182.
11 "From Argument to Argumentation: Fifteen Years of Identity Crises," Proceedings of the Summer Conference on Argumentation, ed. Jack Rhodes and Sara Newell (Annandale, VA: Speech Communication Association, 1980), 8–19.

x    PREFACE TO THE IDEBATE PRESS REISSUE

The first was an expansion of the range of discourses and activities viewed from an argumentative perspective. Toulmin, Richard Rieke, and Allan Janik, for example, described the forms and actions of arguers in such diverse venues as the law, science, the arts, and business.[12] Their work and that of myriad others examined both the discursive forms and the processes involved in the advancing of reasons recommending attitudes and actions.[13] Such study implied a plurality of standards for judging arguments. Hence, a second strain extended *Decision by Debate's* rhetorical take on method by detailing actions and standards supporting argumentative validity. Ehninger addressed argument as "method";[14] Brockriede wrote about "human understanding" and examined the relationships among "constructs, experience, and argument";[15] Robert L. Scott saw rhetoric as "epsitemic";[16] Walter R. Fisher proffered what he termed a "logic of good reasons" as the basis for his narrative paradigm;[17] still others referenced Chaim Perelman and Lucie Olbrechts-Tyteca's "universal audience,"[18] Jurgen Habermas's "ideal speech situation,"[19] and Toulmin's "impartial rational standpoint."[20] In various ways, each of these strains mirrored the framing of method within rhetorical action articulated by Ehninger and Brockriede.[21] Hence, *Decision by Debate* is a seminal work in the study of argumentation and rhetoric because it depicts debate and argumentation as a critical method grounded in rhetorical processes.

Karen Rasmussen
California State University–Long Beach
July 2008

---

12 Stephen Toulmin, Richard Rieke, and Allan Janik, *An Introduction to Reasoning*, 2nd ed. (New York: Macmillan, 1984), 271–392.
13 The following collections addressing both rhetoric and argumentation are indicative of this trend: Robert J. Kibler and Larry E. Barker, eds. *Conceptual Frontiers in Speech Communication* (New York: Speech Association of America, 1969); Lloyd F. Bitzer, Edwin Black, and Karl Richards Wallace, eds. *The Prospect of Rhetoric* (Englewood Cliffs, NJ: Prentice-Hall, 1971).
14 "Argument as Method: Its Nature, Its Limitations, and Its Uses," *Speech Monographs* 37 (1970): 101–111. Ehninger was influenced by the ideas of Natanson and Johnstone. See, for example, Maurice Natanson and Henry W. Johnstone, *Philosophy, Rhetoric, and Argumentation* (University Park: Pennsylvania State University Press, 1965).
15 "Arguing about Human Understanding," *Communication Monographs* 49 (1982): 137–147; "Constructs, Experience, and Argument," *Quarterly Journal of Speech* 71 (1985): 171–163. See also Wayne Brockriede, "Rhetorical Criticism as Argument," *Quarterly Journal of Speech* 60 (1974): 165–174.

16 "On Viewing Rhetoric as Epistemic," *Central States Speech Journal* 18 (1967): 9–17.
17 "Toward a Logic of Good Reasons," *Quarterly Journal of Speech* 64 (1978): 376–384; *Human Communication as Narration: Toward a Philosophy of Reason, Value, and Action*. (Columbia: University of South Carolina Press, 1987).
18 Chaim Perelman, and Lucie Olbrechts-Tyteca, *The New Rhetoric: A Treatise on Argumentation*, trans. John Wilkinson and Purcell Weaver (Notre Dame, Ind.: Notre Dame University Press, 1969).
19 See especially Jurgen Habermas, *Communicaiton and the Evolution of Society*, trans. Thomas McCarthy (Boston: Beacon, 1979) and "Towards a Theory of Communicative Competence," *Recent Sociology* 2, ed. Hans Peter Dreitzel (London: Collier-Macmillan, 1970) 114–148.
20 Stephen Toulmin, *Human Understanding*, vol. 1, *The Connective Use and Evolution of Concepts* (Princeton, NJ: Princeton University Press, 1972).
21 Two 1990's collections that illustrate the way studies in argumentation have continued to develop are: Robert Trapp and Janice Schuetz, eds., *Perspectives on Argumentation: Essays in Honor of Wayne Brockriede* (Prospect Heights, IL: Waveland, 1990); William L. Benoit, Dale Hample, and Pamela J. Benoit, eds., *Readings in Argumentation: Pragmatics and Discourse Analysis* (New York: Foris Publications, 1992).

# Editor's Introduction

VIEWED IN a social context, this book is in the great tradition of public address. The free societies of the Western world—from Plato to the present—have drawn upon the theory and practice of discourse to help nourish public thought and discussion and to sustain representative government. For men who are willing to make up their minds—or who *must* make up their minds—in the formal interplay of intellect upon intellect, the processes of debate have ever been indispensable to efficient deliberation. Viewed in an educational context, this book is for young men and women who wish to use their brains and their unique talent of language to acquire those habits of critical thought that are always revealed when a responsible person freely submits his resolution of a problem to the candid and public test of other minds.

The authors, in my opinion, have not written merely another book in argumentation and debate. They see clearly that debate is an instrument of critical thought, that it requires its practitioners to think reflectively and calls upon the audience as judge to weigh and consider. Its methods are self-critical and self-correcting of error because the form of debate demands that contending ideas be systematically examined. Indeed, the habit of the debater is no less self-critical and self-regulative than the habit of the scientist. Both expect and invite rigorous judgment from their fellows.

The authors are fully aware of the classic relationships between thinking that is directed to theoretical ends and thinking that is intended to influence conduct and behavior. They recognize, accordingly, that the mathematical logic appropriate to scientific thought is not directly useful in discussing those social problems upon which men must come to decision and take action. So in presenting the modes of logical analysis, proof, and evidence they have adopted the point of view of certain modern philosophers. These are the men who bring together logic and ethics and who have identified processes of reasoning held to be more appropriate to action and its values than the logic of science and of the categorical syllogism. For the layout of argument the authors have drawn specifically upon Stephen Toulmin. As a consequence, this book may make a major contribution to the methods of practical argument.

Possibly it contributes more to the textbook literature of debate than any work since Laycock and Scales' *Argumentation and Debate* (1907) and Baker and Huntington's *The Principles of Argumentation* (1905), and, indeed, some may regard it as approaching the significance of a book like Richard Whately's *Elements of Rhetoric* (1828).

At least two other virtues of this book deserve mention. The authors not only view modern debating with a philosophic eye; they confront the problems of oral presentation and of college debate as it is practiced. Style and delivery are treated with sufficient scope and detail to provide self-contained instruction. Neither teacher nor student has to assume prior familiarity with those aspects of speaking. The points of view, modes, problems, and values of college debate are discussed with thoroughness and judicial calm. I believe Professors Ehninger and Brockriede have produced a distinguished book from which discerning directors of debate and their students can profit.

KARL R. WALLACE

# *Preface*

DECISION BY DEBATE reflects ten principles:
1. Debate as a method of decision provides for the rigorous examination and testing of pertinent data and inferences through the give-and-take of informed controversy. Hence, properly employed, it is a means for arriving at judgments that are reflective and decisions that are critical.
2. A debater is not a propagator who seeks to win unqualified acceptance for a predetermined point of view while defeating an opposing view. Rather, when he places himself in the highest tradition of debate, he is an investigator who co-operates with fellow investigators in searching out the truth or in selecting that course of common action which seems best for all concerned, debaters and public alike.
3. Debate is not limited to a particular type of subject matter, a particular sort of audience, or a particular mode of discourse. It is a generic species of deliberation, the principles and procedures of which are applicable to informed, responsible controversy however and wherever it may take place.
4. One learns about debate and becomes skilled in its use in three different but related ways: by the thoughtful observation and analysis of debates, past and present; by guided practice; and by gaining an understanding of the theory of debate, as embodied in the discipline of argumentation. No one of these methods of learning is less important than the others; all deserve equal attention from the student and equal emphasis by the teacher.
5. Research is an indispensable part of reflective decision-making. One does not become a debater at the moment he rises to speak or sits down to write. He becomes a debater long before—when he begins his study of the problem about which he will eventually propound judgments. Debate is a process that reaches from tentative explorations of subject matter to the final decision.
6. Traditional Aristotelian logic provides an imperfect description of how men actually reason today in argumentative controversies. A more accurate and useful logic for today may be inferred from the formulations of the contemporary English logician Stephen Toulmin.
7. Personal and emotional proofs, no less than logical proofs, are

relevant to critical decisions. An extension of Toulmin's analysis of argument provides a formula whereby personal, emotional, and logical proofs may be reduced to a common structure and made subject to comparable tests. The debater is thus able to bring all three modes of artistic proof within the framework of critical controversy.

8. While the ultimate goal of the philosopher may be to exhibit relationships among ideas *per se,* the ultimate goal of the debater is to use ideas as proofs for influencing the beliefs of listeners or readers. A knowledge of how belief functions is, therefore, an essential part of the debater's study.

9. The effective communication of arguments to others depends on adeptness in style and delivery. Clarity and attractiveness are the common criteria, and these criteria urge that debaters express each argument so that it will be given exactly the weight it deserves—no more and no less.

10. Practice debates in the classroom and in college forensics tournaments are not ends in themselves, but means of developing the skills and attitudes necessary for responsible participation in the debating situations of later life where free citizens determine public policy.

These ten principles of *Decision by Debate,* we believe, reveal the major ways in which this book differs from other textbooks in argumentation. The characterization of debate as an instrument for critical investigation is in contrast to the view that debate is a systematic procedure for entering predetermined judgments into conflict. The belief that debate is a generic species of deliberation which encompasses written as well as oral discourse is quite at variance with the view of debate as an exclusively oral activity whose natural habitat is a forensics tournament. The conviction that research is as much a part of the debater's task as presentation accounts for the greater than customary emphasis here given to techniques for finding, evaluating, and recording data. The belief that the formulas of traditional logic provide an imperfect description of real-life argumentative deliberation leads us to our attempt to apply Toulmin's contemporary method. The attempt in this text to reduce personal, emotional, and logical proofs to a common formula, and to relate these modes to the process by which a reader or listener arrives at his beliefs was prompted by dissatisfaction with the still prevalent distinction between "logical" argumentation and "emotional" persuasion. And, finally, the disproportionate emphasis which many argumentation textbooks give to analysis, evidence, and inference at the expense of style and delivery leads us to stress the importance of effective communication in rational decision-making.

The persons who have influenced us in arriving at these points of emphasis are too numerous to list here. Stephen Toulmin deserves special mention. Moreover, we recognize gratefully the help of dozens of students, colleagues, and friends who have helped to shape our thinking and who as this book was being written patiently served as critics of our views and foils for our arguments. Permission to reprint certain materials has been granted, and we specifically acknowledge such permissions in appropriately located footnotes.

At several stages during its preparation the manuscript was read and criticized by Professor Karl R. Wallace of the University of Illinois. On one occasion each, Professors Bower Aly of the University of Oregon and Carroll Arnold of Cornell University read the manuscript and made many helpful suggestions. The section on statistical proof was read and criticized by Professor Roger Nebergall of the University of Oklahoma. Mr. Edward F. Webster, college editor of Dodd, Mead & Company, has offered advice, assistance, and encouragement from the inception of the project to its completion. For the gracious and generous help of these readers we are most appreciative. The responsibility for errors of omission and commission, however, is wholly ours.

In an earlier and somewhat different form the substance of Chapter 2 was published in *The Quarterly Journal of Speech,* and some of the underlying principles of Chapters 8, 10, and 11 were sketched in an article that appeared in the same journal.[1] Materials from many of the other chapters were tested in classroom lectures and exercises at the University of Florida, the University of Illinois, the State University of Iowa, and the University of Oklahoma.

D. E.<br>W. B.

*October 1, 1962*

[1] Douglas Ehninger, "Decision by Debate: A Re-examination," *The Quarterly Journal of Speech,* 45 (Oct. 1959), 282–87; and Wayne Brockriede and Douglas Ehninger, "Toulmin on Argument: An Interpretation and Application," *Ibid.,* 46 (Feb. 1960), 44–53. We are using these materials with the permission of the editor of *The Quarterly Journal of Speech* and the Speech Association of America.

# Contents

EDITOR'S INTRODUCTION xiii
PREFACE xv

## Part I. INTRODUCTION

1. CHOOSING AND DECIDING CRITICALLY 3
2. THE DEBATE PROCESS 14
3. LEARNING TO DEBATE 25

## Part II. BUILDING A SUBJECT-MATTER BACKGROUND

4. OBTAINING INFORMATION: PERSONAL KNOWLEDGE, CONTACTS WITH EXPERTS 33
5. OBTAINING INFORMATION: PRINTED SOURCES 42
6. RECORDING AND FILING INFORMATION 63

## Part III. THE MATERIALS OF ARGUMENT

7. THE ANATOMY OF A DISPUTE 81
8. THE UNIT OF PROOF AND ITS STRUCTURE 98
9. EVIDENCE 110
10. SUBSTANTIVE PROOF 125
11. AUTHORITATIVE AND MOTIVATIONAL PROOFS 158
12. DETECTING DEFICIENCIES OF PROOF 168
13. THE NATURE AND SOURCES OF BELIEF 190

## Part IV. DEVELOPING ARGUMENTATIVE DISCOURSE

14. ANALYZING THE PROPOSITION 211
15. BUILDING THE CASE 233
16. ATTACK AND DEFENSE 252

| | | |
|---|---|---|
| *17.* | STYLE AND DELIVERY: CLARITY | 269 |
| *18.* | STYLE AND DELIVERY: ATTRACTIVENESS | 287 |

## Part V. ARGUMENTATIVE DISCOURSE IN PRACTICE: COLLEGE DEBATE

| | | |
|---|---|---|
| *19.* | A PHILOSOPHY OF COLLEGE DEBATE | 301 |
| *20.* | TYPES OF COLLEGE DEBATE | 318 |
| *21.* | EVALUATING COLLEGE DEBATE | 338 |
| *Appendix A:* | A SAMPLE COLLEGE DEBATE | 351 |
| *Appendix B:* | A SAMPLE PUBLIC DEBATE | 376 |
| *Appendix C:* | THE BRIEF | 393 |
| *Index* | | 413 |

*Part 1*  INTRODUCTION

*Chapter 1*

# CHOOSING AND DECIDING CRITICALLY

*The great impediment to action is, in our opinion, not discussion, but the want of that knowledge which is gained by discussion preparatory to action.* PERICLES

WHEN MEN are called on to make choices or decisions, they proceed in one of two ways. Either they examine the available evidence and survey accepted motives and values to discover what conclusion may be warranted, or, disregarding evidence and values, they leap to a conclusion impulsively on the basis of desire, superstition, or prejudice. Decisions of the first sort are called "critical"; those of the second sort, "uncritical."

## THE VALUE OF CRITICAL CHOICE AND DECISION

For at least three reasons, critical decisions are superior to uncritical ones, and therefore to be preferred.

*A critical decision is more reliable than a decision that is arrived at uncritically, because it is based on a careful study of pertinent evidence and values.* Not only does it have a better chance of proving true when put to the test or of working out successfully in practice, but it is able to withstand what John Dewey described as "the strain of further inquiry." [1] It furnishes a premise for valid predictions, a foundation on which additional beliefs and judgments may safely be erected. When attacked, a critical decision does not weaken or crumble. Instead, by the very act of defending itself it takes on new vitality.

The dependability and productivity of critical judgments may best be seen in science, where no premise is accepted until it has been fully

[1] *Logic: The Theory of Inquiry* (New York: Henry Holt & Co., 1938), p. 6.

warranted by the facts. Science not only yields useful knowledge at the moment, but is self-progressive in the sense that each accepted judgment enables man to advance into new realms of knowledge.

As in science, so in the choices and decisions of everyday life—the student who prejudges the competence or strictness of an instructor; the voter who, instead of studying the issues, acts from prejudice; the man who decides according to desire can be right only by accident, not by design. Each of these persons gambles on arriving at the correct judgment, and he gambles against long odds.

In critical choices and decisions, on the contrary, the gamble is reduced. Because judgment is suspended until facts, motives, and values are taken into account, the chances of making wise decisions are greatly improved. When men decide critically, they guarantee, insofar as is humanly possible, the validity of the decision at which they arrive.

*A critical decision is more flexible than an uncritical one.* Because critical choices and decisions are attuned to accepted facts, motives, and values, they are subject to reexamination in a way that uncritical judgments are not.

When a man or society thinks critically, each new problem is approached without the binding restrictions of earlier commitments. As additional facts become known, conclusions are altered to conform with improved knowledge; as motives and values change, conclusions, too, are modified. The critical attitude cultivates tentativeness, a readiness to learn anew and, if necessary, to start afresh. Its keynote is adaptability, its course a never-ending process of adjustment that keeps conclusions relative to the world as it is known or believed to be.

Uncritical decisions lack flexibility. They are hard set in the cement of desire or prejudice. They tend to categorize things once and for all, to erect permanent barriers and assign labels that can henceforth be resorted to without reflection. As a result, uncritical decisions often become outmoded before they are discarded.

A society whose decisions are inflexible is blind to the changing ways of the world. It sees only a part of the facts or adheres to values that may no longer be valid. It can never fully understand or realistically adjust to the problems that confront it in the present.

*A critical decision is more "human," i.e., rational, than an uncritical one.* The ability to arrive at decisions critically is the trait that chiefly distinguishes man from animal. Animals are bound by instinct and habit. By making choices and decisions that are critical, man rises above instinct and comes to a fuller realization of his potentiality as a rational being. John Erskine has said that man has the "moral obligation to be intelligent."

Do the facts warrant this particular decision? Do socially approved motives endorse it? Do accepted values support it? These are the distinctively human questions on which a judgment may and should be based.

Even the most thoughtful individuals do not always make decisions critically. The scientist or philosopher, when he steps outside his study, may lose the critical attitude and decide without due attention to evidence and values. Nor in the realm of human actions, where problems press and dangers threaten, is it always possible to delay a decision until "all of the facts are in."

Critical choices and decisions are, however, the ideal toward which wise men strive. For though they fall short in the attainment, the striving itself sets them in the proper direction. Hitler bellowed, "Wir denken mit unserem Blut" ("We think with our blood"), and led the world into war. Adlai Stevenson speaks for a saner and happier society when he emphasizes the importance of critical decision-making in our own democratic culture.

The tradition of critical inquiry and discussion informs our entire civilization. Our scientific progress is based upon a final belief in rational order. At its finest, our religious tolerance is based upon the belief that man's dignity demands that he should make his own search—and find, through freedom to know and to see, the truth which he has it in him to find. And in the field to which fate seems particularly to have assigned me—the field of politics—I claim that our political institutions reflect, profoundly and dynamically, the critical view of life. As Walter Bagehot said: "It was government by discussion that broke the bond of ages and set free the originality of mankind." [2]

Today as never before the rational control of individual and collective behavior is imperative. In an age when a bomb can wipe out a city, when an event on a remote island reverberates through the capitals of the world, rational thinking is not a luxury but a necessity. We cannot afford mistakes; we cannot recover from errors. The next Pearl Harbor, as A. Whitney Griswold reminds us, "will be compounded of hydrogen." [3]

## INSTRUMENTS OF CRITICAL CHOICE AND DECISION

Through the ages countless thinkers have given their best energies to developing procedures that will enable men to make critical judgments

[2] "Party of the Second Part," *Harper's Magazine,* Feb. 1956, p. 33. Reprinted by permission of Harper & Brothers, publishers.
[3] "This Tongue-Tied Democracy," *Vital Speeches,* Nov. 1, 1954, pp. 828–32.

6   INTRODUCTION

in all areas of investigation and action.

At the root of their efforts lies the discipline of logic, which has as its task formulating and validating principles which are "field invariant" in the sense that they must guide critical thinking and deliberation in *all* areas where critical method may be applied.

Building on the "field invariant" principles of logic and adding to them "field dependent" methods suited to the subject matter he studies, the physical scientist has forged the critical tools by which the world of nature may be probed and controlled.[4] Similarly, the social scientist and historian have developed instruments for studying the human environment, past and present; the philosopher, instruments for investigating beauty, knowledge, and truth. And to banish dogmatism from disputes and enable groups of men to proceed critically toward collective choices and decisions, the rhetorician has joined the "field invariant" methods of logic with "field dependent" methods of his own discipline to develop the two modes of argumentative deliberation known as "discussion" and "debate."

## THE BASIC SIMILARITY OF CRITICAL INSTRUMENTS

To the extent that they employ "field dependent" principles and methods, critical instruments differ from one another. To the extent that they borrow from the "field invariant" principles of logic, critical instruments share a common character.

A paramount interest in disinterestedness; a greater concern with means than ends; obedience to the laws of valid inference; demand for proof over assertion, for objectivity over desire, for reflection over impulse; a dedication to the proposition that every claim must be grounded in evidence—to these "field invariant" traits all critical instruments adhere.

Moreover, by virtue of their common traits, critical instruments as a class are to be distinguished from other methods of investigation and decision-making. They are distinctive because they alone are consciously reflective, employing only thinking that has itself been thought about and tempered into a sensitive instrument for discovering and communicating "truth."

*Start out from tested facts, endorsed motives, and accepted values, not from ungrounded assumptions; check each new inference as it is intro-*

---

[4] For the terms "field invariant" and "field dependent" we are indebted to Stephen Toulmin, *The Uses of Argument* (Cambridge, England: Cambridge University Press, 1958), p. 15. A field invariant method is one that is useful to a number of areas of study and endeavor. The utility of logical method, for example, is evident in each of the natural and social sciences.

*duced; accept no conclusion that fails to square with the facts, motives, and values employed as premises.* Any critical instrument may be identified by its observance of this injunction.

## TWO METHODS FOR MAKING COLLECTIVE DECISIONS CRITICALLY

When two or more individuals attempt to arrive at a joint decision critically, through a careful study of the pertinent evidence and values, they may regard themselves as a closed group and be content with a decision that satisfies *them*. Or they may regard themselves as part of a larger group and desire that a decision be made by others, by a wider audience, a "public." The one employs methods which we shall call "internal"; the other, "external."

### THE INTERNAL METHOD

When the internal method is used, differences are resolved and a decision reached solely as a result of interaction among the persons concerned. They talk the matter over together, and through the interchange of facts and ideas hammer out a collective judgment. Neither during nor after the deliberation do they appeal to an outside adjudicating agency —a referee, judge, arbitrator, jury, board, or voting body. The decision is exclusively their own—the product of their own trials and efforts.

Under the internal method conflicts among beliefs are settled in one of three ways:

1. *Capitulation.* One or more of the contending parties capitulates, retracting his contention and allowing an alternative view to stand without further challenge. Such capitulation may be voluntary or it may be forced on a protagonist by a majority vote. In either case, the view is withdrawn and its competitor given the field.

2. *Compromise.* Each party sacrifices part of his original claim or so modifies his position that a mutually acceptable decision may be worked out. One point is conceded to save another. Statements are whittled, hacked, and remolded. Competing contentions are reshaped so as to fit together.

3. *Consensus.* Out of the interplay of conflicting ideas a decision emerges that is acceptable to all. This decision may be "created" by the discussion so that it is different from any of the opinions held by the participants at the outset; or it may be the judgment that one of the parties originally advanced. The distinguishing characteristic of a "consensus," however, is that everyone accepts it without reservation. Each

participant feels it is the best possible decision that could be reached under the circumstances.[5]

Sometimes differences are resolved and judgments formed by the three methods working in concert. Certain of the ideas represented in the decision are present because the party who originally opposed them capitulated or failed to win a majority vote. Others are there as a result of compromise or consensus. Whatever its origin, however, a decision produced by the "internal" method is always the product of the participants themselves. Each party to the deliberation plays a double role. He is both protagonist and decision-maker, both advocate of his own ideas and judge of the ideas of others. Proofs and refutations are addressed to one's fellow participants. Judgment is the product of interaction among competing ideas. There is no appeal to an outside adjudicating agency.

DIALECTIC. In earlier centuries the internal method of collective decision-making took the form of dialectic. Most modern students know something about dialectic from their reading of Plato's dialogues. In these dialogues one person questions another in order to win agreement on a question of art or morals. The discussion, directed by the questioner, turns this way and that, delving into all facets of the subject. A new idea is immediately confronted with an opposing idea, as a means of testing its worth. The questioner attempts to win agreement on each point as it is raised, so that in the end the respondent has no choice but to assent to the claim that his previous admissions jointly imply.

In dialectic, as practiced by Plato and his followers, the course of the argument was directed toward a predetermined end. Yet the deliberation itself was highly critical. Claims were made "to stand on their own legs"; evidence was subjected to searching scrutiny. The concern of the participants was for truth rather than victory. Moreover, as has already been suggested, the procedure was strictly "internal." The questioner attempted to convince the respondent. The final decision was made by the participants.

Many philosophers regret that dialectic is no longer used as a tool for probing social, moral, and aesthetic problems. Perhaps modern man lacks the ability to practice dialectic with the consummate mastery of a Socrates or Abelard; perhaps our modern "scientific" world is inhospitable to its nonexperimental method.[6] In any event, dialectic is seldom employed today, except in the graduate seminar or the midnight college "bull session." A related internal method of deliberation called

---

[5] Cf. Franklyn S. Haiman, *Group Leadership and Democratic Action* (Boston: Houghton Mifflin Co., 1951), pp. 179–82.

[6] See Walter J. Ong, S.J., *Ramus: Method, and the Decay of Dialogue* (Cambridge, Mass.: Harvard University Press, 1958).

"discussion" is preferred.

DISCUSSION. Discussion, as distinguished from dialectic, is the pattern of deliberation usually employed in conferences, committees, and other small groups.[7] It is not primarily a question–answer procedure, but an intelligent, purposeful interchange of ideas carried on in a conversational pattern. The atmosphere is informal and permissive. Individuals speak as ideas occur to them, and make brief comments and observations rather than long formal speeches.

Adapted and modified, discussion is also used in larger co-acting groups where all do not have an equal opportunity to participate. Panels, symposia, and open forum meetings, in which questions may be asked and contributions made, are examples of large-group or "public discussion" procedures. Parliamentary deliberation, where business is transacted and decisions reached according to the rules of parliamentary law, is a specialized form of large-group discussion; for here, although factions may emerge and ideas in the form of motions be accepted or rejected by vote, participants still play the double role of protagonist and judge, and decisions are made "internally."

Discussion is a valuable instrument for making collective choices and decisions. Everyone should understand its forms and develop appropriate skill in their use. But the study of discussion is an extensive subject in its own right, and one upon which we cannot enter. Our purpose here is limited to pointing out that, like dialectic, discussion in all of its forms, ranging from small-group interchange to formalized parliamentary procedure, involves an "internal" method of decision-making. The interaction is limited to the participants themselves. Differences are settled by capitulation, compromise, or consensus. A decision originates *within* the group.

## THE EXTERNAL METHOD: DEBATE

Distinguished from the "internal" method of dialectic and discussion is the "external" method known as debate. In debate the contending parties do not appeal to each other directly for judgment or decision. Instead, preserving the same critical attitude characteristic of dialectic and discussion, they deliberately alter the direction of their appeals and, rather than aiming them at each other, aim them at an outside or "external" decision-making agency—a third individual or body whose duty it is to choose among rival claims and arguments.

[7] The terms "discussion," "debate," "public discussion," "dialectic," etc., do not have well-defined meanings in popular discourse, and are, in fact, often used so loosely as to be practically interchangeable. Here we are employing them in their more restricted technical significations, as determined by the basic mode of deliberation—"internal" or "external"—to which they characteristically adhere.

10   INTRODUCTION

The decision-making agency takes many forms. It may be a board of experts called in to settle a labor dispute, or a judge or jury in a courtroom. It may be a critic in a college debate tournament, a business executive listening to an argument between subordinates, or millions of voters as they cast their ballots in a national election. Nor are the appeals addressed to the decision-making agency always the same. Sometimes they are formal, sometimes informal; sometimes spoken, sometimes written; sometimes condensed into thirty minutes or an hour, sometimes extended over weeks or months.

Regardless of the form of the appeals, or who adjudicates the dispute, the requirements of debate as a distinctive mode of deliberation are satisfied if (*a*) the debaters direct their appeals to an "external" agency and agree to abide by its decision, and (*b*) the appeals are critical in nature.

The first requirement—the direction of the appeals—distinguishes debate from the internal method followed by dialectic and discussion, and makes it a form of deliberation in which a decision is sought by "arbitration" rather than by capitulation, compromise, or consensus. The second requirement—that the deliberation be critical—relates debate to dialectic and discussion as an instrument of critical decision-making, and sharply distinguishes it from the uncritical method of decision by prejudice, desire, superstition, or impulse.

Formally defined, *debate is a mode of critical decision-making in which the contending parties appeal to an adjudicating agency acting in the role of arbitrator, and agree to abide by the decision that agency hands down.*

Diagrams will help make clear the distinction between the internal methods of dialectic and discussion and the external method of debate, and will show how debate, as a critical procedure, is related to critical instruments in general.

THE INTERNAL AND EXTERNAL METHODS

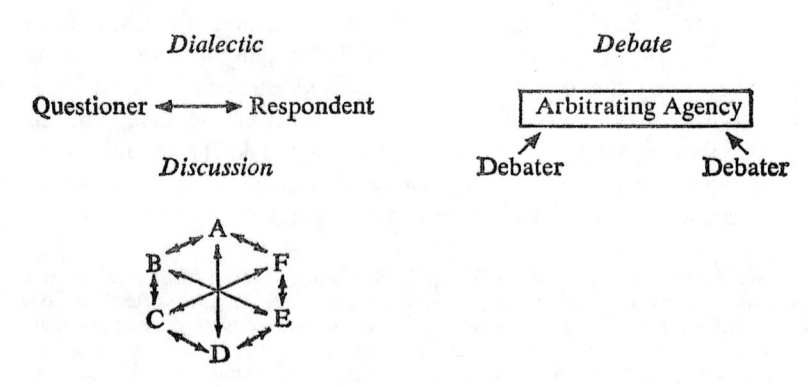

*Dialectic*                                    *Debate*

Questioner ◄─────► Respondent          | Arbitrating Agency |
                                                ↗         ↖
*Discussion*                            Debater      Debater

CHOOSING AND DECIDING CRITICALLY 11

```
                    CRITICAL INSTRUMENTS
        ┌──────────────────────┴──────────────────────┐
Methods for studying problems and      Methods for settling differences and
analyzing subject matter in order to   arriving at collective choices and
arrive at individual beliefs and       decisions
judgments                                            │
                                          ┌──────────┴──────────┐
                                       Internal              External
                                          │                     │
                                    ┌─────┴─────┐               │
                                 Dialectic   Discussion       Debate
```

Methods for studying: Method in the biological and physical sciences; Method in history and the social sciences; Method in philosophy, the humanities, etc.

Discussion subcategories: Group Discussion; Discussion in larger co-acting groups—panels, symposia, forums, etc. (public discussion); Parliamentary Procedure

## QUESTIONS

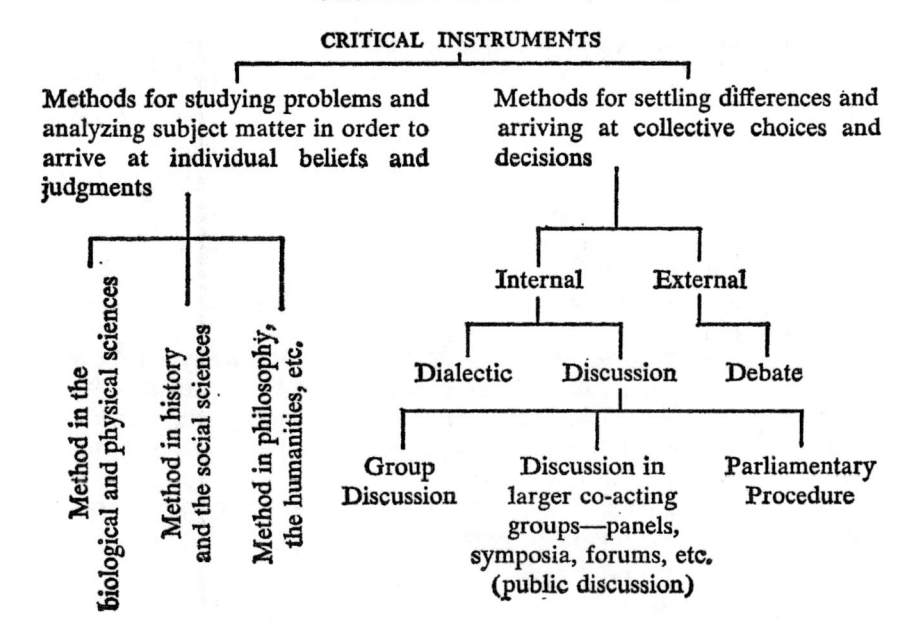

The questions here and at the end of each succeeding chapter fall into two classes. Those under "A" are essentially factual in nature and constitute a self-administering recall and comprehension test. They should be answered, preferably in writing, as soon as you have finished studying the chapter. The questions under "B" involve matters of opinion or interpretation, and are intended as a basis for class discussion. These may or may not be assigned by your instructor.

*A. To Check Your Comprehension and Memory*

1. Distinguish between "critical" and "uncritical" choices and decisions.

2. Explain why critical decisions are usually more "reliable," more "flexible," and more "worthy of man at his best" than are uncritical decisions.

3. From what discipline are the "field invariant" principles of critical thought derived?

4. What are some of the areas of investigation and action in which man attempts to think critically?

5. If man is to choose or decide critically, what must he study besides the "facts"?

6. Distinguish between the "internal" and "external" methods for making collective decisions critically.

7. How are differences resolved in the "internal" method? How in the "external"?

8. Distinguish between "dialectic" and "group discussion."
9. Define "debate."
10. Reproduce the diagram of critical instruments.

*B. For Class Discussion*

1. What reasons, other than the three given in this chapter, might be offered to prove the superiority of critical decisions over uncritical ones?

2. Are there any situations in which uncritical decisions might be preferred—in time of war or national emergency, etc.?

3. To what extent must modern man make certain judgments solely on the basis of authority?

4. What national leaders, other than Hitler, have deliberately sought to make their people think and believe uncritically? What are some of the methods they employed to do this? What were the results of their efforts?

5. Illustrate further Adlai Stevenson's proposition that the critical attitude "informs" our entire democratic culture.

6. Should we attempt to revive Platonic dialectic as a method of argumentative deliberation? Why or why not?

# EXERCISES

*A. Written Exercises*

1. Keep a record of your personal choices and decisions over a half-day, one-day, or two-day period. How many of them would you say were entirely critical? How many were, for one reason or another, essentially uncritical? Think now particularly of those you have decided are uncritical. Would you have reached the same choice or judgment had you employed a strictly critical method?

2. Find in a newspaper, magazine, or in one of your textbooks the record of some statement or action that seems to you to reflect an uncritical choice or judgment. Find another that seems to reflect a critical decision. Tell in each case why you evaluated these instances as you did.

3. Examine carefully the grounds of one of your long-standing beliefs regarding some political or social issue. To what degree does it appear to rest on uncritical grounds?

4. Look up in an unabridged dictionary (the *New English Dictionary* preferably) the etymology and historical development of each of the following terms: debate, dialectic, discussion, fact, rhetoric, compromise, consensus, and arbitration.

5. Examine carefully three advertisements in one of the popular magazines or three radio or television commercials. To what extent does each invite critical judgment? To what extent is each aimed at winning an uncritical response? In those cases where critical judgment is by-passed, what methods or devices are used to influence decision?

B. *Oral Exercise*

Prepare and present to the class a five-minute speech on one of the following subjects or on a similar subject suggested by one of these:

Democracy and the Critical Attitude
Talking It Out vs. Fighting It Out
Criticalness as an Ideal
Attacks on Critical Thought and Deliberation (by propagandists, dictators, advertisers, etc.)
Socrates' Crusade for Examined Ideas and Beliefs
The Social Consequences of Uncritical Beliefs and Choices
"The Moral Obligation to be Intelligent"
Critical Thinking and the Mass Media

## SUGGESTIONS FOR FURTHER READING

Mortimer Adler, *Dialectic* (New York: Harcourt, Brace & Co., 1927). Tackle this only if you are prepared to give your intellectual muscles a strenuous but rewarding workout.

Albert Myrton Frye and Albert William Levi, *Rational Belief: An Introduction to Logic* (New York: Harcourt, Brace & Co., 1941). The whole book is pertinent, but see especially Chapter 15, "The Foundations of Rational Belief," and Chapter 20, "The Spirit and Method of Science."

Irving J. Lee, *How to Talk with People* (New York: Harper & Brothers, 1952). Tells how adherence to certain critical methods and attitudes may help to prevent some of the troubles that arise when people try to make collective choices and decisions.

Martin Meyer, *Madison Avenue, U.S.A.* (New York: Harper & Brothers, 1958). A reporter takes a candid look at the advertising business, its methods and morals.

Clyde R. Miller, *The Process of Persuasion* (New York: Crown Publishers, 1946). An older, but still pertinent and interesting analysis of the non-critical methods of persuasion. Good popular reading.

Vance Packard, *The Hidden Persuaders* (New York: David McKay Co., 1957). An explanation and criticism of the so-called "depth approach" in advertising and selling; how the advertiser often resorts to uncritical means.

Wilbur Schramm, *Responsibility in Mass Communication* (New York: Harper & Brothers, 1958). The role of the mass media in society and the ethics that should govern their use.

## Chapter 2

# THE DEBATE PROCESS

*It is impossible even to discover our misunderstandings except on the basis of a common world which makes possible better understandings.* MORRIS COHEN

## THE FUNCTION OF DEBATE

Debates, like all forms of inquiry and deliberation, originate in a felt difficulty. Is something so or not so? What does something mean? How should something be evaluated? What course of action is required? Such problem-questions lie at the foundation of every debate.

But while all debates originate in problems, not all problems are settled by debates. Consider these two sets of questions: (1) Do more people live in Paris than in Chicago? How cold is it outside this morning? Does the soil in this field contain an alkali? (2) Does capital punishment deter crime? Is progressive education anti-intellectual? Should we strengthen the United Nations?

At first glance, the problems raised by the questions in these two groups may appear similar. When one tries to answer them, however, he soon discovers they are not at all the same. The questions in the first group yield to "empirical" methods of investigation. Answers may be found in an atlas, derived from sense experience, or discovered in a laboratory.

Not so, however, with questions in the second group. Here, although facts, observations, and experiments may contribute toward the answer, they do not in themselves supply the answer. In addition, an element of personal interpretation and evaluation is required; inferences must be drawn, opinions ventured, judgments made. The deterrent effect of capital punishment cannot be measured by a rule or found in a statistical table. Whether or not progressive education is anti-intellectual depends, at least in part, on how "progressive education" and "anti-intellectualism" are defined. The advisability of strengthening the United Nations must be gauged by comparing the apparent effectiveness of the present organization with the probable effectiveness of a strengthened organization.

Questions in the first class—those that can be answered empirically—are said to be *informative;* questions in which personal judgment is also required are called *inferential. The function of debate is to enable men to make collective choices and decisions critically when inferential questions become subjects for dispute.*

To assign debate this function is not to imply that it is inferior to empirical procedures as a method for resolving differences, a court of second choice to be employed only when empirical procedures fail. Rather it is to assign debate a place alongside empirical methods, as an instrument especially adapted to performing a function they cannot serve. In settling the differences that arise in this world, a division of labor is necessary. When collective choices and decisions require personal judgment as well as facts and figures, debate helps insure that these decisions will be made critically.

## THE RATIONALE OF DEBATE

The rationale of debate as an instrument for settling inferential questions critically may be expressed in six premises:

1. Enter contrasting beliefs into full and fair competition, so their relative worth may be assessed.

2. Let such competition consist of two phases. First, set forth each belief in its own right, together with the arguments that support it. Second, test each belief by seeing how well it withstands the attacks of an informed opponent.

3. Delay decision until both views have been presented and defended.

4. Let the decision be rendered, not by the contending parties to the dispute, but by an outside judging agency.

5. Let the judging agency act as an arbitrator, and instead of merely recording the competing arguments, weigh and consider them so as to produce a decision reflectively.

6. Let the debaters agree to abide by the decision which the judging agency awards.

These premises often remain unspoken, and even debaters of long experience may not be aware of them. They are, however, the foundation on which debate as a mode of critical deliberation rests, and in terms of which it must be understood and evaluated.

## ANSWERS TO SOME CRITICISMS OF DEBATE

Failure to recognize one or more of the foregoing premises has led some writers to charge (a) that the end and method of debate are uncritical, (b) that debate is a technique of propagation rather than of investigation, and (c) that debate emphasizes the undesirable attitudes and processes of conflict, not the desirable attitudes and processes of co-operation.[1]

Properly understood, however, the premises of debate point to opposite conclusions. They tell us: (a) *the end and method of debate are critical;* (b) *debate is an instrument of investigation rather than of propagation;* (c) *debate is a co-operative rather than a competitive enterprise.*

### DEBATE AS A CRITICAL INSTRUMENT

On what ground may the end and method of debate be called critical? Cohen and Nagel suggest that the distinguishing marks of a critical instrument are two: (a) The end aimed at by that instrument is a reflective rather than an impulsive judgment. (b) The method employed in arriving at judgment is equipped with controls that render it self-regulative.[2]

Debate meets both requirements. To insure that judgment will be reflective rather than impulsive, debate in the courtroom is surrounded with an elaborate code of rules. These rules determine the types of evidence and appeal that are admissible, the points in the dispute at which they may be introduced, and sometimes even dictate the inference that must be drawn from a given fact. However, even where such regulations are not imposed, any form of debate worthy of the name—whether it occurs in the smoking car, on the street corner, or at the business conference—has embedded in its rationale two important controls that help guarantee a reflective decision: (a) Judgment is suspended until both sides have presented and defended their views (Premises 2 and 3). (b) The decision that finally emerges is made not by the contending

---

[1] Much of the theoretical groundwork for these charges was furnished more than three decades ago by the philosopher John Dewey. See especially his book, *The Public and Its Problems* (New York: Henry Holt & Co., 1927), Chapter 6, "The Problem of Method." Cf. Harrison S. Elliott, *The Process of Group Thinking* (New York: Association Press, 1928), pp. 1–8; and James H. McBurney and Kenneth G. Hance, *Discussion in Human Affairs* (New York: Harper & Brothers, 1950), pp. 3–14.

[2] Morris R. Cohen and Ernest Nagel, *An Introduction to Logic and Scientific Method* (New York: Harcourt, Brace & Co., 1934), pp. 191 ff.

parties themselves, but by a third individual or body acting in the responsible role of arbitrator (Premises 4 and 5).

Both controls are important. The first, by delaying judgment, helps insure that relevant facts and values will be weighed. The second not only promotes impartiality, but calls on the judging agency to exercise thought and reflection. For "arbitration" is an active, creative process, not to be confused with passive "acceptance." As he attends to a debate a judge is expected to be reflective, to *use* the evidence and arguments presented to arrive in his own mind at the decision they appear to warrant.

Whereas the judgment invited by debate is critical because it is *reflective*, the method employed by debate in pursuing that judgment is critical because it is *self-regulative:* (*a*) Each party has an equal opportunity to develop his view (Premises 1 and 3). (*b*) Each debater has the obligation of probing and criticizing the views of his opponent (Premise 2).

Again, the controls are significant. The first guards against victory through the forced suppression of opposition. The second not only allows but *requires* that an informed partisan probe in public a view of a matter which if adopted will result in the rejection of his opposing view. William James in his essay "The Will to Believe" termed this second control "the test of enlightened self-interest." In areas where empirical methods are inapplicable, it is, perhaps, the most searching test of an idea that can be devised.

Any control, internal or external, may, of course, be circumvented, or debate may be so ineptly practiced that much of its effectiveness is lost. Such failure, however, is human and is not to be charged against debate as a method. To do so would be to confuse a manner of discourse with "the disciplinary measures necessary to make human nature capable of the manner of discourse so regulated." [3] Inherent in the method of debate are the internal checks necessary to critical judgment. These checks will operate in proportion as one can discipline his appetites and develop his skills so as to give them effective play.

If built-in controls were not an inescapable part of debate, debate would not invariably be avoided by speakers or writers who seek to "short-circuit" the reflective process. The debater, on the other hand, believes that a reflective judgment produced by the aid of these controls is the only sort worth the winning. Valuable in its own right, such a decision, he is convinced, will also prove best for the group or society concerned.

[3] Mortimer Adler, *Dialectic* (New York: Harcourt, Brace and Co., 1927), p. 185.

## DEBATE AS A MODE OF INVESTIGATION

Why, next, should debate be regarded as a mode of investigation rather than of propagation?

Debate is a mode of investigation for the very reason that its end and method are critical. Unlike the general run of professional public persuaders—the propagandist, the ad writer, the "psychic huckster"—the debater does not seek conviction regardless of the terms. He is more concerned that decision be reflective and that his method be correct than that any particular result be obtained by his appeals. If he were primarily interested in results, he could easily find quicker and surer ways to win acceptance for his claims—ways that involve fewer risks to the cause he espouses. Such methods are available in legion; they range from the blatant devices of censorship and open threat to the subtlest modes of suggestion and indirect persuasion. Most professional persuaders resort to these methods daily. The debater, on the contrary, by the very act of selecting debate as his method, openly renounces them. Foregoing the convenience and easy sureness of "short-circuit" appeals, he shoulders the labors and accepts the risks involved in the premises we have stated. In the debater's code, judgment is delayed until "the facts are in." Argument must run the gamut of the silent criticism of the judge and the open attack of an opponent.

To understand the full significance of the choice one makes in selecting debate as his method, perform five mental experiments: (a) Inquire, "Do fanatics and rigid sectarians appeal for arbitration or for unqualified belief and unthinking acceptance?" (b) Contrast the patient examination of evidence in a court of law with the impulsive, emotionally charged decision of a mob fired by its leader. (c) Recall how frequently a certain type of candidate for political office refuses to meet his opponent in public debate. (d) Ask, "Does the advertiser contract for equal time or space for his closest competitor, and request that buyers delay their decision until both sides have been heard?" (e) Most revealing of all, perhaps, listen to an hour of earnest debating in a courtroom. Then compare it with an hour's run of radio or television commercials.

These experiments help clarify the difference between the debater and the propagandist or professional public persuader; between the way of the truth-seeker and the way of the speaker or writer whose concern is conviction, no matter what the price.

To decide whether a man is essentially an investigator or essentially a propagator, ask: Does he prefer truth at the expense of victory or victory at the expense of truth? When faced with this alternative, the man who chooses "truth" has by that choice rightfully earned the name of investigator. The man who chooses victory can only be regarded as a propagator.

Not that truth and victory are incompatible; often they coincide. As Aristotle argued, they appear to have a natural affinity for each other.[4] Our present purpose, however, is to know whether a man prefers truth to victory or victory to truth. And it is inconceivable that anyone who makes victory paramount would grant an opponent the opportunities and advantages he enjoys in free debate between equals.

Because debate is a critical instrument, it is, then, by virtue of this fact, also an instrument of investigation rather than of propagation.

## DEBATE AS A CO-OPERATIVE ENTERPRISE

How, finally, may one answer the third and last of the criticisms? Why may it be argued that debate is fundamentally a co-operative, rather than a competitive, enterprise?

Understandably, the casual observer may regard debate as a species of competition or conflict. The debater attacks an opponent's view for the purpose of defeating it and thus making his own prevail. Moreover, by the logic of debate method, the contending views are mutually exclusive. When one is accepted, the other is automatically rejected and cast aside.

At the same time, however, two important facts must be recognized. First, in debate competing ideas come into conflict within the broader framework of a distinctly co-operative endeavor—an endeavor that is co-operative because of the premises expressed above. Each party has an equal opportunity to be heard (Premises 1 and 2); each grants the other the right to examine and criticize his arguments (Premise 2); each is willing that judgment be suspended until the facts are in (Premise 3); and each agrees to abide by the decision of an external arbitrating agency (Premises 4, 5, and 6).

Contrast these stipulations with the characteristic attitudes and procedures of conflict. Here, whether the conflict involves words and propagation or physical combat and war, the picture is markedly different. In conflict, instead of granting an opponent an equal opportunity, every effort is made to curb his freedom of statement and action; instead of willingly opening one's resources to inspection, every effort is made to conceal or disguise them; instead of asking that a decision be suspended, effort is directed toward curtailing or terminating the contest; and instead of openly seeking an arbitrated decision, this sort of resolution

[4] *Rhetoric,* 1355a.

which he participates. Viewed as a generic mode of collective decision-making, debate is clearly a co-operative endeavor.

QUESTIONS

*A. To Check Your Comprehension and Memory*
1. How do all forms of inquiry and deliberation originate?
2. What does it mean to say that a question may be answered by "empirical" methods of investigation? What are some of these methods?
3. Distinguish between "informative questions" and "inferential questions."
4. What part do facts play in solving "inferential questions"?
5. Explain the basic method or rationale of debate, as set forth in the six premises.
6. On what ground may it be argued that the end and method of debate are critical?
7. Review the "internal" checks or controls that govern the debate process.
8. What did William James mean by "the test of enlightened self-interest"? Why is it a good test of the worth of a belief?
9. On what ground may it be argued that debate is a mode of investigation or inquiry?
10. Why may it be argued that the debater, unlike many professional public persuaders or propagandists, does not seek victory at any price?
11. What test is suggested for determining whether a man is essentially an "investigator" or essentially a "propagator"?
12. Why is it understandable that debate should so frequently be regarded as a species of conflict?
13. Contrast the characteristic attitudes and procedures of conflict with the stipulations and agreements entered into by the debater.
14. On what level does conflict occur in debate? What end does it serve?

*B. For Class Discussion*
1. Do "facts," as distinguished from "beliefs," ever conflict with one another? Aren't apparent conflicts in "facts" always the result of misinformation or misunderstanding?
2. Why would one be ill-advised to use debate as a means of solving problems that yield to empirical methods?
3. Which is the more reliable test of the worth of an idea: how reasonable it seems in itself, or how well it withstands criticism?
4. Refute as strongly, but yet as fairly and objectively, as you can the argument that debate is a critical instrument.
5. Refute, on the same terms, the argument that debate is a mode of investigation.
6. Refute the argument that debate is essentially a co-operative enterprise.
7. Evaluate Aristotle's argument that truth and victory have an affinity

for each other (i.e., that truth and justice have a natural superiority over untruth and injustice).

8. Do you agree that "conflict" is an inevitable aspect of all intellectual activity?

9. Why must there be an area of agreement behind every difference that causes a debate?

## EXERCISES

*A. Written Exercises*

1. List ten questions or problems that can be solved by "empirical" means, and ten that cannot.

2. Write a short paper in which you contrast the rationale of scientific method with the rationale of debate.

3. Keep a record for a week of questions you hear debated. How many should have been answered empirically?

4. List all of the ways in which debaters have to co-operate in order to make a debate possible.

*B. Oral Exercise*

Present a five-minute informative or persuasive speech on one of the following topics or on a topic suggested by one of these:

Problem-solving in Human Affairs
In Defense of Debate
How the Law Guarantees a Man a Fair Trial
Arbitration in Labor Disputes
Debate in the United Nations
Conflicts in Ideas: The Road to Truth
Testing Ideas by Criticizing Them
Keeping Debate between Political Candidates Critical

## SUGGESTIONS FOR FURTHER READING

Theodore Clevenger, Jr., "Toward a Point of View in Contest Debate," *Central States Speech Journal,* 12 (Autumn 1960), 21–26. Considers five misapprehensions concerning college debate, among them the notion that debate is primarily an exercise in propagation rather than investigation.

Dale D. Drum, "The Debate Judge as a Machine," *Today's Speech,* 4 (April 1956), 28–31. Considers the proper function of the judging agency in rendering decisions.

Halbert E. Gulley, *Essentials of Discussion and Debate* (New York: Henry Holt & Co., 1955), Chapter 1, "Definitions and Relationships." "Discussion" and "debate" as modes of argumentative deliberation are ranged along an inquiry–decision continuum. Discussion is assigned the task of formulating decisions; debate the task of selecting between alternative decisions, or impressing decisions on others. Cf. also Henry Lee Ewbank and J. Jeffery Auer, *Discussion and Debate* (New York: Appleton-Century-Crofts, 1951), Chapter 1, "What This Book Is About"; and Waldo W. Braden and Earnest Brandenburg, *Oral Decision-Making* (New York: Harper & Brothers, 1955), pp. 8–15.

James H. McBurney and Kenneth G. Hance, *Discussion in Human Affairs* (New York: Harper & Brothers, 1950), Chapter 1, "The Nature and Purpose of Discussion." After distinguishing between "inquiry" and "advocacy," the authors associate the first with "discussion," the second with "debate." Hence, they tend to regard debate as (*a*) uncritical, (*b*) an instrument of propagation, and (*c*) competitive.

Wayne N. Thompson, "Discussion and Debate: A Re-Examination," *The Quarterly Journal of Speech*, 30 (Oct. 1944), 288–99. Argues that debate should be regarded as "a device for investigating and testing rather than . . . for persuasion"; that it is critical deliberation applied to a "sharply defined area."

*Chapter 3*

# LEARNING TO DEBATE

*The perfection which is required of the finished orator is, or rather must be, like the perfection of anything else, partly given by nature, but may also be assisted by art. If you have natural power and add to it knowledge and practice, you will be a distinguished speaker.* PLATO

BECAUSE DEBATE enables men to co-operate in arriving at critical beliefs and decisions, all citizens in a democracy owe it to themselves and one another to understand the debate process and be skilled in its use. The well-being of any society depends on collective beliefs that are reliable and public decisions that are wise; and in a democracy such beliefs and decisions are formulated through the free participation of all.

But beyond its connection with the opportunities and duties of citizenship in a democratic society, training in debate is an integral part of a liberal education. In a frequently quoted passage from "The Educated Man," now more than a century old, Cardinal Newman included among the aims of liberal training these habits of mind: "a clear, conscious view of . . . opinions and judgments, a truth in developing them, an eloquence in expressing them, and a force in urging them"; the ability "to see things as they are, to get right to the point, to disentangle a skein of thought, to detect what is sophistical, to discard what is irrelevant." Professor A. Craig Baird, a representative writer of our own generation, sets forth a similar list: "elasticity of thought, power to state great issues, judgment in their solution, [and] increased facility in the communication of those judgments. . . ."[1]

Indeed, most men who have pondered the question agree that a liberal education involves more than the acquiring of knowledge. If facts and values are to be of use in the world, they must be put to the

[1] "Argumentation as a Humanistic Subject," *The Quarterly Journal of Speech*, 10 (June 1924), 260.

task of discovering new facts and arriving at improved values.[2]

Central, then, to the democratic philosophy is the premise that public choices shall be arrived at through the free participation of all; central to the theory of a liberal education is the premise that facts and values must be put to work in deriving and communicating enlightened judgments. Training in debate contributes to both of these ends. It teaches men to test facts and values critically; it teaches them how to use facts in arriving at wise collective judgments. The question is not, Should free men who are liberally educated be skilled in debate? Rather it is, How may they learn about debate most efficiently?

## THREE METHODS OF LEARNING

Long centuries of experience have taught that one may learn about debate and become skilled in its use in three different but related ways: *(a) by the thoughtful observation and analysis of debates, past and present; (b) by guided practice; and (c) by gaining an understanding of the theory of debate, as embodied in the discipline of argumentation.*

### OBSERVATION AND ANALYSIS

The world about us is, and always has been, filled with debates. Some took place long ago and are recorded in books or in old newspapers and magazines. Others are going on today over radio and television, in the courtroom and schoolhouse, on the public platform, and in the press.

There is no surer way to gain an appreciation of the role debate has played in the history of the Western world and plays in our world today than to study the debates great public controversies generate. In addition, such study increases one's own potential as a debater. To read or hear a debate is to enter into a laboratory where textbook rules are given blood and brought to life. But even more important, such observation shows the variety of circumstances in which each principle of analysis, proof, and refutation may appropriately be employed. Just as one never truly understands an idea until he is able to express it in his own words, so he never understands a principle of proof or refutation until he has seen it exemplified in many different situations.

Before long your instructor may ask that you attend a debate held on the campus or in the community or that you report on a debate that has been printed. Welcome such an assignment. At first some of the nuances and finer turns of thought may be missed. Even the basic clash

---

[a] See Hoyt Hudson, *Educating Liberally* (Stanford, Calif.: Stanford University Press, 1945), pp. 32–56.

of arguments may be difficult to follow. Over a period of time, however, observation becomes increasingly meaningful, and should even prove exciting. Two quite different types of debates that might profitably be studied are included in the Appendix (pp. 351–92).

## GUIDED PRACTICE

The second way one learns to debate is to practice in oral and written form the various skills and routines debating involves—the analysis of issues, the proving and refuting of contentions, the organization of arguments, and so forth.

Since debate is not an easy mode of deliberation to master, one best begins, perhaps, by working on these skills separately. Then gradually they may be put together in complete argumentative speeches and full-dress debates. In any event, two considerations are paramount: (1) *Practice must be plentiful and persistent.* (2) *Practice must be carefully guided and evaluated.*

Unless one practices often over a considerable period of time, he cannot hope to gain the facility required by the debate situation, where rapidly changing circumstances often render prepared proofs and refutations useless. Unless practice is carefully guided, the learner may find himself working with a type of subject matter ill suited to his purpose, attempting some exercise beyond his capacity, or practicing errors rather than reinforcing correct habits. And finally, unless practice is followed by constructive criticism, much of its value is lost. In learning to debate, as in acquiring any skill, one progresses best when a trained critic points out what he has done well and suggests how he may improve what he has done badly.

When the foregoing conditions are met, practice is an indispensable means of teaching skills and inculcating attitudes that can be acquired in no other way.

## A KNOWLEDGE OF THE THEORY OF DEBATE

Important as observation and practice are, they would make for a tortuous learning process and might in the end prove unrewarding were they not correlated with a third factor. This factor is a knowledge of debate theory, of the body of principles and procedures that constitute the discipline of argumentation.

A book such as this can be of only modest help in guiding observation and of almost none in directing and criticizing practice. It can, however, be of material aid in teaching the body of theory on which intelligent observation and purposeful practice must be based.

Argumentation is derived from several sources. As we saw in Chapter

1, many of its leading principles are borrowed directly or indirectly from *logic* and reflect man's efforts to develop a valid instrument for arriving at critical choices and decisions.

Argumentation also draws heavily on *psychology,* for it is concerned not with proofs in the abstract, but rather as they are addressed to others in an effort to erase erroneous beliefs and replace them with better ones. What are beliefs? Of what elements are they composed? From what sources are they derived? How may they be altered? Because a debate decision reflects the beliefs of those who decide, answers to such questions help the debater present the strongest possible defense for his point of view.

Third, argumentation draws extensively on *rhetoric,* the art that studies how to render discourse effective. How should arguments be stated to insure maximum intelligibility? How may one win an attentive hearing for his cause? If debate is oral, what manner of delivery is preferred? Without clear and useful answers to these questions the debater could hardly hope to reach his goal of critical judgment.

Logic, psychology, and rhetoric do not represent all of the disciplines on which argumentation draws. They are, however, its most important sources. The serious student of debate should know as much as possible about each. To the degree that he becomes a more skilled logician, a more discerning practical psychologist, and a more apt rhetorician—to that degree he will become a more effective debater, better able to write and speak critically in the many decision-making situations that confront him as a member of a free society.

## QUESTIONS

*A. To Check Your Comprehension and Memory*

1. Why should all citizens in a democratic society understand the nature of debate and be skilled in its use?
2. How does training in debate contribute toward the aims of a liberal education?
3. By what three methods may one learn to debate?
4. What particular values are derived from hearing or reading debates?
5. Name the two conditions practice should meet if it is to be of value.
6. From what three sources is the discipline of argumentation principally derived?
7. What contributions does each of these sources make to argumentation?

*B. For Class Discussion*

1. Study the college debate printed in Appendix A (pp. 351–75). Be prepared to discuss each of the following questions concerning it:

In what order do the participants speak?
Why do you think they use this order and not some other?
Can you notice any difference between the constructive and rebuttal speeches? What seems to be the principal purpose of each?
Does the first affirmative speaker have any special obligations or duties?
Who opens the rebuttal speeches? Who closes them? Why?
How much use is made of factual data? Is one side superior to the other in this respect?
Which side do you think presented the stronger line of constructive arguments?
Which would you say did the better job of refuting the arguments of its opponents?
Do you think that this debate constitutes a fair, well-rounded, and intelligent discussion of the problem? Why, or why not? Be specific.

2. Compare the procedure used in the college debate with that used in the written debate between Professors Murphy and Cripe (Appendix B, pp. 376–92). What advantages and limitations does each style of debate have? How well is each adapted to the purpose for which it is intended? How might each be improved?

## EXERCISES

*A. Written Exercises*

1. As was pointed out in Chapter 2, in ancient Greece arguments concerning ethical and social problems were often carried on as dialogues, one party questioning the other to discover his views on the topic and to see if they were valid. As an introduction to this form of deliberation, read Plato's dialogue *Ion* and answer in writing as many of the following questions as your instructor assigns. If desired, individual questions may be allotted to different members of the class and the written answers used as a basis for general discussion. (The translation by Lane Cooper in *Plato* [New York: Oxford, 1938, pp. 75–93] is recommended, but any standard translation will serve.)

Who asks all of the questions in the dialogue?
In what spirit are the questions asked? Do they seem to be honest and objective requests for information? Are they designed to establish some point? How would you describe them?
How are the questions related to one another?
How is each new question related to the answer that immediately precedes it?
What do you think of the analogy of the iron rings? Is it a good argument? Why, or why not?
In what sort of dilemma does Ion find himself at the close of the dialogue?
Can you trace the steps by which he got into this uncomfortable position?
What do you think is the central idea Socrates is attempting to establish?

Is a dialectical dialogue a good way to establish this idea? Would some other form of critical deliberation be a better way of doing it?

2. Write a brief paper in which you show how training in debate may benefit you as a college student and as an educated citizen.

B. *Oral Exercise*

Prepare and present to the class a five-minute informative speech on one of the following subjects or on a subject suggested by one of these:

Debate and a Liberal Education
The Role of Debate in My Major Field of Study
Abelard and the Disputations of the Twelfth Century
Debating in the Literary Societies of the Early American Colleges
The Role of Debate in Present-Day Political Campaigns
Debate in the Courtroom
How Television Has Affected Debate
Debate and Democracy
The Lincoln-Douglas Debates: Their Nature and Influence
Observation, Practice, and Theory: The Three Roads to Debating Skill

## SUGGESTIONS FOR FURTHER READING

Walter Bagehot, "The Age of Discussion," in *Physics and Politics,* in *The Works and Life of Walter Bagehot,* ed. Mrs. Russell Barrington. 10 vols. (London: Longmans, Green & Co., 1915), VIII, 101–32. A brilliant political economist examines the differences between a static society and a dynamic society. He finds that in a static society public discussion does not exist or is hampered by government and social tradition. In a dynamic society discussion is free and a powerful prod toward progress.

Hugh Blair, Lecture 34, "Means of Improving in Eloquence," in *Lectures on Rhetoric and Belles Lettres* (Edinburgh, 1783). A classic statement of the roles played by nature, art, imitation, and practice in the making of a public speaker. Many editions of Blair's *Lectures* are available.

Marcus Tullius Cicero, *De Oratore,* Book I. One of the world's great orators creates an imaginary dialogue on the subject of learning to speak and write well. This dialogue may also profitably be studied in its own right as a debate. Many usable translations are available, but look first for Cicero, *De Oratore,* tr. E. W. Sutton and H. Rackham (Cambridge, Mass.: Harvard University Press, 1948).

Walter Lippmann, *Public Opinion* (New York: The Macmillan Company, 1927; paperback edition, 1960), Part V, "The Making of a Common Will." Examines how public opinion is formed and communicated in a democracy.

Everett Dean Martin, *The Meaning of a Liberal Education* (New York: W. W. Norton & Company, 1926). An older but still pertinent introduction to the nature of liberal training. Easy and entertaining reading.

*Part II*

# BUILDING A SUBJECT-MATTER BACKGROUND

*Chapter 4*

# OBTAINING INFORMATION: PERSONAL KNOWLEDGE, CONTACTS WITH EXPERTS

*Knowledge is, indeed, that which, next to virtue, truly and essentially raises one man above another.* ADDISON

As we observed in Chapter 1, critical decision-making is pre-eminently a fact-centered process, as attested by three of its cardinal rules. (1) Begin your study of a subject by searching for facts, rather than by making guesses or assumptions. (2) Test each hypothesis and each new step in inference by carefully checking it against the facts. (3) Accept no conclusion that fails to square with the facts.

For a simple question of personal choice, a critical answer may usually be supplied by gathering only a few easily obtainable facts. For example, if one were driving to the beach and wished to arrive as quickly as possible, no more than five items of information would be needed to decide whether to follow Road A or Road B. (*a*) Which road is shorter? (*b*) Which is in a better state of repair? (*c*) Which is leveler and straighter? (*d*) Which passes through fewer cities and congested areas? (*e*) Which is least traveled? On the answers to these queries a sufficiently reliable decision could be reached.

But now consider some of the typical questions about which men deliberate in the courtroom or in public debates. "Is Smith guilty of embezzlement, as charged?" "What should be the distribution of powers between the state and national governments?" "Should laws be passed that regulate labor unions more stringently?" "Is the country headed toward runaway inflation?" Here, obviously, the situation is different. Reaching a critical decision on these questions requires a large supply of many different sorts of facts—statistics; historical records; the texts of laws, constitutions, and treaties; the proceedings of committees and conferences; the recorded opinions and predictions of experts, etc. Here the task of finding, collecting, recording, organizing, and preserving the data essential to a critical judgment assumes the proportions of a major research undertaking. Not only must the investigator expend a considerable amount of time and energy in study, but he must be equipped with a knowledge of standard research procedures. The purpose of this chapter and the two that follow is to describe these procedures.

## THE DEBATER AS RESEARCH WORKER

At the outset the student should reject a common misconception. Many persons believe that the real business of the debater is limited to the development and presentation of persuasive arguments, and that research is only a sort of bothersome preliminary—something of secondary importance which can either be engaged in at random or turned over to an assistant or colleague. The truth of the matter is that research is an essential part of debating itself. There are three reasons why this is so.

First, as Clifford among others has argued, no speaker or writer has the moral right to attempt to influence others until, as a result of long thought and study, he has come to the considered conclusion that his view of a matter is true, or wise, or valuable.[1] To speak without adequate information and mature reflection is to violate the philosophy of critical deliberation and to shirk one's responsibility as a member of society.

Second, thorough research is essential for the highly practical reason that without it the debater stands little chance of making his view prevail. On one occasion, by studying the almanac and thereby showing there was no moon on the night of the crime, Lincoln undermined the central piece of testimony on which his opponent's case rested. This story illustrates that a single pertinent fact overlooked or misevaluated may open a gap through which an alert adversary moves to undermine the entire case.

Third, for reasons rooted deep in the psychology of human communication, listeners or readers are usually quick to sense when a debater's knowledge is meager or when a few surface facts are stretched beyond warrant. As a result, the ill-informed debater seldom inspires

[1] W. K. Clifford, "The Ethics of Belief," in Leslie Stephen and Frederick Pollock, ed., *Lectures and Essays*, 2 vols., 3rd ed. (London and New York: The Macmillan Company, 1901), II, 163–205.

confidence or influences belief.

One does not suddenly become a debater at the moment he rises to speak or sits down to write. He becomes a debater long before—at the time he first begins to investigate his subject and search out the facts on which an intelligent and responsible judgment must be based. When he comes to the platform or takes up his pen he merely enters upon a different stage of a total and unbroken process that reaches from his first tentative explorations to that final moment when judgment is handed down. No part of the process is less important than any other. The conscientious performance of each is necessary to the perfection of the whole. For a debater soon learns, sadly, that a defect anywhere may mean his cause is lost.

Good debating resembles an iceberg, in the sense that the greater part of it is not visible. The brilliant argumentative essay, the campaign speech, the moving jury plea, or, for that matter, the successful constructive or rebuttal speech in a college debate, is seldom a creature born of the moment. Its actual reading or speaking consumes only a fraction of the many hours spent in preparation, and the observable skills of reasoning, language, and arrangement are only a few of the abilities that were required to produce it. The equally essential skills of research, analysis, and audience evaluation remain hidden from view, but to assume that these are without a part in producing the final result is as dangerous as to assume that there is no more to the iceberg than meets the eye.

The ideal debater is, of course, a skilled writer or speaker, at home in the heat of controversy and the atmosphere of public life, but he is also a trained research worker equally at home in the library or study. He is a man who respects facts and who knows how to go about finding them. Brilliance of reasoning or style, the ability to answer an opponent's argument, agility in thought—these, admittedly, are important. But it is in the digging out of facts that most good debating has its birth.

Nor are there many occasions on which a debater may turn the hard work of research over to a colleague, secretary, or library assistant. Only when he patiently studies the facts for himself will they become sufficiently a part of him so that he can use them with maximum effect. Just as observant readers or hearers are quick to sense when a line of argument rests on a feeble factual basis, so are they quick to see when a debater is mouthing undigested ideas fed him by another. To speak or write well demands that the speaker or writer himself be the ultimate authority for what he says.

In short, if the debater is to discharge the moral responsibility assumed by anyone who addresses appeals to the public, and if he is to acquire the broad subject-matter background on which critical judgment ultimately depends, he must view research as an integral part of his task.

What, then, are the research processes in which a speaker or writer must engage? They are three in number and, stated in the order in which they are usually performed, are as follows: (1) *obtaining the information necessary for forming a critical judgment;* (2) *recording portions of this information for future use;* and (3) *organizing and filing the materials recorded.* In the remainder of this chapter we shall be concerned with the first of these processes—considering how one may obtain information by reviewing his own knowledge and experience and by establishing contacts with persons who are experts on the subject he is studying, as well as by talking with friends and acquaintances.

## PERSONAL KNOWLEDGE AND EXPERIENCE

In beginning their study of a new subject, many inexperienced debaters assume they will be breaking into a completely virgin field, one about which they know little or nothing. Sometimes this assumption will be true, and then research must start from the barrier.

More often, however, the debater already knows more about the subject than he at first supposes—if not in the form of specific names, facts, and figures, at least in the way of general background information and applicable bits of theory. Such background knowledge is possessed especially by college students, whose recent studies in the social sciences and elsewhere may often profitably be brought to bear on a wide variety of current problems.

A natural starting point in exploring any subject for debate is, therefore, a careful review of what one may already know about it. Take, for example, the question of free trade. Ask: "What is a tariff?" "Why do nations have tariffs?" "What is the history of our tariff policy here in the United States?" "What tariff policies have some of the other major nations of the world traditionally followed?" "Has free trade ever been tried?" "If so, with what success?" Only a rare individual could supply, without additional study, authoritative answers to all these questions. But any educated man or woman can probably answer one or two of them on the basis of his general knowledge alone.

The amount of previous knowledge which one possesses will, naturally, be greater for some subjects than for others. Sometimes the debater may recall material of sufficient importance to warrant the drawing up of systematic written notes or summaries. On other occasions, he may remember little more than the names of certain books and articles with which he can begin his study. In any case, our advice is this: When confronted with a new subject for debate, do not rush at once to the library and impulsively begin to leaf at random through stacks of books and magazines. Take time first to review and reflect about what you may already believe or know about the subject. Frequently you will be surprised at the number of facts and ideas that come back to you. Almost invariably, such review will help you get your bearings and start your organized research in a more purposeful and productive fashion.

## CONSULTATION WITH EXPERTS

A second important source of information on a subject for debate is consultation with persons who have expert knowledge concerning it. Such persons may be college faculty members, congressmen, officials of state or local government, military officers, journalists, research workers, or world travelers. Information may be secured from these individuals either by personal interviews or by correspondence. In either case, however, certain cautions should be observed if the best results are to be obtained.

### INTERVIEWS

Those principles governing any conversation with a distinguished and busy man should be observed during an interview.

1. Do not request an interview until your study of the subject is well advanced. Only then will you be able to ask the most pertinent questions and fully understand the information offered.

2. Use the interview to best advantage by asking questions on which the expert is particularly qualified, or by seeking information you have not been able to obtain elsewhere.

3. Come to the interview armed with a set of specific questions. Do not insist that the expert adhere rigidly to these questions, or you may not give him an opportunity to bring out important matters that have not previously occurred to you. But it is fruitless to approach an authority with the vague statement that you are studying foreign trade or labor relations or state rights, and would like him to tell you what he knows about the subject. To such a request he has every right to say, "Read my books or take my courses. I have given my life to studying the subject, and in the time we have today I would not even know where to begin."

4. Know something about the man and his general position on the

subject. Not only will such knowledge help you avoid tactless questions, but it will enable you to evaluate more accurately the information he offers.

5. Don't argue with the expert. If he is worth interviewing, he is worth listening to. You are after his ideas, not out to criticize them. Keep your disagreements silent. Listen courteously and attentively to what he has to say.

6. Ask for facts, sources, and ideas, rather than for ready-made arguments pro and con. Do not say, "I am on the affirmative in a debate on compulsory arbitration of labor disputes. How should I build my case?" Such an approach is juvenile and is as dishonest as lifting from a debater's handbook a tailor-made brief prepared by another.[2] Do your own thinking about arguments and cases.

7. If at all possible, make an appointment in advance, so the expert will be able to discuss the subject unhurriedly and without interruption. The professor buttonholed in the hall between classes or the official caught leaving the airport is not in a position to make thoughtful comments. He usually is more anxious to get rid of the questioner than to give helpful information.

8. Be on time for the interview, and don't stay too long. Remember that the person interviewed is doing you a favor.

9. If during the interview you record statements with a view to quoting these directly in a speech or article, write them out and later submit them to the interviewee for his approval. This practice insures that his views will be represented fully and accurately. Always record on such statements the date of the interview and any other information that may be helpful in identifying them for future use.

## CORRESPONDENCE

When consultation takes the form of correspondence rather than of a personal interview, many of the same rules apply.

Ask specific questions and request particular documents or data. Do not send out vague general requests for any information the expert may be able to supply. Avoid, also, asking for materials that may easily be found elsewhere, or writing prematurely, before your own study of the subject has provided a clear notion of what questions are important.

Consultation with experts through correspondence or interviews, when properly planned and conducted, often proves unusually valuable. It is a source of information too little used by most beginning debaters. The dangers and evils lie in misusing the method by employing it with poor judgment or by violating the common rules of courtesy.

[2] A case against the use of debate handbooks is presented on pp. 310–11.

Don't approach an expert prematurely; plan your questions in advance; respect his time and knowledge; solicit only information that is not otherwise available. These rules should always be observed when interviewing or corresponding with an expert.

## CONVERSATIONS WITH FRIENDS

When preparing to debate a subject, conversations with friends—classmates, teachers, business and professional men, members of the community, etc.—may prove a useful supplement to consultations with expert sources. Such conversations are not so much sources of information or ideas as means of testing the effectiveness of the arguments to be used in the debate. By trying his arguments out on a wide variety of persons, the debater may gauge how clearly and effectively he is presenting his ideas and how readily they are accepted. He may discover and repair a fallacy that would otherwise go unnoticed until the debate itself.

While gathering material and formulating arguments, the debater should play the role of Socratic gadfly, presenting his ideas to as many persons as will listen, and carefully noting the questions and objections raised by each. This device was used constantly by President Franklin Roosevelt when preparing his speeches and was also often employed by Winston Churchill. Indeed, many writers and speakers have found that informal conversations not only provide a valuable testing ground for arguments previously thought of, but also stimulate the production of new and better arguments.

## QUESTIONS

*A. To Check Your Comprehension and Memory*
  1. Why is systematic and prolonged research an essential part of debating?
  2. When does one become a debater?
  3. Why is a successful argumentative speech or essay like an iceberg?
  4. Why should the work of research seldom, if ever, be turned over to a colleague, secretary, or assistant?
  5. What three research processes are involved in building up one's knowledge of a subject?
  6. How should one begin the study of a new subject? Why?
  7. What rules should govern interviews with experts? What rules should be followed in corresponding with them?
  8. Why are conversations and informal arguments with nonexperts often helpful to the debater?

*B. For Class Discussion*
  1. How would you explain the fact that listeners and readers are usually

quick to sense when a debater's knowledge of a subject is meager or when a few surface facts are overused and stretched beyond warrant?

2. To what degree does conviction depend on the evident honesty and sincerity of a writer or speaker? To what degree does it grow out of the facts and information he presents?

3. Can you name instances in which you have been convinced by a speech or essay in which almost no facts were presented? In these cases, was the conviction firm and lasting, or tentative and temporary?

4. Do you think that a debater's moral obligation to his readers or listeners is sufficiently discharged once he has acquired a broad and thorough knowledge of his subject? Is this all he must do to satisfy the ethical requirements of good debating?

5. Do you agree that a debater usually speaks or writes better and more convincingly when he has dug out the facts and evidence for himself? Why or why not? Can you cite instances supporting this proposition? instances refuting it?

6. What do you think of the widespread contemporary practice of "ghost writing" articles and speeches?

7. Daniel Webster is reported to have said, "There is no such thing as extempore acquisition." By this he meant that without long and serious preparation one cannot hope to deliver a good speech. Do you agree or disagree? Why?

### EXERCISES

*A. Written Exercises*

1. Select some current problem that might become a topic for debate—the regulation of labor unions, farm prices, our relations with underdeveloped nations, etc. Jot down on a piece of paper all of the facts you now know and all of the ideas you now have about this subject. When you are not certain of a point, put a question mark behind it. See how long a list you can develop without having to turn to new sources of information.

2. Write a short essay on the subject, "The Debater's Responsibility to Know the Facts."

3. Write a short essay on the subject, "Why One Speaks or Writes More Effectively When He Has Dug Out the Facts for Himself." Use whatever textbooks in speech and psychology you may need in order to develop a strong argument.

*B. Oral Exercises*

1. Interview a faculty member or other subject-matter expert on a topic of current interest. Report your findings to the class in a four- or five-minute speech.

2. Practice interviewing techniques and procedures by dividing the class into pairs. Let each student have an opportunity to act as both interviewer

and interviewee. Pay particular attention to getting the interview under way and bringing it to a close courteously and promptly. Try to observe the rules for interviewing outlined in this chapter.

## SUGGESTIONS FOR FURTHER READING

Walter Van Dyke Bingham and Bruce Victor Moore, *How to Interview*, 4th ed. rev. (New York: Harper & Brothers, 1959). Examines the interview as used in a wide variety of situations, including social case work and vocational adjustment. The entire book should be of interest to serious students of writing and speaking, but see especially Chapter 1, "First Principles"; Chapter 2, "Learning How to Interview"; Chapter 13, "The Interview in Journalism"; and Chapter 15, "Conclusions about Interviewing."

R. C. Oldfield, *The Psychology of the Interview* (London: Methuen & Co., 1951). As its title indicates, this little book of 149 pages is primarily concerned with the psychology of the interview, but it contains much practical advice on note-taking, "breaking the ice," maintaining the proper attitude, and bringing the interview to a close.

William P. Sandford and Willard H. Yeager, *Effective Business Speech* [4th ed. of *Practical Business Speaking*]. (New York: McGraw-Hill Book Co., 1960). The final chapters discuss how to plan and conduct interviews, including interviews designed to secure information and persuasive interviews. Special attention is paid to various ways of opening and closing the interview, how to make oneself clear, etc. A direct, simple, practical treatment. The transcript of a portion of a persuasive interview is included.

Lew Sarett, William T. Foster, and Alma Johnson Sarett, *Basic Principles of Speech*, 3d ed. (Boston: Houghton Mifflin Co., 1958). Chapter 12, "Finding and Evaluating Materials," has an excellent section on how to take stock of what you may already know about a subject.

*Chapter 5*

## OBTAINING INFORMATION: PRINTED SOURCES

*Knowledge is of two kinds: we know a subject ourselves, or we know where we can find information upon it.* SAMUEL JOHNSON

ALTHOUGH a debater's knowledge of a subject may be derived in part from a review of information he already has and from consultations with experts, these sources in themselves seldom supply all of the data required to discuss a public question critically. Almost always they must be supplemented by facts and ideas drawn from books, magazines, documents, pamphlets, and reference works.

Some of the printed materials the debater requires may come from his personal library. Others he requests from various organizations, foundations, and agencies, or purchases directly from publishing houses. For most of his needs, however, he will undoubtedly depend on his public or college library. Therefore, he must have some understanding of how a library is organized and be acquainted with the tools designed to help one use it efficiently.

Libraries vary greatly in size and quality and sometimes have many specialized departments and collections. Usually, however, their holdings may be divided into five major classes: *"general" books, newspapers and periodicals, documents, "fugitive materials,"* and *reference works.* We shall discuss these classes in order and then, in a final section of the chapter, make some specific suggestions for using a library's card catalogue.

## GENERAL BOOKS

"General" books are works intended for consecutive and more or less complete reading. They range from erudite research tomes, through textbooks and treatises on the various arts and sciences, to historical romances, "westerns," and paperback "whodunits." In most libraries general books, except for unusually rare or costly ones, are allowed to circulate. That is, they may be charged out and used at home for a period of time.

Since the writing and printing of books is a slow process, a book may be two to four years out of date before it is published. Accordingly, the debater draws most of his information on recent developments from more current sources, using books to furnish background material or information that does not become dated with the passing of time. On some subjects, however, certain books may provide data current enough to be immediately applicable, and these can, of course, be quoted directly.

All of a library's general books are listed in its card catalogue. As we have just indicated, this catalogue and its use will be discussed in the final section of this chapter.

## NEWSPAPERS AND PERIODICALS

Newspapers and periodicals are so numerous and varied that one cannot generalize concerning which of them are most useful to the debater. Some that are valuable for the study of one subject are useless for another.

Among newspapers, special mention must be made, however, of the *New York Times*. Unexcelled in the comprehensiveness of its coverage, the *Times* is one of the few newspapers that still maintain sizable staffs of correspondents throughout the world, rather than depending on syndicated wire and feature services for other than local news. Particularly valuable for anyone writing or speaking on current questions is the section of a dozen or so pages called "News of the Week in Review," which appears in the *Times* each Sunday. This section not only treats important news items in considerable detail but also offers authoritative and impartial comment on the events reported. Because the *Times* is comprehensively indexed, one is able to find a particular item quickly and easily.

Our emphasis on the *Times* does not mean, of course, that all other newspapers lack distinction and that the serious researcher may ignore them. On the contrary, he should regularly consult many different papers to gather editorial views and to sample public opinion in various parts of the world. But for almost any question a debater may be studying, he can disregard the *Times* only at the peril of overlooking a particularly fruitful source of authoritative information.

Among British newspapers the *London Times* and *Manchester Guardian* deserve mention and will be found in most libraries. The *Times* has a comprehensive index.

Magazines or periodicals, viewed as possible sources of debate material, may be divided into several categories. First, there are the general news weeklies, such as *Time, Newsweek,* and *U.S. News and World Report.* These magazines are primarily valuable for keeping abreast of current developments. Read consistently over the years, however, they also provide a broad understanding of the general course of events.

*The Nation,* the *New Republic,* and the biweekly *Reporter* are typical of a group of magazines more given to editorial interpretation than to straight news reporting. Especially valuable for the study of economic and business trends are the various businessmen's newsletters—those issued by Kiplinger, the National City Bank of New York, the Federal Reserve Banks, the Cleveland Trust Company, and Lloyds Bank, Ltd., of London, to mention only a few. *Barron's National Financial Weekly, Business Week,* and the *Wall Street Journal* (a daily newspaper) should also be consulted when studying current economic or business problems. For reprints of recent speeches on a wide variety of subjects, see *Vital Speeches of the Day.*

In England two of the most important and useful weeklies are the *New Statesman* and *Time and Tide.* These publications are especially strong on subjects dealing with Britain and the Commonwealth, but are also useful in the general area of international affairs. For economic topics, *The Economist* is probably the best and most widely available English journal.

As distinguished from the weeklies, the standard monthly and quarterly magazines—*Harper's Magazine,* the *Atlantic Monthly, Foreign Affairs, Current History,* the *Yale Review, Fortune,* etc.—are especially valuable to the debater in providing general background knowledge on a subject. Their longer articles, written for the most part by recognized experts, provide insights based on extensive study and mature reflection. By supplying basic information and suggesting broad and provocative ideas such as are seldom found in newspapers and news magazines, they greatly enrich one's reading of more current sources.

Periodicals in the various specialized fields with which a debater may be concerned—labor, education, foreign trade, agriculture, and the like —are too numerous to mention here. They exist, however, in great profusion, and provide most useful information on some controversies.

All of the weekly, monthly, and quarterly magazines mentioned in the preceding paragraphs are indexed annually or semiannually, and most of them are represented in the *Reader's Guide to Periodical Literature,* or in several more specialized guides.[1] A debater, early in his research, should make a bibliography of magazine articles and newspaper items by consulting recent issues of the *Reader's Guide* and other indexes. With experience in research, a debater develops the ability to distinguish between index references to articles that are valuable and to those that are practically useless. By studying the former, he develops a good backlog of ideas and information.

In addition, however, he must keep his research up to date. Ideally, a number of different newspapers and magazines should be consulted regularly during the period one is working on a subject. Several hours a week may be set aside for browsing through the library, turning the pages of current newspapers and magazines and scanning the contents of those specialized journals that are likely to have pertinent material. Valuable information will often be found in the most unsuspected places—information not only on the subject being researched, but also on a wide variety of related matters. While such random browsing is not a substitute for the systematic digging out of the facts and figures on which proof is based, it is certainly a most valuable supplement to such study.

When using newspapers and magazines, always remember that they vary greatly in authoritativeness and objectivity. To insure a full and fair understanding of a subject, and to avoid presenting colored data to his readers or listeners, the debater should be completely aware of the biases of each newspaper and magazine he uses and of its reliability as an information source.

Because newspapers are bulky to store, many libraries preserve back numbers on microfilm or microcards. These generally must be requested at the main circulation desk, although they are sometimes kept in special collections.

## DOCUMENTS

As used by librarians, the word "document" refers to a publication issued by a governmental unit or agency—local, county, state, national, or international. Such publications are legion and cover almost every conceivable subject. Texts of treaties and trade agreements, transcripts of committee hearings, reports of administrative departments, proceedings of legislative bodies, foreign policy statements, statutes, court decisions, bulletins for businessmen, housewives, and farmers, reports and recommendations of special study groups, technical publications of federal and state research agencies—these are only a few of the many types of

---

[1] See pp. 54–55.

materials that roll from government presses every year.

Because of their great number and variety, documents are difficult for librarians to index and catalogue. Hence, debaters sometimes pass over the mass of valuable information they contain. For not only are documents generally based on primary sources of information—firsthand surveys, actual transcripts of proceedings, etc.—but, for the most part, they are factual in nature, presenting great bodies of detailed information usefully summarized in the form of tables, charts, and graphs. Moreover, with a few easily detected exceptions, documents are unbiased in their selection and handling of data. For these and similar reasons, the time and trouble involved in tracking down a particular document are usually well repaid.

## MUNICIPAL, COUNTY, AND STATE DOCUMENTS

If the debater is concerned with a problem in his own community, such as urban renewal, annexation, or improved police or fire protection, he will probably wish to consult certain local municipal documents.

In most towns and cities the mayor or city manager issues a comprehensive annual report covering the year's activities and outlining plans for the future. In addition, each of the various administrative departments of city government—engineering, sanitation, recreation, housing, education, public library—may issue reports.

County and state documents provide the reports of auditors, assessors, sheriffs, road boards, welfare agencies, game and fish commissions, the proceedings of councils and legislative bodies, tax lists, educational directories, and courses of study for schools.

Sometimes libraries do not catalogue municipal and county documents, and not all libraries organize and file them in the same way. Moreover, for obvious reasons, no very satisfactory bibliographies or indexes of such materials exist. In searching for them, therefore, the debater should enlist the aid of a documents librarian.

For state documents, the *Monthly Checklist of State Publications,* 1910– , assembled by the Library of Congress and issued by the United States Government Printing Office, is the best guide available. Although incomplete, it lists many materials under the name of the issuing state, territory, or possession, and is indexed annually.

## FEDERAL DOCUMENTS

Although municipal, county, and state documents are constantly becoming more numerous, the great flood of government publications is issued on the national level. Within recent decades, the United States, along with most of the other nations of the world, has greatly expanded its printing program, thus reflecting the increased interest of government in all phases of economic and social life, as well as in research in the sciences, engineering, and agriculture.

Only 123 libraries in the United States regularly receive all federal documents, but over 550—including all land-grant colleges—are so-called "depositories," and receive selected items. Even the smallest library will probably have many documents sought by the debater—census reports, Federal Reserve bulletins, and the like.

Federal documents are indexed in *United States Government Publications: Monthly Catalogue,* 1895– , and *Selected United States Government Publications,* July 11, 1928– , both issued by the U.S. Government Printing Office. The *Monthly Catalogue* lists almost all federal documents, congressional as well as departmental. There is a general index in each annual volume and an author and subject index in each monthly issue. Instructions for ordering documents are included. *Selected United States Government Publications* is a brief annotated catalogue of current publications of more general or popular interest, and is published semimonthly. It is arranged by subject, and prices and directions for ordering are supplied.

In addition to these two sources, the U.S. Government Printing Office also issues, from time to time, so-called *Price Lists.* Each of these is devoted to a special subject or type of material, and names publications available in that field.

To single out the three or four federal documents most valuable to the debater is, admittedly, difficult. Any college student or citizen engaged in the deliberation of public questions, however, would do well to be familiar with the following:

*Congressional Record* (Washington: U.S. Government Printing Office, March 4, 1873– ). The *Record,* issued daily while Congress is in session, provides complete transcripts of the President's messages and of congressional debates. It contains the record of votes but does not include the texts of bills. Index is by name, subject, and bill. The "Appendix," bound with the *Record,* contains so-called "extensions of remarks," resolutions, memorials, reprints of articles from newspapers and magazines, and other materials that often prove especially valuable to the debater.

*Statistical Abstract of the United States* (Washington: U.S. Government Printing Office, 1878– ). Contains "quantitative summary statistics on the political, industrial, and economic organization of the United States." Although *Statistical Abstract* is issued annually, the statistics in the tables usually cover the preceding fifteen- or twenty-five-year period.

*Federal Reserve Bulletin* (Washington: Board of Governors of the Federal Reserve System, 1915– ). Issued monthly, the *Bulletin* contains extensive information on economic and financial conditions in the United States.

It also includes comments on financial conditions and developments in foreign countries.

For the discussion of many current problems, various publications issued by the Bureau of the Census, the Bureau of Labor Statistics, the Department of State, and the Department of Agriculture are especially valuable. When attempting to locate census information, see *Census Publications: Catalogue and Subject Guide* (Washington: U.S. Government Printing Office, 1945–   ). For specific information concerning other departmental and bureau publications, a good starting place is the index to Constance M. Winchell's *Guide to Reference Books,* 7th ed. (see p. 50).

For debating some subjects, the transcripts of congressional committee hearings are, of course, almost indispensable. Current hearings are included in the *Monthly Catalogue,* although difficulties in indexing sometimes make them hard to locate in this source. Hearings are also listed—but usually after a considerable time lag—in the irregularly issued *Index of Congressional Committee Hearings* (Washington: U.S. Government Printing Office). A commercial publication, *The Public Affairs Information Service* (11 West Fortieth Street, New York 18), lists important hearings on social, political, and economic matters.

All congressional bills and resolutions of general interest are indexed in the *Congressional Index Service* (Chicago: Commerce Clearing House, Inc., Loose Leaf Services Division of the Corporation Trust Company, 1937–   ).

## FOREIGN DOCUMENTS

Documents issued by foreign governments, while often extremely helpful to the debater, are usually difficult for the beginning research worker to locate. Libraries vary greatly in their holdings and may specialize in only one or two areas—Latin America, the Far East, etc. Although much useful information is contained in *A Study of Current Bibliographies of National Official Publications,* issued in 1958 by UNESCO, probably the best course when searching for foreign publications is to consult a documents librarian.

## UNITED NATIONS DOCUMENTS

A new but extremely important source of documents on a wide variety of subjects is the United Nations. Most of the publications issued by this organization are listed in the *United Nations Documents Index* (New York: United Nations, Jan. 1950–   ).

## FUGITIVE MATERIALS

Because pamphlets, brochures, dodgers, leaflets, and the like are customarily issued at irregular intervals and are not organized into numbered series or volumes, librarians call them "fugitive materials."

Such materials often contain information of great value to the debater. Like documents, however, the "fugitive" items are not always easy to locate and secure. Normally, they are not listed in a library's general card catalogue, and are usually stored in boxes and folders. The only general index of pamphlets and leaflets is the *Vertical File Index* (New York: H. W. Wilson Co., 1930– ), and this source does not pretend to be complete. The items that are included, however, are well described, and prices and directions for ordering are given. Indexing is by title, author, and issuing group or organization.

Sometimes the debater may wish to know if a private organization or foundation has issued materials on the topic he is studying. The names and addresses of such organizations may, for the most part, be found in the *World Almanac*,[2] the *Guide to Public Affairs Organizations,* or *Trade and Professional Associations of the United States,* a publication of the U.S. Chamber of Commerce.

Always be alert, however, when using pamphlets and brochures, for many are sheer propaganda. While some issuing organizations make a genuine effort to present facts impartially, many are primarily pressure groups whose publications are designed to serve their own ends. An item issued by the League of Women Voters, the Brookings Institute, the Institute of Pacific Relations, or the National Safety Council may be completely impartial. On the other hand, one published by the National Association of Manufacturers, the AFL-CIO, the Arab Information Center, or even the United States Chamber of Commerce may need to be analyzed carefully.

## REFERENCE WORKS

Reference works, unlike "general" books, magazine articles, pamphlets, and many documents, are not intended for consecutive reading. On the contrary, they are storehouses of information designed to be consulted in spot fashion for some particular fact or as a means of finding one's way to an organized treatment of a subject under study. To this end, their

[2] See p. 52.

contents are arranged according to some systematic plan—alphabetical, chronological, tabular, etc.—and they are elaborately indexed.

To use a reference work efficiently one should understand how it is organized and become familiar with its system of indexing and making cross references. All good reference books have introductory statements explaining these matters and giving directions and suggestions for their use. A few moments spent with such statements will usually repay one many times over by making use of the book easier and more productive.

Reference works are so numerous and varied that sizable volumes are devoted merely to listing them. The standard bibliography of such materials, Constance M. Winchell's *Guide to Reference Books,* 7th ed. (Chicago: American Library Association, 1951; supplements published in 1954, 1956, and 1960), includes approximately 5500 titles, and it is admittedly selective. Fortunately, however, research for a debate on a public issue normally does not require that one consult more than a handful of these many sources. The reference works the debater is most likely to need are listed on the following pages in the form of an annotated bibliography. They are broken down into six major categories: *encyclopedias; biographical dictionaries; books of facts and figures; summaries of current affairs; indexes to newspapers, periodicals, and books;* and *special publications.*

## ENCYCLOPEDIAS

From time to time the debater will probably find himself consulting many general and specialized encyclopedias. The three on which he usually depends most heavily, however, are these:

*Encyclopaedia Britannica.* A Survey of Universal Knowledge (Chicago: Encyclopaedia Britannica, 1961). 24 vols. Index and atlas in Vol. 24. Although the last formal "edition" of the *Britannica* dates from 1929, it is revised and brought up to date annually under a "continuous revision" policy. The 1961 printing contains 43,500 signed articles, totaling over 38,650,000 words and written by 6134 authorities. Bibliographies and cross references follow most of the articles. All fields of knowledge are covered in this best of all general encyclopedias.

*Encyclopedia Americana* (New York: Americana Corp., 1961). 30 vols. Index in Vol. 30. Also uses the "continuous revision" policy. Many of the longer and more important articles are by outstanding experts and are signed. Especially strong on American subjects, but uniformly reliable. Fewer long articles than the *Britannica,* and in this respect more convenient for some purposes.

*Encyclopaedia of the Social Sciences* (New York: Macmillan, 1937). 8 vols. Index in Vol. 8. As its Introduction states, this encyclopedia endeavors to include "all of the important topics in politics, economics, law, anthropology, sociology, penology, and social work." History is represented only when "historical episodes or methods are of especial importance to the student of society." In the fields of ethics, education, philosophy, and psychology only "those topics of which the social aspects are acquiring increasing significance" are included. Biology, geography, medicine, philology, and art are represented on the same basis, but more briefly and selectively. Alphabetically arranged, with cross references and carefully selected bibliographies following the articles. Each article is prepared by a recognized expert and is signed. Indispensable to the debater for background material, as well as for specific information on many subjects.

## BIOGRAPHICAL DICTIONARIES

Biographical dictionaries are among the most important of the debater's reference tools. He consults them constantly, not only as a means of identifying authors whose books and articles he is studying, but also in order to determine the competence of these persons as authorities, in case he may wish to cite their remarks as evidence or to challenge their citation by an opponent. As suggested in the next chapter, the debater should keep a separate card file of basic biographical information about those authorities whose names are encountered most frequently during debate on a controversy. These are some of the sources from which such information may be obtained:

*Who's Who.* Biographical Dictionary, with Which Is Incorporated "Men and Women of the Time" (London: Adam & Charles Black; New York: Macmillan Co., 1849–   ). This pioneer biographical dictionary, issued annually, lists outstanding *living British* citizens and includes a few prominent names of other nationalities, as well. The biographical data is authoritative, having been checked by the person himself, and is sufficiently detailed to be of real value to the debater. The person's education, titles, membership in organizations, books, etc., are listed.

*Who's Who in America.* A Biographical Dictionary of Notable Living Men and Women of the United States (Chicago: A. N. Marquis Co., 1899–   ). The American counterpart of the British *Who's Who*. On the same general plan, and equally useful and reliable for *living American* men and women. Issued biennially, but with monthly supplements that include names not later admitted to the regular publication.

*International Who's Who* (London: Europa Publications, Ltd., 1935–   ). Many thousands of biographies, although some very short, of prominent men and women of all nations. Useful for an initial check on persons other than American or British. Issued annually.

In addition to these general sources, there are various "who's who" listings for sections or regions and for the different professions. Hence, if you do not find someone in *Who's Who in America,* check *Who's Who in the East, Who's Who in the Midwest, Who's Who in the South and Southwest,* or *Who's Who on the Pacific Coast.* Also try such books as *Who's Who in Commerce and Industry, Leaders in Education, American Men of Science,* and the *Directory of American Scholars.*

For still other specialized biographical dictionaries, including the important *Congressional Directory,* consult a reference librarian. Information about persons no longer living may, of course, be found in earlier editions of these dictionaries, in the *Dictionary of American Biography,* or the *Dictionary of National Biography* (British).

## BOOKS OF FACTS AND FIGURES

Under our discussion of documents we mentioned the *Statistical Abstract,* the various reports issued by the Bureau of the Census, and other government publications containing statistical information of value to the debater. In addition to these, there are certain especially helpful compilations of data prepared by commercial publishers, which, for want of a better name, we shall call books of facts and figures. Five such publications, selected with an eye to the debater's special needs, are listed below. One or all of them should be at hand constantly during the serious discussion of almost any public question.

*World Almanac and Book of Facts* (New York: *World-Telegram and Sun,* 1868– ). The best-known, most comprehensive, and probably the most useful of all fact and figure books. Contains information on educational, financial, religious, and political matters, and records famous events, geographical and governmental data, etc. Many statistical tables on these and related matters. Each volume indexes its own contents and also has a short index of notable articles contained in earlier numbers. Issued annually. Probably one of the basic items that every college debate team should carry with it.

*Statesman's Year-Book.* Statistical and Historical Annual of the States of the World (London and New York: Macmillan Co., 1864– ). Gives organizational information and statistical data about governments. All countries of the world are represented: their populations, areas, rulers, form of government, religions, money and credit, weights and measures, and diplomatic representatives.

*Information Please Almanac* (New York: Macmillan Co., 1947– ). A wide variety of interesting and important information about the United States and foreign countries. Contains a "News Record of the Year," as well as maps, population figures, lists of rulers, etc. Comprehensively cross-indexed.

*International Year Book and Statesmen's Who's Who* (London: Burke's Peerage, 1955). Detailed statistical information about international agencies and the governments of the world. Excellent for population statistics, production figures, imports and exports, revenue, principal industries, etc. A useful biographical section lists facts about statesmen and politicians, ambassadors, heads of government departments, high ranking military officers, leading industrialists, bankers, churchmen, and lawyers.

*Book of the States* (Chicago: Council of State Governments, 1935–   ). Excellent articles and statistical tables on all phases of state government. It deals with the executive, legislative, and judicial branches of the fifty state governments, with their intergovernmental relations, and with the major areas of public service performed by them. Published biennially with supplements.

## SUMMARIES OF CURRENT AFFAIRS

As distinguished from almanacs and similar compilations of facts and figures, a number of publications specialize in summarizing and indexing the course of recent events, either in some part of the world or in the world as a whole. These are useful to the debater in tracing out the background of a subject and in keeping abreast of important developments concerning it. Because such publications present information in a highly condensed fashion, and usually with extensive cross references, they may, in fact, prove more useful than the newspapers and standard news magazines when one is attempting to follow the development of a specific controversy.

*The Annual Register of World Events*. A Review of the Year (London: Longmans, Green & Co., 1758–   ). A review of public events in England and abroad. Part I, "History of the United Kingdom" (by quarters); Part II, "The Commonwealth" (by countries); Part III, "International Organization and Conferences"; Parts IV–IX, the nations of the world (by regions); Parts X–XIV, such topics as religion, science, law, arts and literature, and economics; and Part XV, "Documents and References" (including obituaries, a chronicle of events, and the texts of many documents and political speeches). Emphasizes English affairs, but useful for all countries. Extensively indexed.

*Facts on File* (New York: Person's Index, Facts on File, Inc., 1941–   ). A weekly eight-page news digest, with cross references and cumulative quarterly index. Index is by name, general subject, and specific event. Summarizes, without comment or interpretation, the events of the week, under such headings as World Affairs, National Affairs, Foreign Affairs, Latin America, Economy, Science, Arts, Education, Religion, Obituaries, Sports, and Miscellaneous. There is a cumulative index covering the years 1951–1955.

*Keesing's Contemporary Archives*. Weekly Diary of Important World Events, with Index Continually Kept Up-to-Date (Bristol, England: Keesing's Publications, 1931–   ). The English counterpart of *Facts on*

*File,* and essentially similar. Indexed biweekly, quarterly, and annually.

*Asian Recorder.* A Weekly Digest of Asian Events, with Index (Delhi, India: D. B. Samuel, 1955–   ). Summarizes events week by week for twenty-six Asian countries.

*Britannica Book of the Year* (Chicago: Encyclopaedia Britannica, 1938–   ). Summarizes significant events of the year and tells about the men who made them. Contains statistical and historical data and a chronological calendar of events. Material is organized alphabetically and presented in regular encyclopedia form. Indexed. In recent years has featured, in a special "green section," article-length discussions of some of the year's most important developments.

*Americana Annual* (New York: Americana Corp., 1923–   ). Annual supplement to the *Encyclopedia Americana,* very similar to the *Britannica Book of the Year.*

## INDEXES TO NEWSPAPERS, PERIODICALS, AND BOOKS

The debater's use of newspapers and periodicals for research purposes will become much easier and more productive if he is acquainted with the various guides or indexes to their contents. There are also guides to published books, about which he should know.

Two of the great newspapers of the world are exhaustively indexed, thus furnishing guides not only to their own contents but also indicating the approximate date on which one may expect to find an event recorded in other newspapers.

*New York Times Index* (New York: *New York Times,* 1913–   ). Issued semimonthly, this index not only gives the date, page, and column on which a story may be found, but also contains extensive cross references. Remember, however, it is the *last edition* of the day that is indexed.

*London Times. Official Index* (London: *Times* Office, 1906–   ). Also indexes by date, page, and column. Issued quarterly.

The leading news magazines, *Time, Newsweek,* and *U.S. News and World Report,* have their own indexes, issued periodically. Most of the standard monthly journals have annual indexes. In addition to these sources, however, there are certain general indexes to periodicals, which are of the greatest possible usefulness to the debater in finding a particular article or determining what magazine materials are available on a subject.

*Reader's Guide to Periodical Literature* (New York: H. W. Wilson Co., 1900–   ). Indexes the contents of about 125 magazines, covering nearly all of the general and more popular ones, and also including some scientific and scholarly journals. Index is by author, subject, and title. Issued semimonthly, September to June; monthly in July and August; issues are cumulative.

*International Index.* A Quarterly Guide to Periodical Literature in the Social Sciences and Humanities (New York: H. W. Wilson Co., 1955–   ). Formerly known as *International Index to Periodicals.* On the same general plan as the *Reader's Guide,* but covering 174 more specialized and scholarly journals in the humanities and social sciences.

*Education Index* (New York: H. W. Wilson Co., 1930–   ). Indexes the contents of about 164 educational journals, by author and subject. Published monthly (except July and August) as a cumulative index. Excellent guide for good materials on controversies in the field of education.

*Agricultural Index.* Subject Index to a Selected List of Agricultural Periodicals and Bulletins (New York: H. W. Wilson Co., 1916–   ). Monthly, cumulating annually.

*Business Periodicals Index* (New York: H. W. Wilson Co., 1958–   ). Replaces listing of the materials formerly found in *Industrial Arts Index.* More than 120 journals in all fields of business, advertising, management, finance, etc., are covered. Monthly (except July), cumulating annually.

In locating books, together with their prices and publishers, two sources are especially helpful:

*Cumulative Book Index* (New York: H. W. Wilson Co., 1898–   ). A comprehensive and generally accurate record of all books published *in English* throughout the world. Monthly, except August. Cumulated semiannually, annually, and biannually.

*Publishers' Weekly.* The American Book Trade Journal, 1872–   (New York: R. R. Bowker Co., 1872–   ). Each issue carries a list of the books published in the United States during that week. Hence, a useful source of information about books too new to be found in the *Cumulative Book Index.* Cumulative index by title in the last issue for each month.

For a weekly list of books published in England, see the *British National Bibliography.* Here books are arranged by library call number.

Finally, there is a useful index devoted exclusively to information on current public affairs. It includes in a single listing materials appearing in book, magazine, document, and pamphlet form:

*Bulletin of the Public Affairs Information Service.* A Co-operative Clearing House of Public Affairs Information (New York: Public Affairs Information Service, 1915–   ). Contains a selective index of more than one thousand periodicals. Cumulated bulletins are published five times a year. Especially useful for political and social subjects.

## SPECIAL PUBLICATIONS

A final category of reference works includes publications which are either specifically designed for the college debater or of such great value to him and to all debaters that they warrant the emphasis of separate treatment.

These publications take the form of compilations of materials bearing upon a single subject. Customarily, they include reprints of magazine articles, excerpts from books, selected bibliographies, and perhaps one or more statements prepared by the editors or persons selected by them. Sometimes the material is arranged by subject matter; sometimes pro-and-con discussions of a topic are provided.

Such compilations, based on wholesome educational philosophies, are to be distinguished from "debaters' handbooks"—manuals that attempt to supply ready-made briefs and arguments, and hence to do the debater's thinking for him.[3] Four "special publications" of particular usefulness to the debater are:

*Congressional Digest* (Washington, D.C.: Congressional Digest Corporation, 1921– ). A magazine published monthly, except in July and August. Features in each issue a pro-and-con discussion of some current public question. In fact, except for a short summary of congressional actions during the preceding month, the entire issue customarily consists of such a discussion, in which a number of recognized experts participate. In recent years the November issue has been devoted to the current national intercollegiate debate topic.

*Reference Shelf* (New York: H. W. Wilson Co., 1922– ). A series of books, uniform in size and arrangement, each of which is given over entirely to a single subject of current public interest. Reprints of articles, excerpts from books, etc., give background information and develop pro-and-con positions in such a way as to stimulate thinking and suggest directions for further research. Selected bibliographies are included.

*Editorial Research Reports*, 1924– (1156 Nineteenth Street, N.W., Washington, D.C.). Each issue is devoted to the discussion of a current public question by a recognized expert.

*The NUEA Discussion and Debate Manual.* Committee on Debate Materials and Interstate Co-operation, the National University Extension Association (Columbia, Mo.: Artcraft Press, 1927– ). This annual handbook, edited by Professor Bower Aly of the University of Oregon, contains a collection of materials on the current national high school discussion and debate question. Recommended as authoritative and unbiased.

## THE CARD CATALOGUE

As has already been pointed out, all of the "general" books and most of the other materials a library owns are represented in its card catalogue.

[3] See pp. 310–11.

Nearly everyone knows something about using this helpful tool and has probably used it many times to secure books for class assignments or personal use. Many persons, however, do not know how to take full advantage of the varied information the catalogue provides.

In a large library the card catalogue is bulky not only because it lists many hundreds of thousands of items, but because all "general" books and most documents and reference works are represented in three different ways. Each work is listed *alphabetically,* by the *last name of the author* (or of each author if there is more than one); again by the *first word of the title* (exclusive of articles); and a third time under a *general subject heading*—English Language, Taxation, Labor Law, and the like.

For each type of entry, certain systematic patterns are followed in arranging the cards. For example, when an author—say Stuart Chase or Karl Marx or Charles Beard—is represented many times, the "author" cards are arranged as follows: (1) complete collections of the author's works, arranged chronologically; (2) selections from complete collections; (3) single works, filed alphabetically by title; (4) single works written in collaboration with someone else; (5) works edited or translated; and (6) works about the author—bibliographies, biographies, criticism, etc.—arranged alphabetically by the last names of their authors. A general subject heading, such as taxation, may be followed by several drawers of cards, classified under such subheadings as the names of various states and countries; Bibliography; Corporation, History of; School; etc. Following these there may be a card headed "See also," which will direct the researcher to related subjects—Public Finance, Tax Law, and the like. Thus, in effect, each subject heading in the catalogue provides a comprehensive bibliography on that subject.

On the card itself is a variety of useful information that may enable the skilled researcher to form a good idea of the contents of a particular book and also to make a shrewd estimate of its probable value to him. For instance, consider the author card on page 58.

What may be concluded about the nature of this book and its author, assuming we have not previously heard of either? First, from the date of the author's birth it is evident that at the time the book was published he was a mature individual, some fifty-nine years old. Second, the date of publication (1953) indicates that the work is a relatively recent one. Third, the book is lengthy, consisting of two volumes totaling 1410 relatively large (25 cm.) pages. Fourth, the book is a scholarly treatise, since 128 pages of notes and references are appended. Fifth, the inclusion of "bibliographical references" in the Notes will lead the researcher to related books and articles. Sixth, the list of catalogue headings at the bottom of the card announces the book is also catalogued under U.S. Constitu-

## 58  BUILDING A SUBJECT-MATTER BACKGROUND

tional Law, U.S. Supreme Court, and U.S. Constitutional History. Therefore, if one looks under these headings he can expect to find other books on the same general subject.

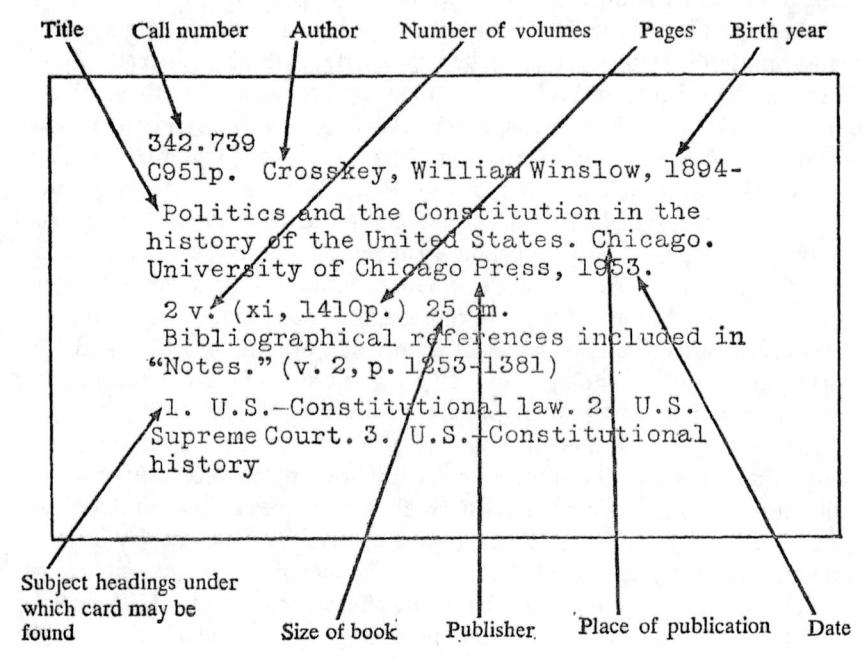

```
342.739
C951p.  Crosskey, William Winslow, 1894-
    Politics and the Constitution in the
history of the United States. Chicago.
University of Chicago Press, 1953.
    2 v. (xi, 1410p.) 25 cm.
    Bibliographical references included in
"Notes." (v. 2, p. 1253-1381)

    1. U.S.—Constitutional law. 2. U.S.
Supreme Court. 3. U.S.—Constitutional
history
```

Labels pointing to the card: Title, Call number, Author, Number of volumes, Pages, Birth year, Subject headings under which card may be found, Size of book, Publisher, Place of publication, Date.

But if these things are known because they are specifically stated on the card, what additional information may more or less safely be inferred? First, since the work is that of a mature author and was issued by one of the best of the university presses, it may be assumed to be an authoritative essay. Indeed, the Chicago "imprint" alone suggests that the manuscript was approved by a number of recognized experts and given careful and intelligent editing. Second, the 1953 publication date, together with the absence of any limiting dates in the title of the book itself, leads one to suspect that it brings the history of the subject down to relatively recent times, probably including the Roosevelt and perhaps even the Truman era. Third, the very length of the book and the presence of notes and bibliographical apparatus suggest it is a detailed and learned, rather than a popularized, treatment of the subject and, for that reason, might not provide a very good starting point for one who knows nothing about constitutional history.

Since these are inferences rather than verifiable facts, any or all of them, of course, may be wrong. But, more often than not, guesses of this sort turn out to be helpful, and as one's knowledge of a given subject

OBTAINING INFORMATION: PRINTED SOURCES      59

grows, his estimates constantly increase in accuracy.

The card just considered, although rich in information, is by no means so detailed and comprehensive as some others that may be found in the catalogue. The main entry for a multivolume work—for instance, *The Works of Aristotle,* edited in eleven volumes by W. D. Ross—will list the particular treatises found in each volume, together with the names of the men who translated them. Each of these individual treatises will, in turn, have a separate card filed by translator and another filed by title. If a work is in a revised or new edition or is part of a series, such as the ten volumes bearing the general title *A History of the South* and published by the Louisiana State University Press, these facts will also be noted on the card. Sometimes the card even briefly describes the contents of the book. Cards listing newspapers indicate what years are covered by the library's holdings, and those for magazines and journals often give the names of editors and other valuable information. In short, for one who has learned how to take full advantage of it, the card catalogue is a rich mine of information about books on any subject and will save the researcher many hours and many, many weary steps.

*A Warning.*   One limitation of card catalogues should, however, be noted. In a large library the ordering, classifying, and carding of books is a slow process that even under the most favorable conditions consumes a period of several months. Therefore, the most recent books on a subject seldom appear in the library's catalogue.

When studying a current problem over a period of time, one should make a habit of scanning the reviews and advertisements in the Sunday *New York Times* Book Review Section, the *Saturday Review,* or such journals as *Harper's Magazine* and the *Atlantic Monthly.* In this way attention is drawn to recent publications that would otherwise escape notice. Moreover, even the best card catalogues are sometimes inaccurate or incomplete. Before concluding that the library does not own a certain book, make a thorough search, looking under several different headings. If in doubt, consult an attendant.

## QUESTIONS

A.  *To Check Your Comprehension and Memory*

1. Into what five major categories do a library's holdings fall?

2. Why should one regularly consult as many newspapers as possible during the period he is studying and debating a subject?

3. What are some of the magazines and newspapers that are especially helpful in studying current business and economic trends?

4. Name several British newspapers and magazines that may prove use-

ful to the debater.

5. How may one discover municipal or county documents that might be useful? state or federal documents? foreign documents? documents issued by the United Nations? transcripts of congressional committee hearings?

6. What sorts of information are contained in the *Statistical Abstract?*

7. How is the *Congressional Record* indexed?

8. What are some of the different sorts of "fugitive materials" in which the debater is especially interested? What index may help him to locate items pertinent to his subject?

9. Under what conditions might a debater consult the *Encyclopaedia of the Social Sciences* rather than *Britannica* or *Americana?*

10. Name some of the general and special biographical dictionaries. How would one use them to find out about a person who is no longer living?

11. Name some of the many sorts of information contained in almanacs and books of facts and figures.

12. Name some of the publications devoted to summarizing and indexing current affairs.

13. What is *Reader's Guide?*

14. What kind of magazines are listed in the *International Index?*

15. What four publications are of especial value to the debater because they contain collections of materials on a single subject?

16. In what three ways is a book represented in the card catalogue?

17. What information about a book is given on the catalogue card?

18. What additional information may often be inferred from the card?

19. Are very recent books usually listed in the card catalogue?

20. How may one find out which numbers of a magazine a library owns?

## EXERCISES

*A. Written Exercises*

1. Name five recent federal documents dealing with agricultural subjects and five dealing with economic or social problems.

2. Look up in the card catalogue three books on international affairs, three on industrial relations, and three on city planning. What are you told about each book and its author? What may you infer about them from the information given on the card?

3. Look up the answers to at least fifteen of the following:
   a. When and where was President John F. Kennedy born?
   b. What is the population of Chicago?
   c. What was the value of United States exports in 1962?
   d. Name the United States Congressmen from Arizona.
   e. What form of government does Bolivia have?
   f. In what year did the present British Prime Minister first enter Parliament?
   g. Who wrote the article on foreign trade in the *Encyclopaedia of the*

OBTAINING INFORMATION: PRINTED SOURCES 61

*Social Sciences?* Who wrote on this subject in the *Encyclopaedia Britannica?*
h. What were the leading news events of the week of June 1–7, 1959?
i. Who was premier of France on May 25, 1958?
j. List five articles on farm price supports published during 1962.
k. How rapidly did the price level climb between January 1, 1960, and January 1, 1962? What happened to wages during this same period?
l. Where did Dean Rusk attend college? Where did he receive his law degree?
m. Do we have reciprocal trade agreements with all of the South American countries?
n. Name four books on American foreign policy that have been published during the last few years.
o. Did the automobile industry make or lose money during 1960? during 1962? How much?
p. How many different books by Stuart Chase does your library own? From studying the card catalogue only, would you say that Chase's interests as a writer have changed much during the last decade?
q. In what year was foreign economic aid the national high school discussion and debate topic?
r. By how large a majority did Kennedy win over Nixon in 1960?
s. What does the National City Bank of New York think about the trend of business in the immediate future?
t. How old is Vice-President Lyndon Johnson?

B. *Oral Exercises*
1. Make a five-minute informative speech on one of the following subjects, or on a similar subject suggested by one of these. Use no less than five books or magazine articles in developing your ideas. List these in a bibliography at the bottom of your speech outline, or hand them to your instructor on a separate sheet of paper.

What's Ahead for the Farmer?
Will the Businessman Be Better Off Next Year?
Editorial Reaction to the Present Administration
Our Growing Urban Areas
The Burden of Taxation on the Average Man
Aspects of Our Foreign Policy

2. Make a three- or four-minute oral report on one of the following:

Finding and Using Federal Documents
How Our Library Handles Pamphlet Materials
Newspapers Available in Our Library
News Magazines as a Research Source
Three Specialized Encyclopedias Useful to the Debater
Recent Volumes in the *Reference Shelf* Series
The *World Almanac:* Its Contents and Organization

## SUGGESTIONS FOR FURTHER READING

Committee on Research of the Amos Tuck School of Administration and Finance of Dartmouth College, *Manual on Research and Reports* (New York: McGraw-Hill Book Co., 1937). "A guidebook of procedures helpful in conducting investigations and presenting reports on subjects in the fields of the social sciences."

W. C. Schulter, *How to Do Research Work* (New York: Prentice-Hall, 1926). Although an older book, gives a highly practical set of instructions for the research worker. Strong chapters on collecting, analyzing, and interpreting data.

Donald A. Sears, *Harbrace Guide to the Library and the Research Paper*, 2d ed. (New York: Harcourt, Brace & Co., 1960). A very simple and practical workbook. See especially pp. 1–8 on the use of the library.

Cecil B. Williams and Allan H. Stevenson, *A Research Manual*, rev. ed. (New York: Harper & Brothers, 1951). The first three chapters on the nature of research and the use of the library and its reference tools are especially important.

*Chapter 6*

# RECORDING AND FILING INFORMATION

*Details are the raw materials of truth. If observation is careless or interpretation faulty, the generalizations or major conclusions based upon them will be unsound.* TYRUS HILLWAY

OBTAINING the data essential to a critical decision is only the first step in building a subject-matter background for debate. To be useful the data must be preserved for ready future reference. Hence, the debater needs to know how to take notes and to organize a note system.

Note-taking, which at first appears to be a relatively simple task, actually presents a number of problems. What information should be recorded? When should the notes be made? What form should they take? How should they be organized and filed? Although any of these matters may at times prove bothersome, the first two are, by all odds, the most difficult.

## WHAT TO RECORD AND WHEN TO RECORD IT

Knowing what information to record and when to record it is difficult because one can never determine the content of an argumentative speech or essay until the research process that underlies it is already well advanced. But, conversely, he cannot know what specific facts and figures will be required as explanation or proof until the theme of the discourse has been set. Therefore, in the early stages of his study the debater is often in the sad plight of the dog who chases his tail. He goes around and around the subject without knowing exactly how to take hold of it. On the one hand, he runs the danger of passing over many items that will be needed later; on the other, he records much that will eventually be discarded as useless.

There is, perhaps, no wholly satisfactory way out of this dilemma. The debater should accept the fact that he will undoubtedly make some mistakes in judgment and engage in considerable waste motion. The following suggestions may, however, prove helpful. They are based on the experience of many different persons and have been tested repeatedly.

1. In the early stages of study read for general background and orientation—for a broad familiarity with the subject, rather than to gather the specific facts on which proof will ultimately be based.

2. Continue this background study until a working knowledge of all important aspects of the problem has been attained. Depending on the scope and importance of the subject under investigation, this study may consume days, weeks, or months. In any event, a debater should spend a considerable portion of his available time for research in background study. If he does not, his knowledge will lack depth and sureness, and his search for specific facts and figures will be more time-consuming.

3. Start by reading (*a*) simpler and more popularized treatments of the subject and (*b*) treatments that appear to be nonpartisan. Look particularly for discussions of the history and development of the problem and for explanations of its nature, scope, and importance. In short, read expository and analytical, rather than argumentative, materials. Keep an open mind; read with a view to learning. Don't worry yet about reaching a decision or about how others may be persuaded.

4. Keep an annotated bibliography, carefully recording on a card the author and title of any book or article that may need to be referred to again. Use the forms illustrated on page 70, adding a few lines summarizing and evaluating those ideas in the source that seem particularly useful. File these bibliography cards in some systematic order—by author, subject, or title.

As yet, take very few, if any, subject-matter notes. Remember, at this stage the purpose is not to collect specific data, but to acquire a general understanding of the subject. Don't pass over any information that will almost certainly be wanted, but don't, as a general rule, stop to take detailed notes.

5. Read with an alert, inquiring mind. Think about the ideas and arguments encountered; analyze and evaluate each. What is true? What seems doubtful or false? What is important? What is trivial? What is interesting? What pertinent? How do the various facts and opinions fit together? What do they all mean?

As reading and thinking continue, a particular interpretation or view of the problem gradually begins to take form. One is able to decide what ambiguous terms mean and in what ways various facts are significant. Soon, also, one begins to decide on the probable causes of the problem, its extent and seriousness, who it affects and how, and perhaps even to think about possible solutions.

At this point review the bibliography cards. Cull out the materials that seem most pertinent. Reread these items, now recording whatever portions of their contents promise to be of future use. Pass on to other books and articles not on the original bibliography. Keep a list of these new sources also, so that a complete record of all noted materials is always available.

6. While engaged in this process of gathering specific facts and figures, continue a program of general background reading. Keep trying to break into previously unexplored areas of the subject. Strive for a fuller and deeper knowledge of all of its parts.

Above all, keep an open mind. Consider interpretations or approaches other than the one being developed. Know as much about alternative views as possible. Not only is it the moral obligation of a debater to have such knowledge, but it makes the argumentative basis of his position stronger and prepares him to answer any attacks that may be made against it.

Keep an open mind, too, about modifying your selected approach as new facts and ideas come to light. Let thinking be flexible. Don't set it once and for all into a hard, unshakable mold.

Read constantly. Begin now to talk with experts. Check what they say and what you are reading against your own previous knowledge and experience. Think hard. Do this not to confirm biases and prejudices—not merely to search out facts that substantiate the view adopted. Do it in an honest effort to understand the subject more thoroughly and interpret it more wisely. Of course, some ways of analyzing or solving the problem will seem better than others, or one would not be justified in advancing them in a debate for the consideration of other people. But don't put on mental blinkers. The strength and validity of any line of argument derives in large measure from a thorough knowledge of the strengths and weaknesses of its possible alternatives. And that argument is always strongest which most clearly accords with all of the facts as one knows or believes them to be.

7. Continue the program of general reading and thinking and the search for specific facts and figures as long as you are speaking or writing about the problem. Do not stop active research until the final word has been spoken or the last line set down.

These, then, are the seven steps we would recommend in determining what information to record and when to record it: (1) Begin by reading for general background and orientation, not for specific facts and figures. (2) Continue background reading until all major aspects of the subject have been explored. (3) Begin with simple and impartial treatments. (4) Keep an annotated bibliography. (5) As a particular interpretation or view of the problem begins to take form, cull out the pertinent items on this bibliography and reread them to gather the specific facts and figures that will be offered in proof. (6) During this stage of searching for specific data, do additional background reading, always keeping a flexible mind. (7) Continue general and specific reading—and hard thinking—until the final debate on the subject is completed.

## FORMULATING THE APPROACH

As suggested in the preceding section, after one has read and thought and talked about a problem for a time, he begins to develop a particular view or interpretation of it. That is, he develops what we call an "approach."

We shall consider at length some of the techniques that expedite the formulation of an approach to a controversy when we discuss the analysis of a proposition in Chapter 14. Our present concern is to decide when the debater should break off his program of orientation reading and attempt to frame and organize his judgments.

Here the danger lies in extremes. The whole purpose of debate is to provide a method by which beliefs may be formed and decisions reached through a critical study of all of the pertinent facts. Therefore, snap judgments must be avoided. Writers and speakers must learn that ideas produced "off the top of the head" are seldom cogent, and that to hurry the period of general reading and thinking is to invite intellectual—and sometimes social—disaster.

But since learning is long and life is short, the opposite extreme is equally undesirable. Debaters customarily deal with problems that press. Tax laws expire and must either be extended or replaced; unemployment and human suffering are immediate; other nations act, and we must react or perish. The control of nuclear energy, the preservation of natural resources, the slaughter on our highways—these problems are not distant and remote, but here and now. The researcher, therefore, must usually ration the time he spends on background reading and get on to the hard intellectual labor of formulating judgments and organizing arguments. Unwarranted delay in moving to this second step is all too common. Nearly every debater has at some time put it off with the excuse that he needs to study a matter more thoroughly.

How may the debater strike the proper balance between precipitance and procrastination? Although no single answer fits all situations and all persons, the following procedure generally applies: After having read and thought—and, if possible, talked with others—for a period of days or weeks, arbitrarily call a halt. Without regarding the result as final, work out a specific "approach" to the problem. Make a judgment about its extent. Form some hypotheses concerning its causes. Develop a possible solution. When preparing for a college debate, confer with your colleague to adjust conflicting ideas and arrive at a common position on each important point. Draw up a rough plan of the intended speech or essay. Get something definite down on paper. There will probably be weak points or even gaps in the arguments recorded. Some ideas will be undeveloped, some relationships still vague or tentative. Don't worry about these. Put down as much as possible and fill in the gaps later. Make at least a one-, two-, or three-page outline, listing leading contentions that might be offered in a debate.

Then put this outline aside to cool. Resume the interrupted program of general reading, thinking always about the meaning and significance of each idea encountered. After a period of days or weeks, work out a second outline similar to the first. Compare the results. Repeat this process until all significant material on the subject has been read and digested.

On even the broadest problems, a point of diminishing returns is eventually reached. Few, if any, new facts or ideas are encountered. The learning process slows down and grinds to a halt. General agreement between colleagues is reached. These conditions signify that the subject is at least temporarily exhausted and that arguments may be put into finished form. At this point, do the hardest thinking of all. Stick at it until the best possible approach has been formulated and the strongest evidence marshaled in support.

Just as general background study should continue so long as a question is under discussion, so should the selected interpretation or approach be re-evaluated periodically. Situations change. What was true or important six months ago may no longer be so today. Strive always to present arguments that are pertinent and ideas that are significant at the moment. The debater whose recommendations are dated is of little use to society.

## HOW TO TAKE NOTES

As the foregoing discussion suggests, deciding what information to preserve in notes requires judgment and experience. The mechanics of recording information may be mastered more quickly but are no less important, if the results of research are to be of maximum use. The note that is illegible, inaccurate, or incomplete is little better than no note at all.

## USE CARDS

The notes taken by the debater should be put on cards or slips of heavy paper. Only in rare instances, when recording complex tables or diagrams, are loose-leaf notebooks or separate sheets of paper to be preferred. Cards are easier to file and store while gathering material and more convenient to use while speaking or writing.

The size of the cards employed is a matter of personal preference. Most persons, however, find $3 \times 5$'s too small to hold much information and $5 \times 8$'s too large to carry and file conveniently. Hence, by a process of elimination, they settle upon the $4 \times 6$ size.

## RECORD INFORMATION ACCURATELY AND COMPLETELY

In newspaper work there is an old saying, "Be quick, be complete, be accurate." In note-taking there is seldom need for speed. Completeness and accuracy, however, are of prime importance. A single word omitted from a quotation or a single figure inaccurately reproduced from a statistical report may alter the meaning of the data drastically, rendering a critical decision impossible.

When copying words or figures verbatim, or taking down the title of a book or article, recheck the finished note against the source to insure accuracy. Indicate the verbatim character of the note with quotation marks. When condensing or summarizing a passage, take pains to represent fully and fairly the material telescoped.

Similar care should be exercised when recording the source from which a note is derived. Be sure to get the name of the author or authors, the exact title and date of the publication, and the page from which the data are taken. Write these immediately. Do not trust to memory or put it off until later. The danger of forgetting the source of an important note is always great.

Follow also the practice of putting only one unit of information—one connected passage, one set of statistics, one book or article title—on a card. In writing or speaking, notes are used as independent units, and one great advantage of cards is that they can be sorted so as to make data fall into different organizational patterns. If diverse pieces of information are recorded on the same card, this mobility is lost.

Above all, when taking notes write legibly and large enough so that the information on the card can be read easily. In oral debating notes must be referred to during the heat of the argument when time is at a premium and excitement runs high. Often quotations must be read aloud to the audience. For these reasons, legibility is essential.

## TYPES OF NOTES

Customarily a debater requires three types of notes: bibliography notes, biography notes, and subject-matter notes.

### BIBLIOGRAPHY NOTES

A bibliography note records the author, title, and date of a printed source of information. A note on a magazine article also indicates the pages on which the recorded material appears. A bibliography note should always be made as soon as an important source is encountered.

Bibliography notes serve three important purposes: (*a*) They "flag" materials that may be returned to later for more careful study. (*b*) They supply a ready store of information if, during the course of a controversy, the authenticity or source of data is challenged. (*c*) They save time and labor by enabling one to use a shortened form for recording sources on subject-matter notes. (For examples of such condensation, see the sample subject-matter notes on pp. 72–73.)

Bibliography notes should be placed in a separate file and carefully preserved. Some debaters record them on colored cards or slips so they are easily distinguished from subject-matter notes, which are usually recorded on white.

In recording bibliographical information, standard forms should be followed. The proper forms for listing a magazine article and a book are illustrated on p. 70. Variations suitable for newspaper articles, documents, and the like may be worked out by the individual debater or found in *A Manual of Style* (Chicago: University of Chicago Press, 1949), pp. 150–53. For bibliographical purposes a pamphlet, or other separately bound and unnumbered publication, is treated as a book, whereas chapters or sections of books are treated as magazine articles.

If a book has more than one author, record each name accurately. Failure to do so is a common cause of confusion. If a book consists of a collection of essays by different persons, indicate the name of the compiler or editor. Make certain also to include the date of publication, since knowing exactly when data appeared is often crucial to determining their worth as evidence. Finally, when using library materials write the call number of the book or magazine at the bottom of the card, for convenience in rechecking a source.

The sample bibliography cards shown below—the first of a magazine article and the second of a book—are "annotated." That is, they carry a short statement describing and evaluating the contents of the work cited. While not always essential, annotations are frequently useful jogs to the memory.

---

Brogan, D. W.

"Australia: The Innocent Continent," Harper's Magazine, June 1958, pp. 62-68

Australia today—its geography, culture, people, and economy. Prospects for future development.

Especially good analysis of socioeconomic factors.

051
H294

---

Scharr, John H.

Loyalty in America (Berkeley and Los Angeles: University of California Press), 1957.

The psychology and sociology of the concept of "loyalty." Its relations with other political concepts and doctrines. An historical sketch of the development of the theory of political loyalty in the U.S. The problem today—loyalty oaths, investigations, etc.
A philosophic and synthetic treatment.
See especially Chapter 6 on loyalty and mass democracy.

320.158
S2911

---

BIOGRAPHY NOTES

Biography notes constitute a miniature *Who's Who* for the problem under discussion. They contain biographical data concerning frequently cited authorities, public officials, and other persons whose actions or decisions may come into question. Their purpose is to enable the debater to identify these persons quickly should it become necessary to do so, and to help him evaluate their authoritativeness.

Biography cards may be made in any convenient form. Usually they are copied from one of the standard biographical dictionaries.

---

LUCE, CLARE BOOTH, MRS.

B., N.Y.C., 1903. Grad. Miss Mason's School, Tarrytown, N.Y. Honorary degrees Colby Coll., Creighton Univ., Georgetown Univ.

Assoc. ed. Vogue, 1930. Assoc. ed. Vanity Fair, 1931; managing ed., 1933.

Married Henry Luce of Time, Life, and Fortune, 1935. World War II correspondent in Europe and Asia. Congresswoman, 4th Conn. Dist., 1943-47. Appointed by Eisenhower as Ambassador to Italy 1953-57. Writer and lecturer on public affairs; playwright.

---

Many debaters find it helpful to put biography notes on paper of a distinctive color, so they may readily be separated from bibliography and subject-matter cards.

## SUBJECT-MATTER NOTES

Subject-matter notes contain the data on which proof, and hence decision, are based.

The important rules governing the preparation of subject-matter notes are the same as for notes in general, and have, therefore, already been discussed. Be accurate, be complete, write legibly, put one unit of information on a card—each of these principles must be faithfully observed.

The subject-matter notes used by the debater may be divided into three types: (*a*) the verbatim quotation, (*b*) the paraphrase summary, and (*c*) the personal reaction or reminder statement.

When the data being recorded are of unusual importance, when the exact wording used by the source is significant, or when the strength of proof depends on direct statement, take the note as a *verbatim quotation*. Enclose the reproduced material in quotation marks, indicate omissions by ellipses . . . , and interpolations by brackets [ ]. How to do this is

72  BUILDING A SUBJECT-MATTER BACKGROUND

shown in the first sample note below.

When exact statement is not necessary, use the second type of note, the *paraphrase summary*. Remember, however, the injunction to summarize fairly. The note must always reflect as accurately as possible the view expressed by the source.

In certain instances, instead of drawing information from others, the debater wishes to record his own observations or reactions. Notes of this sort serve as *personal reaction* or *reminder statements*. Write personal reaction notes in the form best suited to their future use, and initial them for identification.

VERBATIM QUOTATION

Descriptive heading

First part of sentence omitted

Word inserted

Single quotation marks because quotation is within a quotation

---

Income-Cost Plight of the Farmer

". . . the [farm] problem is a grave one. . . . Nearly a third of all non-military Federal expenditure goes to supporting agriculture, the largest single 'civil' item. . . . Meantime the income-cost plight of millions of farmers has been harsh. . . . They have seen their net income drop forty-one per cent from 1948 to 1957, down from $17 billion to $10 billion while all their costs have risen. . . . [Yet] today's farmer . . . lives on practically the same cash basis as the rest of us, even buys his eggs in the grocery store."

Chase "America's Farm Problem," Commonwealth, June 27, 1958, p. 319.

---

Source given in condensed form. Complete information appears on bibliography card

Only one unit of information

Last of sentence omitted (ellipsis plus period)

Quotation marks at beginning and end of quotation

Experience is the best teacher in learning what sorts of information to record verbatim and what to put in paraphrase summary form. When in doubt, however, take a statement verbatim. It can always be condensed later if that seems desirable, but changing a paraphrased statement back to a direct quotation necessitates relocating the source.

HEADINGS. A good rule for all research purposes, but especially for debate, is to give each subject-matter note a heading describing its contents. Such a heading is an aid not only in filing information systematically, but also in locating it quickly. The heading should be as brief and simple as possible and should summarize accurately the information contained in the note. It may be put on at the time the note is made or added later.

SAMPLE SUBJECT-MATTER NOTES. Study carefully the sample subject-matter notes and accompanying marginal comments on these two pages.

PARAPHRASE SUMMARY

---

Baruch's Recipe for Recession Cure

Testifying before Senate Committee on Finance, April 1, 1958, Bernard Baruch counseled against a tax cut, arguing that our real problem is to organize and employ our resources so as to insure our defense, raise our standard of living, and promote economic security for all.

To do this we must gain technological superiority, guard against further deterioration of credit, place Federal Works program on self-liquidating basis, end wage-price spirals, and ameliorate suffering of unemployed.

Testimony reprinted in The Congressional Digest, June-July, 1958, pp. 181, 183, 185.

---

PERSONAL OBSERVATION

---

U.S. Tariffs and Communist Bloc Trade

If U.S. tariffs were abolished or appreciably lowered at this time, would it not enable the Communist Bloc countries to flood our markets with cheaper products, thus greatly enhancing their position in world trade?

CKT

## FILING INFORMATION

The filing of biography and bibliography notes presents no particular problem. Organizing subject-matter notes is more difficult.

The difficulty arises because in debate many subject-matter notes serve a double function. First, they are aids in building up the debater's knowledge of a subject; second, they are aids in proving his contentions to others. Notes valuable for the first purpose may be useless for the second. Moreover, the same note may at one time be used constructively to establish a point, at another destructively to refute the argument of an opponent.

In organizing a note system recognize the double function that subject-matter notes serve. During the period of preparation that precedes actual writing or speaking, file them in any way that facilitates study of the subject. Do not worry about how they will be used in an actual debate. As thinking changes and new ideas and relationships emerge, rearrange the notes accordingly.

Eventually, certain vital questions arise that must be answered in arriving at a decision on the question under debate. These vital questions, as we shall learn in Chapters 7 and 14, are called "issues." "Is the proposed policy needed?" "Would it remedy alleged problems?" "Would it entail worse evils?" These questions are typical of the "issues" that often emerge when debating the advisability of adopting a new policy.

Once the issues become clear, overhaul the note system and refile the cards under the issue to which each applies. Such organization adapts the notes to the specific needs that arise as one writes and speaks. It groups together under a single head all of the information that has been assembled on each of the potential points of contest, and makes it readily available for use either in attack or defense. If, as sometimes happens, a single note applies to several issues, a system of cross-indexing may be worked out.

When the notes have been refiled according to the preceding scheme, write in the upper right-hand corner of each card, in large letters, the issue to which the note applies. If, during the course of writing or speaking, the notes become scattered, this "issue" label makes easy the reassembling of the data.

Here is a note card with an "issue" label affixed. Observe that, unlike the three notes considered above, it contains statistical data in tabular form. This is a type of note the debater frequently needs to make.

RECORDING AND FILING INFORMATION 75

NEED

NORTH CAROLINA (cities over 25,000)

Dwelling Units, 1950

|  | Total | Hot water, bath Not dilapidated | Occupied Total | Owner Occupied |
|---|---|---|---|---|
| Asheville | 15,965 | 68.7 | 15,029 | 51.4 |
| Charlotte | 37,847 | 70.0 | 36,899 | 44.1 |
| Durham | 18,810 | 51.2 | 18,414 | 37.8 |
| Fayetteville | 9,579 | 54.3 | 9,293 | 41.3 |
| Greensboro | 19,539 | 66.2 | 18,997 | 45.2 |
| Wilmington | 13,409 | 63.4 | 12,794 | 48.6 |
| Winston-Salem | 24,869 | 51.3 | 24,362 | 42.8 |

County and City Data Book. A Statistical Abstract Supplement. Prepared by the Bureau of the Census (Washington: U.S. Government Printing Office, 1957), p. 397.

## QUESTIONS

*A. To Check Your Comprehension and Memory*

1. Why is it difficult to know what information to preserve in notes until the study of a subject is relatively well advanced?

2. Explain the seven-step program that may help to solve the problem of what to record and when.

3. What part does systematic thinking or reflection play in this process?

4. Why should the debater keep an open mind?

5. When should general background reading on a subject stop?

6. At what point in his study of a subject should the debater begin to formulate a specific view or "approach"?

7. Explain why the "extremes" of precipitousness and procrastination are to be avoided.

8. Why must the debater, unlike the scientist, sometimes make decisions before he is entirely ready to do so?

9. How may the debater combat the tendency to procrastinate in formulating an approach?

10. What are good signs that one has pretty well exhausted a subject?

11. Why must a debater thoroughly reevaluate his thinking about a subject every few weeks or months?

12. Why must correct habits of note-taking be formed at the very beginning?

76  BUILDING A SUBJECT-MATTER BACKGROUND

13. Explain why the debater's notes must be accurate and complete.
14. What are some good rules that insure these qualities?
15. Why should each note card contain only one unit of information?
16. Name the three general types of notes a debater needs.
17. What purposes does a bibliography note serve?
18. Where may the information for biography notes be obtained?
19. What are the three different types of subject-matter notes?
20. When should a note take the form of a direct quotation?
21. What is especially important when paraphrasing or summarizing?
22. Why should each subject-matter note be given a descriptive heading?
23. How are omissions from a quoted passage indicated? How interpolations?
24. When should subject-matter notes be refiled? How?
25. What is an "issue" label, and why is it important?

*B. For Class Discussion*
1. Chapter 3 stated that no debater has the right to advocate to others a view in which he himself does not firmly believe. In this chapter, however, the debater was urged always to preserve an open mind. Reconcile these statements.
2. Recall the statement made on p. 65: "The strength and validity of any line of argument derives in large measure from a thorough knowledge of the strengths and weaknesses of its possible alternatives." Do you agree or disagree? Why?
3. How would you explain the fact that ideas produced "off the top of the head" are seldom convincing?
4. In preparing a speech, report, or term paper, have you ever found yourself delaying unduly the actual organizing and writing? Can you analyze the reasons for this? On the other hand, have you ever been guilty of undue precipitousness? What was the result?
5. Recall that the debater, unlike the scientist, cannot always delay decisions until he is entirely ready to decide. Does this mean that his decisions are inferior to the scientist's?

EXERCISES

*A. Written Exercises*
1. Interview a faculty member who has done considerable research and writing in the humanities or social sciences. Discuss with him the problem of organizing material and formulating an "approach." Ask for any practical suggestions he may have on note-taking, etc. Hand in a written report, summarizing what you have learned.
2. Talk with several members of your college debate team. Find out how they go about note-taking, selecting an approach, etc. Compare what they have to say with the suggestions offered by the faculty member. Write

up your results.

3. Select a subject of current interest and do some reading on it. Then prepare and hand in the following: (1) five bibliography notes—one on a magazine article, one on a book, one on a newspaper story, one on a document, and one on a pamphlet; (2) one biography note concerning an author whose book or article you have cited; and (3) three subject-matter notes—a direct quotation, a paraphrase summary, and a personal reaction statement. Give your subject-matter notes appropriate headings and carefully follow the forms illustrated in the sample notes in this chapter.

*B. Oral Exercises*

1. Present a five-minute informative or persuasive speech on a subject of current interest. In addition to an outline, hand in three bibliography notes (citing a book, a magazine article, and a pamphlet or document); two biography notes of persons quoted or referred to; and five subject-matter notes, of which at least two are direct quotations.

2. Read what Schmitz or Williams and Stevenson (you will find their books listed in Suggestions for Further Reading) have to say about note-taking and the building of note systems. Make a five- or six-minute oral report summarizing their recommendations. Use examples of different types of notes drawn on the blackboard, or any other visual aids you think will be helpful in communicating this information to the class.

## SUGGESTIONS FOR FURTHER READING

Mortimer Adler, *How to Read a Book*. The Art of Getting a Liberal Education (New York: Simon and Schuster, 1940; paperback, 1956). Just what its title indicates. Gives practical rules for analyzing the contents of a book, grasping the relationships between its parts, following the author's ideas, etc. Part 2, "The Rules," is especially valuable to the debater.

John Dewey, *How We Think* (New York: D. C. Heath & Co., 1933), Chapter 7, "Analysis of Reflective Thinking"; Chapter 8, "The Place of Judgment in Reflective Activity"; and Chapter 9, "Understanding: Ideas and Meaning." These chapters explore the mysterious process by which ideas, meanings, and hypotheses arise out of the study of data.

Homer Carey Hockett, *The Critical Method in Historical Research and Writing*, 3d ed. (New York: The Macmillan Co., 1955). On pp. 134–42 you will find a discussion of what to record in notes, how to record it, and how to file your results. Don't be fooled by the title of the book. The straightforward advice is very much to the debater's purpose.

E. Wayne Marjarum, *How to Use a Book* (New Brunswick, N.J.: Rutgers University Press, 1947). Excellent chapters on how to increase your reading speed and still remember what you read.

R. Morell Schmitz, *Preparing the Research Paper*. A Handbook for Undergraduates, 4th ed. (New York: Holt, Rinehart & Winston, 1957). A useful guide to all phases of library research—finding materials, note-taking, bibliography building, etc.

Cecil B. Williams and Allan H. Stevenson, *A Research Manual*, rev. ed. (New York: Harper & Brothers, 1951), Chapter 6, "Notes and Note Taking." Perhaps the best available treatment of this subject for the debater.

*Part III*

# THE MATERIALS OF ARGUMENT

# Chapter 7
## THE ANATOMY OF A DISPUTE

*When men are brought face to face with their opponents, forced to listen and learn and mend their ideas, they cease to be children and begin to live like civilized men. . . .* WALTER LIPPMANN

CHAPTER 2 considered the function and rationale of debate. This chapter will cut beneath the surface of the debate process to examine the functioning parts—or, as they may figuratively be called, the anatomy—of a dispute.

### A HYPOTHETICAL EXAMPLE

It is a hot August afternoon. Mr. N on his way home from the office comes to the bus stop and, finding a single spot of shade just large enough to cover him, steps into it gratefully. Soon Mr. A, a fellow worker, approaches and, seeing the only spot of shade already occupied by Mr. N, resigns himself to waiting in the sun. A certain order of things— a certain pattern of relationships among Mr. N, Mr. A, and the spot of shade—is thus established and persists until the bus arrives.

But now suppose that instead of being a peaceful, timid soul, Mr. A is an aggressive, belligerent individual, and that he attempts to push Mr. N out of the shady spot, by words or manner challenging him to retain it. Under these circumstances, one of two reactions is possible: (*a*) Mr. N may let the challenge pass, and move as Mr. A desires, so that a new pattern of relationships is established, with Mr. A now in the shade and Mr. N out in the sun. (*b*) Mr. N may try to repel Mr. A's aggression, with the result that blows are exchanged and a fight develops.

Either way, two facts are to be observed: (*a*) Mr. N and Mr. A want the same spot of shade, a spot too small for both of them to occupy at once; and (*b*) when Mr. A attempts to push Mr. N out of the shade he takes a certain risk, a risk on which he has to make good if he is to achieve what he wants, and even, perhaps, avoid physical harm to himself. For Mr. N may respond to A's shove by knocking him down and beating him soundly. Then Mr. A would not only fail to win the place in the shade, but might sustain injuries, as well.

Now let us vary the story in one respect. Assume that the altercation between Mr. N and Mr. A, instead of involving shoves and blows, is confined to words.

In this new situation Mr. A, on approaching the bus stop, might say: "By rights, N, that spot of shade belongs to me." Again, Mr. N has two courses of action open to him: (*a*) He may reply, "Yes, that is so," and move out of the shady spot, allowing Mr. A to occupy it; or (*b*) he may answer, "I deny this spot of shade belongs to you. Prove that such is, indeed, true."

Three observations are to be made about this second version of the story:

1. Although less direct physical danger may be involved in the verbal declaration than in the shove, Mr. A still takes a risk when he asserts that the shade by rights belongs to him, for, unless his claim is to be idle talk, he must be able to prove the necessity, expediency, or justice of the state of affairs he seeks. This, too, is a "risk," not only because failure to make good his claim means that it will be impossible for A to achieve the goal he seeks, but also because defeat may cause him to lose status in the eyes of N and of the community as a whole, so that in the end he will be less well off than he was before.

2. The verbal assertion, no less than the physical blow, is an agitating force. It has the effect of stirring up and throwing into turmoil what had previously been a static and ordered situation, a situation which, it may be assumed, would have remained static had the challenge not been issued.

3. The verbal assertion, no less than the physical blow, specifies the particular reordering—the new pattern of relationships—that A believes should replace the old order. It says that instead of N being in the shade and A in the sun, A should be in the shade and N in the sun.

## PRESUMPTION, BURDEN OF PROOF, AND BURDEN OF GOING FORWARD WITH THE DEBATE

Keeping these points in mind, one must consider two concepts that are of the greatest possible importance in understanding what happens when contending parties engage in a debate. They are *presumption* and *burden of proof*.

PRESUMPTION

As the two versions of the story about Mr. N and Mr. A showed, the battle of fists and the battle of words arose for the same reason: Mr. N was occupying a particular piece of ground that Mr. A believed N should not be on.

In this respect, the story is completely typical. Every debate that ever has or ever will take place concerns, if not an actual, at least a figurative piece of ground. One of the disputants *preoccupies*—figuratively stands upon—an idea, interpretation, or value that the other thinks he should not be occupying. Indeed, unless some actual or figurative piece of ground is preoccupied, there can be no debate. There is no established order or pattern of relationships that may be challenged. The situation is chaotic or formless and hence not subject to reordering. There is nothing to argue about, no matter concerning which the parties can disagree. For a debate to occur, the occupancy of a piece of argumentative ground must be contested. Here, as at many other points in a description of debates and verbal disputes, the analogy to a physical order or event is both close and pertinent.

The technical term for the preoccupation of a piece of argumentative ground is *presumption*. The party who at the beginning of the debate stands upon the disputed ground—in our example, Mr. N—is, therefore, said to have the presumption.

Presumption is, however, neither more nor less than such preoccupation. As a concept, it makes no evaluation of the situation it labels. To say that one of the parties to a dispute has the presumption does not mean that the ground which he occupies is occupied legitimately or illegitimately or that he should or should not be standing on it. The term only describes a situation that exists and points out the prevailing order of things by declaring that one of the disputants stands at a particular place within that order.

NATURAL AND ARTIFICIAL PRESUMPTION. As a description of an existing system of relationships, presumption may be either *natural* or *artificial*.

Natural presumption reflects things as they are viewed in the world about us. If an argument involves a belief concerning existing institutions, practices, customs, mores, values, or interpretations, the presumption is automatically in favor of that belief simply because the institutions, etc., are thought to exist.

Artificial presumption, on the other hand, is the result of ground arbitrarily assigned, a preoccupation by agreement rather than by the present order of things. That a man brought to trial is to be presumed

84   THE MATERIALS OF ARGUMENT

innocent until proved guilty is an example of presumption of this second sort.

The point to bear in mind, however, is that neither natural nor artificial presumption evaluates. The former does not say that a belief about existing institutions, practices, customs, mores, values, or interpretations is intrinsically good or even better than anything that might be substituted for it. Presumption merely recognizes that the belief now stands on the ground that any alternative belief would have to occupy. Nor does the artificial presumption of innocence mean that an accused man is more apt to be innocent than guilty, or that the judge thinks him innocent, or that most men brought to trial are not guilty.[1] Here the presumption is only a man-made convention, invoked so that an order may be established and debate proceed. The accused must be placed on some piece of ground to begin with; and American legal tradition assumes that the interests of justice and expediency will best be served if he is assigned the ground of "innocence." In short, presumption is always descriptive, never evaluative.

### BURDEN OF PROOF

Whereas presumption is the preoccupation of argumentative ground, burden of proof is the obligation devolving upon the party who advances a statement—or, as it is called when formally worded, a *proposition* [2]—that challenges that occupancy. In most debates outside the courtroom, the burden of proof is twofold. It entails (*a*) showing that the person, idea, institution, or practice now occupying the disputed ground should not be there; and (*b*) specifying what person, idea, institution, or practice should be there. Hence, burden of proof both criticizes the present order and recommends a new one, the specific content and scope of the "burden" being determined by the wording of the proposition that is advanced. (In the hypothetical case outlined above, for example, Mr. A would have to prove (*a*) that Mr. N should not be in the spot of shade, and (*b*) that he, Mr. A, should be.)

Unlike presumption, which merely describes, burden of proof evaluates and recommends. Instead of reporting what is, it declares what should be. And because it does evaluate, assuming the burden of proof involves taking the risk described on pp. 81–82.

There is no risk in description. Descriptions are merely reports, and as such accurate or inaccurate, complete or incomplete, clear or unclear. But when the debater criticizes and recommends, he takes the risk that he will not be able to prove his criticism justified or his recommendation

---
[1] Richard Whately, *Elements of Rhetoric* (London: 1828), 1.3.2.
[2] See Chapter 14.

sound. The burden of proof may, therefore, most accurately and usefully be defined as *the risk involved in advancing the proposition.*

## THE BURDEN OF GOING FORWARD WITH THE DEBATE

Having defined presumption as the preoccupation of a piece of argumentative ground and burden of proof as the risk involved in advancing the proposition, we return to Mr. A and Mr. N.

All was calm and at rest—in technical language, the "universe" of the bus stop was quiescent—until Mr. A declared, "By rights, N, that spot of shade belongs to me." By advancing this proposition A disturbed the situation initially. Moreover, his proposition specified the exact burden of proof that A, as the party standing outside the disputed ground, must now be prepared to assume.

But the proposition alone did not start the dispute. Had Mr. N, without replying, surrendered the shady spot to A, no interchange would have taken place, even though a proposition had been advanced. Instead, a new order would have been established quickly and peacefully. The debate began only when N answered A's challenge by saying, "I deny this spot of shade belongs to you. Prove that such is, indeed, true."

This reply, operating in conjunction with A's challenge, produced the controversy, by forcing A to do more than mouth assertions. Now he was required to produce proof to support the proposition he had advanced.

If, for instance, at this point A were to say, "I have no proof. Let's just forget the whole matter," he obviously would fail to make good on the risk he took in initiating the dispute. Under these circumstances, not only would any impartial judge be forced to declare against him, but, as a practical matter, he would lose all hope of gaining the desired place in the shade. Therefore, if he is to attain the end for which he began the debate in the first place, A must now make good his claim. He must do as N asks and present proof designed to show its expediency and justice. In other words, he must *go forward with the debate.* Unless he does so, obviously his case will fail.

This obligation of going forward with the debate is a new and additional one, quite distinct from the risk A took in advancing his original proposition. Of course, if he had not challenged N, he would not now be called on to carry the debate forward. But it was not merely the advancing of the proposition that gave rise to the new burden. What directly motivated this second obligation was not A's challenge, but N's response. Had N not answered, the obligation would not have risen. Had N answered differently from the way he did, the obligation would have assumed a different form. But since N did deny the challenge in the fashion stated, A is now called on to make good his claim by proving that the shady spot is "by rights" his.

PRIMA FACIE CASE.  The first thing A must do in discharging his obligation of going forward with the debate is to make out what is technically called a *prima facie case* [3]—that is, *a case that any reasonable judge would consider strong enough to stand, unless or until refutation is offered against it*. If A cannot make good his claim at least to this extent, he can hardly expect a further hearing. To have any validity at all, his case must at the minimum be able to stand by itself.

But making out a *prima facie* case is only the first step involved in carrying the debate forward. In a second, and equally important, phase of this process, N as well as A participates. For when A has successfully made out a *prima facie* case, his obligation is for the moment discharged. Now N must bestir himself. If he wants to maintain his place in the shade, he must counter A's *prima facie* case strongly enough so that it can no longer stand without additional support, or without A's showing the invalidity or irrelevance of N's attacks upon it.[4]

Assuming that N does attack successfully, the burden of going forward then shifts back to A. It is once more his duty to offer proof or refutation so that his *prima facie* case may be reconstituted and his cause strengthened. But A's action only calls for a new response from N, to which A must again reply. And so the debate proceeds, with each party alternately bestirring the other into action, until the evidence and proofs have been exhausted or a predetermined time limit has expired. Then he who by this process of alternating action and counteraction has achieved a preponderance of proof, thus establishing his "right" beyond the point where it can reasonably be disputed, may be awarded the decision.

The importance to each party of this alternating obligation to carry the debate forward may be seen by supposing the arrival of the bus at various stages during the course of the controversy between N and A. If, for example, the bus arrives after A has issued his challenge but before he has an opportunity to develop a *prima facie* case, any reasonable judge, being called on to decide the dispute at this point, would have to declare in favor of N. If, however, it arrives after the *prima facie* case is completed and before N has an opportunity to reply, the award would have to be for A; if after a successful attack upon that case, for N; etc. Not until both sides have had a fair and equal chance to present all of their proofs, or an agreed time limit is exhausted, is a final or summary decision possible.

[3] See the definition of "case" on p. 233 of Chapter 15.
[4] See James M. O'Neill, Craven Laycock, and Robert L. Scales, *Argumentation and Debate* (New York: The Macmillan Company, 1917), pp. 33–38.

THE BURDEN OF PROOF DOES NOT SHIFT. A discussion of the difference between the burden of proof and the burden of going forward with the debate requires attention to a frequently misunderstood matter.

While the burden of going forward with the debate constantly shifts back and forth between the contesting parties, the burden of proof does not. From beginning to end it always rests with him who challenges the existing order. Unlike the burden of going forward, it is not a subsequent or contingent obligation. Rather, the burden of proof represents the risk involved in originating the action by advancing the proposition in the first place. Since the challenger puts forward the proposition, he must accept as his permanent and unshiftable obligation the task of making good on whatever risk it entails.

Moreover, this obligation requires that the challenging party maintain his proof throughout the debate at a level above equilibrium. Unlike the defendant, he cannot be satisfied with a balance or standoff. Although a draw in proof may subject the existing order to severe tests and put it on its mettle to defend itself, in the end it leaves that order unaltered, with the original occupant still in control of the contested ground. To make good his claim the challenger must do more than threaten or annoy; he must effect a rearrangement.

Consider, again, the dispute at the bus stop. N may maintain the existing order of himself in the shade and A in the sun simply by parrying or countering the attempts of A to alter it. He need not show cause why the situation should not be altered. A, on the contrary, must offer affirmative proof why it should. In conducting his defense of the present order N must, of course, from time to time go forward with the debate by advancing proof or refutation. This requirement, however, represents only a temporary shift in the center of gravity of the controversy, not a shift in the fundamental obligations of the parties. These obligations remain constant. A must strike and maintain throughout a level of proof sufficiently above equilibrium to effect the rearrangement he desires. This margin of proof above equilibrium represents the unshiftable obligation he assumed in initiating the action. Hence, another way to define the burden of proof is to say it consists of such a margin.

## QUESTION, ISSUES, AND POINTS FOR DECISION

Although the dispute between N and A has been traced in some detail, certain of its most important elements remain to be examined. This examination involves the introduction of three additional terms: *Question, issues,* and *points for decision.*

## THE QUESTION

The Question (for reasons made clear below, we shall always write it with a capital "Q") is that element in a dispute that arises directly out of the clash between the proposition and the answer that is made to it. For example, A's assertion, "By rights, N, that spot of shade belongs to me," coupled with N's reply, "I deny that that spot of shade by rights belongs to you," gives rise to the Question, "To whom does the spot of shade by rights belong?"

Since the Question is the joint product of the proposition and the answer made to the proposition, its form and content are determined by the form and content of these two elements. If, instead of the declaration just considered, A had made his point by saying, "N, you are a selfish hog," and N had answered, "I am not a selfish hog," the Question would have been, "Is N a selfish hog?" If A had said, "Although I admit that the shade properly belongs to you, if you were any sort of gentleman you would let me stand in it," and N had replied, "Giving up shade is no part of being a gentleman," the Question would have been, "Is refusing shade to another an ungentlemanly act?" As it was, however, the specific proposition and answer made to it combined to produce the Question, "To whom does the spot of shade by rights belong?"

## ISSUES

Once the proposition and answer have been put forward and the Question thus delineated, the party who advances the proposition, thereby assuming the burden of proof, must, as we have seen, proceed to make out a *prima facie* case.

Since this case must be of sufficient strength to stand unless or until refutation is offered against it, it will, as a matter of expediency, nearly always contain the major contentions by which the challenging party proposes to support his claim.

To understand this point, suppose that in developing his *prima facie* case A advances the following contentions as the strongest he can muster: This spot of shade by rights belongs to me because (*a*) you have promised that I can stand in the shade whenever I am ill; and (*b*) this afternoon I am ill.

Since these are the strongest contentions A can command, they are also the contentions N must attack if he wishes to undermine that case or weaken it to the point that A must bestir himself in its defense. N's attack may, as we shall learn in Chapters 15 and 16, take any of several forms. For simplicity's sake, however, assume that he elects to make a direct denial of each of these contentions. That is, he answers, (*a*) I have made no such promise, and (*b*) you are not ill.

Just as A's original proposition, combined with N's answer, gave rise to the Question in which the dispute as a whole centers, so does each of these contentions of A's *prima facie* case, combined with N's denial, give rise to a narrower or more specific kind of question: (*a*) Did N make such a promise? (*b*) Is A actually ill? These more specific questions, arising out of the principal contentions of A's *prima facie* case as denied by N, are known as *issues*.

The questions raised by the issues bear upon the central Question directly and immediately. How one answers them will automatically determine how he answers the Question itself. No intervening steps of reasoning or inference are necessary. If one believes that N did make such a promise and that A is ill, he may immediately conclude that the spot of shade belongs to A. If, on the other hand, he answers these questions negatively, he may immediately conclude that the shade does not belong to A. Any specific question which does not bear directly on the central Question, no matter how important it may seem, is not, in the proper sense of the term, an issue.

Because of its direct bearing on the central Question, each issue is vital to the life of the challenger's cause and is in itself capable of determining the success or failure of that cause.

In the mythical bus stop situation, if A can successfully prove both of the issues indicated—the existence of a promise by N and his own illness—he has doubtless established his case. But unless he can prove *both* of the issues he has no case at all. One alone will not do. To prove the existence of a promise, without proving present illness, would gain him nothing; nor, conversely, would it avail to prove illness, without also proving the existence of a promise.

Formally defined, *an issue is a question so vital to the life of the challenger's cause that unless it is answered in his favor his cause as a whole must fail.* Any specific question that does not provide an immediate answer to the central Question is not an issue; any contention that the challenger may fail to prove and still make out a case is not an issue. The issues are vital to the life of the proposition. They are like the links in a chain; all must work together to carry the load, and the cause as a whole is no stronger than the issue that is least firmly supported.

But if the party who brings the charge must establish all of the issues to make his cause succeed, the party who denies the charge—in our example, N—need win on but a single issue to destroy that cause entirely. If he can create sufficient doubt at only one point—either about the existence of an agreement or about the illness—he may leave the other issue untouched and still succeed in the eyes of a reasonable judge. As a matter of insurance, the attack mounted by the denying party will usually be directed at more than one point, and under most circumstances his strongest case will be made by attacking as vigorously as possible all along the line. Such diversification of attack is, however, a matter of strategy rather than necessity. As the example suggests, the destruction of a single issue is sufficient to destroy a challenger's cause.

ACTUAL AND CONTESTED ISSUES. While the party who advances the proposition must win on all of the issues, whether he will be called on to submit proof beyond the point of making out a *prima facie* case depends on the actions of his opponent.

In our example, N denied both issues directly. Therefore, assuming that he presented sufficient proofs to justify these denials, A is called upon to come to the defense of each. Suppose, however, that N had admitted the first issue—the existence of his promise—and denied only the second—that A is ill. The question concerning the promise would then automatically be answered in A's favor and drop out of the debate, so that the dispute centers entirely on the remaining issue of A's illness.

But N's decision to leave the first question uncontested does not mean that this question ceases to be an issue in the debate. It is still vital to the life of A's cause and, as such, must be proved at least to the extent necessary to make out a *prima facie* case. Support beyond this point, however, is unnecessary.

A distinction between *actual* and *contested* issues is, therefore, to be recognized. The actual issues are those subquestions, growing directly out of the central Question, which the challenger must prove, at least to the point of making out a *prima facie* case. The contested issues are the actual issues to which the challenger must bring additional support because his attempts to prove them have been more or less successfully countered by his opponent.

Actual issues are never a matter of choice. They are determined by what the challenger needs to prove in order to make out a *prima facie* case. Contested issues, on the contrary, always result from choice. They depend on which of the actual issues are disputed by the party who undertakes to rebut the challenger.

THE ACTUAL ISSUES ARE INHERENT IN THE QUESTION. In the courtroom the actual issues in a dispute are usually embedded in the Question by definition. For example, to prove murder, one must establish motive, because motive is part of the definition of murder. Similarly, in English law of an earlier day, to prove burglary, one had to show (*a*) breaking, (*b*) entering, (*c*) a dwelling, (*d*) at night, (*e*) with felonious intent, because all these were included in the definition of burglary.[5]

In nonlegal debates the actual issues are not so conveniently predetermined. Yet here, too, they are embedded in the Question and the situation out of which the Question arises. They may be uncovered through careful study and analysis.

By way of illustration, consider yet another time the case of N and A at the bus stop. Observe that in advancing the proposition that initiated the dispute, A did not merely say, "N, that spot of shade belongs to me." He said, *"By rights,* N, that spot of shade belongs to me." In so doing, he added a significant phrase—one that states an important fact about the situation out of which the Question arose. This phrase immediately suggests that the relationship between N and A is, to some extent, formalized—that in A's judgment, at least, a mutually recognized agreement or arrangement exists, which grants the parties certain "rights" and obligations and which sets up rules of precedence that may be observed or violated.

Acting on this cue, the debater is motivated to look into the history and present status of the relationship between N and A and to search for any information that may bear upon the question of "rights" and obligations. Assume that such a search reveals the following seven items. Further assume that this list is exhaustive and that no additional items of fact or principle relative to the relationship remain to be discovered.

Here are the results of the study: (1) N has occupied the spot of shade every afternoon for the past two weeks; (2) while N is a young man, A is now approaching retirement and expects the courtesies and considerations usually accorded the elderly; (3) whenever A arrives at the bus stop first and takes the shady spot, he always offers it to N when the latter arrives; (4) both men recognize that public property is the special preserve of no one, but is to be shared and enjoyed by all; (5) because A is sometimes ill, N has promised that at such times he may stand in the shade; (6) by common consent, both N and A always readily give up the spot of shade to a lady when one is present; and (7) today A is ill.

Provided the foregoing list is accurate and contains all possible items bearing upon the matter of "rights" and obligations between N and A, it will, of necessity, contain the issue or issues on which their dispute turns. And just so will a study of the pertinent matters of fact or principle in any other dispute uncover the issues in that case.

Which of the preceding seven items, then, are issues? Which, if proved beyond reasonable doubt, automatically establish A's right to the shade?

[5] See O'Neill, Laycock, and Scales, *Argumentation and Debate,* p. 43.

Which, if not so proved, automatically result in A's failure to establish his right? On which points can A not afford to lose?

As reflection will show, only two of the seven items are "vital" in the sense just described. These are Nos. 5 and 7. If A can prove that N has agreed to give him the shady spot whenever he is ill (No. 5), and if today he is ill (No. 7), then reasonable judges must conclude that today the spot "by rights" belongs to A. If A cannot prove this, although he may present some very strong arguments and appeals, he will not—under the particular set of facts supposed—establish his "right" to the degree that makes his claim conclusive. Because Nos. 5 and 7 are crucial to A's case, they are issues; because they are the only crucial points, they are the only issues in the dispute.

Students of debate must clearly understand, however, that the contending parties did not invent these issues at the time the disagreement occurred. The issues already existed as part of the history of their relationship. Instead of being invented, they were discovered by examining all of the stored-up matters of fact or principle that had anything to do with an agreement, spoken or unspoken, concerning "rights" and conventions. Once the challenge and answer had moved the dispute into the area of "rights," by searching in that area the issues were uncovered.

Chapters 14 and 15 will have more to say about ferreting out issues and will give directions for systematizing that process. The point now to be observed is that issues are inherent in the Question and in the situation out of which the Question arises. If twenty or a hundred or a thousand persons were to look into the N–A relationship and uncover all of the pertinent information, they would emerge with the same issues. Issues exist for the disputants and are not created by them.

To say that the issues exist is not, of course, to say they are always found. They may be missed in analysis or mistaken for unimportant points. High school and college debaters sometimes study a Question for weeks or months without discovering the issues. Eventually, however, careful analysis will reveal those subsidiary questions which the challenger, if he is to succeed, must cause to be answered in his favor. These subsidiary questions are the actual issues.

## POINTS FOR DECISION

As the preceding discussion implies, the decision in a debate is properly determined by the answers to two questions: (1) Did the party bringing the challenge succeed in making out a *prima facie* case on all of the issues? (2) If so, did he successfully maintain a preponderance of proof on each of the issues his opponent chose to contest? If the answer to both questions is "yes," clearly the decision belongs to the challenger. If the answer to either or both of them is "no," then the decision belongs to the party who denies the charge. Because these questions decisively determine the success or failure of the contesting causes, they are known as the *points for decision*. On the *points for decision* rather than on any vague impressions concerning the merits or demerits of the cause as a whole, judgment should always be rendered.[6]

Because an issue sometimes raises an extremely narrow question, so also may a point for decision sometimes be narrow. If N does not contest the existence of an agreement between himself and A, the determination of A's rights will rest entirely on the question of whether he is ill. In burglary, if the definition includes, as one of five essential elements, the act of "breaking," an entire case may rest on the question of whether a door was inches ajar. How narrow or specific such a question may be is immaterial. If it is directly related to one or more of the issues, the narrowest conceivable point for decision can determine the success or failure of an entire cause.

A debater should, therefore, keep in mind the two vital points on which judgment depends. He must never forget the importance of the challenger's making out a *prima facie* case, nor must he forget that even a narrow question, provided it is really an issue, is crucial to the debate as a whole. In successful debating the smallest detail cannot be overlooked. Here, if anywhere, for want of a shoe a battle may be lost.

## SIDE AND POSITION

In describing how the contending parties in a debate proceed toward a decision, we introduced a number of technical terms and concepts. Two terms, however, were deliberately avoided. For until one understands something of the inner workings of the debate process, their definitions have little or no meaning. These terms are (*a*) *side* (with its subordinate terms *affirmative* and *negative*) and (*b*) *position*.

### SIDE

As used in debate, *side* is a descriptive term that locates a disputant relative to the contested ground, i.e., places him in*side* or out*side* of it. The party who is located inside the contested ground, and who, as a result, has the presumption, is known as the *negative* (Mr. N in our example). The party who is located outside the contested ground, and who,

[6] Cf. Chapter 21, pp. 338–39.

as a result, has the burden of proof, is known as the *affirmative* (Mr. A).

Because of their relative locations within and without the contested ground, the negative may also be defined as the party who resists the reordering specified by the proposition; the affirmative as the party who seeks the reordering specified by the proposition and who will be dissatisfied if it is not achieved.

## POSITION

Whereas *side* describes a disputant as inside or outside the contested ground, *position* locates him more precisely by naming the point within his assigned territory at which he *takes a stand* for the purpose of attacking or defending the proposition.

Because a disputant must either be inside or outside the contested ground, there can be only two sides in a debate. One must either seek the reordering that the proposition specifies, or he must resist it. But because there are many places in both areas from which an attack may be launched or a defense conducted, there are many positions at which a disputant can take his stand.

For example, in advancing a charge of murder, counsel may locate his *prima facie* case at the position of motive as financial gain, motive as jealousy, motive as revenge, and the like. In rebutting the charge, opposing counsel may take his stand at the point of direct denial, at that of insanity, etc. Similarly, in denying a proposition of policy, a legislator may take the stand that the proposal is not only unnecessary but potentially dangerous, or the stand that it should be rejected because a better plan is available, etc.[7]

Note, however, that these different positions are merely alternative ways of achieving the same end—the acceptance or rejection of the proposition advanced. No matter which stand the debater takes he remains on the affirmative or negative side, i.e., outside or inside the contested ground. He merely locates himself at a different point or *position* on his chosen ground. The decision as to whether he will favor or resist reordering has been made earlier. Now the problem is one of "means" rather than of "ends." How may the proposition most successfully be attacked or defended? Where shall I "stand" to do the job? These questions are the ones that are answered by the selection of a position.

[7] See Chapter 15, pp. 240–49.

# THE ANATOMY OF A DISPUTE

## AN ILLUSTRATIVE DIAGRAM

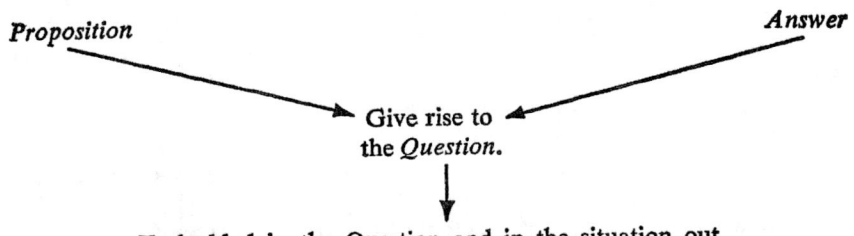

*Proposition* → Give rise to the *Question*. ← *Answer*

↓

Embedded in the Question and in the situation out of which it arose are certain vital subquestions which are the *actual issues* in the dispute

↙ ↘

In order to win the right to a hearing the *affirmative* must make out a *prima facie* case on each of the *actual issues*.

The actual issues which the *negative* chooses to dispute become the *contested issues* in the debate.

↘ ↙

As *points for decision* the judging-agency asks: (*a*) Did the *affirmative* make out a *prima facie* case on each of the *actual issues*? (*b*) Did it maintain a preponderance of proof on each of the *contested issues*?

## QUESTIONS

*A. To Check Your Comprehension and Memory*

1. In what sense does A take a risk when he asserts, "By rights, N, that spot of shade belongs to me"?
2. Why is the verbal assertion, no less than the physical blow, a disturbing or agitating force?
3. How does the verbal assertion specify the particular reordering of the situation which A desires?
4. What is presumption?
5. Does presumption evaluate the situation it describes?
6. Distinguish between natural and artificial presumption.
7. Define burden of proof.
8. Why in most debates outside the courtroom is the burden of proof twofold in nature?
9. Does the burden of proof evaluate?
10. Distinguish between the burden of proof and the burden of going forward with the debate.

96    THE MATERIALS OF ARGUMENT

11. What is the first thing the challenger must do in carrying the debate forward?
12. Define a *prima facie* case.
13. Why does the burden of carrying the debate forward alternate between the contending parties?
14. Does the burden of proof shift? Why?
15. What is the Question, and how does it arise?
16. How are the specific form and content of the Question determined?
17. What are issues?
18. In what sense is an issue vital to the life of the proposition?
19. Why must the challenger win on all of the issues to make his cause prevail?
20. Distinguish between actual and contested issues.
21. How are the actual issues derived?
22. What are the points for decision?
23. How broad or all-inclusive must a point for decision be?
24. How many sides are there to a debate?
25. Define the term "position."

*B. For Class Discussion*

1. Mention all the ways you can think of in which a debate is analogous to a physical combat. What are some of the common terms and expressions used to describe both a battle of fists and a battle of words?
2. In a murder trial when the defense attorney pleads that the accused is insane, doesn't he assume a burden of proof?
3. In a debate involving some existing institution or practice that is obviously evil and dangerous, shouldn't the proposed reform have the presumption, so that the party who favored the undesirable existing situation would be called on to assume the burden of proof concerning it?
4. If a challenger must establish all of the issues and his opponent successfully rebut only one, how can the challenger ever hope to win a debate?
5. The statement that there are many sides to every argument is often made, but in this chapter we say there can be only two. Explain.

EXERCISES

*A. Written Exercises*

1. Study the sample college debate printed in Appendix A. Pick out what you believe to be the issues. Then, keeping in mind the two points for decision outlined in this chapter, determine the winning side. Hand in a paper listing the issues and points for decision you have selected. Justify your judgment as to which side won.
2. Work out an imaginary dispute similar to the one between Mr. N and Mr. A. Frame a proposition and answer, and from these derive a Question. Then isolate the issues that are inherent in the situation you are supposing,

and determine the points for decision which will emerge. Write up the dispute in outline form, or summarize it in a diagram similar to the one given at the end of the chapter.

*B. Oral Exercise*

Give a five-minute persuasive speech on a controversial problem. Use as the main heads of this speech contentions that you believe represent the issues involved in the problem. Let the instructor and other students challenge your choice of heads, at the conclusion of the speech, and if they feel that any one of them is not a true issue, proceed to show them why in your opinion it is.

## SUGGESTIONS FOR FURTHER READING

Cicero, *De Inventione*, 1.8–14. A discussion of four types of disputable questions and a description of the successive stages through which a dispute passes. Although Cicero had the legal situation primarily in mind, his analysis will prove interesting to any serious student of argumentation. Difficult but rewarding reading.

James Milton O'Neill, Craven Laycock, and Robert L. Scales, *Argumentation and Debate* (New York: The Macmillan Co., 1917), Chapter 3, "The Burden of Proof," and Chapter 4, "The Issues." An earlier statement and useful supplement of the basic philosophy expressed in this chapter. Distinguishes clearly between "burden of proof" and "burden of going forward," and argues that issues are inherent in the proposition.

Robert L. Scott, "On the Meaning of the Term *Prima Facie* in Argumentation," *Central States Speech Journal*, 12 (Autumn 1960), 33–37. Objects that the term *prima facie* is often loosely used as synonymous with "good case," and suggests that it should lead the debater to raise "formal questions" on three levels: "the case as a whole, the primary units (the contentions), and the facts alleged."

Richard Whately, *Elements of Rhetoric* (London: 1828), 1.3.2. Although for centuries a part of the law of evidence, the concepts of presumption and burden of proof were first introduced into the field of general nonlegal argument in 1828 by Richard Whately. In taking these concepts out of their traditional legal environment, Whately encountered certain difficulties but also laid the groundwork for most subsequent treatments of the subject.

John Henry Wigmore, *A Student's Textbook of the Law of Evidence* (Brooklyn: Foundation Press, 1935), Book 3, "Burdens of Proof; Presumptions." A well-known authority on the law of evidence presents a brief and not too technical explanation of presumption and burden of proof as the lawyer views them. Burden of proof is distinguished from the burden of going forward with the argument, and various types of legal presumptions are described.

*Chapter 8*

# THE UNIT OF PROOF AND ITS STRUCTURE

*Keeping our eyes on the categories of applied logic—on the practical business of argumentation, that is, and the notions it requires us to employ—we must ask what features a logically candid layout of arguments will need to have.*
STEPHEN TOULMIN

BECAUSE the debater participates in making decisions critically, not by snap judgment, he must seek to establish each of his contentions through the materials of argument rather than by blind appeals to personality, emotion, or prejudice. In so doing, he employs *proof*.

What is proof? What are the elements and the structure of a unit of proof? What are the sources, ethics, and rhetoric of evidence? What are the types of proof? How may deficiencies of proof be detected? What are the sources and standards of belief that determine the acceptance or rejection of proofs? These are the questions investigated in this and the following five chapters.

## TOULMIN'S ANALYSIS OF REASONING

Our analysis of reasoning is based on the structural model in Stephen Toulmin's *Uses of Argument* [1] rather than on the apparatus derived from formal logic. Although the rules, moods, and figures of syllogisms are sometimes summarily discussed in argumentation textbooks, they are seldom employed by debaters.

For several reasons, Toulmin's analysis seems more useful for debaters. (1) In the Toulmin model, proofs are displayed in a spatial pattern to help debaters see a *dynamic* relationship between evidence and

[1] (Cambridge: Cambridge University Press, 1958).

claim as certified by principles of reasoning actually used by debaters; in the syllogism, proof consists of a series of statements that reflect the relatively *static* relationship of compartmentalization. (2) The Toulmin model provides explicitly for the material support of warrants; the major premises of syllogisms are supportable only by a sort of extralogical operation. (3) The Toulmin model emphasizes the *factual* analysis of a unit of proof and *material* validity by investigating a proof within the context of all related information; the syllogism, more concerned with class relationships, emphasizes *formal* validity and achieves a sort of factual analysis only through a complex series of syllogisms. (4) The Toulmin model provides explicitly for ways of qualifying and limiting the force of a claim; the conclusion of a syllogism can often be properly qualified or limited only through tortuous and involved propositions.

Although we have departed in several instances from Toulmin's terminology in favor of traditional language, we have retained two of his terms that are not a part of the usual vocabulary of argumentation. No traditional terms say adequately what Toulmin means by *warrant* and *claim*. "Inference" approximates in meaning "warrant," but inference signifies a relationship between evidence and claim, whereas a warrant is the statement that certifies such a relationship. "Conclusion" has a meaning similar to "claim," but conclusion implies the final statement in a line of argument, whereas claim can stand for either a final or an intermediate statement in a chain of reasoning.

## THE INDISPENSABLE ELEMENTS OF A UNIT OF PROOF

*Proof is the process of securing belief in one statement by relating it to another statement already believed.* A unit of proof has six elements, three of which, *evidence, warrant,* and *claim,* are absolutely indispensable.

### EVIDENCE

Evidence may be described initially as the information to which a proof appeals, the factual foundation on which it rests, the terminus from which it starts. No unit of proof is possible without some sort of informative data, for without data, there is no accepted ground to which a claim may be referred.

Not all information a debater collects on a proposition, however, functions as evidence. Two conditions must be met. First, some principle of reasoning must warrant the connection between a bit of information and some claim a debater wants to advance. Only *germane* information can become evidence. Second, the informative statement must be *believed* by the listener or reader before it becomes evidence in a unit of proof.

Some writers distinguish between evidence of *fact* and evidence of *opinion*. But if evidence is considered from the point of view of the listeners or readers to whom it is addressed, the "factual" character of any information ultimately depends on the "opinion" of the audience.

Evidence may be described more meaningfully by placing it on a verifiability continuum. For a given group of listeners or readers at some point in time, information may range from statements that cannot be verified, through those susceptible of verification with varying degrees of difficulty, to those needing no verification at all.[2] If a debater cannot verify an informative statement to the satisfaction of his listeners or readers, he may as well leave out of his discourse any proof based on it. If an informative statement needs no verification, he can proceed immediately to the proof which is grounded on it, for such a statement can function as evidence.

If the information is questionable but verifiable, on the other hand, a debater must present the necessary preliminary proofs. For not until the information is agreed to does it become evidence for a unit of proof. For example, suppose a debater claims that savings and consumption among American industrial workers is increasing, and cites as evidence a statement by Professor X that the income of industrial workers is higher than a year ago. If the listener or reader doubts that Professor X is competent to make acceptable statements concerning the income of industrial workers, the debater must present the professor's credentials. Not until the professor's statement about increased income is accepted is the debater ready to prove that increased income is causally related to increased savings and consumption.

Sometimes in the process of verifying evidence a series of several proofs is necessitated. In such a chain, the evidence needing certification becomes the claim of a prior proof; if the evidence of that proof needs verification, it becomes the claim of still another proof, etc., until some informative statement is believed by the listener or reader.

Evidence may be defined, then, as *an informative statement believed by the listener or reader and employed by an arguer to secure belief in another statement.* As the preceding discussion indicates, evidence may range from highly specific statements of statistical compilation, descrip-

[2] The idea concerning evidence verifiability comes from conversations with Professor Roger Nebergall of the University of Oklahoma.

tion, direct quotation, or narrative, to far more generalized statements that have previously been certified by means of prior proofs.[3] Always, however, evidence answers the questions, "How do you know?" "What have you got to go on?"

In the actual presentation of a proof, the evidence may not need explicit statement. Evidence must always be "present," however, if only by implication. To analyze critically his own proofs or those of his opponents, a debater may have to make explicit the implied evidence. For unless the evidence is clearly understood and accepted as true or probable, a unit of proof cannot be carried forward successfully to its claim.

## WARRANT

Whereas evidence supplies the informative data on which a unit of proof rests, the warrant provides the *method* by which the proof is derived. It answers the questions, "So what?" "How does the person advancing the proof get from these data to this contention?"

Because a warrant is the means by which one moves from evidence to claim, it states an inference; it involves a mental leap. Its function in a unit of proof is to bring believed data to bear upon a claimed statement, certifying that statement as true or false, desirable or undesirable, and therefore warranting a statement to that effect. "From evidence of such and such a nature," the warrant assures one, "men are entitled to draw such and such a conclusion."

As distinguished from evidence, which is categorical and bound to the subject matter of the controversy, the warrant is hypothetical and content-free. If the evidence is believed, and if it is related to another statement in one of certain prescribed ways,[4] the warrant authorizes one to reason from the data in a particular way. The pattern employed in the warrant may be used over and over again when dealing with different aspects of the same subject or with entirely different subjects.

Moreover, unlike evidence, which is given and static, the warrant is dynamic and creative. It "does" rather than "is"; "acts" rather than is "acted upon"; is "form" rather than "matter"; is "method" rather than "substance." By relating accepted evidence to a claim, the warrant bridges these two statements and causes them to be associated in such a way that the truth or probability of the first comes to stand as certificate for the truth or probability of the second.

[3] Other distinctions among types of evidence are considered in Chapter 9.
[4] The kinds of relationships expressed in warrants are discussed at length in Chapters 10 and 11.

## CLAIM

The claim is the explicit appeal produced by the evidence and warrant, the specific stand which, as a result of accepting the data and recognizing the validity of the reasoning, one is now prepared to take on the question under consideration. Thus, when formally worded, a unit of proof says, "On the basis of these data, reasoned from in this way, one may claim that such and such is so."

Any claim advanced during the course of any dispute will be intended to answer, either directly or by means of intervening proofs, one of four questions.

1. Claims that answer *questions of definition*—whether something is, or was, or will be—are *definitive*. For example, whether a certain percentage of men accepted for military service establishes physical fitness, whether a certain extent of genetic and somatic radiation damage can be defined as extensive radiation harm, or whether Jones' action constitutes burglary are all questions of definition to be established in proofs as definitive claims.

2. Claims that answer *questions of fact*—whether something is, or was, or will be so—are *designative*. For example, to what extent the young men of the United States are acceptable for military service, whether radioactive fallout from nuclear weapons testing causes extensive genetic and somatic harm, or whether Jones broke and entered a dwelling at night with felonious intent are all questions of fact to be established in proofs as designative claims.

3. Claims that answer *questions of value*—of what value something is, or was, or will be—are *evaluative*. For example, to what degree physical fitness, radiation harm, or burglary are good or bad are all questions of value to be established in proofs as evaluative claims.

4. Claims that answer *questions of policy*—what proposal should be accepted—are *actuative*. For example, whether we should revise our present physical education curricula, whether we should enter into an international agreement to control the testing of nuclear weapons, or whether Jones should be given a certain kind of sentence are all questions of policy to be established in proofs as actuative claims.

A claim may be a final proposition in an argumentative discourse, or an intermediate statement that may serve as evidence for a subsequent proof in the controversy.

## RELATIONSHIPS AMONG THE INDISPENSABLE ELEMENTS

The way in which evidence, warrant, and claim are related may be represented diagrammatically:

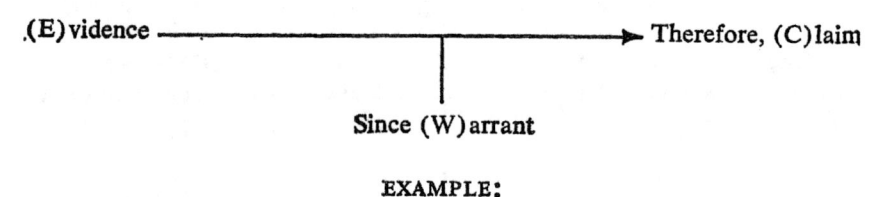

(E)vidence ──────────────────────► Therefore, (C)laim
                        │
                  Since (W)arrant

**EXAMPLE:**

(E) The income of industrial workers is higher than a year ago. ──────────► Therefore, (C) consumption and savings have increased.

Since (W) workers usually spend and save more when they earn more and only when they do so.

The line EC, connecting evidence and claim, represents the specific contention advanced by the proof and, for this reason, may be regarded as the *main proof line*. When read in normal order from left to right as EC, this line always contains or implies the word *therefore*. The income of industrial workers is higher than a year ago; *therefore*, consumption and savings have increased. In some instances, the main proof line also contains the word *therefore* when the order of the elements is reversed and the line read as CE. Consumption and savings have increased; *therefore*, the income of industrial workers is higher than a year ago. Convertibility is not, however, an essential property of a valid proof line. Whenever one is justified in asserting, "E, *therefore*, C," a legitimate claim has been inferred from the evidence.

As the diagram shows, the *warrant* does not stand on the main proof line. The warrant may appear, therefore, only incidental to the explicit appeal made by the proof. Yet one must not for this reason underestimate the importance of the role it plays in establishing a claim. Without the general assumption it expresses, the accepted data could not be brought to bear upon the claim, nor could the relationship between these elements be validated. Evidence and claim would merely continue to exist as independent and unrelated entities. For the warrant, by exhibiting one of the approved relationships that may exist between any evidence and claim, establishes a connection between these two elements. The warrant, therefore, actually gives birth to the proof as a whole.

The role of the warrant in determining the validity of a proof may be shown by a variation of the example introduced earlier:

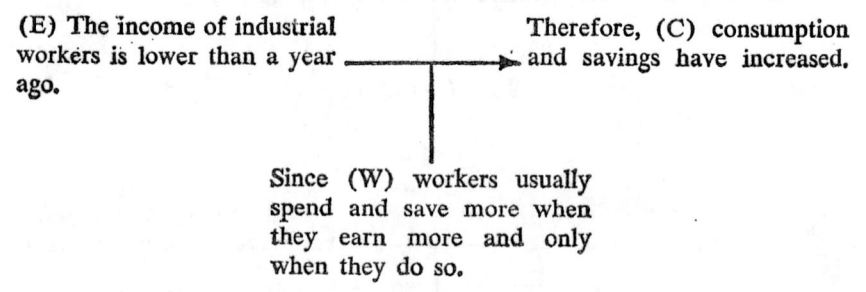

(E) The income of industrial workers is lower than a year ago. ⟶ Therefore, (C) consumption and savings have increased.

Since (W) workers usually spend and save more when they earn more and only when they do so.

This proof is invalid because the connection between the evidence and claim is not certified by what is stated in the warrant. Indeed, instead of authorizing the claim that consumption and savings have increased, the warrant justifies the opposite claim that consumption and savings have not increased. Hence, if one were to represent this situation diagrammatically, he would have to draw a new proof line leading to a very different conclusion. The original line has been blocked or turned back by the warrant.

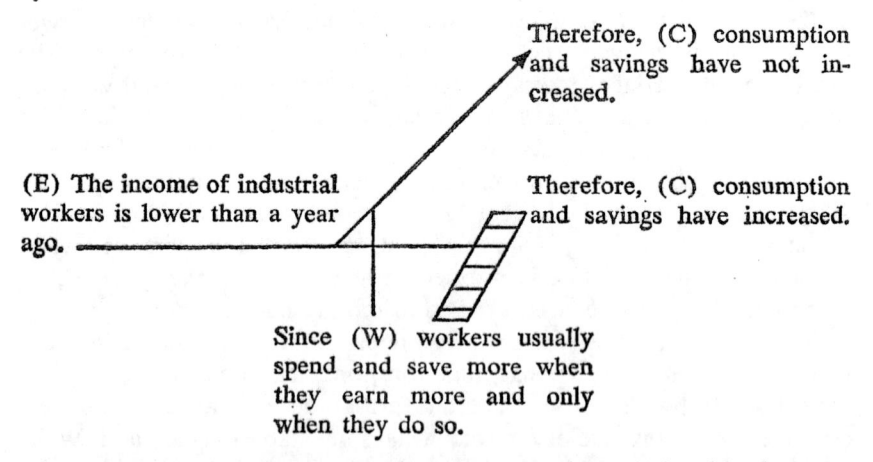

Therefore, (C) consumption and savings have not increased.

(E) The income of industrial workers is lower than a year ago.

Therefore, (C) consumption and savings have increased.

Since (W) workers usually spend and save more when they earn more and only when they do so.

The original proof line is blocked because the relationship between evidence and the original claim does not conform to the general relationship expressed in the warrant. The new proof line *is* justified because the relationship between the evidence and the new claim *does* fit the pattern stated in the warrant.

The warrant is so fundamental to an understanding of the structure and functioning of a unit of proof that in Chapters 10 and 11 proofs are classified into types on the basis of the kinds of general relationships that warrants may express.

## THREE ADDITIONAL PROOF ELEMENTS

Evidence, warrant, and claim, functioning together as just described, constitute the indispensable elements of any unit of proof. If any one of them is missing, the proof cannot exist.

In many of the proofs that one encounters three additional elements may be present: the *support for the warrant* (S for W), *reservations* (R), and a *qualifier* (Q). When these additional elements of a unit of proof are called for, their function may vitally affect the establishment of the proof as a whole.

### SUPPORT FOR THE WARRANT

The claim of a unit of proof is not accepted critically unless the reader or listener is willing to believe the assumption stated by the warrant. Support for the warrant (S for W) is intended to certify the acceptability of the assumption that the warrant expresses.

The warrants of different kinds of proof require different types of support, but one of three methods is appropriate in most controversies. (*a*) An entire proof is advanced and structured so that the warrant needing the support is the claim of the proof. (*b*) A group of acceptable standards is applied to evaluate the warrant. (*c*) The doubted assumption of the warrant is related to some principle or value acceptable to the listener or reader. The purpose of the support for the warrant in any of these forms is to give assurance that the warrant as stated is probable or true and therefore should be endorsed.

Materials introduced as support for the warrant are quite distinct from those data on which the main proof line rests, the evidence. While the function of the evidence is to furnish a *direct* foundation for the claim, the purpose of any material used to support the warrant is limited to underwriting the acceptability of the warrant that the proof employs. Thus S for W certifies a claim only *indirectly*.

If the warrant is accepted from the outset, no amplification or support of any kind is needed. On other occasions, since the claim is no stronger than the warrant that helps to produce it, the material introduced as support for a questionable assumption in the warrant may be vital to the establishment of the proof as a whole.

## RESERVATIONS

Even when the warrant, accepted or supported, authorizes one to move from the evidence to a claim along the main proof line, the authorization is only a general one. Specific circumstances or special conditions surrounding the proof may set aside or reduce the force of the warrant on the claim. The arguer will then have to append reservations (R) to the statement of the claim, as a sort of "safety valve" or "escape hatch" clause.

By thus recognizing certain exceptional circumstances that reduce or refute the force of a claim, the reservation qualifies or limits the area to which the claim may apply. In this way the arguer anticipates the possible refutations that may be advanced against his claim, and discovers, if possible, how to eliminate them. A reservation is customarily expressed by the word *unless,* so a proof may read, "On the basis of this evidence, as inferred by this warrant, one may claim such and such, *unless* he must account for exceptional circumstances that might set aside the claim or reduce its force or applicability."

Three kinds of reservations are applicable to certain types of proof: (*a*) An intervening or counteracting cause may completely or partially block the main proof line. (*b*) Special circumstances in the factual context surrounding the specific relationship between evidence and claim may not conform to the general relationship expressed in the warrant. (*c*) Counterproofs may have greater validity or force than the proof under consideration.

Citing a reservation is not an indispensable element of all units of proof, because some claims may be affirmed without a reservation of any kind.

## QUALIFIER

Since claims vary considerably in the degree of strength with which they may be believed, one needs a set of qualifying terms that declare how strongly a claim is affirmed. These terms, *qualifiers* (Q), register the degree of force a claim is judged to possess.

The need to qualify claim statements stems from either or both of two sources. If the evidence or the warrant is in any way qualified, then the claim should have corresponding qualification, by such terms as "possibly," "probably," "at the 5 per cent level of confidence," "almost certainly," and others. A second need for qualification arises when the claim is accepted only under the condition that reservations can be cancelled out. Until one has satisfactorily disposed of the doubt cast by the reservations, he must qualify his claim with "presumably," "probably," or a similar term.

When the debater has established a claim that his listeners or readers will regard as necessary or certain, no qualifier need be inserted into the statement of the claim.

## RELATIONSHIP AMONG THE SIX ELEMENTS OF A UNIT OF PROOF

These additional elements of *support for the warrant* (S for W), *reservations* (R), and a *qualifier* (Q), may be superimposed upon the earlier diagram:

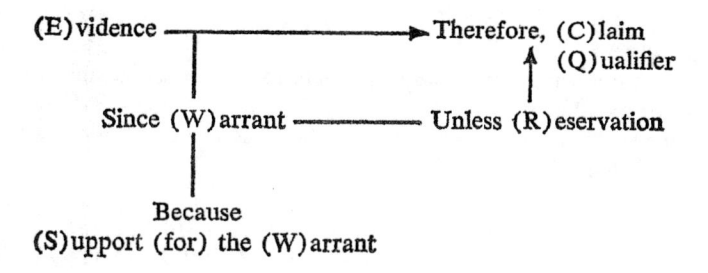

```
(E)vidence ─────────────────► Therefore, (C)laim
               │                      ▲ (Q)ualifier
               │                      │
          Since (W)arrant ─────── Unless (R)eservation
               │
               │
           Because
    (S)upport (for) the (W)arrant
```

### EXAMPLE:

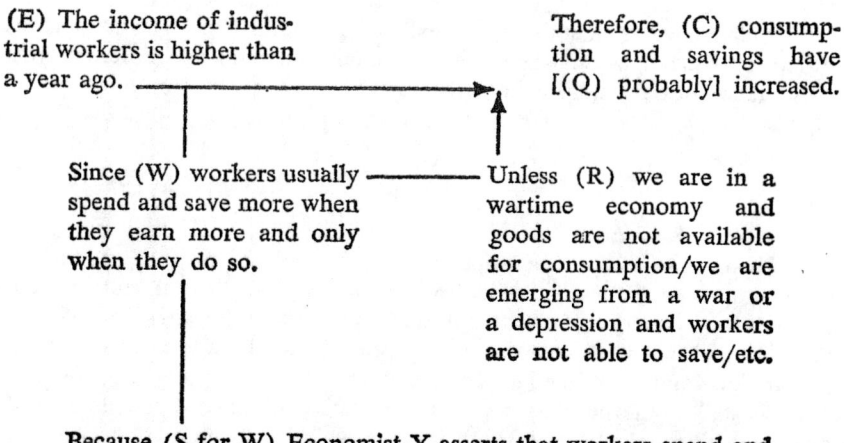

(E) The income of industrial workers is higher than a year ago. ─────────────► Therefore, (C) consumption and savings have [(Q) probably] increased.

Since (W) workers usually spend and save more when they earn more and only when they do so. ─────── Unless (R) we are in a wartime economy and goods are not available for consumption/we are emerging from a war or a depression and workers are not able to save/etc.

Because (S for W) Economist Y asserts that workers spend and save more only when they earn more/in the past $x$ instances of increases in the income of industrial workers, consumption and savings have increased/etc.

108  THE MATERIALS OF ARGUMENT

## QUESTIONS

*A. To Check Your Comprehension and Memory*
1. Define proof.
2. What are the indispensable elements of a unit of proof?
3. Why is no proof possible without evidence?
4. What two conditions must be met before an informative statement functions as evidence?
5. What is evidence verifiability?
6. How may the warrant be distinguished from evidence?
7. What are the four types of claims? What kinds of questions does each attempt to answer?
8. What proof elements appear on the main proof line?
9. What function is performed by the warrant?
10. When does the warrant need support? How can it be supported?
11. How is support for the warrant to be distinguished from evidence?
12. What is the function of reservations in a unit of proof? What forms may they take?
13. What are two reasons why qualifiers may need to be inserted into a statement of the claim?
14. Reproduce in diagrammatic form the structure of a unit of proof. Include all six elements.

*B. For Class Discussion*
1. In what ways does the structure of a unit of proof, as analyzed in this chapter, imply a critical kind of decision-making?
2. Which of the six elements of a unit of proof must function critically if the proof as a whole is to become a part of critical decision-making?
3. Read Chapter 4 of Castell's *A College Logic* (see Suggested Readings) or a similar chapter in some other textbook or manual in logic. How is the structure of proof as analyzed in this chapter similar to and different from the structure of the syllogism in formal logic?

## EXERCISES

*A. Written Exercises*
1. Using materials in the Appendix of this book, or texts of speeches in a newspaper or *Vital Speeches*, diagram four proofs. Invent and insert in brackets any element of proof not stated explicitly. Comment on whether the "missing" proof element makes the proof as a whole less valid. Identify the kind of claim established in each proof.
2. Read one of the chapters on the structure of proof in another argumentation textbook. Write a short paper in which you compare and contrast the method of treating proof structure there with the treatment in this textbook.

## THE UNIT OF PROOF AND ITS STRUCTURE

**B.** *Oral Exercises*

1. Present orally a unit of proof. Include each of the six elements. Your hearers will try to diagram your unit of proof after its oral presentation.

2. Present a three-minute speech in which you claim that _____ is an important element in establishing a unit of proof critically. Include all six elements of proof in the establishment of your claim.

### SUGGESTIONS FOR FURTHER READING

Wayne Brockriede and Douglas Ehninger, "Toulmin on Argument: An Interpretation and Application," *The Quarterly Journal of Speech*, 46 (Feb. 1960), 44–53. Covers some of the same ground considered in this chapter, but on a somewhat more theoretical level.

Alburey Castell, *A College Logic* (New York: The Macmillan Co., 1935), Chapters 1 and 4. Chapter 1 presents a discussion of inference as "If P, then Q," and Chapter 4 discusses the syllogism clearly and simply.

F. S. C. Schiller, *Formal Logic* (London: The Macmillan Co., 1912), Chapter 1. A technical and philosophical discussion of what the author believes to be the problems, failures, and self-contradictions of formal logic.

Stephen Toulmin, *The Uses of Argument* (Cambridge: Cambridge University Press, 1958), Chapter 3. Toulmin believes that formal logic lacks utility in the practical arena of argumentation, and he constructs a comprehensive and useful model for the structure of argument. Your efforts will be rewarded if you are prepared to "stretch" while reading Toulmin's book.

## Chapter 9

# EVIDENCE

> *The chief way in which we approach certainty as a limit is by the discovery of converging lines of evidence. Any single piece of evidence must be respected, but the chance of avoiding error is vastly increased if there is support from independent sources. The difference between one line of evidence and two or three, pointing in the same direction, is tremendous.*
>
> DAVID ELTON TRUEBLOOD [1]

IN CHAPTER 8 evidence was defined as consisting of informative statements which, because they are believed by a listener or reader, may be used as means for gaining his assent to a further statement.

## EVIDENCE CLASSIFIED

Evidence has been classified traditionally in many ways. It has been described as (*a*) real or personal, (*b*) original or hearsay, (*c*) direct or circumstantial, (*d*) preappointed or casual, (*e*) written or unwritten, (*f*) positive or negative, and (*g*) eager or reluctant.[2]

These categories are not mutually exclusive, nor are they intended to be so. They represent functional, rather than theoretical, distinctions and are designed to bring out certain important facts about evidence that will guide the debater in using it critically.

### REAL OR PERSONAL EVIDENCE

Real evidence consists of things one can see, hear, taste, or handle—things immediately perceptible to the senses. The items entered as ex-

---

[1] *Logic of Belief* (New York: Harper & Brothers, 1942), p. 41. Reprinted with the permission of the publisher.

[2] Evidence is frequently also classified as testimony, statistics, examples, etc. We are treating such forms in Chapters 10 and 11 as principles of reasoning (warrants) rather than as types of evidence—in Aristotelian language, artistic rather than inartistic proofs.

hibits in a murder trial—the powder-stained gun, the glasses with the accused's fingerprints, the torn coat or dressing gown—are examples of real evidence that any reader of detective stories will immediately recognize.

In the discussion of public questions real evidence seldom plays as important a role as it does in the courtroom. Yet there are many occasions on which it may be employed to advantage. A headline held up as real evidence that a certain newspaper has reported a story unfairly may be worth many written or spoken words to that effect. A demonstration which reveals that a product fails to meet the manufacturer's claims concerning size, weight, or durability may speak more eloquently than the statement of a respected authority. Pictures, diagrams, charts, and models may also be employed with effect. Indeed, for the debater who is alive to the possibilities, real evidence is often available and of great potential usefulness. When appropriate, real evidence underwrites a unit of proof vividly.

As distinguished from real evidence, personal evidence consists of information reported by a human agent. As recorded in books or other printed sources, or derived from personal contacts with experts, personal evidence provides the great bulk of the data used in the discussion of public questions.

The worth of personal evidence depends on the competency and objectivity of the source offering the data, as well as on the relevancy, recency, completeness, and clarity of the testimony offered. Was the person reporting the information in a position to observe the facts? Did he have sufficient knowledge of the subject to recognize and interpret what he saw? Was he relatively unbiased?[3] Do the data bear upon the point in question? Are they recent enough to be applicable to the situation as it now exists? Are all relevant aspects of the problem taken into account? Is the intended meaning of the source clear and unmistakable? These are some of the questions that should be asked when personal evidence is offered in support of a claim.

## ORIGINAL OR HEARSAY EVIDENCE

As their names imply, original evidence consists of reports based on firsthand observation or experience, while hearsay evidence is evidence that has been told to the reporter by someone else.

If Mr. A, who has just traveled through India, reports from personal observation that the economic conditions of the Indian villagers is improving as a result of the government's agricultural program, this is original evidence. If, however, Mr. B, who has never been to India,

---

[3] These three questions are discussed further in Chapter 11, pp. 159–60.

reports this conclusion as having been told him by Mr. A, the evidence is hearsay—or, as it is sometimes called, *secondary* rather than *primary*.

Except in rare instances, hearsay evidence is not admissible in the courts, and because of the intensely personal and emotionally charged questions which are dealt with there, the reasons for excluding it are strong. The nonlegal debater, on the other hand, uses hearsay evidence extensively. He repeats declarations of public officials as reported by newspaper columnists; he cites statistics from summary accounts given in magazines rather than from the raw data of official publications; he repeats what a radio or television newscaster says someone has told him, etc.

Such practices are not only permissible, but, in fact, necessary if the deliberation of public questions is to be carried on by the average citizen who cannot speak directly with Washington or London officialdom, and who has little opportunity to examine for himself hard-to-obtain foreign and domestic documents.

The dangers involved in the transmission of information from one person to another should, however, be understood. The popular party game of whispering a message to one's neighbor and having him pass it on illustrates these perils. After a message has been communicated to seven or eight persons it nearly always emerges in a considerably different form.

If debate is to be critical, original evidence must be used whenever it is available, and hearsay evidence employed only when it is reasonably close to the original source. Moreover, the transmitter of the data must meet the same rigid tests of competency that are applied to the source itself. Irresponsible or biased statements, rumors, unfounded gossip, and vague or indefinite reports concerning what someone thought another person may have said must be carefully avoided. In using information of this sort one not only runs the risk of reaching unreliable decisions, but he is employing data which are seldom convincing to an intelligent reader or listener.

## DIRECT OR CIRCUMSTANTIAL EVIDENCE

Direct evidence offers an immediate answer to the question in contention. Circumstantial evidence answers that question only indirectly or by inference.

Official statistics showing the high income level of farmers in a certain part of the state furnish direct evidence that these farmers are prosperous. If, however, upon driving through the region one observes fine new homes and barns, an abundance of expensive farm machinery, lush crops, many new cars, and large herds of fine looking cattle, these items provide indirect or circumstantial evidence of what the statistics tell directly.

Sometimes the argument is advanced that because circumstantial evidence is indirect, it is less strong and compelling than direct evidence. Perhaps in general this evaluation is correct, and in the courts the use of circumstantial evidence is surrounded by many special strictures. Again, however, as with hearsay evidence, what is true in the legal situation need not necessarily hold in the freer field of nonlegal argumentation.

In debates on public questions, circumstantial evidence may at times provide strong support for a claim. The conditions observed in one's travels through X part of the state demonstrate its prosperity as convincingly as the income figures themselves. Similarly, if an industrial plant has a large labor turnover, is plagued by strikes and walkouts, and is ill spoken of by its employees, one is reasonably safe in concluding that its personnel policies are deficient.

Insofar as observation is faulty or incomplete, circumstantial evidence may, of course, mislead. Moreover, as will be pointed out in Chapter 10, there is always the possibility of misinterpreting the signs or indications on which a circumstantial claim is based. Even so, to conclude that circumstantial evidence is never as strong as direct evidence would be a serious error. The best conceivable evidential bases for some claims is a combination of the two forms, one supporting and corroborating the other.

## PREAPPOINTED OR CASUAL EVIDENCE

Preappointed evidence is created and preserved for the specific purpose of later being used as evidence. Casual evidence is not uttered or set down with any thought that it may some day be employed as an element of proof.

In law, such papers as deeds, notes, contracts, and witnessed or notarized documents come under the head of preappointed evidence, since they are drawn up with a view to enforcing a right or obligation should it ever be contested. In general argumentation preappointed evidence usually consists of informative statements especially prepared to uphold one side of a contested proposition. If a debater who opposes placing additional regulations on labor unions invites a union official to make a statement that may be cited in support of his cause, such a statement is preappointed evidence. If his opponent uses material specifically prepared by an organization interested in encouraging additional regulation, this, too, falls into the preappointed class.

At first thought, casual evidence seems preferable to preappointed, because material prepared for a specific purpose is apt to be biased in favor of that purpose, whereas a statement made casually reflects the opinion actually held by the source. This danger must, however, be balanced against a counterpossibility: Casual evidence, since it is not uttered with a future use in view, is often thoughtlessly or carelessly given. Statements made in an informal conversation with friends are not as closely considered as statements intended for a published book or article, or for an important speech.

No blanket evaluation of the relative worth of preappointed and casual evidence is, therefore, possible. Each piece of information must be examined individually, in the light of the circumstances out of which it arose and the use for which it is intended.

## WRITTEN OR UNWRITTEN EVIDENCE

The distinction between written and unwritten evidence is obvious. Although most of the statements the debater cites are taken from printed sources and, therefore, fall under the head of written evidence, occasionally he may report what an authority has told him orally, thus using the unwritten variety.

Although too great a tendency exists on the part of most people to believe a statement merely because they see it in print, for purposes of critical deliberation written evidence has one important advantage. An opponent, judge, or interested observer can check the source for himself to see if the information has been fully and fairly reported. Moreover, by examining the book or article from which the evidence is drawn, he can form a more accurate opinion of its reliability and worth. With unwritten evidence such tests are impossible. Except in those rare instances in which the evidence is preserved on a tape or record, one is forced to take the debater's word concerning what somebody else told him.

Unwritten evidence should not be ruled out of critical deliberation, but it should always be used with caution and, whenever possible, corroborated by written sources. To decide an important public question on the basis of unwritten evidence alone is seldom a desirable procedure not only because oral statements are more difficult to check, but also because they are highly susceptible to unconscious alteration.

## POSITIVE OR NEGATIVE EVIDENCE

Positive evidence gives direct affirmative support to the contention in question; negative evidence is the absence of evidence to the contrary. It says, in effect, that something is so because it cannot be proved otherwise.

Using positive evidence, one might claim that A has paid his taxes, because his name appeared on the published list of paid-up freeholders. Using negative evidence, one would claim that A has paid his taxes, because his name *did not* appear on the list of delinquents.

For the most part, negative evidence is not admissible in the courts. In nonlegal argumentation, also, it should be viewed with caution. The absence of evidence to the contrary seldom establishes a claim as firmly as does direct positive evidence. Which provides stronger proof that a bill has been paid: a stamped receipt or the fact that a statement was not received the first of the month? Which goes farther toward proving a soldier brave: a citation for heroism or the absence of a court-martial charge for cowardice?

Mark Twain once pointed to the inherent weakness of negative evidence by asking in his inimitable way, "How do you know a fish can't climb a tree? Did you ever see one not do it?" Yet if some "fact" almost certainly indicates the presence of a given condition, the absence of the "fact" may serve as reasonably strong negative evidence that the condition does not exist.

## EAGER OR RELUCTANT EVIDENCE

A final distinction is between eager and reluctant evidence. Eager evidence appears to work toward the reporter's advantage. Reluctant evidence appears to work against him.

The classics teacher who testifies that a knowledge of the ancient languages is an essential part of a liberal education gives eager evidence; the classics teacher who testifies that such knowledge is not important gives reluctant evidence. The public official who admits the failure of a policy he has fostered, the critic who confesses that his earlier judgment concerning a book or play was wrong, the parent who testifies against his child—these persons, too, probably give reluctant evidence. It would appear advantageous for them to report a conclusion opposite to the one they do report. Yet they cross our expectancy and in so doing tend to work against their apparent interests.

Reluctant evidence, sincerely given, possesses great probative value. The man who openly confesses that his judgment was wrong, his policy a failure, or his guiding value worthless seems to speak from the depths of conviction. Hence, the debater should always be on the watch for reluctant evidence; and if upon analysis he finds it reflects the witnesses' honest convictions, he should give such evidence an important place in the development of his proofs.

## PRESENTING EVIDENCE

If evidence is to play its proper role in debate, it must, in addition to meeting the standards suggested in the preceding section, also be fairly and effectively presented to those persons with whom the decision rests.

Underlying all rules for the presentation of evidence in critical deliberation is this basic test: *Is the evidence set forth in such a way that the reader or listener is able to assign it exactly the weight it deserves— no more and no less?* When this question can be answered affirmatively, the evidence has been presented in an acceptable manner; when it must be answered negatively, the presentation has in some respect failed to meet the standard that a reader or auditor has the right to expect.

### AN ETHIC OF EVIDENCE

Deliberate attempts to manipulate data, so as to give them greater weight than they deserve, violate what may be termed an ethic of evidence. Such violations fall into two major classes: selective reporting and altered or colored reporting.

SELECTIVE REPORTING. There are several methods by which evidence may be reported in a selected, mutilated, or otherwise incomplete form. Below are some of the most common devices.

1. *Suppressing data unfavorable to the position one is supporting.* A familiar device of the propagandist is known as "card stacking." A writer or speaker stacks the cards in his favor when he selects for presentation only those facts and values that support his position and leaves unmentioned those that refute it. Such deliberate suppression of unfavorable evidence throws a reader's or listener's view of a problem out of balance and renders a critical decision impossible.

2. *Omitting words or sentences from quoted passages, or figures from sets of statistics, thus altering the meaning or significance of the evidence.* For example, the statement actually made by the source from which a debater quotes reads: "While the danger admittedly is not very great, the possibility of a serious depression does loom on the horizon more strongly today than at any time during the past few years." The debater, omitting the qualifying phrase and altering the wording accordingly, reports: "According to Senator John Doe, ' . . . the possibility of a serious depression looms on the horizon more strongly today than at any time during the past few years.' " By this omission the tone of the original statement is entirely changed.

3. *Citing a statement or statistic out of context.* In this device no

words or figures are omitted, but the datum is reported in isolation, without reference to the nature of the book or article from which it is drawn or the situation of which it is a part.

Condemning a certain politician, a debater quotes him as having said, "An aggressive war is sometimes justified." What the debater does not add is that this statement was embedded in a long speech, the central theme of which was the desirability of settling international disputes by peaceful means, and was immediately followed by the phrase, "but these occasions almost never occur." Nor does the debater report that the speech was given at a time when our own security was seriously threatened by the warlike acts of an unfriendly nation.

Such surrounding facts do not deny that the statement was actually made. Nor do they condone aggression as a national policy. But by taking a single sentence out of context, the debater gives it an emphasis quite different from that intended by the speaker.

4. *Failure to date information.* In arguing that a community's tax rate should be lowered, a debater says, "Figures show it to be the highest in the state." He conveniently forgets to mention, however, that the "figures" referred to date from 1956, and that later statistics show that several other cities are now taxed more heavily. By failing to mention the date he leaves an impression no less false than if he had deliberately lied.

5. *Failure to state the source of information when a knowledge of that source is essential to a fair evaluation of the facts reported.* A debater asserts, "According to several articles that have appeared recently in influential newspapers, the foreign policy of the present administration has failed to win friends and enhance our national prestige." By omitting the names of these newspapers, however, he suppresses vital information. If they were mentioned, his readers or listeners would immediately recognize them as avowed organs of the "out" party and would evaluate the statements accordingly.

ALTERED OR COLORED REPORTING. The five devices just considered are unfair because they do not report the facts completely. The three now to be examined do not omit essential data, but alter or color evidence to suit a particular purpose.

1. *Deliberate falsification.* Here the debater willfully alters facts or distorts values to make them support the claim he is advancing. Such alterations may involve changes in the wording of statements, the fabrication of cases and examples, or the unfair use of statistics.[4] Deliberate falsification not only violates the principles of critical delibera-

[4] Standards for the proper use of statistics are discussed in Chapter 12, pp. 180–81.

tion, but constitutes dishonesty of the worst sort.

2. *Putting information into an emotional setting, or exerting irrelevant emotional pressures to help gain its acceptance or rejection.* In the reaching of critical decisions, appropriate motives and values, as well as pertinent evidence, must always be taken into account. Weighing motives and values for what they are worth, however, differs significantly from deliberately surrounding a claim with irrelevant emotional pressures designed to promote its acceptance or rejection. Impassioned pleas to "mother and country," or deliberate attempts to arouse fear, anger, or revenge, when such appeals are unrelated to the issues, give arguments an unwarranted emotional coloring. When a question involves matters about which a debater feels strongly, he has every right to state this fact. But to exert irrelevant pressures is to undermine the central purpose of debate.

3. *Withholding information until a point in the debate when it can no longer receive careful consideration, or when an opponent has little or no chance to answer it.* If a decision is to be critical, it not only must be based on *all* the pertinent facts and values, but on these facts and values *fully and carefully considered*. To withhold data beyond a point when they may receive such consideration by judge and opponent alike renders the co-operative testing of rival claims impossible.

## A RHETORIC OF EVIDENCE

An ethic of evidence aims to insure that the evidence entered into argument will be given no more weight than it deserves. A rhetoric of evidence seeks to guarantee that it will not be undervalued. For just as one may exaggerate the worth of data by the use of unfair devices, so may one detract from their worth by ineffective presentation. In debate, claims must "stand on their own legs," but they must stand unhampered by unnatural burdens and barriers. The following principles help insure that evidence will not be undervalued.

1. *An effective argument is more than a string of quotations and statistics.* In settling certain questions of fact—say whether College A is larger than College B or whether George Washington smoked cigars—authority and statistics alone are sufficient. As was pointed out in Chapter 2, however, these questions should not be decided by debate, but by direct recourse to data.

In resolving the kind of questions appropriate to debate, facts and figures are not all-sufficient. Instead, the decision always rests, at least in part, on judgment. The facts do not provide an immediate answer but must be interpreted and evaluated; inferences and conclusions must be drawn from them.

Because an element of personal judgment is always involved in the decisions a debater seeks, his own ideas and convictions form an important part of his arguments. The reader or listener looks upon him as an informed student of the subject and wants to know what he recommends.

The English statesman William Ewart Gladstone wisely observed, "Truth is not necessarily loved when seen, [and] not necessarily seen when shown." [5] Centuries earlier, Plato had made a similar comment.[6] To make "truth" loved and seen, the debater must do more than rehearse data or transmit what others have said. Unless he is a student of his subject, who expresses significant original ideas concerning it, he fails both in his purpose and in his responsibility.

2. *The evidence used in debate often requires explanation. Readers or listeners must be told how it applies and, sometimes, what it means.* The debater who has studied a complex problem long and carefully often forgets that the persons to whom his arguments are addressed are less well informed concerning it. He assumes they understand the meaning and significance of the data as quickly and fully as he does. The truth, unfortunately, is quite otherwise. Statistics on the balance of trade, statements about the structure of UNESCO, or opinions of geneticists about the effects of radiation on future generations may go entirely over the head of the uninformed reader or listener.

Whenever the slightest chance exists that the meaning or pertinence of data will not be appreciated, the debater should stop to clarify them. His discourse should be studded with such phrases as, "The following statistics show . . ."; "Further evidence bearing on the point of growing economic instability is . . ."; "Most significant of all is President Kennedy's statement that . . ."; "In direct contradiction to my opponent's assertion that wage rates are falling, a recent Labor Department report shows. . . ."

If evidence is to be given the full weight it deserves, such clarifying statements are indispensable.

3. *Facts and figures must undergird each unit of proof presented.* As already remarked, an effective argument is more than a string of quotations and statistics. Equally undesirable, however, is an opposite tendency to cut loose from facts completely and advance claims that lack a suitable evidential basis. Rhetorical effectiveness, as well as reliable judgment, demands that claims be based on facts and not offered as unsupported assertions. Data and warrant, each present in the proper

---

[5] "Public Speaking," cited in Loren Reid, "Gladstone's Essay on Public Speaking," *The Quarterly Journal of Speech,* 39 (Oct. 1953), 267.
[6] *Phaedrus,* 277.

proportion, must be woven into an integrated pattern: facts as the base; warrants constructed upon this foundation; claims that follow from the warrants and can be checked back against the facts. This formula at once describes the critical method and the method best calculated to convince others.

4. *Special care must be taken to present statistics clearly.* Statistics, especially when presented in quantity, are difficult for the average reader or listener to follow. To make them easier to understand, observe the following suggestions:

*a.* Do not compound statistics needlessly. Use only the minimum required to support the claim or warrant.

*b.* Insofar as one may do so without violating the standards of truth and fairness, use round numbers rather than exact figures. Say "nearly two and a half billion" rather than "2,497,868,442"; "approximately two hundred and fifty thousand" rather than "249,903."

*c.* When presenting very large or very small numbers supply a standard for comparison. Break the national debt down on a per capita basis; tell how many times one would have to split a human hair to get a segment .0017 of an inch thick.

*d.* Use visual aids. Line or bar charts, maps, pictures, diagrams, and the like, help clarify statistical data by putting them into graphic form.

*e.* If the statistics are presented orally rather than in writing, speak slowly and with a careful use of pause and emphasis.

5. *Evidence must be entered into argument in specific and concrete terms.* The probative value of evidence is, in most instances, directly proportional to the specificity with which it is stated.

In answering the argument of an opponent the inexperienced debater may say: "Mr. Jones has contended that over the past decade labor relations in the automobile industry have deteriorated. In refutation, I would refer him to a recent article in *Harper's Magazine*. If he will read this article, he will find the facts quite otherwise." From the point of view of proof, such an answer is no answer at all. To judge the facts of the situation, a reader or listener would have to know what the article said and to recognize the relationship between its contents and the point at issue. Because the debater's reference is vague and general rather than specific, no appropriate conclusion may be drawn.

Similarly, evidence becomes stronger in proportion as its source is stated specifically. Do not say, "According to an eminent economist. . . ." Give his exact name and position, and if he is not already well known, tell why his opinion should be listened to with respect. Avoid such phrases as, "In a recent book . . ."; "Facts suggest . . .";

"Statistics reveal . . ."; "Several articles show . . ."; "Reliable sources indicate. . . ." State the author, title, and date of the work quoted. Vague citations leave room for doubt in the mind of the listener or reader and, therefore, do not give data as much weight as they deserve in the making of critical choices and judgments.[7]

## RELATION OF ETHICS AND RHETORIC OF EVIDENCE

As the experienced debater will testify, the strongest attack that can be made on an argument is to expose it as uncritical—to show it is based on a mutilated quotation, a faulty statistic, or the deliberate suppression of data. Such exposure immediately undermines confidence in the debater's integrity and hence not only destroys the argument in question but casts suspicion on his entire case, as well.

On the other hand, nothing is so persuasive as arguments based on valid reasoning from authenticated facts and accepted values, fully and fairly reported. If, in the face of such arguments, untruth or deceit triumphs, the victory is, with few exceptions, temporary rather than permanent. In the end, truth breaks through.

*An ethic of evidence and a rhetoric of evidence, therefore, coincide.* If one seeks to write and speak persuasively, he should write and speak truthfully and give to each fact or value exactly the weight it deserves. Only when one is more concerned with truth than with victory are his chances for victory at their best. To be persuasive be truthful; be truthful to be persuasive.[8]

## QUESTIONS

*A. To Check Your Comprehension and Memory*
  1. Define "evidence."
  2. How may evidence be classified?
  3. What are some of the ways in which real evidence may be used in nonlegal debate?
  4. What dangers must be avoided when using hearsay evidence?
  5. Distinguish between direct and circumstantial evidence.
  6. Is circumstantial evidence always weaker than direct evidence?
  7. What are the strengths and weaknesses of casual evidence?
  8. Under what circumstances, if any, does negative evidence provide reasonably strong proof?
  9. Define reluctant evidence.

---

[7] See Chapter 12, pp. 181–82.
[8] See Bertrand Russell, "Best Answer to Fanaticism, Liberalism," *New York Times Magazine,* Dec. 16, 1951, p. 9.

10. What basic principle underlies all rules for the use of evidence?

11. Name some of the ways in which evidence may be mutilated or otherwise reported in an incomplete form.

12. Name three ways in which evidence is sometimes altered or colored to suit an unscrupulous debater's purpose.

13. Name the principles which help insure that evidence will be entered into argument at its full worth.

14. Give four rules to be followed when presenting statistics.

15. Explain why an "ethic of evidence" and a "rhetoric of evidence" coincide.

*B. For Class Discussion*

1. Is it possible to present evidence in such a way that a reader or listener can assign it exactly the weight it deserves? Isn't this an impossibly high ethical standard? Won't there always be some distortions or shadings in the sheer act of presentation—in getting the facts down on paper or in expressing them orally? In the latter case, how about the tone of one's voice, the degree of force or emphasis with which one speaks, and so on?

2. Can you think of instances in which negative evidence may provide stronger proof of a claim than certain forms of positive evidence do?

3. Review some of the famous criminal cases that have been decided very largely on the basis of circumstantial evidence. (Kidnaping of the Lindbergh baby, for example.)

4. Which do you think is worse: suppressing information unfavorable to one's side, or deliberately falsifying facts? Why?

5. Develop the strongest argument you can to refute the proposition that an "ethic of evidence" and a "rhetoric of evidence" coincide. Cite cases in which you believe this is not true. Use reason to support the contention that it is possible to win belief by unfair means, and sometimes to continue to do so over a period of many months or years.

EXERCISES

*A. Written Exercises*

1. Write a short paper analyzing the evidence used by each team in the sample college debate printed in Appendix A. What types of evidence were used? How well did the teams meet the standards for evidence suggested in this chapter?

2. Evaluate the evidence offered to support the claims advanced in five magazine advertisements. Was the evidence presented in such a way that the reader could assess its exact worth? Turn these advertisements and your evaluations of them in to your instructor.

3. Keep a record for two or three days of how your professors and your friends and classmates attempt to prove the claims they advance. In how many cases do they offer any evidence at all? When they do offer evidence,

how well do they meet the standards suggested in this chapter? What is your general conclusion about how most people use evidence in their everyday speaking and conversation? Are your professors more or less scrupulous in supporting their statements with evidence than are your friends and classmates?

4. The reading list at the end of this chapter includes articles on "Evidence" in the *Encyclopaedia Britannica* and the *Encyclopaedia of the Social Sciences*. As the annotation indicates, these essays are chiefly concerned with the history of legal evidence and the principles that now govern the use of evidence in the courtroom. Read these articles and any of the other materials listed in the bibliographies that accompany these articles, and then write a short paper entitled "Legal Evidence."

B. *Oral Exercise*

Present a five- or six-minute one-point speech to persuade, in which you use at least four different types of evidence—real, original, circumstantial, reluctant, etc.

In organizing your speech, begin by stating as an hypothesis the proposition you seek to prove. Then marshal in an orderly fashion the various pieces of evidence that support it. Close with a reaffirmation of the proposition, now viewing it as a claim established by the evidence rather than as an hypothesis to be proved. (You may say at the beginning of your speech, "I am going to consider with you the question concerning. . . ." At the end, you may conclude, "Therefore, in view of these facts, I have proved to you. . . ."). Here are some suggested subjects:

It Pays to Advertise
Businessmen in Our Community Would Benefit from Daylight Saving Time
Progressive Education Develops the Student's Ability to Think for Himself
Today's Farmer Is Caught in a Price Squeeze
Americans Read Fewer Books Than Do Englishmen
You Are Safer in an Airplane than in an Automobile

## SUGGESTIONS FOR FURTHER READING

Edwin Leavitt Clarke, *The Art of Straight Thinking* (New York: D. Appleton-Century Co., 1934). Chapter 10, "Circumstantial Evidence and the Proof of Hypotheses"; Chapter 11, "Oral Testimony"; and Chapter 12, "Written Sources." These chapters provide an interesting and useful discussion of the various types and sources of evidence. They are abundantly illustrated with both real and hypothetical examples that show how evidence is used and the tests it must meet in order to produce sound proof. (Remember in reading these examples, however, that the book was published in 1934, so that some of them are now a bit out of date.)

*Encyclopaedia Britannica* and *Encyclopaedia of the Social Sciences*. Articles on "Evidence." The articles in both of these encyclopedias treat evidence from the legal point of view and therefore should be of special interest to students who are planning to go to law school. They give the history of the law of evidence, and present rules and principles. Each is followed by a bibliography that suggests additional readings.

Rudolf Flesch, *The Art of Clear Thinking* (New York: Harper & Brothers, 1951), Chapter 10, "Why Argue?" An interesting discussion of the role facts play in initiating and prolonging disputes, and why they sometimes prevent agreement altogether.

# Chapter 10
# SUBSTANTIVE PROOF

> *Certain basic similarities of pattern and procedure can be recognised, not only among legal arguments but among justificatory arguments in general, however widely different the fields of the arguments, the sorts of evidence relevant, and the weight of the evidence may be.* STEPHEN TOULMIN

THE SAME *structure* of proof, described in Chapter 8, applies to all proofs a debater may advance in the course of any controversy. The way the elements of proof *function,* however, varies widely, and proofs may accordingly be classified into types on this basis.

The determining element in classifying proofs has traditionally been the warrant. Since the warrant performs the function of connecting evidence and claim, and since the support for the warrant and the reservations are both profoundly influenced by the type of warrant, a classification of proofs has been essentially synonymous with a classification of warrants.[1]

Since evidence may be carried to a claim through one of three routes, three general categories of proof patterns may be employed to establish or deny any statement:

1. Proofs in which the warrant asserts a relationship among phenomena of the external world—these may be called *substantive* proofs.

2. Proofs in which the warrant asserts an assumption concerning the credibility of the source from which the evidence is derived—these may be called *authoritative* proofs.

---

[1] Although we are following the traditional principle in classifying proofs, we apply the principle more broadly than is customary. Since Aristotle divided the modes of proof into *logos, pathos,* and *ethos,* rather definite boundaries have been erected between "logical" argument, emotional appeal, and the character of the speaker. The boundaries are perhaps more theoretical than functional. Only the first of these proofs is ordinarily assigned to the province of the debater. We believe strongly, however, that the debater must understand and employ units of proof from all three modes, and that he may do so within the context of the same structure.

3. Proofs in which the warrant asserts an assumption concerning the emotions, values, or motives which direct the behavior of those persons to whom the proof is addressed—these may be called *motivational* proofs.

This chapter describes and illustrates various patterns of *substantive* proof and indicates what types of claims may be established by each pattern. In Chapter 11 *authoritative* and *motivational* proofs are similarly treated.

As the student examines each of these classes of proof patterns, he should note that the same structure prevails, that proof elements of each pattern function somewhat differently, that different types of claims are made good by different patterns, and that each pattern may be employed critically in certain argumentative situations.

## GENERAL CHARACTERISTICS OF SUBSTANTIVE PROOFS

Each pattern of substantive proof employs a warrant that expresses a relationship among data of the external world. All such warrants make three common assumptions: (*a*) The facts of our world are not separate and isolated, but interdependent and connected. (*b*) Such connections are not disorganized and random, but systematic and regular. (*c*) These systematic connections are not temporary and fluid, but sufficiently permanent and invariable to support present judgments and values and to provide a ground for predictions concerning future policy.

Each substantive proof pattern, then, employs a warrant that states a relatively *interdependent, systematic,* and *permanent* relationship among the data of the external world. By pointing out how the specific item or items reported in the evidence of a substantive proof fit into one of the general categories of relationship recognized to exist among data of the external world, one may infer a claim concerning those items.

What, then, are the patterns of relationship? Seven such patterns may be recognized: (1) *cause,* (2) *sign,* (3) *generalization,* (4) *parallel case,* (5) *analogy,* (6) *classification,* and (7) *statistics.* Let us analyze and illustrate the patterns of substantive proof that are based on these seven kinds of relationship.

### CAUSE

CAUSE TO EFFECT. Two kinds of proofs involve causal relationship. The first of these, cause to effect, assumes that one set of data, as *cause,* may be related to another set of data, as *effect.* When one argues, for example, from the evidence that the income of industrial workers is higher now than it was a year ago, to the claim that, therefore, both consumption and savings may be expected to rise, he is arguing from cause to effect. Or if one moves from evidence that many high schools offer no course in mathematics, to the claim that a shortage of trained engineers is not likely to be alleviated, he is similarly arguing from an accepted cause to a controversial effect.

*Evidence* in a proof from cause to effect consists of one or more accepted items of information about a person, object, institution, event, or condition. The *warrant* attributes to the information a generative power and designates the result that will be produced. The *claim* relates such results to the person, object, institution, event, or condition named in the evidence. Such relationships are illustrated diagrammatically:

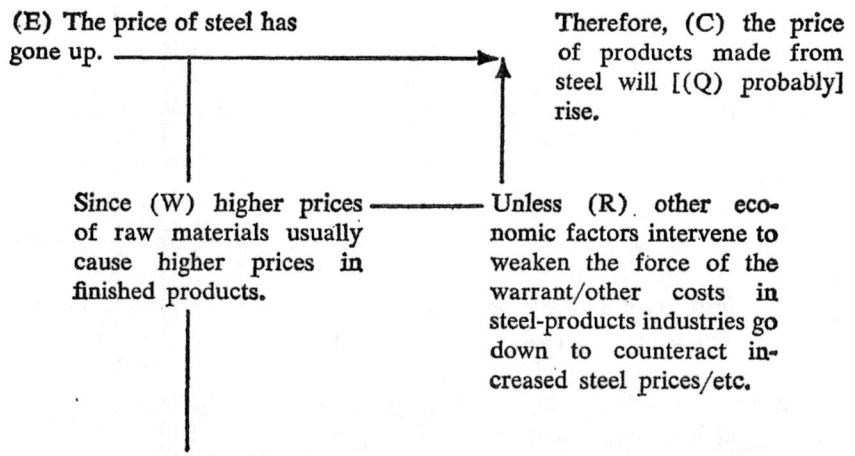

(E) The price of steel has gone up. ⟶ Therefore, (C) the price of products made from steel will [(Q) probably] rise.

Since (W) higher prices of raw materials usually cause higher prices in finished products. — Unless (R) other economic factors intervene to weaken the force of the warrant/other costs in steel-products industries go down to counteract increased steel prices/etc.

Because (S for W) Expert X asserts that the price of finished products almost always reflects the price of raw materials/a study of a large sample of industries indicates that changed prices of raw materials generally cause changes of prices of finished products/etc.

The *warrant* states a general cause–effect relationship between the cost of raw materials and the price of finished products. That the relationship expressed in such a warrant fits the subject matter of steel and steel-products industries is probably self-evident. In some instances, however, the *applicability* of the warrant may need proof or explanation.

If the listener or reader does not believe the causal relationship itself, the arguer must offer *support for the warrant*. He may do so by advancing a unit of proof in which the warrant functions as a claim. In the above example an authoritative proof and a generalization support the dependability of the causal relationship of the warrant. Although support for the warrant has nothing directly to say about the subject matter on the main proof line, it certifies the validity of the principle expressed in the warrant.

Even if the warrant is accepted or adequately supported, its force upon the main proof line may be removed or weakened by *reservations*. In the cause–effect proof, reservations take the form of other causal forces that intervene or counteract the cause asserted in the warrant. A cause may be thought of as an active force sending off a series of waves or impulses directed toward some effect. An *intervening* cause sends off forces of its own that cut across the forces of the original cause, thus nullifying its energy:

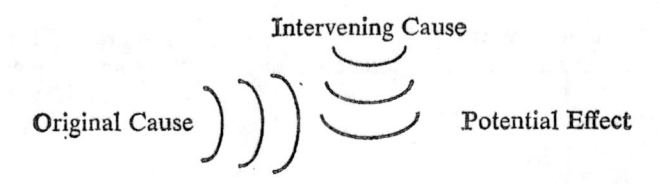

Intervening Cause

Original Cause  )))  Potential Effect

An increase in the price of steel, a raw material, would potentially create the effect of boosting prices of products made from steel. Other economic factors, however, might intervene. For example, if in a particular steel-products industry conditions were highly competitive, the producer might not be able to pass along the increased cost of steel to the consumer.

Whereas an intervening cause checks the force of the original cause by cutting across its path, a *counteracting* cause impedes progress by sending off impulses that travel in the opposite direction:

Counteracting Cause

Original Cause  )))  (((  Potential Effect

A decrease in other production costs in steel-products industries may counteract the increase in the price of steel. If either intervening or counteracting causes are operative in a cause–effect proof, a claim may safely be made only with reservations.

Claims derived from cause–effect proofs vary widely in the degree of assurance with which they may be held. The effect expressed in the claim may be predicted with relatively great assurance if (*a*) the evidence reports events or conditions accurately, (*b*) the warrant states a dependable causal relationship, and (c) intervening and counteracting causes are not present. To the extent that a unit of proof lacks these conditions, the claim must be *qualified*. Although the evidence in the example concerning the price of products made from steel is presumably accurate, the claim must be qualified because higher prices of raw materials only *usually* cause higher prices in finished products, and because an intervening and a counteracting cause may be present. Hence the qualifying "probably" is included in the claim statement.

EFFECT TO CAUSE. In the other kind of causal proof, a set of data, as *effect,* is related to another set of data, as *cause*. When one argues from the evidence that both consumption and savings have increased during the past year, to the claim, therefore, that the income of industrial workers must be higher than a year ago, he is employing an effect–cause proof. And when one moves from evidence that persons who are released from a particular penal institution rarely commit further crimes, to a claim, therefore, that that penal institution is successfully rehabilitating its inmates, he is, again, arguing from effect to cause.

*Evidence* in an effect–cause proof consists of one or more believed items of information about a person, object, event, institution, or condition. The *warrant* asserts that a particular causal force is sufficient to account for the kind of information asserted in the evidence. The *claim* then relates this cause to the particular person, object, event, institution, or condition named in the evidence. The effect–cause proof is illustrated in the following example:

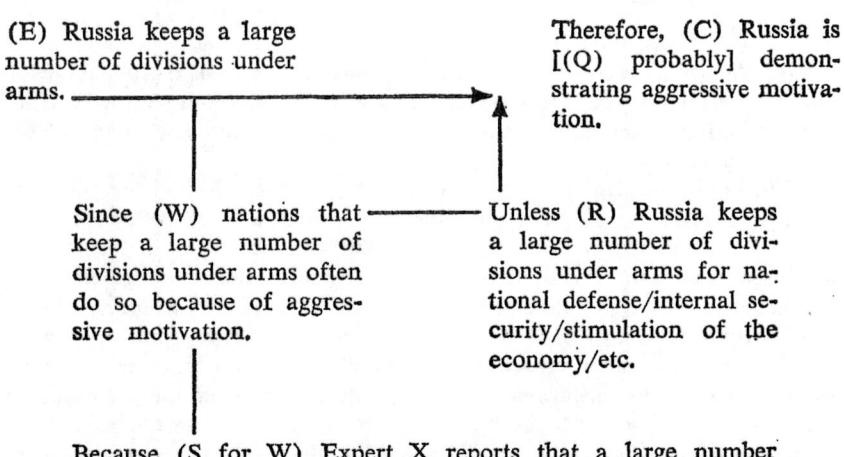

(E) Russia keeps a large number of divisions under arms. ⟶ Therefore, (C) Russia is [(Q) probably] demonstrating aggressive motivation.

Since (W) nations that keep a large number of divisions under arms often do so because of aggressive motivation.

Unless (R) Russia keeps a large number of divisions under arms for national defense/internal security/stimulation of the economy/etc.

Because (S for W) Expert X reports that a large number of divisions under arms almost always indicates aggressive intent/a large sample of instances exist in which aggressive motivation caused the arming of large numbers of divisions/etc.

Like those of cause–effect proofs, a warrant in an effect–cause proof must be accepted as relevant to the main proof line and as embodying a credible principle. In the example above the relevance of the warrant is obvious. Its credibility is attested to by the *support for the warrant,* which consists of one proof by authority and one by generalization.

*Reservations* function in effect–cause proofs as a sort of countercausal claim. Whereas reservations are made in cause–effect proofs if intervening or counteracting causes are present, an effect–cause proof requires a reservation if other causes are recognized that better account for the effect reported in the evidence. One can safely conclude that Russia's aggression accounts for the large number of divisions under arms only if he has discounted other suggested causes.

METHODS FOR DETERMINING CAUSAL FORCES. Since the discovery of causal forces presents a difficult problem—especially when dealing with complex social, moral, political, and economic questions—the reservation is a very important element in an effect–cause unit of proof. A debater deals with situations arising out of multiple causes that form a complex network. Often he can attribute an effect to a cause only with the reservation that other causal forces are also present.

Especially useful in sorting out causal forces are the so-called *experimental methods* of John Stuart Mill, a nineteenth-century English philosopher. While these methods do not guarantee success, they do aid the search for causes and effects by suggesting useful tests. Since Mill's own statement of the methods makes sufficiently clear the nature of the tests, we shall reproduce his language without additional comment or explanation.

*The Method of Agreement* If two or more instances of the phenomenon under investigation have only one circumstance in common, the circumstance in which alone all the instances agree, is the cause (or effect) of the given phenomenon.

*The Method of Difference* If an instance in which the phenomenon under investigation occurs, and an instance in which it does not occur, have every circumstance in common save one, that one occurring in the former; the circumstance in which alone the two instances differ, is the effect, or the cause, or an indispensable part of the cause, of the phenomenon.

*The Joint Method of Agreement and Difference* If two or more instances in which the phenomenon occurs have only one circumstance in common, while two or more instances in which it does not occur have nothing in common save the absence of the circumstance; the circumstance in which alone the two sets of instances differ, is the effect, or the cause, or an indispensable part of the cause, of the phenomenon.

*The Method of Concomitant Variation* Whatever phenomenon varies in any manner whenever another phenomenon varies in some particular manner, is either a cause or an effect of that phenomenon, or is connected with it through some fact of causation.

*The Method of Residues* Subduct from any phenomenon such part as is known by previous inductions to be the effect of certain antecedents, and the residue of the phenomenon is the effect of the remaining antecedents.[2]

Since the determination of causes is so difficult in most debatable questions, the claims of effect-to-cause proofs almost always require a *qualifier*. If the warrant states a relationship that only "often" occurs, and if countercausal claims appear in the reservation, one may make only a qualified claim that certain causal forces account for, or contribute to, the effect reported in the evidence.

Both kinds of causal proofs answer only questions of fact and, therefore, establish only *designative* claims. The only purpose of a causal proof is to determine whether a cause or an effect exists.

## SIGN

Just as the detective uses clues to reconstruct a crime, or the doctor employs symptoms to diagnose a disease, so the debater resorts to proof by *sign,* a second kind of substantive proof.

Consider this example. During the course of an argument Smith wants to show that the nation is very probably moving toward a serious business recession. He cannot actually "see" or "feel" a nation-wide recession any more than a doctor can "see" or "feel" measles germs, or the detective can relive a crime that took place last week. But Smith, like a doctor or a detective, can work indirectly by inference and employ certain *signs* as a means of proving his claim: Employment in the basic industries has fallen sharply; bank deposits and loans to businesses have decreased; the stock market is in a slump; inventories are at a five-year peak—these, he argues, are signs that the nation is on the brink of a recession.

RELATIONSHIP OF EFFECT AND SIGN. The distinction between the proof from effect to cause and the proof from sign, as Archbishop Richard Whately pointed out nearly a century and a half ago, is "a fruitful source of confusion." This confusion arises because *effect* and *sign* are sometimes one and the same. The observed increase in consumption and savings is at once an effect and a sign of the rise in income of industrial workers. That persons released from a particular penal institution rarely commit further crimes is both effect and sign of the successful rehabilitation measures of that institution.

But such a coincidence of effect and sign is by no means universal. One may believe something by means of signs, without understanding what causes that to which the signs point. Indeed, the causes may be irrelevant to such a belief. A friend is distant and surly. He fails to respond to a greeting and does not stop to chat in his customary way. Has

[2] *A System of Logic* (London: 1843), 3.8.

some word or act offended him? Did he have an argument with his wife? Is his ill temper the result of a headache? One is at a loss to name the cause of his behavior even though the signs and their meaning are obvious.

When the cause is clearly known, there is sometimes not the least relationship between it and the signs on which one bases his belief. The gong ringing on shipboard is a sign that dinner is ready, but not the cause. The sounds of reveille are a sign to the soldier that it is time to get up, but not the cause. On many such occasions one reasons from sign relationships with no interest in raising questions about causation.

The point to remember is that effect and sign are products of two different reasoning processes that are based on quite different kinds of warrants. Even though a cause may be lurking somewhere in the background of a proof by sign, the cause is not really essential to the functioning of the proof, since the sign relationship itself may warrant the claim.

*Evidence* in a proof by sign consists of symptoms or clues. The *warrant* states that the information presented in the evidence is usually symptomatic of a certain sort of condition. The *claim* then affirms that some particular person, object, institution, event, or state of affairs possesses a condition of which the clues are thus declared to be symptomatic. Consider an example:

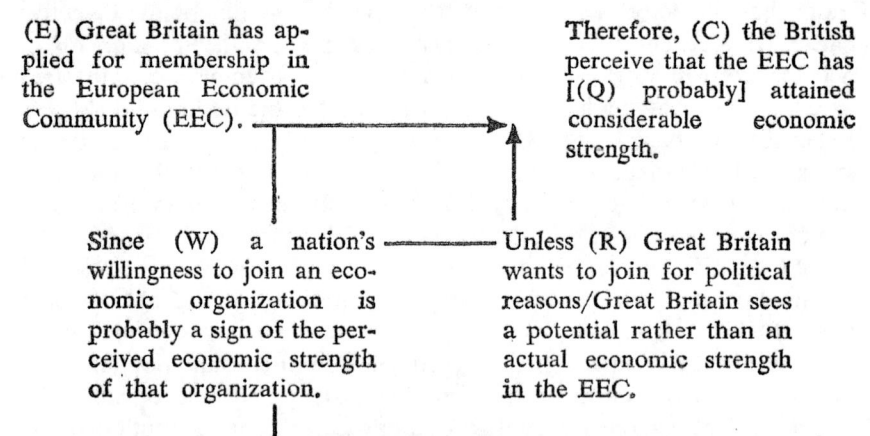

(E) Great Britain has applied for membership in the European Economic Community (EEC).

Therefore, (C) the British perceive that the EEC has [(Q) probably] attained considerable economic strength.

Since (W) a nation's willingness to join an economic organization is probably a sign of the perceived economic strength of that organization.

Unless (R) Great Britain wants to join for political reasons/Great Britain sees a potential rather than an actual economic strength in the EEC.

Because (S for W) one can assume, in view of Great Britain's network of trade relations with the commonwealth nations and other nations not in the EEC, a network threatened by membership in the EEC, that she would not seek membership in the EEC if she thought the organization were weak/nations X, Y, and Z in the past have joined organizations they thought strong and stayed out of organizations they thought weak.

The *support for the warrant* in the above example consists of a proof from effect to cause and a proof from parallel cases to certify the reliability of the sign relationship expressed in the warrant. If the sign is unreliable, the proof fails. To interpret decreased attendance at the movies and baseball games as a sign that the American people are reading more books, or the fact that a neighbor drives a new car as a sign that the car is paid for, may assume the association of facts that in reality are quite independent of each other. Only after one is certain of the probability of the sign relationship should he proceed to examine the proof as a whole.

RESERVATIONS IN PROOF BY SIGN. The warrant in the above example, as supported, reports a sign relationship between a nation's wanting to join an organization and its perception of the strength of that organization. Specific circumstances surrounding the contention on the main proof line, however, as indicated in the example, may reduce or set aside the usual force of the warrant. In short, a claim may sometimes be made only with *reservations*.

For at least two good reasons, one must examine carefully the whole context of the proof by sign to determine whether reservations are applicable. In the first place, *that which at one time or under one set of conditions may be a valid sign will not necessarily be a valid sign at another time or under other conditions*. Fifty years ago owning an automobile was a fairly dependable sign of wealth and a mark of social prestige. Today, however, when nearly everyone owns one or more automobiles, mere ownership of a car no longer signifies status, at least in the United States. In certain other countries, on the other hand, the sign would be a good one.

In the second place, *the corroboration of several signs is generally required to establish the existence of a certain state of affairs*. A competent physician would not base his diagnosis of a serious disease on a single symptom. Nor should the debater ordinarily be satisfied with a single sign. Although armed troops on a border is a meaningful sign, war is not thereby inevitable. A rise in food prices, disturbing as it may be, does not in itself mean that a nation is entering a period of "runaway inflation." Only after examining a proof in its whole context with all relevant circumstances taken into account can a debater know how closely the facts surrounding the controversy conform to the sign relationship of the warrant, and, consequently, whether reservations need to be made.

QUALIFICATION IN PROOF BY SIGN. If the evidence or warrant of a unit of proof by sign, like cause, is qualified in any way, or if reservations can be identified, the claim must include a *qualifier*. Since the warrant in the example concerning the British application for membership in the

EEC is qualified, and since reservations have been attached, the claim is qualified.

*Only when a sign is infallible may the claim of a proof by sign be made without qualification.* In an infallible sign the mere existence of a sign may be taken as proof that a certain condition also exists: "There is ice on the pond; therefore, the temperature is thirty-two degrees Fahrenheit or below." "This strawberry is red; therefore, it is ripe."

Most of the signs debaters employ do not, unfortunately, yield necessary claims. Because man's actions are unpredictable, because the solution of political, social, moral, and economic problems must depend on informed guesses more often than on demonstrable judgments, usually debaters must be satisfied with fallible signs that yield only probable claims—biased news stories and highly colored editorials as signs that a newspaper is the tool of special interests; a rising crime rate as a sign of inefficiency or corruption in a city's police department; the arms race as a sign of fear and mistrust among nations. Such signs warrant only qualified claims.

Since a debater argues from signs only to determine the past, present, or future condition of some person, object, institution, or state of affairs, he establishes only *designative* claims with the proof.

## GENERALIZATION

In a *generalization* the arguer moves from a statement about a sample of items to the same statement about other items in the same class. Thus, one reasons from *some* to *more*. When someone argues that many athletes are poor students, because certain individual athletes have been poor students, or when one moves from information about increased unemployment in certain areas to the claim that unemployment is generally increasing throughout the country, he is employing a proof by generalization.

*Evidence* in a generalization consists of a series of assertions about a number of individual instances of persons, objects, institutions, events, or signs, which together are taken as constituting a sample of some class of phenomena. Because a class, by definition, exhibits a certain uniformity, the *warrant* assumes that what is true of the items forming the sample is also true of other members of the class not included in the sample. The *claim* makes explicit the assumption embodied in the warrant. The example on page 135 illustrates these relationships.

EVALUATION OF THE EVIDENCE-SAMPLE IN PROOF BY GENERALIZATION. In proofs by cause and sign the general assumption stated in the warrant may be supported without any direct consideration of the evidence. The warrant in a generalization, however, relates the sample

SUBSTANTIVE PROOF    135

to other items in the same class. The *support for the warrant*, therefore, consists of several criteria that may be applied to evaluate the sample reported in the evidence. Three general criteria may be applied to support the warrant in a generalization.

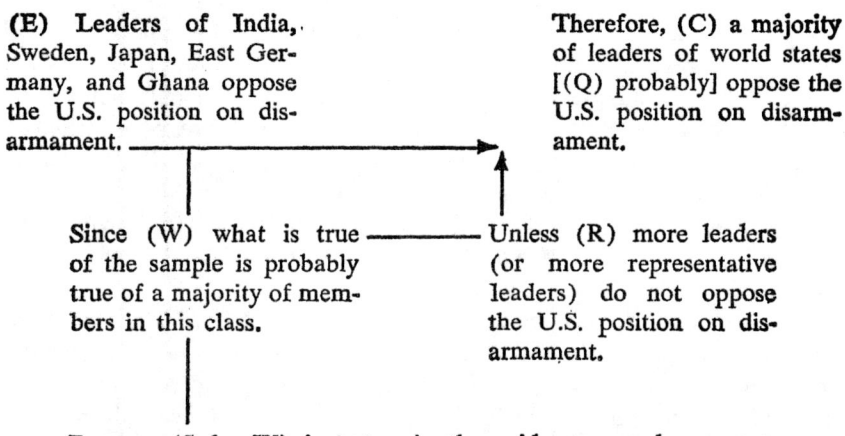

(E) Leaders of India, Sweden, Japan, East Germany, and Ghana oppose the U.S. position on disarmament. ─────────────▶ Therefore, (C) a majority of leaders of world states [(Q) probably] oppose the U.S. position on disarmament.

Since (W) what is true of the sample is probably true of a majority of members in this class. ─── Unless (R) more leaders (or more representative leaders) do not oppose the U.S. position on disarmament.

Because (S for W) instances in the evidence sample are germane to the claim/adequate in number/and fairly selected on the basis of political alignment and geographical location.

1. *Are the instances included in the sample germane to the class generalized upon in the claim?* To generalize concerning brickbats, goose feathers, or china plates, one obviously must employ those items in the evidence-sample. One draws no reliable conclusion about brickbats from studying flower pots. Debaters frequently encounter situations, however, that are not quite so pat. In the diagrammed example the leaders of the five world states in the evidence are certainly germane to the claim that is based on them. But consider another example: As evidence for a generalization about nations in the communist bloc, does a debater include Yugoslavia? In short, are the instances cited as evidence actually germane to the claim? A good answer to this question may sometimes require a careful definition of the class cited in the claim.

2. *Is the sample large enough to justify the assumption in the warrant that what is true of "m" is also true of "m" plus "n"?* Well-developed statistical techniques can determine the size of a sample required to render reliable certain kinds of claims. For general purposes of proof, however, one simple rule is helpful: other things being equal, the predictive power of a generalization is the *ratio of instances adduced to instances possible*. If an event has occurred "m" times, the probability that it will happen "m" plus "n" times increases as "m" increases.

Whether a sample is large enough, however, depends on at least three special considerations:

(a) *The adequacy of an evidence-sample varies in size according to the degree of homogeneity of the class.* Since a high degree of uniformity and regularity exist among the members of such classes as brickbats, goose feathers, and china plates, a comparatively small sample will support the generalizations, "Brickbats are heavy," "Goose feathers are light," and "China plates break easily." Suppose a debater, however, sought to establish the generalizations, "All women are poor drivers," "Most poets are eccentric," and "Lawyers are crooks." Since women, poets, and lawyers are not, as classes, homogeneous, but widely different, at least in the respects here mentioned, a much larger sample would be required. Since leaders of world states also vary widely, the warrant in the above example might be hard to support.

(b) *The adequacy of an evidence-sample varies in size according to one's knowledge of the cause that is responsible for the characteristic concerning which he generalizes.* Thus people demand relatively fewer instances of brickbats, goose feathers, and china plates, not only because of the homogeneity exhibited by such items, but also because they understand more or less clearly *why* brickbats are heavy, goose feathers light, and china plates breakable. If one's listeners or readers understand why certain leaders of world states are opposed to the U.S. position on disarmament—if common causal forces exist—they require relatively fewer instances in the evidence-sample.

(c) *The adequacy of an evidence-sample varies in size according to the care with which the instances were observed and reported.* A large number of observations made carelessly by untrained observers may be of little or no value as evidence, while a few made carefully by trained observers may furnish the basis for a valid generalization. Physical scientists commonly speak of a "crucial experiment"—an observation so carefully planned, controlled, and reported that it is in itself regarded as sufficient to underwrite a general principle. The type of subject matter with which the debater deals does not lend itself well to measurement or analysis by a "crucial experiment." Yet, in proportion as care and expert knowledge are employed in making a series of observations, a relatively smaller number of instances will yield an acceptable sample.

In applying the second criterion, then, concerning the adequacy of the size of the sample, one may support his warrant by considering the homogeneity of the class represented, the state of knowledge concerning the causes of the phenomenon being studied, and the care with which the observations were made and reported.

3. *Have the instances included in the sample been fairly selected?* By

deliberately choosing biased or loaded instances, one may find information to support almost any generalization. Suppose, for example, that during the course of an argument concerning the ability of individual states to support their public school systems, Jones cited as an evidence-sample the amounts spent per student in New York, Michigan, Pennsylvania, and Wisconsin, and concluded that state appropriations were sufficient and federal aid unnecessary. Brown, on the other hand, cited expenditures per student in Arkansas, Mississippi, Alabama, and Georgia, and concluded that state support was inadequate and, therefore, must be supplemented by federal funds. Each debater, knowingly or unknowingly, offered a badly biased sample to support his view. The first principle of selection of instances to be included in a sample is to *avoid a biased or loaded collection.*

A second principle need not be considered in supporting the warrant of every generalization. Often, however, the evidence-sample must avoid excessive homogeneity. If one is to conclude that the majority of leaders of world states have a particular opinion about the U.S. position on disarmament, he ought not draw all his instances from the same type of world state, nor from the same geographical area. A debater may not validly infer that what is true of the opinions of leaders of communist-bloc nations will prove true of a majority of leaders of world states; nor can he validly infer from opinions of leaders of Southeast Asian countries that he can generalize the claim on a world-wide basis. In short, a warrant must in some instances be supported by showing that the evidence-sample has been chosen on a *representational* basis.

In summary, warrants of generalizations are supported by applying criteria for evaluating the selection of the evidence-sample. Instances included in the sample should be germane to the class generalized upon in the claim, adequate in size, and fairly chosen.

RESERVATIONS IN PROOF BY GENERALIZATION. Two kinds of situations require that *reservations* be appended to claims derived from generalizations. In the first place, a *counter-generalization* based on an evidence-sample that better meets the criteria discussed above may set aside the claim of the original generalization. A better sample of statements may show that many world leaders are *not* opposed to the U.S. position on disarmament.

In the second place, *negative instances* may call for reservations. Assume that a professor observed instances of individual college students and arrived at the generalization that few undergraduate students read much in the newspapers beyond the comics and the sports page. But during the course of his inquiry he also encountered several exceptions—

students who read the papers thoroughly and intelligently.

He may deal with his negative instances critically in either of two ways: (*a*) He may show that every negative instance is the result of some special cause that does not negate his claim concerning representative undergraduates. One exception is the son of a congressman, raised in a home frequented by men in public life, where discussion of current problems was the order of the day; a second is planning to enter a career in politics; a third is majoring in journalism, with a special interest in foreign affairs. (*b*) He may simply report the negative instances and qualify his claim accordingly: "Despite a few striking instances to the contrary, the great majority of students interviewed. . . ." "Even when the exceptions are taken into account, we are warranted in making the general statement that. . . ."

QUALIFICATION IN PROOF BY GENERALIZATION. All claims derived from generalizations require a *qualifier* of some kind. There is no certain claim by generalization. The reason, as the eighteenth-century Scottish philosopher David Hume pointed out, is that in every generalization the claim is always more inclusive and comprehensive than the evidence on which it rests. That generalization involves reasoning from *some* to *more* means that he who uses it must always make an *inductive leap*—a leap into the dark, as far as immediately verifiable knowledge is concerned. This leap dooms a generalization to be *probable* rather than *necessary*.

Since the warrant of a generalization permits one to move from a statement about *some* to the same statement about *more* items in the same class, a second function of a qualifier is to limit how far one may go in his generalizing. The proportion of items within a class to which the claim statement applies is indicated by the qualifier. The whole class of items, on occasion, may be included in the claim, qualified only by *probability*. More often, the claim is more limited, since not all leaders of world states are opposed to the U.S. position on disarmament, not all athletes are poor students, and so on. Our evaluation of the evidence-sample may require the use of such qualifiers as "some," "many," "a majority of," "nearly all," or a similar expression. Also, as observed earlier, negative instances recognized in the reservation may force the arguer to limit the area within the class to which his claim safely applies.

Since the example concerning U.S. disarmament policy tries to answer a question of fact, the claim is *designative*. Proofs by generalization, unlike those by cause or sign, may, however, also be used to establish *evaluative* claims. An adequate evidence-sample of good administrative actions of City Manager Jones entitles one to claim that Jones has generally been a good administrator.

## PARALLEL CASE

Although they are similar, proof by parallel case differs from proof by generalization in one important respect. An arguer generalizes by moving from a statement about a cluster of related items of a class to a claim concerning some or all of the remaining members of the class. In a proof by parallel case, however, he moves from a statement about a sample of one instance to a similar statement about a parallel instance within the same class.

If a debater argues that because a smoke control system was effective in Pittsburgh, St. Louis, and Los Angeles, it will be effective in many cities, he is *generalizing*. If he argues, on the other hand, that because the system was effective in Pittsburgh, it will be effective in his city, he is employing a unit of proof by *parallel case*.

*Evidence* in this kind of proof consists of one or more statements about a person, object, institution, event, or condition. The *warrant* states that the instance reported in the evidence bears a similarity in essential characteristics to a second instance in the same class. The *claim* then affirms about the new instance what had already been accepted about the first instance. The instance reported in the evidence thus becomes a parallel case for the instance included in the claim. An example follows:

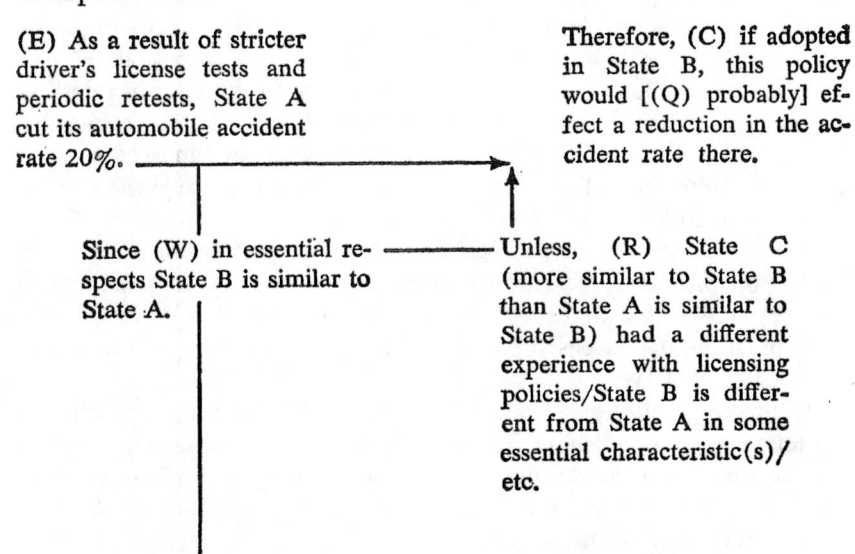

(E) As a result of stricter driver's license tests and periodic retests, State A cut its automobile accident rate 20%.

Therefore, (C) if adopted in State B, this policy would [(Q) probably] effect a reduction in the accident rate there.

Since (W) in essential respects State B is similar to State A.

Unless, (R) State C (more similar to State B than State A is similar to State B) had a different experience with licensing policies/State B is different from State A in some essential characteristic(s)/ etc.

Because (S for W) the two states are similar in highway networks, systems of law enforcement, climate, geography, and past policies of driver licensing.

Warrants of proofs by parallel case involve the relationship of similarity: the instance stated in the claim is said to be similar in essential respects to the parallel instance reported in the evidence. The *support for the warrant* in a proof by parallel case, then, consists of an analysis of the similarity of the two instances or cases.

Obviously, a debater must distinguish carefully between those similarities that are and those that are not pertinent to a particular claim. A considerable similarity between the two cases, if it has no direct bearing on the claim, has little or no effect on the strength of a proof. A consideration bearing immediately on the claim, however, although in itself seemingly trivial, may make or break the entire proof.

That State B was admitted to the Union a century before State A, that it has a Republican rather than a Democratic administration, four instead of two state universities, etc., probably makes no difference in driver's licensing policy. More important to the comparison are their highway networks, their systems of law enforcement, their climates, their geographies, and their past policies of licensing. If the two states are similar in these relevant respects, the warrant is supported and the proof has some measure of validity.

The support for the warrant of this type of proof, then, involves (*a*) a recognition of the *essential* aspects of comparison, and (*b*) a presentation of data supporting the assumption that the two cases are parallel.

RESERVATIONS IN PROOF BY PARALLEL CASE. The claims of proofs by parallel case require *reservations* in either of two situations: (*a*) If another parallel case bears a stronger similarity to the case in question, the claim is accepted only with reservation. If a third state, which has had a different experience with licensing policies, bears an even stronger resemblance to State B, an arguer may be forced to set aside the warrant based on a similarity to State A. (*b*) If, in spite of some essential similarities, some essential dissimilarity can be found, the force of the warrant upon the claim would be reduced or negated. If, for example, in spite of similarities, States A and B differ in population or distribution of population, the successful results of the policy in State A may not be achieved in State B.

In the reservations, as in the support for the warrant, care must be exercised in distinguishing between what is and what is not essential. Just as only pertinent similarities warrant the movement from evidence to claim, only pertinent differences should block this movement or append reservations to the claim.

In estimating the strength of a claim based on a proof by parallel case, the test is this: *Do the essential points of similarity outweigh the essential points of difference, or do the differences predominate?* If the latter is true, the proof is refuted. Otherwise, assuming acceptable evidence, the reliability of the claim may be measured by the degree to which similarities outweigh differences.[3]

QUALIFICATION IN PROOF BY PARALLEL CASE. Since proofs by parallel case, like generalizations, make an inductive leap, taking one beyond what is reported in the evidence, and since parallel cases are never altogether identical, a *qualifier* must always be attached to claims of proofs by parallel case. Thus, the policy of stricter driver's license tests and retests, if adopted in State B, would only *probably* result in a reduction in the accident rate there.

Proofs by parallel case may establish all four kinds of claims. Since the example concerning licensing policy considers a question of fact, it establishes a *designative* claim. A debater may establish a *definitive* claim: for example, that in this election, majority should be defined as a majority of members present and voting (as in a parallel election). He may make good an *evaluative* claim: for example, that the critical nature of the discussion process should be highly valued (as it is in the parallel process of debate). He may also establish an *actuative* claim: for example, that the court should hold such and such in this particular case (as it did in a parallel case).

INVENTED PARALLELS. All examples of proof by parallel case cited in this chapter so far have assumed that the case characterized in the evidence is an actual one, a *real parallel*. Assuming relevance, however, a hypothetical case, an *invented parallel*, may serve as the basis for proof. For example, when recommending a course of action one believes an official should follow, one may say, "Suppose that Thomas Jefferson (or Woodrow Wilson) had been faced with this problem? Is there any doubt but that he would have acted thus and so?"

Invented parallels, just because they are invented and not the result of actual experience, seldom have the probative force of a real parallel. Yet they are not completely worthless as evidence. As Richard Whately, among others, has pointed out, the important consideration is whether an invented parallel is *probable*. Does it report an action or attitude that seems intrinsically reasonable? Is this the way Jefferson or Wilson *would* have acted? To the extent that such questions may be answered affirmatively, then the cases possess probability. Consequently, although invented parallels are fictional, they have some worth as evidence, if they are closely parallel in essential respects to the case considered in

[3] By "outweigh" we do not imply a principle of majority rule. We do not mean that four similarities automatically outweigh three differences. One sufficiently potent dissimilarity can outweigh many similarities.

142   THE MATERIALS OF ARGUMENT

the claim.

PROOF BY A COLLECTION OF PARALLEL CASES. The examples thus far have also involved a *single* comparison. One may also support a claim by referring to several parallel cases. For example, consider the famous passage from a speech by Patrick Henry: "Caesar had his Brutus, Charles I his Cromwell, and George III . . . may he profit by their example." Similarly, a lawyer does not confine himself to a single case, but tries to include in his brief or argument as many relevant cases as possible.

The point to clarify, however, is that the process of citing a number of parallel cases is not the same as proof by generalization. In generalizing one assumes that the instances in his evidence-sample are bound together by a common underlying cause or principle that extends beyond the sample and makes more or less probable the presence of that same principle in additional instances of the same class. But in proof by parallel case no such common relationship or cause among the evidence items is assumed. Each case is related to the claim independently and separately. They are then brought together to amass a body of autonomous parallels, and not amalgamated through the assumption of a common cause into a unified evidence base. The difference between the two proof patterns may be illustrated diagrammatically:

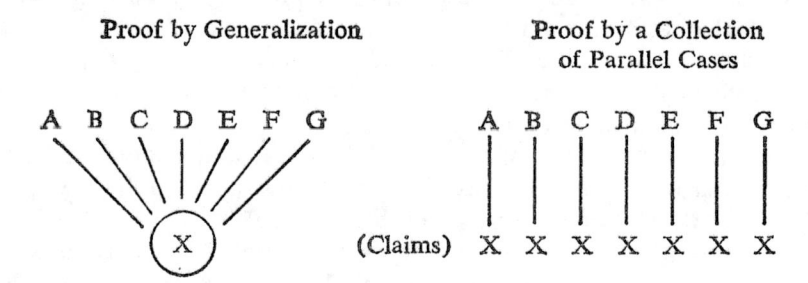

Proof by Generalization                Proof by a Collection
                                        of Parallel Cases

A  B  C  D  E  F  G          A  B  C  D  E  F  G
 \  \  \  |  /  /  /         |  |  |  |  |  |  |
         (X)         (Claims) X  X  X  X  X  X  X

ANALOGY

Proof by analogy is sometimes defined to include both the proof we are calling an *analogy* and the one we have labelled *parallel case*. We make a distinction between these types, because the proof by parallel case depends on a direct similarity between two *cases*, whereas an analogy involves a similarity in the *relation* which each of two cases bears to something else.

Suppose a debater wanted to establish the claim that the president should keep Congress thoroughly informed of his plans and policies.

Employing a proof by *parallel case,* he might say, "The president should do this because Roosevelt (or Taft or Truman) always did so." Or, "The president should do this because the British Prime Minister always keeps his Parliament so informed." Using a proof by *analogy,* however, his procedure is quite different. Now he might say, "Just as it is the duty of a congressman to keep his constituents informed of his plans and policies, so it is the duty of the President to keep Congress informed of his."

*Evidence* in an analogy reports that a relationship of some sort exists between two items. Each "item" may be a person, object, institution, event, or condition, and the related items may fall within the same or a different category. The *warrant* states that an alleged relationship between a second pair of items is similar to the relationship existing between the first pair. The *claim* affirms that the alleged relationship between the second pair of items, therefore, does exist. Consider this example of the structure of a proof by analogy:

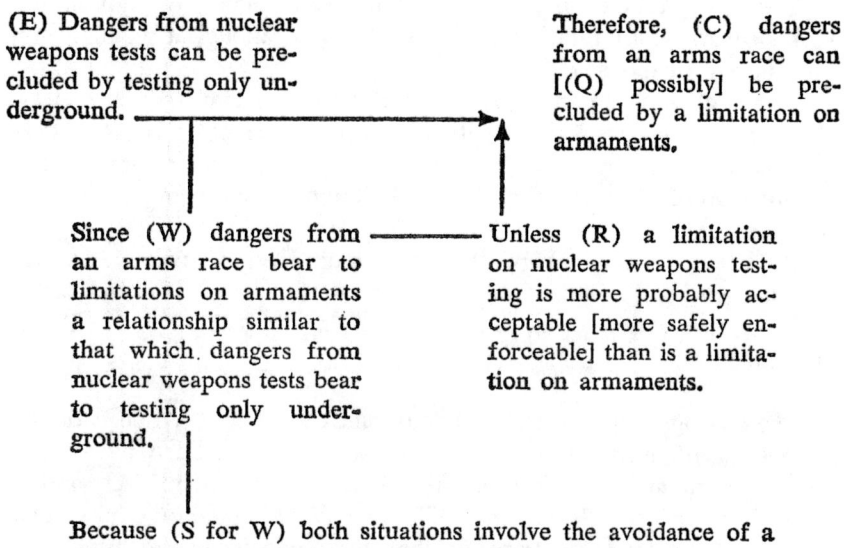

(E) Dangers from nuclear weapons tests can be precluded by testing only underground. ⟶ Therefore, (C) dangers from an arms race can [(Q) possibly] be precluded by a limitation on armaments.

Since (W) dangers from an arms race bear to limitations on armaments a relationship similar to that which dangers from nuclear weapons tests bear to testing only underground. — Unless (R) a limitation on nuclear weapons testing is more probably acceptable [more safely enforceable] than is a limitation on armaments.

Because (S for W) both situations involve the avoidance of a danger by limitation rather than complete elimination.

Whereas the warrant of a proof by parallel case must be supported by comparing two cases in essential respects, the *support for the warrant* in an analogy consists of identifying the kind of relationship that exists in both pairs of items. In the above example the support for the warrant points out that the avoidance of dangers from an arms race by limiting armaments is analogous to the avoidance of radiation dangers from nuclear weapons testing by conducting tests only underground. The function and effect of "limitation" in the one context is the same as the function and effect of "limitation" in the other context.

The relationship identified in the support for the warrant may perhaps be clarified if the proof is cast in the form of a proportion:

$$\frac{\text{dangers from nuclear weapons tests}}{\text{precluding dangers by testing only underground}} = \frac{\text{dangers from arms races}}{\text{precluding dangers by limiting armaments}}$$

RESERVATIONS AND QUALIFICATIONS IN PROOF BY ANALOGY. Even if the warrant and its support show that the relationships existing within two pairs of items are clearly similar, essential differences in circumstances may require a debater to attach *reservations* to his claim. Such differences are almost certain. For example, limiting armaments may not be as acceptable or as enforceable as an agreement to test nuclear weapons only underground. One might be forced to conclude, therefore, that the relationship of "limitation rather than total elimination" will not warrant a limitation on armaments even though it justifies limiting nuclear weapons tests.

Since a claim in an analogy is inferred only by a similarity in relationship, an analogy has less probative force than any other proof pattern. Claims supported by an analogy should very probably be supplemented by other proofs. Perhaps the primary function of an analogy is to clarify a claim and state it more vividly.

The claim in an analogy, therefore, must have a *qualifier*. Because the warrant itself is more indirect, open to more questions, and subject to more reservations, the strongly qualifying "possibly" is usually appropriate.

The analogy is relevant to all four kinds of claims. When a debater argues that dangers from an arms race may be precluded by a limitation on armaments, he is trying to answer a question of fact, and his claim is *designative*. When the evidence reports a *definitive,* an *evaluative,* or an *actuative* relationship, then the analogy aims at establishing a corresponding kind of claim.

Since the warrant assumes only a similarity in *relationship,* and not *cases,* the actual items included in the evidence may or may not be similar in kind to those comprising the claim. For example, one could argue that dangers from an arms race bear to limitations on armaments the same *relationship* that dangers from overeating bear to dieting. The similar relationship here, as in the earlier example, is in the avoidance of a danger by limitation rather than by complete elimination.

## CLASSIFICATION

A sixth substantive proof pattern is *classification*. When a debater argues that what is true generally of union leaders, fifty-year-old houses, summit conferences, or fluoridated water may be claimed about a particular union leader, fifty-year-old house, summit conference, or supply of fluoridated water, he is arguing from classification.

In this type of proof pattern the *evidence* is a generalization about known members of a class of persons, objects, institutions, events, or conditions. The *warrant* states that what is true of the items reported in the evidence is also true of a hitherto unexamined item under consideration that is known (or believed) to fall within that class. The *claim* then applies the generalization in the evidence to the particular class member. An example should illustrate these relationships:

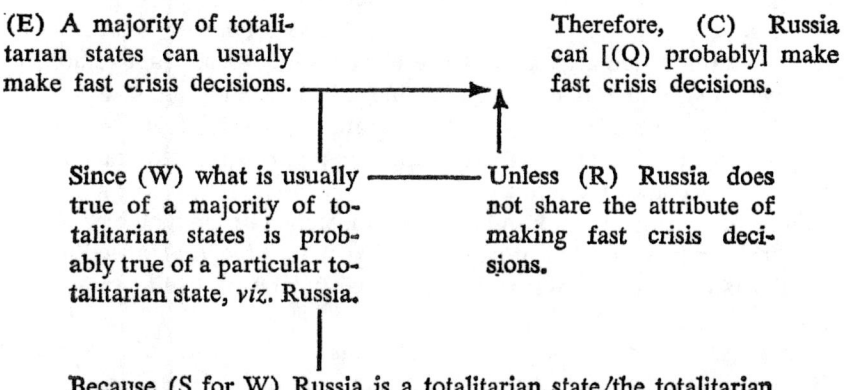

(E) A majority of totalitarian states can usually make fast crisis decisions. ⟶ Therefore, (C) Russia can [(Q) probably] make fast crisis decisions.

Since (W) what is usually true of a majority of totalitarian states is probably true of a particular totalitarian state, *viz.* Russia. ⟶ Unless (R) Russia does not share the attribute of making fast crisis decisions.

Because (S for W) Russia is a totalitarian state/the totalitarian class is reasonably homogeneous and its attributes relatively stable and predictable.

As stated above, the *evidence* in a proof by classification is a generalization, and two of its characteristics should be noted. First, evidence in a classification is a *qualified* claim ("majority" and "usually" in the example diagramed). If listeners or readers readily agree that *all* totalitarian states *necessarily* make fast crisis decisions *at all times*, then to say that Russia makes fast decisions in crises is organizational analysis and not a proof by classification.[4] But unless a qualified generalization is acceptable to the reader or listener, no evidence generates a proof by classification.

[4] That *all* members of a class have an attribute automatically means that a member of that class shares the attribute. Rarely, however, in disputable propositions, are attributes shared by *all* members of a class.

Second, since the evidence has usually been verified as a claim in a prior generalization, it may frequently be qualified both by "someness" and by "probability." Unlike the formal logician who restricts himself to statements of certainty and seems to prefer dealing with those of "allness," the person who advances arguments in the arena of practical affairs *must* base proofs on *probable* evidence that applies only to *some* members of a class. For example: Only *a majority of* totalitarian states make fast crisis decisions (a complete induction is unnecessary and may be impossible), and they only *usually* decide speedily.

The *warrant* states that what is usually true of a majority of totalitarian states is probably true of a particular member of that class, for example, Russia. The arguer here is making two assumptions in his warrant, and either or both may require support.

One kind of *support for the warrant* serves the function of justifying the placement of the member within the class. Is Russia a totalitarian state? If it is not, the proof is not valid. If the reader or hearer doubts the assumption, the arguer must present an added proof that establishes the *definitive* claim that Russia is, indeed, a totalitarian state.

The other assumption that may require support is that the class is reasonably homogeneous and its attributes relatively stable and predictable. If the class of totalitarian states lacks homogeneity, or if the attribute of speedy decision-making is not stable or predictable, then a debater is not warranted in assuming that what is true of a majority of totalitarian states will probably prove true of one particular totalitarian state.

Suppose a debater argues that because a majority of leaders of European nations have expressed a certain opinion, the leader of a particular European nation probably has the same opinion. The warrant is relatively unreliable because leaders of European nations do not constitute a very homogeneous group whose opinions are stable and predictable. On the other hand, suppose he argues that a certain leader of a communist-bloc nation will hold a particular opinion because leaders of a majority of communist-bloc nations have stated such an opinion. This warrant is stronger because leaders of communist-bloc nations, in comparison with those of European nations, exhibit a greater homogeneity, and their opinions are much more stable as a group.

RESERVATIONS IN PROOF BY CLASSIFICATION. *Reservations* may be applicable in a proof by classification because the class member may not share the particular attribute cited in the evidence, although it may share enough other attributes to deserve delineation as a member of the class. Although Russia is proved to be a totalitarian state, she may lack the specific attribute of making crisis decisions rapidly, an attribute generally shared by a majority of totalitarian states.

QUALIFICATION IN PROOF BY CLASSIFICATION. To what extent the claim resulting from a proof by classification requires *qualifiers* depends on how the evidence and warrant have been qualified and on the strength of any relevant reservations. If totalitarian states only *usually* make fast crisis decisions, or if only *a majority of* totalitarian states do so, then Russia only *probably* makes fast crisis decisions. If the warrant is qualified by probability, then the claim must be similarly qualified. If any reservations apply, the claim may be entirely refuted, or at least some qualifier may be needed.

Although classifications may be employed to prove *designative* claims, as our diagramed example illustrates, such proof is useful only when understanding of a class exceeds an understanding of the specific class member. To prove a question of fact about a member of a class—for example, Russia—by means of some other substantive proof pattern is usually easier and is certainly more direct than to prove it in relation to the entire class of totalitarian states and then apply the designation to the particular class member, Russia.

The establishment of *evaluative* claims by this type of proof also has limited value. Suppose a person argues that since fifty-year-old houses are generally undesirable, a particular house of this class will prove undesirable. Such a claim is valid only if the standards determining the general evaluation of fifty-year-old houses may be justly applied to the particular house. The evaluative claim may usually be determined better by more direct proof.

A more direct pattern is often proof by parallel cases. Instead of employing examples to build a generalization and then applying the general conclusion to a particular member of the class, a debater can relate his examples directly to the case at issue if his examples are sufficiently similar to warrant the comparison.

Neither definitive nor actuative claims are made good in a critical way by classification. To establish *definitive* claims by means of such a proof is pointlessly repetitious; for in making good a claim through classification, one must define the very term the proof seeks to define. Obviously, a term's place within a class is not assured unless that term is carefully defined.

Proof by classification is a roundabout, and may even be a dangerous, method of making good *actuative* claims, since specific questions of policy can usually be determined more critically by a direct examination of the facts immediately involved than by referring to a general class of policy decisions.

## STATISTICS

*Statistics* may be defined as "numerical expressions of facts after they have been systematically selected and analyzed." Statistics indicate relationships among phenomena or summarize and interpret bodies of data. The serious deliberation of almost any public question requires some use of figures.

Statistics is a form of evidence out of which a debater can build any of the proofs already considered in this chapter. From statistical information he can infer a cause or an effect, perceive a sign relationship, draw a generalization, cite a parallel case, claim an analogous relationship, or apply a classification.

Before generating any proof from statistical evidence, however, a debater may need to present a prior proof to verify the acceptability of such evidence. Just because data comes in quantitative form rather than in words provides no magical guarantee of its reliability. The critical opponent and judge should demand that statistics, no less than other forms of evidence, be verified.

The most common method of verification is by advancing an authoritative proof. One may get statistical evidence accepted by indicating that it comes from a reliable *source,* for example, a report from the U.S. Census Bureau. If such an authoritative proof satisfies a critical listener or reader, the debater need go no further.[5] If it does not, he may employ a second procedure by validating the *method* of interpreting the statistical information. Do the figures accurately represent what has been counted or measured? Do the statistical procedures make valid assumptions? Are there hidden implications in the management of the data? When a debater copes with such questions, he is analyzing *statistical proof.*[6]

The *evidence* of a statistical proof is the raw data from which computations are made, together with the method by which the data are collected and interpreted. Only rarely do debaters participate in collection or interpretation. Rather, they get the evidence from a government bureau, a research institute, a philanthropic foundation, or some other organization. Occasionally, the data are presented with little or no statistical manipulation, and one is invited to draw his own conclusions. More often, the person or group reporting the data also makes computations and draws conclusions.

---

[5] Authoritative proofs are analyzed and illustrated at length in Chapter 11.
[6] The student must distinguish between statistical proofs and other substantive proofs that utilize statistical evidence. The purpose of a statistical proof is to verify statistical data so they may be employed as evidence in substantive proofs.

A debater may be sorely tempted to relay such conclusions without critically inspecting the information or the methods employed. Yet unless a debater, his opponent, and a judge are willing to accept these claims on authoritative faith, the debater must prove them.

The *claim* of a statistical proof may be stated in the form of a number, a comparison, a percentage, or a measure of central tendency.

Many kinds of *warrants* exist in statistical proofs. Each method of organizing data employs its own warrant embodying its own set of assumptions. Three methods of managing statistics are frequently encountered by debaters.[7] For each of them debaters must learn the appropriate criteria for evaluating the warrant and should know the reservations and qualifiers that might prove relevant. The methods are (*a*) *counting and measuring,* (*b*) *making comparisons,* and (*c*) *determining central tendencies.*

COUNTING AND MEASURING. Perhaps the most simple statistical manipulation is counting the units of some "population" or measuring its magnitude. A population may be defined as any class of elements that is the object of a statistical investigation, and may refer to such diverse phenomena as a collection of biological specimens, the members of a labor union, victims of automobile accidents, etc. The warrant certifies the accuracy of the count or measure and may be evaluated by several criteria.

One criterion is: *Are the units represented by the statistics clearly and consistently defined?* Unless the units of information are precisely defined, and the same definition holds for all of the units included in the figures, a statistical count or measure is neither valid nor meaningful. Is a "senior citizen" someone over sixty or someone over seventy? Is a "successful teacher" one who earns more than the average or one whose students do superior work? Is a "large university" a school with more than ten thousand students or one with more than twenty thousand? In short, does each collector of data throughout the study know precisely what he is counting or measuring? If he does not, the resulting sum or magnitude may be misleading.

Two other criteria grow out of the impossibility of counting every unit in a large population and the consequent necessity for some sort of *sampling* method. Although a debater unsophisticated in sampling theory can evaluate a sample only in a gross way, certain tests are still worth applying.

Thus, a second criterion: *Is the sample large enough to warrant a*

---

[7] Although these are the methods debaters most often must evaluate, a good elementary statistics textbook may be consulted with profit from time to time to analyze these methods and other kinds of statistical interpretation.

*projected estimate of the magnitude of an entire population?* A sample based on a few isolated cases can be highly inaccurate. Suppose someone interviews a sample of ten union members of a total membership of ten thousand and discovers that one member is dissatisfied with the union leadership. Is the statistician justified in estimating that a thousand members are dissatisfied? No, clearly he is not. A debater encountering an estimate of the magnitude of some population based on a small sample not validated by the statistician should regard the data suspiciously.[8]

A third criterion: *Does each unit of the population have an equal opportunity to be included in the count?* If the researcher has properly employed a *random* or *representative* sample, the answer is affirmative. If he has not, the sample may be biased.

The classic example of a biased sample is the 1936 *Literary Digest* public opinion poll that predicted Landon would defeat Roosevelt by securing 370 electoral votes. Instead, he carried only two states. Although the sample was large enough, bias was probably introduced in two ways. First, the sample was selected from *Digest* subscribers and from telephone directories. People who could not afford magazine subscriptions or telephones had no chance of being included in the sample. Thus, although they were part of the voting population, they were not represented in the poll's sample. Second, the decision of individuals whether or not to respond to the poll may have introduced a bias. One may speculate that Democrats, more confident of success in the election, may not have responded in as many cases as did Republicans, who were anxious to register their desire for a change.

A *random* sample is the best method of guaranteeing by statistical assumptions that the sample represents the population to be counted. Tables of random numbers and methods for drawing a random sample are included in many statistics books. For some purposes a *representative,* or *stratified random,* sample may be preferable. The important point is this: The magnitude claimed for any sampled population is accurate to the extent that each unit had an equal opportunity of being included in the count.

*Reservations* concerning a statistical proof based on counting or measuring may be attacked if the statistical procedure reveals any errors not covered by any of the three criteria just discussed.

A claim concerning the magnitude of a phenomenon based on counting or measurement must be *qualified* in several ways. First, the claim is valid only for the time the enumeration or measurement was made. A debater may not assume that a count made in 1959 and published in

---

[8] The tests for the size of a statistical sample correspond to the criteria for evaluating the evidence-sample of a generalization. See pp. 135–37.

1960 is valid for 1961.

Second, if the data are secured by a questionnaire or interview method, the claim may not automatically register the magnitude of what is purportedly counted but, rather, may tabulate only the guesses, exaggerations, or downright lies of the subjects. The population then consists of the responses of the subjects, and the claim should accordingly be qualified.

Third, if a questionnaire is employed, the population is reduced to those persons who return the questionnaire, and the claim should exclude those who did not.

Fourth, sampling errors are inevitable and should be treated statistically. The claim may be qualified by stating a range of magnitudes rather than a single unqualified figure and by indicating how confidently that range may be accepted. For example, instead of saying, "Program X was viewed by 47,238,694 persons," a qualified statement is preferable: "One is assured at the 5 per cent level of confidence that between forty-five and fifty million persons viewed Program X." Such a statement means that in only five chances out of one hundred could such a range be a result of chance or statistical error.

COMPARISONS. A second statistical method common among debaters is the claim that X is the same as, more than, or less than Y. Such a claim is warranted if two general criteria are met.

Since two statistical magnitudes are involved in any comparison, the first criterion is: *Are the magnitudes of each compared item accurate?* The three standards just applied to evaluate the procedure of counting or measuring are again applicable. The units must be clearly and consistently defined, the sample must be large enough, and each unit of the population must have had an equal opportunity of being included.

A second criterion is: *Are the compared units really comparable?* Statistical comparisons can involve two or more classes of phenomena at the same point in time or a single population at two or more points in time. The former is valid if the compared units are similarly defined. For example, in determining which of two communities is constructing the most classroom space in their public school systems, the number of new schools would *not* be a comparable unit if one community built larger schools than the other.

The latter, a "before–after" type of comparison, must meet two standards: (1) The items, again, must be similarly defined. One of the common violations of this principle occurs when dollars, income, debt, or other financial indexes are compared across time. A dollar in 1947 is not the same measure of value as a 1962 dollar. Either the comparison must be made in "constant dollars," or one or the other "dollar" must be

152    THE MATERIALS OF ARGUMENT

converted in value, before any comparison is meaningful. (2) A before–after comparison requires a certain amount of time. For example, if after rising uninterruptedly for nearly three years, the price level were to show no increase over a two-months period, one is hardly justified in asserting that a major trend has been reversed. He would have to wait and see if he were witnessing a trend or merely a variation of a temporary or accidental nature.

*Percentages* are a particular kind of comparison, a quantified one. Instead of utilizing such expressions as "larger than" or "smaller than," a percentage states the quantitative magnitude of one item in relation to another. Although percentages seem simple enough, they are actually highly deceptive and are often misused by debaters. In addition to the two general criteria applicable to any comparison, several specific tests may be applied to determine whether a computation of percentage is warranted.

First, the percentage *base* must be carefully defined and properly employed in the calculation. The base is that item to which another item or items may be compared. If "X" is to be compared to "Y," then "Y" is the base and is converted to a value of one hundred; "X" is treated proportionately and becomes a percentage of "Y." In other words, "X" is divided by "Y."

For example, if in one year one hundred strikes took place, and in a second year fifty strikes occurred, then the second year had 50 per cent as many strikes as the first. Or, the comparison could be stated as a percentage of decrease in the number of strikes: From the first year to the second, strikes decreased 50 per cent.[9]

Second, the units must be large enough to permit meaningful percentages. Darrel Huff relates an amusing case in point. When John Hopkins University first started to admit women students, someone reported that 33⅓ per cent of the women had married faculty members. One of the three women students at that time had married an instructor.[10]

Third, comparisons among percentages must be made very cautiously, if at all. Adding or subtracting percentages that have different bases is grossly fallacious. If strikes are reduced by 10 per cent in one industry and increased by 5 per cent in each of two other industries, the assumption is not warranted that in all three industries, taken together,

---

[9] A common error is to reverse the base year and conclude that strikes decreased 100 per cent. To say that something has been reduced 100 per cent, however, asserts that the item compared to the base has become zero. A 100 per cent reduction in strikes heralds the millennium in labor-management relations!

[10] *How to Lie with Statistics* (New York: W. W. Norton & Co., 1954), pp. 128–29.

the number of strikes has remained constant. Percentages can be compared only if they share a common base.

*Reservations* are appropriate in statistical comparisons, whether in the form of percentages or not, if other variables affect the significance of the comparison in question. For example, to cite an increase in production without also taking into account a variation in "unit cost" will not give an accurate picture of the change in efficiency in a particular industry.[11]

The claim of a statistical comparison often requires a *qualifier*. Certain statistical methods make possible an unusually precise qualification. If the data meet prescribed standards, a difference between two sets of data is said to be *statistically significant* at the 5 per cent (or 1 per cent, or 10 per cent) level of confidence. At what level of confidence a difference is significant depends on the data, the size of the sample, and the errors that have not been eliminated by the statistical method.

CENTRAL TENDENCIES. A third computation often employed by debaters for their proofs is the determination of the central tendency of a body of data. Two general criteria determine the warrantability of a central tendency.

First, since the accuracy of a central tendency is no better than the accuracy of included items, the now-familiar criterion is again applicable: *Is the magnitude of each item represented in the central tendency accurate?* [12]

A second criterion is: *Has the right kind of central tendency been selected and identified?* The most misleading practice in treating central tendencies is an indiscriminate use of the term "average." Actually, "average" may refer to any of three measures of central tendency: mean, median, or mode. The *mean* is a figure obtained by dividing the sum of a series of items by the number of items. The *median* is a figure so chosen that half of the items in a series are on one side of it and half are on the other. The *mode* is that item that occurs in a series most often. When one encounters the term "average," he must first decide whether it refers to a mean, a median, or a mode, before he can evaluate its appropriateness.

Since means, medians, and modes serve different purposes and express different facts about a set of figures, the selection of a meaningful

[11] Even if a comparison is significant and a claim to that effect warranted, a debater must be careful when he employs it as evidence in a substantive proof, e.g., a proof from effect to cause. Attributing an increase or decrease to a single, accessible cause is a frequent hazard debaters must avoid after they make their statistical interpretation.

[12] See pp. 149–50 for an analysis of this criterion.

central tendency depends on the nature of the data. Suppose a multimillionaire student were to join a college class. The *mean wealth* of the class would jump tremendously; the *median* would be affected only slightly; and the *mode*, one would assume, not at all. A proof based on the "average" wealth of the students in that classroom is evaluated only by determining "which average."

In the above example, a *skewed distribution,* the median is the most accurate measure; at other times the mean or mode may be more reliable. To cite a mode rather than a mean, or a mean rather than a median, for the purpose of either confusing the issue or presenting a figure more favorable to the view one is upholding, can only be regarded as flagrant dishonesty. The informed opponent or judge can make such dishonesty a costly practice for a debater.

*Reservations* may have to be attached to a claim concerning a central tendency if the "average" conceals a good deal of variation in the series of figures. A badly skewed distribution may change the whole meaning of any central tendency of data. That the mean wage of a particular class of workers varies from $2 to $5 per hour from one part of the country to another may be more significant than a statement that the mean national hourly wage of such workers is $3.07. Information about the range and distribution of a series of figures may have to be included in the claim about a central tendency.

Unless a central tendency is based on exact figures (not estimates) and includes a total population (not a sample), a *qualifier* must be included in the claim. One useful statistical qualifier for the mean, assuming that the data follow the curve of a normal distribution, is its *standard deviation*. The standard deviation is a statistical tool that indicates how widely a set of scores disperses about the mean. The larger the standard deviation, the greater the dispersion of the items about the mean. Plus or minus one standard deviation from the mean defines a range in which 68.27 per cent of the items will lie. For example, if the mean is 50 and the standard deviation 5, then 68.27 per cent of the cases will fall in a range from 45 to 55.[13]

Statistical proofs can be employed only to establish *designative* or *definitive* claims. They may not answer questions of value or policy since their only function is to certify the validity of statistical interpretations.

---

[13] Debaters must carefully examine how a claim derived from a computation of a central tendency may function as evidence generating a substantive proof. A central tendency is a kind of statistical generalization and, like other generalizations, may tell one relatively little about a characteristic of any item which is a part of the "average."

## CLAIMS ESTABLISHED BY SUBSTANTIVE PROOFS

The information concerning which of the four kinds of claims are established by each of the patterns of substantive proof may be summarized diagrammatically:

|                | Designative | Definitive | Evaluative | Actuative |
|----------------|:---:|:---:|:---:|:---:|
| Cause          | X |   |   |   |
| Sign           | X |   |   |   |
| Generalization | X |   | X |   |
| Parallel Case  | X | X | X | X |
| Analogy        | X | X | X | X |
| Classification | X |   | X |   |
| Statistics     | X | X |   |   |

## QUESTIONS

*A. To Check Your Comprehension and Memory*
1. Which element of proof determines the classification of proofs?
2. What are the three general classes of proof patterns?
3. What general assumptions does the warrant of any substantive proof make?
4. What are the seven patterns of substantive proof?
5. Answer the series of questions below in relation to each of the patterns of substantive proof:
    a. What is the nature of the evidence?
    b. What is stated in the warrant?
    c. How is the warrant supported?
    d. Under what conditions are reservations needed?
    e. What determines what kinds of qualifiers are needed?
    f. What kinds of claims may be established?
6. What are the five experimental methods? Who formulated them?
7. Why must the whole factual context surrounding a proof by sign be examined carefully?
8. What is a fallible sign? What is an infallible sign? What kind will debaters most often employ?
9. How may one distinguish between proofs by effect to cause and proofs by sign?
10. What special considerations determine whether the sample of a generalization is large enough?
11. What must the debater avoid in selecting the sample of a generalization?
12. How may one deal with negative instances in a generalization?

13. What is the best test of the strength of a claim based on a proof by parallel case?
14. What is the difference between a real parallel and an invented parallel? Which type usually has the greater probative force?
15. What is the difference between arguing from a number of parallel cases and generalizing from an evidence-sample?
16. How does an analogy differ from a proof by parallel case?
17. Which proof pattern may be restated in the form of a proportion?
18. Which substantive pattern has the least probative force?
19. When may one usefully establish designative claims through classification?
20. How may statistical evidence be verified?
21. What are three methods of organizing statistical data?
22. What criteria must be met by a sample?
23. What criteria must be met by a percentage?
24. What are the three measures of central tendency? How may each be computed?

B. *For Class Discussion*
1. Are some proof patterns intrinsically more convincing than others?
2. What are the relative merits of proof by classification, as treated in this chapter, and syllogistic reasoning as customarily discussed?
3. Is the analogy a proof pattern or merely a colorful method of clarification?
4. Is statistics a form of proof as well as a type of evidence?
5. Are distinctions between the following patterns of proof valid?
    a. effect to cause–sign
    b. generalization–parallel case
    c. parallel case—analogy

EXERCISES

A. *Written Exercises*
1. Invent an example of each of the proof patterns discussed in this chapter. Diagram each example.
2. Find an example of each proof pattern in one of the debates in the Appendix. Diagram each example.
3. Identify and criticize as many proofs as you can locate in a first affirmative speech.

B. *Oral Exercises*
1. Prepare a short speech in which you make one claim, and support it with two different proof patterns. Your audience will:
    a. identify the kind of claim.
    b. identify each of the two proof patterns.

c. ask questions designed to test the adequacy of each proof.

2. Present a brief oral report in which you describe and evaluate the classification of proofs made in some other speech textbook.

## SUGGESTIONS FOR FURTHER READING

Aristotle, *Rhetoric*, in *The Rhetoric and the Poetics of Aristotle*, tr. W. Rhys Roberts, with an introduction by Friedrich Solmsen (New York: Modern Library, Random House, 1954), 1.2. Note particularly the discussion of the three artistic modes of proof and the treatment of enthymemes, examples, signs, and probabilities.

Winston L. Brembeck and William S. Howell, *Persuasion: A Means of Social Control* (New York: Prentice-Hall, 1952), Chapters 11 and 12. The authors discuss nine methods of supporting argumentative conclusions.

Wayne Brockriede and Douglas Ehninger, "Toulmin on Argument: An Interpretation and Application," *The Quarterly Journal of Speech*, 46 (Feb. 1960), 44–53. Covers some of the same ground considered in this chapter, but on a more theoretical level.

John Stuart Mill, *A System of Logic* (London: J. W. Parker, 1843). Read particularly Book 3, Chapter 8, for a discussion of the experimental methods.

William A. Neiswanger, *Elementary Statistical Methods* (New York: Macmillan, 1943; rev. ed., 1956). One of a number of suitable textbooks in statistics that debaters may find useful for reference purposes.

James M. O'Neill, Craven Laycock, and Robert L. Scales, *Argumentation and Debate* (New York: The Macmillan Co., 1917), Chapter 7. A thorough and traditional treatment of the types of argument in rhetoric and logic.

Richard Whately, *The Elements of Rhetoric* (London: 1828). A nineteenth-century classical rhetorician and logician divides argument into (1) such arguments "that the premiss would account for the conclusion were that conclusion granted," and (2) all other arguments.

Hans Zeisel, *Say It With Figures*, 4th ed. (New York: Harper & Brothers, 1957). See particularly Chapters 1 and 2 for an unusually lucid discussion of percentages.

*Chapter 11*

# AUTHORITATIVE AND MOTIVATIONAL PROOFS

> *Paraphrasing the old couplet, If your authority be not authority to me, what care I how authoritative he be?* JAMES A. WINANS
>
> *Motives are the premises of persuasive argumentation. . . . To say then that it is desirable to appeal to motives is not enough; it is futile and suicidal not to base a plea in some way on motive.*
> JOHN GENUNG

AUTHORITATIVE and motivational proofs are similar in structure to the seven patterns of substantive proof. Unlike substantive warrants, however, the warrants of authoritative and motivational proofs assume no relationship among facts of the external world. Furthermore, since the warrants of authoritative and motivational proofs state only one kind of relationship each, these two classes of proof, unlike the substantive, are not divisible into species.

In this chapter we shall examine the kinds of assumptions stated in the warrants of authoritative and motivational proofs, the way the elements of proof function together in arguments of each class, and the kinds of claims each may establish.

## AUTHORITATIVE PROOFS [1]

As a culture becomes increasingly specialized, people tend to rely more and more on the experience and judgment of others. Such reliance on others is the basis for *authoritative* proofs. Debaters depend on the authority of someone else in two ways. First, they may accept the opinion of someone who can better interpret the relationships among certain

---
[1] See p. 161, footnote 2.

## AUTHORITATIVE AND MOTIVATIONAL PROOFS

kinds of facts in the external world: the judgment of the ballistics expert, the economist, the nuclear scientist, and others must sometimes be accepted. Second, debaters may rely on the experience of other people to supply them with the data for substantive proofs. The purpose of an authoritative proof is to verify the credibility of the *source*—whether the testimony presents factual data or an opinion.

The *evidence* of an authoritative proof is a factual report or a statement of an opinion, together with an identification of the source of the data. Sources could include subject-matter experts, witnesses who testify only to matters within their experience, documents such as the Bible or a constitution, or the authoritative sanction of some institution, cultural mores, group of persons, or organization. The *warrant* states that the source of the evidence is credible. The *claim* then reiterates the statement appearing in the evidence as now certified by the warrant. Consider the following example:

(E) Klaus Knorr states, "Soviet leaders . . . calculate that a minor build-up of nuclear power in the NATO countries of Western Europe . . . will add only marginally [to the danger of American striking power.]"

Therefore, (C) Soviet leaders [(Q) probably] calculate that a minor build-up of nuclear power in the NATO countries of Western Europe will add only marginally to the danger of American striking power.

Since (W) what Knorr says about the opinions of Soviet leaders is worthy of belief.

Unless (R) other authorities more qualified than Knorr say otherwise/substantive proofs of greater probative force yield a different claim/etc.

Because (S for W) Knorr is a professor at Princeton's Center of International Studies and is an expert in the field/is in a position to get at the facts/is reasonably unbiased/has made past statements that have proved reliable/etc.

The *support for the warrant* evaluates the source of the evidence by applying three well-established criteria and by investigating the past reliability of the witness's statements on the same subject covered in the evidence.

1. *Is the witness an expert in the field?* Because a man is an expert in one field, some people attribute to him a sort of universal wisdom and regard him as an authority on all subjects. Perhaps this tendency is encouraged by the popular practice of having athletes endorse razor blades and movie actors sing the praises of cigarette filters. Or perhaps it is because people are often influenced more by the personality or reputation of an individual than by his knowledge of a subject. Yet expertness in one field obviously does not validate a person's authority in another. The critical listener or reader is warranted in believing an authoritative claim only if the witness is an expert in the *relevant* subject. If the person quoted is not known to be an authority, the debater should present information about his experience, background, or position, to support the authoritative warrant.

2. *Did the witness have an opportunity to get at the facts?* Even if a person has the training and experience necessary to qualify him as an expert, his testimony may be of little value if he has not had the opportunity to study a subject, preferably at first hand. The greatest heart specialist can hardly make a reliable diagnosis by mail. The most profound student of Russian affairs cannot arrive at valid judgments if he is denied access to vital data. Even an expert can only make reliable statements when necessary data are before him.

3. *Is the witness reasonably unbiased?* A pamphlet published by a pressure group may lack authority because its statements are merely those expected from such an organization. The national chairman of a political party, who issues predictions concerning the outcome of an election, is certainly an expert in the field in which those judgments lie; and he is in an excellent position to gather and evaluate the pertinent data. Yet his statements should not be taken at face value. The partisanship inherent in his position introduces a bias that renders his statement suspect.

In addition to applying such criteria, a debater may support a warrant of an authoritative proof by evaluating past testimony of his witness on similar questions. If past statements by Knorr have proved reliable, the statement he makes now on a similar matter is probably also reliable. In short, a unit of proof by parallel case may support the warrant.

In college debating and elsewhere the support for the warrant of an authoritative proof is quite important. All too often a college debater will support a contention with a few "quotes" from "noted authorities," without taking the trouble to inform his listeners of the qualifications that make the opinions and information of his experts worth believing. Such a debater might as well attribute the statements to himself. Unless an authoritative warrant is supported adequately, no proof exists at all. For it is the warrant certifying the credibility of the source that carries testimonial evidence to the status of a claim.

*Reservations* may be needed in an authoritative proof for two reasons. In the first place, even if the general reliability of a source is accepted, the idea may be rejected if a more respected authority presents a counterclaim. One may agree that Professor Knorr is usually a reliable authority and yet reject a particular statement of opinion if Professor Kissinger's differing testimony seems more authoritative. Second, a reservation is required if a substantive proof of greater probative force yields a counterclaim. One is often more justified in believing what can be proved substantively—for example, through causal reasoning—than to rely on what may only represent the speculation of an authority.

Claims derived from authoritative proofs almost always require some sort of *qualifier*. As with substantive proofs, claims may need qualifiers for any or all of three reasons: (*a*) If the evidence is in any way qualified, the claim must also be qualified. If Knorr had stated, "Soviet leaders *probably* calculate . . . ," the "probably" would have to be attached to the claim. (*b*) If the warrant is qualified, the claim must also be qualified. If Knorr's opinions, for example, are of limited reliability, some sort of qualifier is needed. (*c*) If reservations are present, the claim may have to be set aside or qualified.

The discussion of authoritative proofs so far has assumed that the source of the evidence is external to the arguer. When the testimony comes from the speaker or writer himself, however, the structure and function of an authoritative unit of proof remain the same. One moves from evidence to claim by means of the same sort of assumption embodied in the warrant, and the warrant may be supported in the same way—by applying criteria and by examining past testimony. When the arguer is his own source of evidence, reservations and qualifications function in precisely the same manner as when the source is external to the arguer. One may infer a claim from Professor Knorr's testimony whether someone else is reporting it or whether he is making the statement himself in an essay or speech. Although the speaker-audience relationship may dictate a change in the manner of presenting the "personal" proof of a speaker, the structure of a proof and its leading characteristics remain unchanged.[2]

Whether the source of the testimony is the writer or speaker, or someone else, authoritative proofs may make good only certain kinds of claims. The critical listener or reader does not accept an authoritative proof designed to establish the *ultimate* claim of a controversy. The decision in a debate is not critically determined merely by acquiescing to the opinion of an expert, no matter how qualified he may be. Authorita-

---

[2] Therefore, the classical doctrine of *ethos* and the modern concept of *source credibility* may illuminate one's understanding of proof by authority, and vice versa.

tive proofs are best employed in establishing *intermediate* claims in a chain of argument.

Proof by authority is also limited to establishing critically *designative* and *definitive* claims. The critical listener or reader will not accept an *evaluative* or *actuative* claim just on the say-so of an authority. Within the limits of establishing intermediate claims on questions of fact or definition, however, authoritative proofs can influence even the most critical listener or reader. The claim takes on the form of the evidence. Designative testimony leads one to a designative claim; definitive testimony, to a definitive claim.

## MOTIVATIONAL PROOFS

Writers in the field of speech have long persisted in distinguishing between the so-called "logical mode" of proof, which emphasizes evidence and argument, and the so-called "emotional mode," which emphasizes the motives, values, and emotions of the listener. Such writers have generally excluded the emotional mode from their treatment of argumentation and have discussed it only as a part of the study of persuasion.

What we are calling *motivational* proof, however, is not only appropriately considered as a part of the instrument of proof employed in argumentation, but a necessary part. The warrant of a motivational proof states that a certain set of emotions, values, or motives can direct the behavior of the persons to whom the proof is addressed. Certain claims necessary for a decision in some disputes can be established for critical listeners or readers in no other kind of proof.

The question is not whether the "emotional mode" of proof is best included or excluded, but whether substantive, authoritative, and motivational proofs are all to be employed critically or uncritically. The use of snap judgment or blind appeals to prejudice, desire, or emotion should have no place in debate.

The critical use of motivational proofs has one important limitation: *Through motivational proofs a debater can establish evaluative and actuative claims, but not designative or definitive ones.*

Whether the price of products made from steel will go up, whether Russia is demonstrating an aggressive intent, or whether Russia can make crisis decisions speedily—these are questions of fact that are best decided in complete independence of one's wishes in the matter. Such questions must be answered critically through substantive or authoritative proofs, and not by investigating the desires or motives of the debaters or their judges. Motivational proofs should not be advanced to establish *designative* claims.

Nor can they critically establish *definitive* claims. Whether a series of acts may fairly be defined as "burglary," whether an institution may properly be called "democratic," or whether a policy is "discriminatory" —these questions, once again, are best answered in complete independence of the wishes of debaters or their readers or listeners. Substantive and authoritative proofs are appropriate. To the extent that motivation influences the answer to a question of definition, to that extent the proof is less critical.

Debaters can employ motivational proofs critically in making good *evaluative* and *actuative* claims. The function of any proof is to lead men from one belief to another. When the claim calls for an evaluation or a willingness to act, the warrant must state some motive which underwrites it. As James A. Winans long ago observed, "Motives stand as the major premises in persuasive arguments." [3]

Motivational proofs of evaluative or actuative claims may be analyzed and illustrated in the same manner as may substantive or authoritative proofs. *Evidence* in a motivational proof consists of either designative or definitive statements that are acceptable from the outset, or those established in prior proofs. The *warrant* states a motive for accepting the claim. The *claim* is either evaluative or actuative: One may accept some person, object, institution, event, or state of affairs as having some degree of value, or one may agree to perform or not perform some action, or adopt or not adopt some policy. The following example shows how a motivational proof functions in establishing an *evaluative* claim:

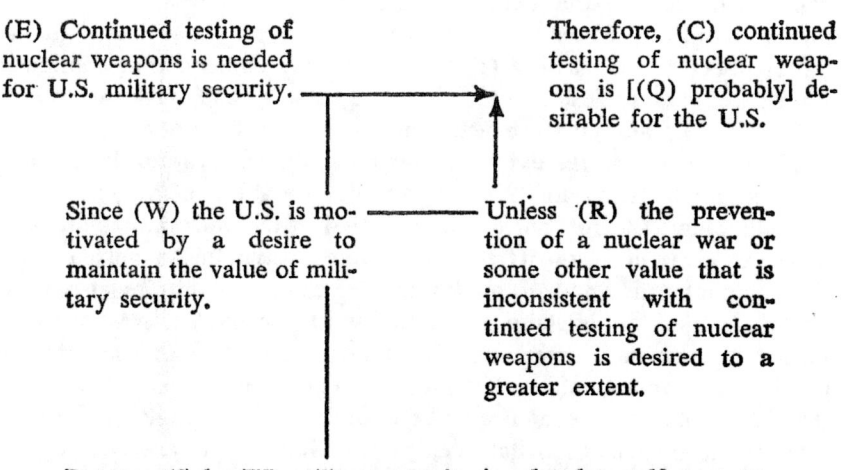

(E) Continued testing of nuclear weapons is needed for U.S. military security. ⟶ Therefore, (C) continued testing of nuclear weapons is [(Q) probably] desirable for the U.S.

Since (W) the U.S. is motivated by a desire to maintain the value of military security. ——— Unless (R) the prevention of a nuclear war or some other value that is inconsistent with continued testing of nuclear weapons is desired to a greater extent.

Because (S for W) military security is related to self-preservation/the maintenance of our high standard of living/the preservation of democracy/patriotism/etc.

[3] *Public Speaking*, rev. ed. (New York: D. Appleton, 1924), p. 196.

The *evidence* in this example is probably a claim resulting from a series of proofs. Perhaps the debater in this example proved a definitive claim stating what constitutes "military security." Perhaps he established a designative claim asserting that the United States now lacks conditions necessary for its military security. Perhaps he made good another designative claim stating that without continued testing such conditions cannot be achieved, or that with continued testing they can. Some such claims must be proved if the debater is able to employ *as evidence* the statement that continued testing is needed for the military security of the United States.

The *warrant* states a motive that authorizes the evaluative claim. If one is indifferent concerning military security, his reaction to the proof is, "So what!" If he accepts the evidence and if he is *motivated* to achieve military security, he is warranted in agreeing with the claim.

Such a warrant may need no support; it may not even need explicit statement. For purposes of analysis, however, a debater, his opponent, or his critic may have to identify the motivational warrant and consider how it may be supported. If military security is not accepted as a sufficient motivational value, the *support for the warrant* may relate it to some drive, value, desire, or emotion that does motivate the listener or reader.

*Reservations* in motivational proofs commonly appear in the form of counterclaims. Even if one accepts a value stated in the warrant as motivational, he may be unwilling to accept an evaluative claim if he recognizes other values that have greater motivational force and that deny the claim. If he believes that continued testing of nuclear weapons increases the probability of a nuclear war (evidence), and if he strongly abhors the prospect of such a war (warrant), he may contend that continued testing would be undesirable for the United States (counterclaim).

Such a reservation may be dealt with by either or both of two methods: (*a*) One may refute the evidence implied in the reservation, by arguing that continued testing does not increase the probability of a nuclear war. (*b*) One may contend that the value stated in the warrant should have higher motivational priority than the value of avoiding a nuclear war.

The debater may have to qualify the degree to which he regards valuable the subject of his claim. Continued testing of nuclear weapons may be just "somewhat" more desirable than undesirable, or "among the highest" of national values. The kind of *qualifier* needed will depend on the probability of the evidence and the motivational strength of the warrant. If the evidence is established as a claim in an earlier proof, its degree of probability should already have been determined. The motivational strength of the warrant may frequently be evaluated only in relation to whatever other motivational forces are considered in the reservation.

Motivational proofs function to produce *actuative* claims in much the same fashion as *evaluative* ones. The *evidence* in either event is a designative or definitive statement probably established as a claim in another proof or series of proofs. The *warrant* in either event provides a motive for accepting the claim.

An actuative claim may require a stronger motive than an evaluative claim since one may be more easily led to assent to a value judgment than to perform an action or make a policy decision. For this reason, warrants yielding actuative claims may more often need support, and perhaps more convincing support, than those producing evaluative claims. The *support for the warrant* in any event, however, relates an apparently inadequate warrant to some inner drive, value, desire, or emotion deemed adequately motivational.

An actuative claim may require *reservations* for the same reason evaluative claims need them, i.e., a countervalue may have stronger motivational force than the motive stated in the warrant.

The *qualifier* also functions similarly. One may attach a qualifier to register the degree of force with which the warrant motivates the adoption of the action or policy stated in the claim.

The similarity with which motivational proofs function in proving evaluative and actuative claims should become apparent as we repeat the preceding example and change only the nature of the claim:

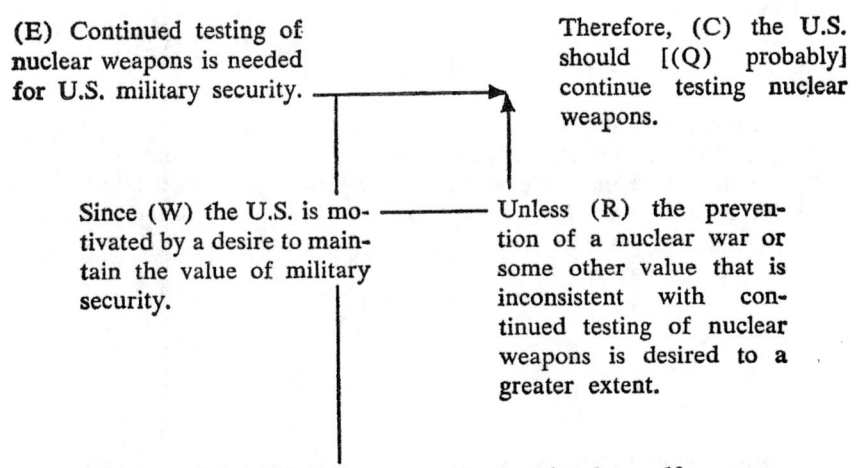

(E) Continued testing of nuclear weapons is needed for U.S. military security.

Therefore, (C) the U.S. should [(Q) probably] continue testing nuclear weapons.

Since (W) the U.S. is motivated by a desire to maintain the value of military security.

Unless (R) the prevention of a nuclear war or some other value that is inconsistent with continued testing of nuclear weapons is desired to a greater extent.

Because (S for W) military security is related to self-preservation/the maintenance of our high standard of living/the preservation of democracy/patriotism/etc.

Thus, the same desire to maintain military security which motivates a favorable evaluation of continued testing of nuclear weapons may also motivate endorsing the policy of continued testing. Whether the claim is evaluative or actuative, the motivational proof functions in the same manner.

## QUESTIONS

*A. To Check Your Comprehension and Memory*
1. What constitutes the evidence of an authoritative proof? of a motivational proof?
2. What is stated in the warrant of an authoritative proof? of a motivational proof?
3. How are warrants supported in an authoritative proof? in a motivational proof?
4. What kinds of reservations may be required in an authoritative proof? in a motivational proof?
5. How may reservations in motivational proofs be treated by the arguer?
6. What kinds of qualifiers must be included in the claim of an authoritative proof? Why? In a motivational proof? Why?
7. What kinds of claims may be established critically by authoritative proofs? by motivational proofs?
8. Compare and contrast the functioning of authoritative proofs when the source of the evidence is (*a*) the speaker or writer himself, and (*b*) someone else.
9. Compare and contrast the functioning of motivational proofs in establishing evaluative and actuative claims.

*B. For Class Discussion*
1. Why is authoritative proof not a pattern of substantive proof?
2. We have said that emotions and values may serve critically as warrants for certain kinds of claims in a motivational proof. Do emotions and values also have a place in substantive or authoritative proofs? If so, in what element of proof may they be placed? If not, why not?
3. Are motivational proofs "logical"? Explain.

## EXERCISES

*A. Written Exercises*
1. Enumerate the authorities employed in one of the speeches of one of the sample debates in the Appendix, and decide whether each usage was proper. Apply the criteria discussed in this chapter.
2. What is the central motive appealed to by the affirmative in one of the sample debates in the Appendix? What is the central motive appealed to by

the negative in the same debate? Evaluate the motivational proofs advanced by both sides.

B. *Oral Exercises*
1. Assume that one of the authorities in some controversy you are preparing to debate is going to speak to your class. Introduce him to the class in a short speech.
2. Present the conclusion to a speech advocating a policy change of some sort. Assume you have proved several statements; use these as evidence for a motivational unit of proof.

## SUGGESTIONS FOR FURTHER READING

Aristotle, *Rhetoric*, in *The Rhetoric and the Poetics of Aristotle*, tr. by W. Rhys Roberts, with an introduction by Friedrich Solmsen (New York: Modern Library, Random House, 1954), Book 2. In what chapters of Book 2 is Aristotle discussing authoritative or personal proof (*ethos*) and in what chapters motivational proof (*pathos*)?

Richard Whately, *Elements of Rhetoric* (London: 1828), 1.2.4. Whately treats argument from testimony as a species of argument from sign.

Charles Woolbert, "Conviction and Persuasion: Some Considerations of Theory," *The Quarterly Journal of Speech*, 3 (1917), 249–64. Woolbert develops the point of view that rhetoric be viewed as aiming at a unitary response and not divided into conviction and persuasion.

*Chapter 12*

# DETECTING DEFICIENCIES OF PROOF

*Sophistry is a hydra of which, if all the necks could be exposed, the force would be destroyed.* JEREMY BENTHAM

THE DEBATE process is made critical primarily through the confrontation of opposing debaters. Although unopposed persuasive speakers may hope that the weaknesses of their proofs will be charitably overlooked, debaters expect their opponents to detect the deficiencies of proof.

One can debate effectively only if he understands various proof deficiencies. If he understands them, he can avoid them in his own proofs and search them out in the proofs of his opponents.

Unfortunately, inadequacies of proof are numerous and often cleverly disguised, so that the task of detection is not easy. Proof elements are not always clearly presented in a prescribed and uniform order. Furthermore, debaters and judges can often spot weaknesses only by supplying unstated assumptions and implied proof elements.

Nor are weak and strong proofs readily distinguished. The strength of proof is a matter of degree to be decided by each reader or listener. Although some units of proof would be evaluated highly by virtually all critical observers, and other proofs almost universally denounced, many arguments in the middle of the "proof-strength spectrum" may be accepted by some and rejected by others. In later chapters we shall consider problems in adapting such proofs as these to the beliefs and motivations of the audience.[1] Our present concern is to discuss those gross deficiencies of proof that are unacceptable to most critical persons.

Although for the sake of analysis we shall consider units of proof separately, no proof can be safely evaluated except in comparison with

[1] See Chapter 13, pp. 203–06, and Chapter 15, pp. 245–49.

the counterproofs that an opponent might present. A proof acceptable when offered in isolation may be justly called deficient when confronted by a stronger counterproof.

Furthermore, any system of classifying deficient proofs must take into account an important fact: A single portion of an argumentative discourse may involve simultaneously several deficiencies. The "multiple fallacy" principle will be illustrated often in this chapter. Labeling a fallacy one type or another is less important to the debater, however, than clearly establishing that the proof is deficient. Any one gross weakness of proof, clearly identified and exposed, may make the entire case deficient.

In this chapter we shall describe and illustrate each of the more common proof deficiencies, and we shall classify them under five headings: (1) *deficient evidence,* (2) *unwarranted claims,* (3) *deficient warrants,* (4) *ignored reservations,* and (5) *overstated claims.*

## DEFICIENT EVIDENCE

A unit of proof will not convince a critical listener or reader unless it is based on evidence he will believe. He may reject evidence as deficient if it is (a) *incomplete,* (b) *inaccurate,* (c) *ambiguous,* or (d) *absent.*

Evidence may be *incomplete* if debaters practice selective reporting. It may be *inaccurate* if they engage in altered or colored reporting. It may be *ambiguous* if debaters violate the rules of rhetoric in presenting their evidence.[2] Claims based on incomplete, inaccurate, or ambiguous evidence are unlikely to yield a critically derived judgment or decision.

Nor can such decisions be reached through claims based on no evidence at all. As indicated in Chapter 8, a unit of proof is not possible when evidence is *absent.* No matter how vigorously or how craftily a debater asserts that federal aid to education entails federal controls, or contends that Supreme Court decisions have harmed the American people, or maintains that socialized medicine has failed miserably in Great Britain, unless he presents evidence to support such claims, or unless his personal credentials make him authoritative, the critical opponent will call him to task and the critical judge will decide against his cause.

[2] Practices of selective reporting are discussed and illustrated on pp. 116–17; altered reporting, on pp. 117–18; and a rhetoric of evidence, on pp. 118–21.

## UNWARRANTED CLAIMS

A second class of deficient proofs results when a claim is not warranted by any of the relationships discussed in Chapters 10 and 11. Either the warrant is absent (*missing links*), or it states without proof an assumption that is the very question to be settled by the claim (*begging the question*), or it establishes—perhaps even very well—some claim other than the one in dispute (*ignoring the question*).

### MISSING LINKS

Logicians commonly include among the fallacies they discuss the *non sequitur*, an argument in which the claim does not follow from the evidence. For example, "Meteorologist X predicts rain for tomorrow; therefore, Congressman Y will win the primary election." Or, "The Public Works Director erred in handling the bids for the addition to the City Building; therefore, the city-manager form of government should be repealed in this community."

Surely, these are examples of the *non sequitur*. Yet a debater seldom deliberately presents evidence he believes is unrelated to the claim he is making. Careful analysis usually reveals that, although no single warrant can bridge the evidence and claim in such proofs, a series of proofs may put together a sensible argument. The deficiency said to be a *non sequitur* is usually an omission of important links; hence the deficiency may be called the fallacy of the *missing links*.

One of the above examples, actually comprising four distinct proofs, may illustrate the fallacy:

1. Meteorologist X predicts rain for tomorrow; therefore, we can accept the fact that it will rain tomorrow (authoritative warrant).

2. It will rain tomorrow; therefore, farmers will be unable to work tomorrow (cause–effect warrant).

3. Farmers will be unable to work tomorrow; therefore, the farm vote will be heavy in the election (cause–effect warrant).

4. Political Analyst Z states that Congressman Y will win the primary election if the farm vote is heavy; therefore, Congressman Y will win the primary election (authoritative warrant).

The individual proofs in a missing links fallacy may themselves be quite satisfactory. The deficiency consists in concealing them; for, until they are identified, they cannot be evaluated critically. The critic must first supply the concealed proofs; then he may approve the argument or expose one or more deficiencies. A debater can avoid the missing links fallacy by clearly presenting each of the individual proofs in the series.

## BEGGING THE QUESTION

In question-begging fallacies a debater assumes what ought to be proved. Such fallacies take the form of (a) *persuasive prefaces,* (b) *emotional language,* or (c) *circular reasoning.*

PERSUASIVE PREFACES. *"We all know* that the removal of price supports will work a serious hardship on farmers everywhere." *"All intelligent students of the problem* recognize that to discontinue testing nuclear weapons is a dangerous policy." *"Obviously. . . ." "There can be no doubt. . . ."* Such prefaces beg the question because they invite the listener or reader to accept a claim without asking to see the evidence or warrant that certifies it. The judge or opponent is coaxed to lower his guard. The preface is presented in lieu of proof, as if it *were* proof. Any claim that has no better support than a comforting prelude is not warranted.

EMOTIONAL LANGUAGE. "We must never adopt the *radical* plan of my opponent." "We must elect that *great freedom fighter,* the *Honorable* Mr. X." Before one can understand how the italicized words beg the question, he must consider a curious fact about language. As Jeremy Bentham, a British philosopher, put it, words have a tripartite vocabulary. Statements can be made in three ways: (1) They may merely refer to a person, object, event, or idea; they are then said to be *neutral.* (2) They may also indicate the arguer's favorable attitude toward the referent; they are then said to be *eulogistic.* (3) Or they may also reveal the arguer's anger, fear, hatred, or contempt toward the referent; they are then said to be *dyslogistic.*[3]

Thus the same person may be described as "cautious toward change" (*neutral*), "a dynamic conservative" (*eulogistic*), or a "reactionary" (*dyslogistic*). The same animal may be termed a race horse, a thoroughbred, or a nag.

When inserted in a unit of proof, emotional words have two effects. First, like the persuasive preface, they invite acceptance of a claim without critical thought. The reader or listener is expected to acquiesce gracefully to the implied attitude of the debater. To ask someone to decide against a plan only because it is "radical" is to beg the question. The dyslogistic label has replaced proof.

Second, emotional language smuggles into a unit of proof a bogus,

---

[3] For a further discussion of Bentham's tripartite vocabulary, see Wayne E. Brockriede, "Bentham's Philosophy of Rhetoric," *Speech Monographs,* 23 (Nov. 1956), 242–44.

question-begging issue that hides the real issue. "Is freedom-fighting not to be applauded by red-blooded Americans?" replaces "Are the credentials of Mr. X better than those of his opponents?" Similarly, "Shall we adopt a radical plan?" confuses the issue of whether a given proposal will result in net value.

When confronted with emotional language, the critically minded person must translate it into a neutral expression and remember what the issue is.

A warning against this kind of question-begging fallacy is not a directive to employ only neutral language in debate. In the first place, neutral language is not always possible without clumsy circumlocutions. Bentham observed that neutral language is particularly scarce in morals and politics. Secondly, the use of emotional language, *per se,* does not constitute a question-begging fallacy. The prosecuting attorney may reasonably denounce a prisoner as a scoundrel, if he explains what species of scoundrel he is and presents evidence to support each charge. Acceptable and fallacious use of emotional language are distinguished by three tests: (1) Does the arguer speak to the issues? (2) Are his claims supported by evidence? (3) Are his claims warranted or begged?

CIRCULAR REASONING. "Communist China is not in the UN because she does not have the respect of peace-loving nations. . . . Communist China does not have the respect of peace-loving nations because she is not in the UN." "We send considerable technical aid to nations X, Y, and Z because they need it. . . . We know that nations X, Y, and Z need our technical aid, because they have had to accept so much of it."

The fallacy of arguing in a circle consists of two mutually-supported units of "proof." X is so because of Y; Y is so because of X. Circular reasoning begs the question because at no time is any proof advanced. The argument does not move forward, only around. Consequently, the two claims of a circular fallacy are equally unwarranted.[4]

Circular reasoning would be easy to detect if the two "proofs" were plainly presented in quick succession. Unfortunately, however, the second "proof" is often set forth much later than the first, and the opponent or judge may not join the two in his mind and see the circularity.

IGNORING THE QUESTION

Whereas question-begging fallacies smuggle counterfeit warrants into a unit of proof, the debater who ignores the question *applies actual*

[4] Even if such claims are initially acceptable to some readers or listeners, the reasoning is deficient because it represents an attempt to pass off for real what is only counterfeit.

*warrants to irrelevant claims.* The relevant claim, the one at issue, is neglected and thus unwarranted.

Various methods of ignoring the question may be grouped under three headings: (*a*) irrelevant appeals; (*b*) diversions; and (*c*) attacks on personalities.

IRRELEVANT APPEALS. As indicated in Chapter 11, motivational appeals legitimately establish evaluative and actuative claims. They are inappropriate, however, in answering questions of fact or definition. Irrelevant appeals, however, make *any* unit of proof deficient. Five types of irrelevant appeals are especially common.

First, the appeal is sometimes to an irrelevant *emotion.* "I need only remind you of the suffering at Hiroshima to convince you that the health hazard alone justifies a ban on nuclear weapons testing." This appeal may be appropriate as the warrant of a motivational proof if the arguer has proved that harm to world health is a consequence of continued testing. If the appeal is presented instead of proof, however, he has ignored the question, and his proof is deficient.

Second, an irrelevant appeal to *humor* is sometimes employed. "My opponent has quoted Mr. X as saying in *Life* that the Russian-trained engineer may not fairly be compared with the American-trained engineer. May I suggest that one cannot hope to learn of life in Russia by reading *Life* in America." Humor may help keep interest alive; and if the debater relates his jest to an attempt to refute the testimony, no harm is done. Humor presented instead of proof, however, ignores the question and constitutes a deficiency.

Third, some debaters appeal to *tradition.* "Federal aid to education violates one of the most hallowed American traditions, the local control and financial support of public education. We must at all cost keep this tradition alive." Tradition is not relevant in determining whether federal financial assistance is needed or whether the advantages of such a program outweigh the disadvantages. The affirmative side must assume the burden of advocating the end of a "tradition" in any debate on a question of policy. The appeal to tradition constitutes relevant proof only when the preservation of a tradition is itself an issue. For example, if part of the attraction of a fraternal order lies in its rituals and traditions, then the value of one of the traditions to the association is relevant to the question of discontinuing it.

Fourth, appeals are addressed to *popular prejudice.* "Are we going to let those politicians in Washington tell us who can and who cannot vote in our elections? No! The sovereign state of X can decide full well for herself what kind of civil rights legislation she needs." (The appeal to popular prejudice was aptly described by Francis Bacon as an appeal to "idols of the market place.") The quotation concerning civil rights makes at least two irrelevant appeals to popular ideas. The reference to "politicians" is decidedly irrelevant. Although the allusion to "Washington" and "sovereign state of X" could lead to a relevant argument, showing that states can more advantageously pass civil rights legislation than can the federal government, unless proof is advanced, the appeal to "states' rights" is likewise irrelevant. Not only do the two appeals ignore the question, but they also beg the question with such emotional language as "politician," "sovereign state of X," and "full well for itself." No proof is offered, for example, that legislators in the state of X are "statesmen," whereas those in Washington deserve the dyslogistic label, "politicians."

Fifth, debaters can appeal to what has been called the *ignorance of the opposite*. "My opponent questions whether a federal fair employment practices law could be enforced in Southern states. I contend the proposal is practicable, and I challenge him to prove conclusively that it is not." Debatable questions can never be answered "conclusively." The debater who ignores the question and presents no probable proof to support his own claim may try to hide behind the impossibility of presenting certain proof for a contradictory claim. Since the debater in the above example has advanced the proposition, he must fulfill his burden of (probable) proof.

DIVERSIONARY PROOFS. The fallacy of diversionary proofs consists of starting with a claim at issue and then meandering gradually to some related but different claim that is more easily established. The fallacy may be difficult to detect because listeners or readers, impressed with a well-developed proof, may never realize that the wrong claim is being proved. Diversionary proofs may take several forms.

First is the *simple diversion*. "My opponent has argued that we must maintain compulsory unionism to strengthen the collective bargaining power of labor unions. We must consider, however, that many labor leaders are corrupt. For example, the McClellan Committee discovered. . . ." And the debater goes on to present an excellent proof of the corruption of a significant number of leaders of large labor unions. Although a simple diversion is clearly irrelevant to the issue at hand, opponents and judges who are not sufficiently alert may accept proof of corruption as proof that compulsory unionism is not needed to maintain labor's collective bargaining power. The arguer thus proves an irrelevant claim and ignores the claim at issue.

Second, a diversion repeated several times during the course of a controversy is called a *red herring*. "Like the others, my opponent's fourth argument, that compulsory unionism makes for stable industrial relations, ignores the fact that we have proved earlier—that many unions have corrupt leaders. How can stable labor relations be maintained with such corrupt leaders?" If the debater goes on to prove that corrupt leaders cannot maintain stable labor relations, he has a reasonable argument. If not, his repeated and irrelevant references to corruption constitute a "red herring."

A third diversion is to set up a *straw man*. "My opponent will tell you that the present system gives Congress adequate methods of removing harmful Supreme Court decisions through the ratification of the appointment of justices. Such a power, however, does nothing to reverse specific harmful decisions." The straw-man diversion consists of refuting the weakest of alternative opposing positions. The proof becomes irrelevant when an opponent replies, "Yes, but two other recourses adequately deal with specific decisions alleged to be harmful— the amendment process and the re-enactment of statutes." To establish a *prima facie* case an affirmative debater may have to show that no adequate recourse exists to remedy harmful decisions, but he should refute real objections, not straw men. Similarly, a negative debater should refute arguments actually advanced, not those straw men he hoped his opponents would present.

Fourth, a real issue may be ignored through the diversion of *assuming a more general truth*. "To permit the Supreme Court to rule a congressional act unconstitutional is to deny the basic democratic principle that laws should be made by the people. We must repeal at once this mockery of our democratic system." The debater has shifted ground from a specific issue to a larger question easier to uphold. Instead of arguing whether the *specific* procedure of judicial review is disadvantageous and ought to be repealed, he tries the easier tack of arguing that undemocratic procedures should be repealed. He ignores the question of whether making judicial decisions *in a democracy* must be influenced directly by the people. Furthermore, the phrase, "basic democratic principle," puts a confusing eulogistic gloss over the entire argument.

Fifth, a diversion may be created by making a distinction between theory and practice. "The adoption of a federal world government is good in theory, but it simply will not work in practice." The *impractical theory* diversion is surprisingly common. The German philosopher Arthur Schopenhauer shows its weakness:

The assertion is based upon an impossibility: what is right in theory *must* work in practice; and if it does not, there is a mistake in the theory; something has been overlooked and not allowed for; and, consequently, what is wrong in practice is wrong in theory, too.[5]

[5] "The Art of Controversy," in *The Essays of Arthur Schopenhauer*, tr. T. Bailey Saunders (New York: Willey, n. d.), p. 37.

Sixth, attention may be diverted from the alleged harmfulness of one evil by *pointing to a second wrong*. "We have heard a great deal about the dangers of radiation allegedly caused by the testing of nuclear weapons. Well, if radiation is so dangerous that we must give up our military security, then we must also eliminate the radium dials on watches, medical and dental X rays, and background radiation." Here, the debater ignores the real issue—whether radiation from nuclear tests justifies eliminating the tests—to point to something irrelevant to the proposition. Whether a "second wrong" needs remedy does not settle the question of a need for curing the first.

Finally, a debater makes a diversion by a *shift in meaning*. "The preceding speaker alleged that minority groups were being discriminated against in employment practices, and that the discrimination was harmful to everyone. But all people discriminate. Actually, since discrimination is simply selecting among alternatives, the more educated persons discriminate better." The argument may appear strong until one examines what has happened to the reference to "discrimination." The "preceding speaker" referred to unequal treatment in a collective and political sense, as governed, for example, by the federal constitution. The second reference was to an individual's freedom to "discriminate" in ways not deemed unlawful by the body politic.

UNRELATED ATTACKS ON PERSONALITY. In addition to irrelevant appeals and diversionary proofs, a debater may ignore the question by *attacking the personality* of his opponent or some other person associated with the controversy. Personality attacks occur frequently in campaign oratory and are sometimes found in other kinds of debate.

"Our opponents have not dealt adequately with our argument regarding the law of comparative advantage. Obviously, they do not understand it. Perhaps they may some day be able to take an elementary course in economics." If the refutation of an argument by an opposing debater is weak, explain why your argument still stands. If your opponent did not understand your argument, perhaps the judge also missed it. The educational background of an opponent is in no way related to the argument that the law of comparative advantage provides a good reason for adopting a policy of free trade.

In addition to their irrelevance, personality attacks are deficient in two other ways: First, they more often than not will prejudice the cause of the attacker, for the audience may well sympathize with the person attacked. Second, such attacks tend to multiply. One attack provokes another. The critical attitude is abandoned, and a decision is awarded by adding up the score on irrelevant mutual personality assaults, not by carefully analyzing the issues and weighing the relevant proofs.

## DEFICIENT WARRANTS

The class of deficient proofs just considered reveal no warrants for the claims at issue. In another group of proofs the debater tries to warrant the claim, but the warrant is either insufficient or inadequately supported. Different kinds of deficiencies occur in the employment of each type of warrant discussed in Chapters 10 and 11.

### INADEQUATE CAUSAL WARRANTS

There are at least three kinds of weak causal warrants. The first results from *insufficient cause*. "For the past eight years we have given a substantial amount of economic aid to the 'uncommitted nations' of Southeast Asia. We have not only failed thereby to win their friendship, but we have suffered a steady and severe deterioration in our relations with them, as a result of the economic assistance." The evidence and the resulting "effect" may be perfectly true. The weakness of the unit of proof lies in claiming an effect (deteriorated relations) that the cause *by itself* (economic aid) very probably cannot produce. Although a causal relationship may indeed exist, it is insufficient to generate the effect.

Second, a causal warrant may be *inadequately supported*. "For the past eight years we have given a substantial amount of direct economic aid to the 'uncommitted nations' of Southeast Asia. The effect has been distrust of our motives, general ingratitude, and open criticism of the directness with which our aid program has been administered." The alleged effects here are less ambitious, and the cause *may* be sufficient to produce them. But the debater should advance proof that the alleged distrust, ingratitude, and criticism exist and are causally related to the directness of our foreign assistance program.

Third, a causal warrant may be guilty of a special weakness and given the Latin name, *post hoc, ergo propter hoc*, "after this, therefore because of this." "In 1949 many nations recognized that the Communist government of China was the legal *de facto* government. The United States did not. Our government assumed that Red China was not there and that the republican government on Formosa would return to the mainland and be reinstated. What has been the result of the refusal to recognize the Communist government of China? We have forced that government into an increasingly closer political relation with, and economic reliance on, Soviet Russia." The deficiency consists of mistaking time sequence for a cause–effect relationship. The *post hoc* fallacy, a common weakness of proof in debate, lies at the bottom of all superstition. References to the four-leaf clover, the horseshoe, the black cat, walking under a ladder, and countless others represent *post hoc* reasoning.

### INADEQUATE SIGNS

In a proof by sign a causal relationship need not be imputed. Only a correlation between sign and what is signified is necessary to warrant a claim. The warrant itself is not very likely to be deficient [6] if it is adequately supported.

"The average attendance at union meetings is 3 per cent of the membership. Such a poor turnout is a sign of the general apathy so common among union members." The proof may become a good one if the debater supports his warrant and shows *why* poor attendance at meetings may be taken as a sign of apathy—if, in short, the warrant is adequately supported.

### INADEQUATE GENERALIZATIONS

Warrants of generalizations have three kinds of weaknesses. The most common is the so-called *hasty generalization*. "Premier Nehru of India and Prime Minister U Nu of Burma have made strong statements criticizing the United States' foreign aid program. So we can see that our program is generally unpopular among world leaders." The claim may or may not be true, but a mere two examples do not warrant it. The validity of the assumption that what is true of an evidence-sample is true of the class generalized upon in the claim depends in part on the size of the sample. Whether the sample is large enough, in turn, depends on three considerations discussed in Chapter 10: the homogeneity of the sampled class, the arguer's knowledge of underlying causes, and the care with which the evidence-sample was observed and reported.[7]

The example concerning the U.S. foreign aid program also illustrates a second kind of inadequacy, the *unrepresentative generalization*. Even if the sample were large enough, the opinions of leaders of "uncommitted nations" of Southeast Asia are not a firm basis for generalizing to a statement about world leaders. "World leaders" also include those from countries in the Communist and Western blocs. Furthermore, India and Burma are not representative geographically.

A third deficiency of generalizing warrants is the *fallacy of composition*. "The United Nations includes men of great ability, for example,

---

[6] If no warrant at all is present, of course, the deficiency falls into the second general class, unwarranted claims.

[7] See pp. 134–37.

U. Thant, Mongi Slim, Lester Pearson, Adlai Stevenson, and Valerian Zorin. The UN is obviously, therefore, an effective organization." A generalization is warranted only when the "some" in the evidence bears a "part-whole" relationship to the "more" in the claim. The fallacy of composition assumes a part-whole relationship that is not justified. The abilities of certain delegates do not necessarily "add up" to an effective United Nations. The effectiveness of any organization depends on other attributes—the goals of the group, interpersonal relations among members of the group, power and status relationships, the distribution of members' talents, and the loyalty of members to that group in preference to others. For example, if the men enumerated above pledge their primary allegiance to their own national governments, the UN will not have the full benefit of their abilities. For this reason and others, it may not be an effective organization. Thus, even when a generalization may *seem* warranted, the fallacy of composition conceals a deficient causal relationship between able members and effective organizations.

## INADEQUATE PARALLEL CASES

The strength of the warrant in a proof by parallel case depends on the degree to which the parallel cases are similar in essential characteristics. The warrant is deficient when similarities are few or do not involve essential attributes. Unlike some of the other types of proof, warrants of proofs by parallel case do not often contain clearcut fallacies: the strength or weakness of such warrants is usually a matter of degree.

## INADEQUATE ANALOGIES

The warrant of an analogy may be termed inadequate if the relationship expressed in the claim is not similar to the relationship stated in the evidence, or if such a relationship is not clearly communicated. Like the proof by a parallel case, the power of the warrant in an analogy is a matter of degree.

## INADEQUATE CLASSIFICATION

The principal deficiency of a warrant by classification is the *fallacy of division,* the reverse of the composition fallacy of generalizations. "My opponent, as you know, has represented this district in the State Legislature during the past session. The inactivity of this past legislative session is appalling: only two bills of any substance passed, and these are likely to do more harm than good. My opponent should not, therefore, be re-elected." Even if a debater can prove that a legislative group is justly condemned, the conduct of any member may be totally blameless. If the generalization in the evidence refers to a class having group attributes and structural relationships, as well as characteristics of the members of the class, then what is true of a class (evidence) is not necessarily true of one of the members of a class (claim). Proof by classification is properly applied only when the generalization in the evidence is based on additive attributes, and the whole is indeed equal to the sum of its parts.

### INADEQUATE STATISTICS

Any failure to meet satisfactorily one of the criteria for evaluating the warrant of a statistical proof is a fallacy.[8] Debaters should particularly beware of three common statistical fallacies. Proofs are frequently deficient because they employ (a) *units in a comparison that are not comparable;* (b) *a faulty base in computing a percentage;* or (c) *misleading "averages."*

First, the warrant of a statistical proof often involves a comparison of *units that are not commensurate.* "The lowest quartile of states spent only $227 per pupil in 1956–1957, whereas the highest quartile of states spent $307. This index points clearly to the tremendous variation among states in the quality of their public school systems."[9] On the surface, the statistics seem to justify the claimed comparison. Yet, by itself, dollar expenditure is not a comparable unit for evaluating the quality of the schools, because a dollar can buy more school construction in those states in the lowest quartile, and lower wages for teachers in those states are consistent with the lower costs of living.

Second, statistical proofs are fallacious when a *faulty base* is utilized in computing a percentage. "Between 1929 and 1951 teachers fared better than dentists. When 1929 dollars are converted to 1951 values, annual earnings of dentists increased only 21 per cent, while the salaries of teachers went up 53 per cent."[10] One must consider what the base was for each of the percentages before he evaluates the comparison. The 1929 earnings for dentists, converted to 1951 values, was $6460; for teachers it was $2120. Comparing percentages is meaningless when the two base figures are so different. The teacher who earned 53 per cent more money drew a 1951 salary of $3235 (a converted dollar increase

[8] To review criteria for evaluating warrants of proofs based on counting and measuring, comparisons, and central tendencies, see pp. 149–50, 151–53, and 153–54.

[9] Information for this example is taken from Roger Freeman, *Taxes for the Schools* (Washington, D.C.: Institute for Social Science Research, 1960), pp. 80–81, 141.

[10] Information for this example is taken from Roger Freeman, *School Needs in the Decade Ahead* (Washington, D.C.: Institute for Social Science Research, 1958), p. 136.

of $1115 since 1929). He may well wonder if he "fared better" than the dentist whose salary represented only a 21 per cent increase, but who actually earned $7820 (a converted dollar increase of $1360 since 1929). A comparison of percentages is valid only when each has the same or a similar base.

The percentage base is also faulty when selected in a *biased* way. "The salaries of teachers increased only 4 per cent in an eleven-year period ending in 1940."[11] The base year of 1929 represents a biased selection, since it was the peak year of the boom of the 1920's that preceded the depression of the 1930's. Actually, a 4 per cent increase shows a relatively good recovery from the depression; the earnings of all workers in 1940 was still 7 per cent below the 1929 level.[12]

Third, the warrants of statistical proofs are often inadequate because of *misleading "averages."* Which of the central tendencies an "average" refers to should be indicated in the proof.[13] In addition, the proper measure should be employed. "The average annual wage of our workers is $7500." If the "average" is a mean that includes the high salaries of executive "workers," the distribution of wages may be highly skewed and the figure misleading. The median would be a more proper measure of central tendency.

## INADEQUATE AUTHORITATIVE WARRANTS

One of the principal weaknesses of an authoritative unit of proof is that *inadequate credentials* are presented for the authority. Credentials are deficient, first, if they are *missing*. "Jasper Jorgenson assures us that. . . ." "We find in the August issue of *Current History* the statement, 'Our foreign policy today. . . .'" In both statements the authority's credentials are missing. The first example identifies the witness. But unless the listener or reader accepts Mr. Jorgenson as an authority, the mere name provides no warrant for agreeing to the claim. The second example does not even identify the writer. Unfortunately, debaters too commonly cite only the publication in which a bit of testimony appears. Yet the writer is the one responsible for a statement, and only his qualifications provide a critical basis for evaluating it.

Second, credentials may be *irrelevant*. "Professor Waldo Waldemar, President of the American Psychological Association and former editor of the *American Psychologist,* very properly warns us against the fal-

[11] Information for this example is taken from *School Needs in the Decade Ahead,* p. 133.
[12] This comparison does not have the same flaw as the one between teachers and dentists. The base earnings of teachers in 1929 was $1400; during the same year the base earnings of all workers was $1405.
[13] For a review of means, medians, and modes, see pp. 153–54.

lacy of the principle of comparative advantage, sometimes used to support the free trade proposal." The professor (mythical in this case) is not only identified, but given a full pedigree. The credentials are irrelevant, however. The reader or listener is informed of no special competence that prepares Waldemar to speak authoritatively about free trade. Note also the question-begging phrase, "very properly."

Third, credentials may be too *indefinite*. "Statistics prove that surpluses in agricultural products are caused by high price supports." "Professor Waldemar, a noted psychologist, has proved conclusively the existence of extrasensory perception." In these examples, the credentials of the authority are too indefinite to justify accepting the claim.

Even when an authority's credentials are adequate, however, an authoritative warrant may not be employed critically to establish claims that are *too broad*. "We should adopt a permanent police force for the UN because Sir Leslie Munro, long-time delegate to the UN from New Zealand and former president of the General Assembly, supports such an idea." Sir Leslie Munro undoubtedly has good credentials to speak about UN affairs. But the proposition itself must be examined critically before a wise decision is reached. The need for such a force, the cost, and the probable effectiveness in dealing with international disputes should be analyzed. Authoritative statements made by Sir Leslie Munro and others may well support specific assertions about the need, cost, or effectiveness of the proposal. But the acceptance of a whole proposition because of one man's opinion represents a short circuit of the debate process.

The foregoing deficiencies also apply when the authority is the speaker himself. The assertions of a speaker function as evidence in a reasonably strong unit of proof only if he is viewed as having adequate credentials for such assertions, and if his claims are not too broad.

## INADEQUATE MOTIVATIONAL PROOFS

In Chapter 11 motivational appeals were deemed admissible only in establishing evaluative or actuative claims. In that chapter references to irrelevant emotional appeals were considered a species of the fallacy of ignoring the question. Do relevant motivational warrants ever result in deficient proof of evaluative or actuative claims? They do when the motive is *insufficient*.

"Recognizing Communist China would mean a show of weakness in a part of the world where 'saving face' is important. The loss of prestige we would suffer is reason enough to reject the proposal to extend diplomatic recognition to the Communist government of China." Assuming the debater has proved that recognition of Communist China would reduce U.S. prestige and that U.S. policy is determined in part by motives of national pride, then the proof may be satisfactory as far as it goes. But propositions such as the one here illustrated are usually too complex to prove or disprove by reference to one motive—unless the motive is potent. If a debater combines his reference to prestige with other motivational proofs, and if no stronger countermotives are cited, he may successfully establish the actuative claim. But he may fail to prove his cause by invoking only the motive of national pride.

## IGNORED RESERVATIONS

Thus far valid claims have been shown to depend on the relationships among the indispensable proof elements—*evidence, warrant,* and *claim.* Proofs have been termed deficient if the claim is unwarranted, or if either the evidence or warrant is inadequate.

A fourth class of deficient proofs includes those that *ignore reservations* that ought to be appended to the claim. Such deficiencies occur when the debater fails to investigate the *whole factual context* of a controversy.

One weakness in this class results when a debater overlooks a *counteracting cause.* "In trying to demonstrate a need to adopt a guaranteed annual wage, the preceding speaker pointed out that state unemployment benefits were too small to provide for the minimum expenses of laid-off workers. This situation may have existed a few years ago, but we submit that increased benefits to the extent of X by Y states will be adequate to meet the alleged need." This proof has a good cause–effect warrant: increased income ordinarily helps one meet expenses, or more nearly meet them. If the debater presents evidence showing that Y states have increased benefits to X amount, the argument would appear valid. The factual context of the whole argument must be investigated, however. For example, a corresponding increase in the cost of living may *counteract* the causal force of increased income.

A second weakness is to ignore an *intervening cause.* "Therefore, we should strengthen the UN by eliminating the veto privilege and establishing a permanent police force. By releasing the fetters that now prevent immediate and decisive action by the will of a clear majority of member nations, we can transform the UN into an effective instrument for maintaining the collective security of the world." This argument illustrates another good cause–effect warrant that may also be deficient if the total factual context is not clearly understood. Unless nations are compelled to abide by UN decisions, the unwillingness to submit to such decisions and help finance them would *intervene* to thwart the causal warrant of the proposal.

Third, in effect–cause proofs debaters may neglect *"other causes."* "Two years ago we reduced the tariff on X products. Since that time two of the major producers have gone out of business. The combination of the competition of cheap foreign labor and the low tariff caused these companies to fold." Since lower costs of production and distribution may permit one set of producers to out-compete another, the effect–cause warrant is adequate to justify the claim. The judgment is not a careful one, however, unless one searches for *other causes* that might better account for the effect—and fails to find them. In this example, other causes might include a general financial weakness or operating inefficiency of the two hypothetical producers, or a general national depression. Only an examination of the total factual context of a controversy can provide reasonable assurance of what produced an effect.

Fourth, a sign relationship in a warrant could be countered by *other signs.* "My opponent questions whether the vast majority of union members are really apathetic about their membership. A clear sign of such apathy is that the mean attendance at union meetings is less than 3 per cent." That poor attendance is generally a sign of member apathy is an adequate warrant if properly supported. Since this sign, like most, is fallible, however, a close inspection of the factual context of the argument may weaken the proof. The number of strikes and the persistence with which the rank and file members carry them out may signify member enthusiasm, not apathy. A sign or group of signs not apparent in the evidence or warrant may entirely refute a claim based on sign, or at least limit its scope and force.

Fifth, a statistical relationship, although seemingly warranted, may *conceal facts* that necessitate the addition of a reservation to the claim. In the example above, the mean attendance is 3 per cent. The mean may include instances of very small attendance at routine meetings and very high attendance when collective bargaining disputes are aired. If such an analysis is correct, then the claim requires a reservation: union members are apathetic in attending meetings *unless vital matters are discussed.*

Sixth, in a classification, the debater may ignore *differences between the general evidence and the particular claim.* "From these examples we can see that arms races are generally unable to preserve peace. So it is with the present nuclear arms race, which actually increases the likelihood of a nuclear war." This proof by classification applies a generalization about arms races to the present nuclear arms race. However, even if the present nuclear arms race has enough attributes to justify placement in the class of "arms races" generalized upon in the evidence, the factual context of the argument must be examined to see if differences occur that might require reservations. If, unlike the weapons of earlier arms races, nuclear weapons have sufficient destructive power to deter aggression, then the proof is weakened. What has proved true of past arms races may not prove true of the present nuclear arms race.

Seventh, proof by parallel case or analogy may be deficient if *significant differences among compared cases or relations are ignored.* "In 1787 the thirteen colonies were united only by the Articles of Confederation, which lacked powers to levy taxes, regulate commerce, administer justice, and in other ways to legislate and execute the majority will of the colonies. Today, similarly, powers needed to maintain peace and justice among nations are denied the UN. If the UN is given new powers, the change will prove as successful as did the similar change made by the establishment of the U.S. Constitution." Even if a claim is adequately warranted by parallel case or analogy, the proof is deficient if differences between the compared cases or relationships have a direct bearing on the claim. In the example, the difference in degree between the emerging patriotism of the colonies in 1787 and the well-developed nationalism of present world states may be enough to refute or qualify the claim.

## OVERSTATED CLAIMS

The most common way debaters overstate a claim is *to assert a degree of certainty not justified by the evidence, warrant, and reservation.* If the evidence or warrant is probable, the claim can be no more than probable. If reservations are relevant, they should be appended to the claim statement. Making the degree of acceptability of the claim fit the other proof elements is important in all proof patterns.

Second, claims may be overstated in generalizations by being *broader in scope than justified.* "Responsible public officials from India, Burma, Indonesia, and Ceylon have all issued statements opposing the U.S. policy of not recognizing the Communist government of China. Thus, nations are generally opposed to our nonrecognition policy." Because an inductive leap, discussed in Chapter 9, has been made, a "generally" must be included to qualify the claim. But further qualification is needed. The nations represented by the "responsible public officials" are restricted to the group of "uncommitted nations" of Southeast Asia. *The scope of the claim should correspond to the scope of the evidence:*

"The uncommitted nations of Southeast Asia are generally opposed to our nonrecognition policy." Incidentally, the debater should support the assumption that the "responsible officials" speak for their nations.

Third, claims may be overstated through *concealed qualifiers*. "The leaders of nations A, B, C, and D have criticized the political connotations of our direct economic aid. The world is opposed to the policy." What is the meaning of "the world"? Every nation in the world? Every leader of every nation in the world? The majority of leaders of every nation in the world? The majority of leaders of the majority of nations in the world? The majority of Communist leaders? The vagueness of the claim statement makes impossible a clear answer to these questions.

## PROOF DEFICIENCIES AND BELIEF

The deficiencies of proof discussed in this chapter are not purely logical fallacies that *must* be rejected on some absolutist ground. A proof is deficient only when the listener or reader *believes* it is deficient.

Such a definition of proof deficiency should not be construed as giving a debater license for knavery or deceit in his attempt to influence belief. Because the debater is confronted by an opponent, who in a very real sense can keep him honest, and because he is trying to influence the belief of a *critical* decision-maker, he must make his proofs achieve the highest standards possible.

In this chapter we have outlined some of the grounds whereby most *critical* listeners and readers will *believe* proofs to be *deficient* and hence reject them. The next chapter presents an analysis of the nature of belief.

QUESTIONS

A. *To Check Your Comprehension and Memory*
  1. Describe each of the following types of proof deficiency:
     I. Deficient Evidence
        A. Incomplete evidence
        B. Inaccurate evidence
        C. Ambiguous evidence
        D. Absent evidence
     II. Unwarranted Claims
        A. Missing links
        B. Begging the question
           1. Persuasive prefaces

## DETECTING DEFICIENCIES OF PROOF

      2. Emotional language
      3. Circular reasoning
   C. Ignoring the question
      1. Irrelevant appeals
         a. to emotion
         b. to humor
         c. to tradition
         d. to popular prejudice
         e. to the ignorance of the opposite
      2. Diversionary proofs
         a. simple diversion
         b. red herring
         c. straw man
         d. assuming a more general truth
         e. impractical theory
         f. pointing to a second wrong
         g. shift in meaning
      3. Unrelated attacks on personality
III. Deficient Warrants
   A. Inadequate causal warrants
      1. Insufficient cause
      2. Causal warrant inadequately supported
      3. *Post hoc, ergo propter hoc*
   B. Inadequate signs
   C. Inadequate generalizations
      1. Hasty generalization
      2. Unrepresentative generalization
      3. Fallacy of composition
   D. Inadequate parallel cases
   E. Inadequate analogies
   F. Inadequate classifications
      1. Fallacy of division
   G. Inadequate statistics
      1. Units not commensurate
      2. Faulty percentage base
      3. Misleading "average"
   H. Inadequate authoritative warrants
      1. Inadequate credentials
         a. credentials missing
         b. credentials irrelevant
         c. credentials indefinite
      2. Claim too broad for authoritative proof
   I. Inadequate motivational proof
IV. Ignored Reservations
   A. Ignoring counteracting causes
   B. Ignoring intervening causes

## 188   THE MATERIALS OF ARGUMENT

      C. Ignoring other causes
      D. Ignoring other signs
      E. Ignoring concealed facts in a statistic
      F. Ignoring differences in a classification
      G. Ignoring differences in compared cases or relations
  V. Overstated Claims
      A. Degree of certainty not justified
      B. Scope of claim broader than scope of evidence
      C. Concealed qualifiers
2. What is Bentham's tripartite vocabulary?
3. What are two weaknesses in attacking personalities?
4. What is the relationship between deficient proofs and critical belief?

B. *For Class Discussion*

1. Is proof strength a matter of degree, or is a unit of proof either valid or not valid? Defend your point of view.

2. Which of the proof deficiencies discussed in this chapter will interfere seriously with the critical method of reaching decisions? Why?

3. Distinguish between motivational proof as a valid form of proof, and the appeal to emotions as a deficient form.

## EXERCISES

A. *Written Exercises*

1. Make a list of the fallacies exhibited by the hypothetical examples employed in this chapter—*other than the deficiencies the examples were meant to illustrate.*

2. Invent ten examples of ten different kinds of proof deficiency discussed in this chapter.

3. Read an argumentative article, editorial, or letter to the editor. List the proofs included, label the adequate proofs, and identify the deficiencies.

4. Enumerate the proof deficiencies of one of the speeches or essays in one of the sample debates in the Appendix.

B. *Oral Exercise*

Prepare a "one-point" speech in which you support one claim by several different kinds of proof. Include at least two proof deficiencies as cleverly disguised as you can manage. See if your classmates can spot and identify the deficiencies; be prepared to offer help if needed.

## SUGGESTIONS FOR FURTHER READING

Jeremy Bentham, *The Book of Fallacies,* in *The Works of Jeremy Bentham,* 11 vols., ed. John Bowring (Edinburgh: William Tait, 1838–1843), II, 375–487. An interesting classification and discussion of a number of political fallacies, complete with colorful labels for each fallacy.

Max Black, *Critical Thinking*, 2d ed. (Englewood Cliffs, N.J.: Prentice-Hall, 1952). Defines fallacy as weakness in an argument that sounds strong, and discusses the common fallacies.

W. Ward Fearnside and William B. Holther, *Fallacy: The Counterfeit of Argument* (Englewood Cliffs, N.J.: Prentice-Hall, 1959). Discusses and illustrates fifty-one fallacies. The examples are especially interesting.

Darrel Huff, *How to Lie with Statistics* (New York: W. W. Norton, 1954). A lively and highly popularized account of how statistics may fool you, if you don't watch out.

Arthur Schopenhauer, "The Art of Controversy," in *The Essays of Arthur Schopenhauer*, tr. T. Bailey Saunders (New York: John Wiley, n. d.). A satiric and amusing treatment of political fallacies. Thirty-eight "stratagems" are discussed briefly and illustrated.

Robert H. Thouless, *Straight and Crooked Thinking* (New York: Simon and Schuster, 1932). A very practical discussion of fallacies in arguments, together with examples from controversies of that time. Appendix I usefully catalogues the thirty-four dishonest tricks discussed in the text, and Appendix II presents a delightful imaginary conversation that manages to illustrate most of the tricks.

*Chapter 13*

# THE NATURE AND SOURCES OF BELIEF

*When we find ourselves entertaining an opinion about which there is a feeling that even to inquire into it would be absurd, unnecessary, undesirable, or wicked—we may know that that opinion is a non-rational one.* A. E. MANDER

WHAT MEN choose or decide is determined by what they believe. Therefore, if the debater is to help them decide wisely, he must understand what beliefs are and how they function.

What are beliefs? Why do men believe? From what sources are beliefs derived? Of what elements are they composed? How may they be evaluated? What should the debater know about the existing beliefs of his readers or listeners? These are the questions with which the present chapter will be concerned.

## DEFINITION OF BELIEF

A belief may be defined as *an attitude of affirmation or acceptance,* as a disposition to endorse rather than deny an idea that is presented to us.

### BELIEF AS APPREHENSION AND FEELING

A belief is composed of two ingredients: (*a*) an apprehension of some event or condition, and (*b*) a distinctive "feeling" about that apprehension, a "feeling" that differentiates it from mere awareness and identifies it as something we are willing to accept as true.

Why belief involves apprehension is not difficult to understand. Unless one is first aware of something, he can hardly hold a belief concerning its nature, cause, seriousness, or probable results. To know nothing is to believe nothing.

But that belief entails more than awareness is equally obvious. Everyone knows about many things in which he does not for a moment believe—dragons, rock candy mountains, tunnels under the oceans. These and a host of similar ideas, concrete or abstract, one can bring into consciousness and describe at length. But he does not believe them.

In addition to awareness, belief involves a confident impulse to affirm that our item of knowledge exists or is "so." As John Stuart Mill put it: "We believe a thing [only] when we are ready to act on the faith of it; to face the practical consequences of taking it for granted. And therein lies the distinction between believing the facts to be conjoined and merely thinking of them together." [1]

## APPREHENSION AND FEELING AS INDEPENDENT ELEMENTS

Although apprehension and feeling join to create belief, they are independent elements in consciousness. They may come into being at different times, as the second develops gradually out of the first. We hear of something, and not until later do we come to believe it; or at first we only "suppose," and then "believe." To borrow a phrase from Brentano, in belief an object is "twice present in consciousness, as thought of and as held for real or denied." [2]

## BELIEF DISTINGUISHED FROM DOUBT

While the difference that sets off belief from apprehension is easy to recognize, trying to describe how belief *feels* presents a difficult problem. So skillful a writer as William James was eventually forced to admit, "Belief is an emotion . . . perfectly distinct, but perfectly indescribable in words." It "feels like itself—that is about as much as we can say." [3] A century and a half earlier the Scottish philosopher David Hume had come to the same conclusion. "It is impossible," he said, "to explain this feeling. . . . We can go no farther than assert that belief is something felt by the mind, which distinguishes the idea of judgment from the fictions of the imagination." [4]

Faced with this difficulty, most writers have contented themselves with contrasting the radically different sensations that accompany belief and doubt.

[1] Note in James Mill, *Analysis of the Human Mind* (London: Longmans, Green, Reader and Dyer, 1869), I, 403.
[2] F. Brentano, *Psychologie* (Leipzig: 1847), p. 226.
[3] All quotations from William James in this chapter are from *The Principles of Psychology* (for complete reference see p. 207).
[4] *An Enquiry Concerning Human Understanding* (London and Edinburgh, 1758), 5.2.

How does one "feel" when he doubts? John Dewey suggested the appropriateness of the words "obscurity," "conflict," "disturbance," and "agitation" as representative of these states.[5] James offered "theoretic agitation"; McDougall, "anxiety in respect of a proposition"; and Cohen, that condition "where all is double," and hence bewildering, difficult, and unpleasant.[6]

But we do not require authorities to tell us that doubt is characterized by mental irritation and discomfort. Everyone has experienced for himself the itching uncertainty it brings. Doubt resembles the frustration we know when unable to recall a familiar face or a bit of verse or melody. Yet doubt also has a magnetlike quality that fascinates as it repels. We try to put the matter out of mind, but it persists in returning. To doubt is to suffer.

Belief, on the contrary, presents, in Dewey's words, a "situation that is clear, coherent, settled, harmonious." Uncertainty gives way to comforting calmness. Pain stops; a peaceful satisfaction emerges. For the present at least, the matter seems closed—settled, sealed, and finished. The believer steps out with sprightliness and assurance, even though his belief may be false.

To experience again the familiar difference between belief and doubt, try the following experiment: Take a common everyday belief, and for a few minutes try earnestly to doubt it. For example, instead of believing that the book now in your hands is an actual physical object occupying space and time in the external world, assume that it is only an image existing in your mind. Make a genuine effort to believe this.

What is the result? From the first, the assumption is difficult to accept. If the book is not actually there, how does it happen that I am able to see and feel it? Why does my roommate confidently assert that I am holding it in my hands? Why do I hear a noise if the book drops? Why do I feel a pain if I strike it sharply against my arm? Question after question arises.

Eventually, the mental agitation that accompanies the attempt to believe becomes unbearable. You give up the assumption that the book is a mental image and return to your original belief that it has existence as a discrete physical object.

Now doubts mysteriously disappear. There is a ready answer to each of the problems that previously plagued you. Man's senses, you conclude, are reliable; the judgments of other persons, acceptable; the

---

[5] *How We Think* (Boston: D. C. Heath & Company, 1933), p. 100.
[6] William McDougall, *Outline of Psychology* (New York: Charles Scribner's Sons, 1923), p. 367; and Morris Cohen, "Belief," in *Encyclopaedia of the Social Sciences* (New York: The Macmillan Company, 1930).

objects of the external world, "real." The matter is sealed off from attention, and you have a "feeling" of assurance and repose.

## WHY MEN BELIEVE

Why do men believe? Why do they hold opinions about things? The simplest answer is that man desires the mental peace and repose that belief brings. He is by nature a believing animal.

Let us call the roll of the authorities:

W. P. MONTAGUE: "Man is . . . suggestible . . . and tends to believe what is said to him unless he has some positive reason for doubting the honesty or competence of his informant. . . . We have an almost unconquerable temptation to shun uncertainty and to commit ourselves definitely either for or against a given proposition." [7]

BERTRAND RUSSELL: "When an idea is entertained without belief, the impulse to believe is not absent but is inhibited. Belief is not something added to an idea merely entertained, but something subtracted from an idea by effort." [8]

WILLIAM JAMES: "The primitive impulse is to affirm immediately the reality of all that is conceived. . . . As a rule, we believe as much as we can. We would believe everything if we only could." [9]

W. B. PILLSBURY: "Doubt, not belief, is the positive process. Whatever is not doubted is believed." [10]

RALPH BARTON PERRY: "It is characteristic for the living mind to be *for* some things and *against* others. . . ." [11]

Again, experience confirms these statements. Consider the belief habits of small children. They often accept the most improbable tales about goblins, giants, and fairy godmothers. They endorse whatever their parents or elders assure them is so. Adults, although less credulous than children, have a strong impulse to believe something about everything. As soon as one belief is discredited, it is replaced with another; a vacuum among beliefs is abhorred. Nothing is harder to learn than to suspend judgment while the facts of a situation are studied. To the untrained researcher, doubts, like ripe olives and raw oysters, are at first decidedly unpleasant.

[7] *The Ways of Knowing* (New York: The Macmillan Company, 1925), p. 39.
[8] *Human Knowledge* (New York: Simon & Schuster, 1948), p. 102.
[9] *Principles of Psychology*, II, 299, 319.
[10] *The Psychology of Reasoning* (New York: D. Appleton Co., 1910), p. 58.
[11] *General Theory of Value* (New York: Longmans, Green & Co., 1926), p. 115.

## SOURCES OF BELIEF

Most beliefs come from one of three sources: (a) *experience*, (b) *authority*, or (c) *other beliefs*.

### EXPERIENCE

"Seeing is believing." "Show me." "Experience is the best teacher." "The tongue of experience has the most truth." These and similar adages emphasize the reliance traditionally placed on experience as a source of belief. Nor can it be denied that many beliefs are the direct result of what one has himself seen, tried, felt, or undergone.

We believe that alum is tart; ice, cold; lemons, sour; and cotton, soft, because these substances have actually produced such sensations. Similarly, our beliefs about the competence of army doctors, the fairness of teachers, and the eccentricities of traffic policemen may be based entirely on chapters out of our own biographies.

Beliefs founded on firsthand experience are more vivid than other beliefs. The man who "has actually been there or done it" is, in the court of his own mind at least, always the final authority. Others, too, customarily regard such an individual as an "expert" and respect his opinions. The ultimate appeal in advertising is to try the product for oneself, the assumption being that nothing is quite so convincing as direct experience.

More than fifty years ago A. E. Phillips recognized the authority of experience:

What things are real to us? Of what things are we most positive? Those things which we have experienced. . . . The certainty is born of our actual life, and if someone asserts the opposite we refuse to believe it. It is contrary to our experience.[12]

Even earlier James had written:

The certainty of sense is fundamental, whilst the certainty of thought, as concerned with objects of higher order, presupposes sensory *fundamenta*. . . . *What ever things have intimate and continuous connection with my life are things of whose reality I cannot doubt.*

### AUTHORITY

The limitations of firsthand experience require a second source of belief. No man, even in the longest and busiest of lives, can come into

[12] *Effective Speaking* (Chicago: Newton Co., 1908). Quotation as here reproduced is from rev. ed. (1938), p. 30.

contact with more than a fraction of the physical, social, and intellectual worlds in which he dwells. He cannot visit all the cities, meet all the people, hold all the jobs, know all the emotions, or experience all the events that compose his environment. Nor can he have firsthand experience with the world of the past. D. Elton Trueblood has called the area of immediate experience open to any person "a mere slit in the world's expanse." [13]

Outside the narrow realm of what one has himself seen, felt, or heard, he is forced to depend on the say-so of others, to know what to believe. This say-so of others is called *authority*.

Authority takes many forms. It may consist of the judgment of a single individual offering advice or information—the international affairs expert analyzing the significance of a recent event, the lawyer interpreting a law, the soil chemist asserting that a lawn needs nitrogen. Or it may be the voice of many, as one defers to a majority opinion, does something because "everyone is doing it," or votes for the more popular candidate. Or it may be the voice of ages past, encased in the folkways and mores or in the institutional patterns that form our culture.

In each instance one turns to authority to make up his mind about matters he cannot investigate for himself, or when he thinks an authoritative pronouncement should take precedence over the conclusion his own experience suggests.

### OTHER BELIEFS

Some beliefs do not depend directly on either firsthand experience or authoritative sanction, but rather grow out of other beliefs. Like the corollary of a demonstration in geometry, the derivative belief has its source and its full strength in prior beliefs.

A belief concerning a particular labor–management dispute may have its source in other beliefs concerning the value of labor unions, the importance of the profit incentive, or the character of the disputants. A belief that the federal government should or should not provide medical care for the aged may be based on beliefs concerning the extent to which the government is responsible for the welfare of its citizens, the extent of need among the aged for health care, principles underwriting fiscal policies, the effect of the proposal on various health agencies, etc.

Since the acceptance of one belief may involve the acceptance of others, beliefs tend to form themselves into clusters. A belief that democracy is a desirable form of government may lead one to another belief that voters generally exhibit sound political judgment. A cluster

[13] *The Logic of Belief* (New York: Harper & Brothers, 1942), p. 66.

of beliefs on race relations will influence one's belief on any particular dispute in this area.

Because of such a tendency to cluster, most beliefs involve not only a direct intellectual and emotional commitment to the belief itself, but also an indirect commitment to a whole series of other conclusions that are directly implied by it. Some beliefs may set off a chain reaction that leads one into regions far removed from his starting point.

## THE STRUCTURE OF BELIEF

### THE COMPONENTS AND AXES OF A BELIEF

When one takes a belief apart, he finds that it is composed of the three elements represented in this diagram:

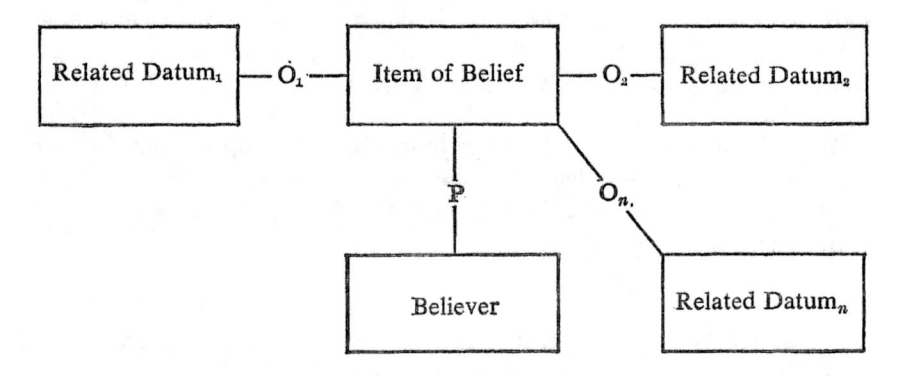

```
[Related Datum₁] — O₁ — [Item of Belief] — O₂ — [Related Datum₂]
                              |         \
                              P          Oₙ
                              |           \
                        [Believer]    [Related Datumₙ]
```

Each of these elements is an indispensable component of a total act of belief. The *item of belief,* located in the upper center of the diagram, is the idea that forms the subject matter of the belief—blondes are fickle, candy is fattening, gambling should be legalized, Brutus slew Caesar. The square at the bottom of the diagram represents the *believer,* the individual who holds a particular item of belief as part of his accumulated stock of attitudes. Third, completing the complex, are a number of *related data* about the external world, data which in one way or another bear upon the belief item in question. Such related data may come from experience, from authority, or from other beliefs.

The components of an act of belief are not independent units, but, as the diagram shows, are associated by means of two axes.

Line P, connecting belief item and believer, is the so-called *personal* or *subjective* axis. By introducing the motives, emotions, and values of the believer into the belief act, the personal axis transforms the belief from a mere cognitive apprehension to a state in which the feelings and motives of the believer play an important role.

One may be indifferent to an item of information; one cannot be indifferent to a belief. Challenge some belief held by another person, and see how he reacts. Or see how you feel when one of your own beliefs is questioned. To have a belief challenged is never a completely objective experience, because the feelings of the believer are brought into play through the personal axis.

Lines $O_1$, $O_2$ . . . $O_n$, connecting the item of belief with related data about the external world, represent the belief's *objective axes* and keep it from being purely a creature of "feeling."

"A belief," said John Dewey, "refers to something beyond itself by which its value is tested." [14] Belief is not blind impulse, nor is it willful desire or wish fulfillment. In the words of McDougall, belief is "confidence on the intellectual level." [15]

Even when the evidence on which one bases his belief is inadequate, or his reasoning invalid, he still engages in a sort of pseudo-rational activity in arriving at judgment. To his own satisfaction at least, his opinion has been tested by being referred "to something beyond itself" for verification. He is always ready to give reasons—be they good or bad—why a belief is "so."

Because they supply the "reasons" that make a belief acceptable, objective axes play an indispensable role in the process of belief formation. To quote from Bertrand Russell, "In every assertion [of belief] two sides must be separated. On the subjective side, the assertion 'expresses' a state of the speaker; on the objective side, it intends to indicate a fact, and succeeds in this intention when true." [16]

### BELIEF AS COMPULSORY

Because a belief has objective axes, it must, at least to the believer's satisfaction, square with the facts and related beliefs that constitute its natural environment.

As a result, although associated by means of its personal axis with the wishes or desires of the believer, a belief is not responsive to these forces alone. Beliefs cannot be created, abolished, or reshaped at will. In large measure, they are imposed upon us by our apprehension of experiential and authoritative data and by related beliefs we also hold.

Many writers distinguish belief from imagination or apprehension by pointing out that, unlike belief, these states may be entered upon voluntarily. Others openly declare that compulsion is the essence of belief.

---

[14] *How We Think*, p. 6. See also Bertrand Russell, *Human Knowledge, Its Scope and Limits* (New York: Simon & Schuster, 1948), p. 145.
[15] *Outline of Psychology*, p. 364.
[16] *An Inquiry into Meaning and Truth* (New York: W. W. Norton & Co., 1940), p. 23.

DAVID HUME: Belief "depends not on the will, but must arise from certain determinate causes or principles of which we are not masters." [17]

WILLIAM McDOUGALL: "It is the resistance offered by things to our desires and our efforts that is the foundation of our belief in their reality." [18]

G. F. STOUT: "Whenever belief or judgment exists, it involves the control of our activity as thinking beings by conditions which are fixed for us and not by us. In so far as we are left free to think otherwise than we do think belief is absent; in so far as it is present, the range of subjective selection is confined within definite limits. . . . The whole process is like testing a foothold in climbing, to see whether it will bear us or not; the more resistance the ground makes to our pressure, the more ready we are to trust ourselves to it. . . . The more easily we find it possible to realize in thought opposite alternatives, we become less confident and less energetic in our pursuit of the object along this special line." [19]

G. F. STOUT: "Belief . . . involves restriction of mental activity. Objective coercion is the very essence of belief. Whatever influences subjective needs as such may have in determining belief, they can never be the sole factor. In framing a belief, we endeavour to represent real existence as it is in its own nature, independent of our own individual consciousness. . . ." [20]

## EGO- AND OBJECT-ORIENTED BELIEFS

Although every belief must have both a personal and an objective element, the relative importance of these elements in shaping the belief may vary. The personal component exercises the dominant influence in some instances; the objective component, in others. Moreover, the same belief as held by different individuals may vary in this respect. The hypothetical cases of Harold Leslie and Gordon Berger, students at State University, will illustrate the point.

Harold, a sophomore, strongly holds the opinion that college social fraternities are undemocratic. As even he will admit, however, his belief is largely influenced by the fact that only recently he was refused a pledge pin by Eta Eta Eta, the group he particularly wished to join. Moreover, as Harold will in a candid moment further admit, he finds his belief about the undemocratic nature of fraternities congenial and comforting. Not only does it help salve a keen personal disappointment, but it conveniently protects his pride when he is discussing fraternities with friends.

Gordon, a senior at State University, also believes that fraternities are undemocratic. The grounds for his conclusion, however, are strikingly

[17] *A Treatise of Human Nature* (London, 1739), Appendix.
[18] *Outline of Psychology*, p. 372.
[19] *Analytic Psychology* (New York: The Macmillan Company, 1896), II, 239–41.
[20] *A Manual of Psychology* (New York: Hinds & Noble, 1899), pp. 548–49.

different. Since Gordon has himself been a member of Eta Eta Eta for three years, disappointment and wounded pride played no part in forming his opinion. Instead, over a period of time, repeated instances of social snobbery and intolerance—instances he could not in conscience justify—have forced this conclusion upon him. As a result, instead of finding his conviction pleasant, he finds it decidedly unpleasant. He wishes with all his heart that he did not feel morally bound to accept it, for translated into action his belief would mean breaking his own affiliation with Eta Eta Eta and sacrificing many close, personal friendships.

Harold's belief, dominated largely by his own wishes and feelings, may be called *ego-oriented*. Gordon's belief, forced on him by the apparent weight of related data, is *object-oriented*.

Ego- and object-oriented beliefs may be illustrated by variations of the diagram introduced earlier:

### EGO-ORIENTED BELIEF

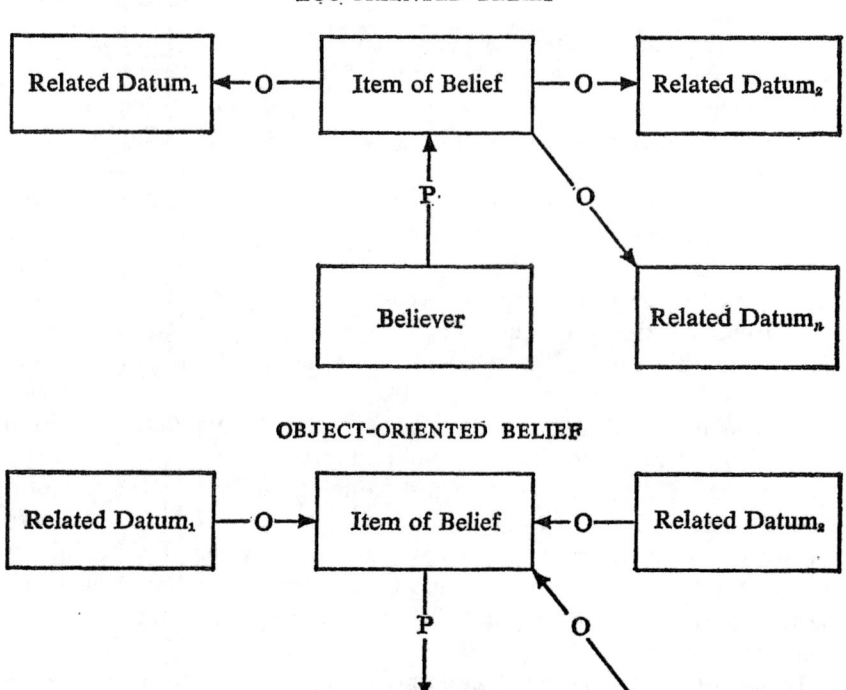

Related Datum$_1$ ←O— Item of Belief —O→ Related Datum$_2$

Believer —P→ Item of Belief

Item of Belief —O→ Related Datum$_n$

### OBJECT-ORIENTED BELIEF

Related Datum$_1$ —O→ Item of Belief ←O— Related Datum$_2$

Item of Belief —P→ Believer

Related Datum$_n$ —O→ Item of Belief

As the directional arrows indicate, in *ego-oriented beliefs* the impulse to believe originates principally within the believer and, figuratively speaking, travels upward and outward, encompassing his other beliefs and his judgments about related experiential and authoritative facts. Upon occasion, related beliefs and facts may even be colored or reshaped to bring them into line with the desired conclusion.

In *object-oriented beliefs,* on the other hand, the impulse to believe has its origin principally in the complex of related beliefs and facts and travels downward and inward, imposing itself on the believer.

Although many of the beliefs that any man holds are heavily ego- or object-oriented, others cannot be clearly delineated. The personal and objective elements may be equally prominent, or their relative influence may have become diffused and obscured.

## EVALUATION OF BELIEFS

### THE HEALTH DIMENSION

Not infrequently, either the personal or the object component of a belief, instead of merely being dominated by its counterpart, is completely blocked off so it can no longer play a part in molding the conviction. Belief then ceases to be normal, and becomes *pathological.* Consider two final variations of our diagram which appear on the next page.

The first variation illustrates how an object-oriented belief may become pathological. A conclusion dictated by judgments about the external world or by other beliefs is so repugnant to the believer that he refuses to accept it, with the result that the normal belief pattern is destroyed. Either the conclusion is consciously or unconsciously rejected and shut out of the mind, or fictitious substitutes in the form of fantasies or daydreams are created to take its place. In extreme cases, the denial of a belief dictated by related data takes the form of a psychosis and must be dealt with clinically.

The second diagram represents a pathological belief of a personal or ego-oriented nature. Here the situation is reversed. The desire or motive of the believer is so strong and persistent that by one means or another he succeeds in discounting whatever opposition related experience, authority, and other beliefs may raise against the wished-for conclusion.

In its milder form, the discounting of opposing facts is known as *rationalization* and consists in making only a few minor and temporary adjustments among data in order to bring them into line with the desired conclusion. Rationalization is an activity in which everyone engages from time to time, and unless carried too far or resorted to habitually does not have permanently harmful results. In its extreme form, however, this same distortion of the normal belief pattern results in a total disregard of all related data—sometimes of reality itself. The wish-motivated believer assumes with sincerity and consistency any role he chooses, or entertains any conviction he desires, no matter how unrealistic or improbable. His denial of the facts of the world about him results in a typically schizophrenic personality.

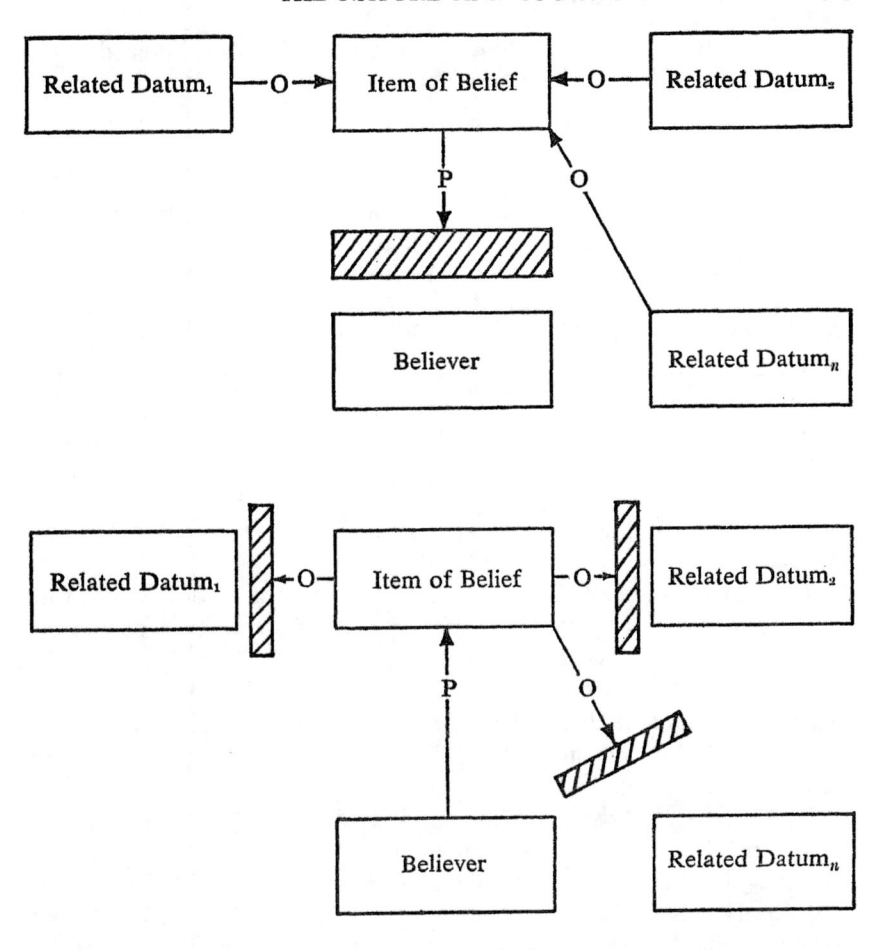

From the description of pathological beliefs may be inferred the two conditions that must be met if beliefs are to be *healthy:* (a) *All related facts and beliefs must be taken into account in arriving at a conclusion.* (b) *The belief, once established as true or probable, must be accepted as such by the believer.*

Insofar as these two conditions are met, beliefs will have the glow and stability of health. Insofar as these qualities are lacking, beliefs will be pathological, and hence dangerous to the believer and to others.

## THE VALIDITY DIMENSION

Although the notion may at first seem curious, a healthy belief need not necessarily be valid. To be healthy, a belief must be factually oriented and fully accepted by the believer. But if it is to be valid, two additional requirements must be met: (*a*) *The data on which the belief is based must themselves be true or probable.* (*b*) *The connections asserted to exist among the three components of the belief must be warranted.*

To a thirsty man in the middle of a desert the mirage of an oasis with abundant shade and water may appear very real. The person who reads only one partisan newspaper during a political campaign and votes for the candidate it supports honestly believes his decision rests on the "facts."

In neither instance is belief unhealthily grounded in wishes or desires at the expense of objective factors, nor is there any refusal on the part of the believer to face frankly the conclusion the "facts" dictate. The difficulty arises not because the belief act is incomplete or distorted, but because *the factual data on which it is based are faulty.* The thirsty man's belief rests on an illusion; the newspaper reader mistakes some of the "facts" for all.

The beliefs of Aristotle, Plato, or Francis Bacon were certainly not unhealthy. Our improved knowledge of social and physical phenomena, however, has shown many of them to be invalid. These men reasoned objectively, but their understanding of some "facts" was, as we now know, incomplete or faulty. Just so will a future generation, with improved knowledge of the social and physical environments, write off as invalid many beliefs that today are accepted as true.

A valid belief, then, first rests on facts that represent the situation accurately and completely. The conclusion must actually accord, and not merely be thought to accord, with the evidence.

But besides reflecting an existing situation accurately, valid beliefs must be based on warranted inferences. The item of belief is connected with judgments about related data concerning the external world along *objective axes* through *substantive* and *authoritative* warrants. Unless the belief item squares with the believer's best inferences from all the facts to which it is related, it will not be certified objectively. To a superstitious man a whole cluster of "facts" seem to support the belief

THE NATURE AND SOURCES OF BELIEF 203

that walking under a ladder brings bad luck. Such a belief, however, is not valid because it is based on faulty causal connections.[21]

The item of belief is related to the feelings and desires of the believer along the *personal axis* by means of *motivational* warrants. Unless the emotions and motives of the believer certify the reasonableness of the personal belief axis, he will be unwilling to act on the basis of his "belief."

We can, then, have healthy beliefs by learning to think critically and as emotionally mature men and women. We can acquire valid beliefs only by learning more about the ways of the world in which we live and by making valid interpretations of such information through acceptable reasoning. *All valid beliefs are healthy beliefs, but not all healthy beliefs are valid.*

## BELIEF AND THE DEBATER

Some debaters have the misconception that their sole task is to formulate "logical" proofs that meet the test of abstract "validity." To understand the nature and function of beliefs, however, is of vital concern to debaters since debate decisions represent not abstract conclusions but the actual beliefs of listeners and readers.

Each claim the debater tries to prove is an attempt to influence belief, and each proof element—evidence, warrant (or its support), reservations, and qualifications—must be believed if the claim as a whole is to be accepted. The concept of proof is meaningless when divorced from the person to whom the proof is offered.[22]

As the debater designs and criticizes proofs, he should ask three questions: (1) What do my readers or listeners now believe about the question under discussion? (2) From what sources are their beliefs derived? (3) To what extent are their beliefs ego- or object-oriented?

### EXISTING BELIEFS

When a claim is first advanced, readers or listeners may believe it, disbelieve it, or reserve judgment. Which of these attitudes they display depends, in large part, on what they already believe about data and values related to the subject.

[21] Our analysis of belief validity corresponds to our classification of the types of proofs in Chapters 10 and 11. The tests of the various kinds of warrants may be applied to determine the validity of beliefs.
[22] An additional reason why debaters must understand beliefs is presented in Chapter 15, pp. 245–49.

If a claim is believed, it is usually because that claim accords with previously accepted data and values. Here a simple statement by the debater or, at most, a brief reinforcing proof will suffice.

Judgment may be reserved for two reasons: First, the listener or reader may have no body of related data by which to test the worth of the claim, and no motives or values that endorse its acceptance. Here acceptable related facts must be provided and a suitable motive for believing supplied. Second, the listener or reader may have conflicting data or motives which result in indecision. The debater must verify the set of data and reinforce the motive that would justify the desired belief.

If a claim is disbelieved, more often than not it is because that claim contradicts accepted related data or violates accepted motives and values. Here the debater must do two things: First, he must effectively refute the contradictory data and mitigate the motives that stand in the way of the claim's acceptance. Second, he must replace these destroyed elements with evidence that supports the claim he advances, and with motives and values that urge its acceptance.

Determining what listeners or readers believe about a disputable question is seldom easy. Even in those rare instances when interviews or other direct contacts are practical, pride, fear, or the desire to conform may prevent people from reporting what they actually think. Such information, however, will make decisions more critical. The debater who knows what people already believe and why they believe it can intelligently determine what proofs to present and how to structure them to achieve their intended purpose.

## SOURCES OF BELIEFS

Whether he seeks to confirm an existing belief or to alter an opposing one, the debater will be helped in his task if he knows the sources of his audience's beliefs.

Beliefs based on personal experience, it must be remembered, are particularly strong and tenacious. Therefore, one can often build convincing proofs to reinforce an existing belief by referring to events which the audience has directly experienced. When refuting a belief, however, one will not likely succeed by directly attacking the truth of experiential data. To question the interpretation given an experience, to show that the reasoning from experience to claim is invalid, or to present new counterevidence based on other experience will be more apt to bring the desired result.

Beliefs based on authority vary greatly in tenacity and strength. Authoritative pronouncements often bear great weight when experiential data are unavailable. In other instances, reliance will depend on (*a*) the credibility of the source, and (*b*) the extent to which the authoritative sanction is corroborated by experience and related beliefs. To refute beliefs derived from authority, the debater may directly criticize the believability of the authority or present counterproofs based on experience, other authorities, or stronger beliefs.

The strength of derivative beliefs depends ultimately on the experiential and authoritative weight of the beliefs from which they are derived. They may be refuted by denying the validity of these originating beliefs or by criticizing the reasoning employed to connect the data of experience or authority with the derivative belief claim.

## EGO- AND OBJECT-ORIENTED BELIEFS

For several reasons, the debater must understand whether the beliefs of his audience are primarily ego- or object-oriented.

First, the degree to which a belief is ego-oriented largely controls how the believer will behave with respect to it. Whether he is ashamed or proud of his conviction; whether he will act on it in public, in private only, or not at all; whether he will assume the defensive when it is challenged or examine criticism objectively—these and similar behavior patterns often reflect the extent to which a belief is shaped by desire and emotion.

Second, the degree to which a belief is ego-oriented often goes far toward determining the stubbornness with which it is held. Does the believer find his conviction pleasant or repugnant? Does he feel a close personal attachment to the ideas, or does he view them with detachment? Are his basic drives or desires involved? Although a relatively objective belief can also be deep-seated and tenacious, an ego-oriented belief grounded in a long history of fear, hatred, or envy may be very difficult to modify and practically impossible to abolish.

Third, the extent to which subjective factors sustain a belief helps determine the sort of proof that should be employed to dislodge it. If the belief is ego-oriented, the debater cannot easily deny the evidence of the believer's feeling or desire. He may, however, (*a*) show that the feeling or desire is not relevant to the item of belief, (*b*) claim that it is insufficient to motivate an endorsement of the belief, or (*c*) present counterproofs based on stronger values that motivate altering the belief. If, on the other hand, the belief is object-oriented, substantive and authoritative proofs are required. The debater may gain assent to a belief if he shows that it is compatible with beliefs his listeners or readers already hold, or he may refute an opposing belief by proving it inconsistent with related beliefs already accepted. Whether the belief is ego- or object-oriented, the debater must identify his claim with the relevant judgments and motives of his readers or hearers.

Finally, the study of the personal and objective axes of a belief may show why that belief has been singled out as a controversial subject among men. For most disputes arise because the contending parties differ (*a*) in their desires or feelings with respect to some item of belief (*unlike personal axes*); (*b*) in their backgrounds of experience, knowledge, and other beliefs (*unlike objective axes*); and (*c*) both in their feelings about a belief item and in their backgrounds of experience, knowledge, and other beliefs (*unlike personal and objective axes*).

Conversely, if men are to agree about a belief, without compromise or reservation, two conditions must be met: (*a*) their "feelings" about the belief must come into accord; and (*b*) they must recognize a common set of related data and must interpret and evaluate it in essentially the same way.

## QUESTIONS

A. To Check Your Comprehension and Memory
 1. What are the two ingredients that make up belief?
 2. Which element appears first?
 3. Distinguish belief from doubt.
 4. Why do men believe?
 5. What are the three principal sources of belief?
 6. What is a belief cluster?
 7. What are the three components of a belief?
 8. What are the two kinds of belief axes?
 9. In what sense is belief compulsory?
 10. In what two ways may belief be oriented?
 11. When does belief become pathological?
 12. What are the two conditions of a healthy belief?
 13. What are the two conditions of a valid belief?
 14. What kinds of proofs connect the item of belief with related data about the external world?
 15. What kinds of proofs connect the item of belief with the believer?
 16. Why must the debater understand the nature and function of beliefs?
 17. What should the debater do if his listeners or readers initially believe the claim he is advancing? if they disbelieve the claim? if they are reserving judgment?
 18. What should the debater do if the beliefs of his readers or listeners have their source in experience? in authority? in other beliefs?
 19. Why should the debater understand whether the beliefs of his readers or hearers are primarily ego- or object-oriented?
 20. What three reasons account for most disputes?

B. *For Class Discussion*
1. If "feeling" is an indispensable part of belief, can one ever arrive at a belief critically?
2. To what extent should one make a conscious effort to suspend judgment when hearing or reading a debate, and how long should he suspend it?
3. What is the role of belief in detecting deficiencies of proof?

## EXERCISES

A. *Written Exercises*
1. Examine your beliefs concerning some controversial question of current interest. Try to determine which were derived (directly or indirectly) from experience, which were derived from authority, and which came from other beliefs you also hold. List each set of beliefs in a separate column.
2. Reexamine your beliefs on the same question, with a view to determining the extent to which each is ego- or object-oriented. Be as detached and fair as possible in making your analysis. Again record the results of your investigation in two columns.

B. *Oral Exercise*
Carefully analyze the existing beliefs of your classmates concerning a controversial question. Decide what claims they will probably accept without proof, what claims they may doubt, and what claims they will probably disbelieve. Then prepare and present a five-minute speech in which (*a*) you provide reasons and motives for believing doubted claims, and (*b*) by refuting present reasons and motives you pave the way for the acceptance of disbelieved claims. Indicate in the margin of the speech outline you hand your instructor your estimate of the probable reception each claim will receive.

## SUGGESTIONS FOR FURTHER READING

William James, *The Principles of Psychology* (New York: Holt, 1890), Vol. II, Chapter 21, "The Perception of Reality." See especially the discussions of belief and doubt, the influence of emotion and active impulse on belief, and the relation between belief and will (Vol. II, pp. 283–87, 307–24). Although much of what James said must be discounted in the light of present-day psychology, his discussion is still extremely valuable for anyone who wishes to understand the nature and properties of belief.

Harold A. Larrabee, *Reliable Knowledge* (Boston: Houghton Mifflin Co., 1945), Chapter 4, "Observation—'Get the Facts.'" Discusses the requirements that observation and fact-gathering must meet in order to lead to beliefs that are reliable.

A. E. Mander, *Logic for the Million* (New York: Philosophical Library, 1947), Chapter 2, "Groundless Beliefs," and Chapter 3, "What May We Believe?" Mander explores how we get our beliefs and points out why most of them are groundless. He then sets forth a criterion by which the "truth" of a belief may be determined.

W. P. Montague, *The Ways of Knowing* (New York: The Macmillan Co., 1925). A technical but provocative critique of five sources of belief: testimony, intuition, abstract reasoning from universal principles, sensory experience, and practical activity having successful consequences.

# Part IV

# DEVELOPING ARGUMENTATIVE DISCOURSE

## Chapter 14
# ANALYZING THE PROPOSITION

*If we were not always trying to reduce diversity to identity, we should find it almost impossible to think at all. The world would be a mere chaos, an unconnected series of mutually irrelevant phenomena.* ALDOUS HUXLEY

AN IMPORTANT distinction must be recognized between the task discussed in this chapter and the one to be considered in Chapter 15. *Analyzing a proposition* depends entirely on the facts and issues of a controversy, and the beliefs of debaters and audience alike must be disregarded. *Building a case,* on the other hand, is a process in which a debater selects and organizes proofs to influence the critical beliefs of a particular set of listeners or readers. Since proofs must be related to the issues of a proposition, analysis logically precedes case construction.

As suggested in Chapter 7, a proposition formulates a challenge advanced by someone who assumes the burden of proving that one idea, value, or practice should be replaced by some other idea, value, or practice.[1] There are four types of propositions: *definition, fact, value,* and *policy.*

The proposition advanced by one disputant (affirmative) clashes with the reply of another (negative) to form the *Question* that is debated. Thus the proposition and the reply represent the central claims each side respectively must make good. To establish these claims, each side must find the *issues,* those questions so vital to his cause that unless they are answered in his favor his cause as a whole must fall.

To locate the issues is the primary purpose of analyzing the proposition, a process that includes four steps: (*a*) *discovering the immediate causes of the controversy;* (*b*) *understanding the historical background;* (*c*) *defining the terms of the proposition;* and (*d*) *determining the issues.*

[1] See pp. 84–87.

## DISCOVERING THE IMMEDIATE CAUSES

To understand the function of the "immediate causes" of a controversy calls for answers to three questions: (1) *What are the immediate causes?* (2) *How does the debater discover them?* (3) *Why must he discover them as part of his analysis of a proposition?*

1. *What are immediate causes?* Perhaps two examples will illustrate what is and what is not an immediate cause of a controversy. A state legislature is debating whether to repeal a law that permits capital punishment for specified crimes. A city planning commission is holding a public hearing to consider revising the zoning status of a street that has recently become a main thoroughfare into the business district.

Before identifying the immediate causes of these controversies, consider what are *not* immediate causes. Man's first murder or society's first execution as punishment for a capital crime are not immediate causes of the debate in the state legislature. Nor are the invention of the automobile and the origin of municipal zoning provisions immediate causes for the public hearing. On the other hand, the immediate causes are not introducing a bill in the state legislature or distributing a petition requesting a public hearing. Rather, these actions are immediate causes for bringing the controversies to decisions.

In each example, the *immediate cause* is a recent or present lamentable occurrence or condition that provokes persons to question the wisdom of the present order of things out of which that occurrence or condition grew. Among other things, instances in which someone confessed a crime for which another person had been executed caused persons to question and then challenge the existing legislation. Similarly, the traffic conditions following the decision to make the street in question a main route into the business district caused home-owners to question and then challenge the present zoning status of their street.

The immediate cause, therefore, is *a problem-situation sufficiently disturbing to challenge a present fact, definition, value, or policy.*

2. *How are immediate causes discovered?* A debater is often an interested party in a dispute from the beginning, and thus has firsthand experiences that reveal the immediate causes of a controversy. Sometimes, however, he may enter after a dispute is well under way and must learn the immediate causes as a part of his early research. In Chapter 5 the debater was advised to begin his research by reading for general background and orientation. During such reading he should look specifically for immediate causes of a controversy.

The immediate causes may sometimes be perceived easily because some event brings the problem into clear focus. For example, vague and general dissatisfaction with the nation's schools was transformed sharply into definite and specific condemnations when the Soviet sputnik went into orbit. Many community school boards subsequently debated proposals to place more emphasis on mathematics and science. At other times, the immediate causes of a controversy develop slowly and almost imperceptibly over a long period of time.

3. *Why discover immediate causes?* The same two examples introduced earlier, plus a moment's reflection, show why debaters must understand what has disturbed the present order and set the stage for debate. The home-owner attending the public hearing cannot debate intelligently unless he knows why the proposal to rezone the street has been made. Those for and against the repeal of the capital punishment law may be better able to analyze dissatisfaction with the present law by discovering the significance of recent confessions and executions.

Discovering the immediate causes of a controversy is important in leading the debater to an understanding of the history, terms, and issues of the dispute.

## THE HISTORICAL BACKGROUND

When he has learned what the immediate causes of a controversy are, a debater is ready to take a second and equally important step in analyzing the proposition—to become informed about the historical background of the dispute. He must find historical materials of two kinds, those concerning (*a*) a dissatisfaction with some judgment, value, or policy, and (*b*) past and present attempts to change the allegedly unsatisfactory situation.

Suppose a senator plans to participate in a debate on a particular agriculture bill. He has determined that the immediate causes of the controversy are widespread concern about increasing surpluses of agricultural products, and a growing dissatisfaction among farmers with the present agricultural program.

The senator must find out all he can about the relevant history of problems in agriculture—the origin and development of the problem of surpluses, trends in the income of farmers as compared with other workers and in relation to the cost of living, information about the amount of tillable land, the number of farms, the sizes of farms, etc. Such information helps him discover issues related to the unsatisfactory conditions that provoked the dispute and provides evidence for proofs he will later build.

He should also know the history of such past policies and proposals as the Agricultural Adjustment Act, the emergence and development of various price support systems—rigid and flexible, high and low—the Brannan Plan, and the Soil Bank. What were the effects of past policies on problems already analyzed? What were the apparent strengths and weaknesses of proposals not put into practice? What have been the positions of national agriculture associations and other interested groups? Answers to these and similar questions will help a debater discover issues related to remedying the unsatisfactory problem-situation in agriculture, and suggest proofs he may later develop.

Research on the weaknesses of the existing judgment, value, or policy in dispute, as well as on the changes that have been proposed to improve them, must be brought up to the last possible moment. The date with which one begins his research varies from one controversy to another. A debater preparing to argue about the power of the Supreme Court will need to study more historical background than someone involved in a controversy over missile development. When one doubts how far back to carry his study of history, he will do better to get information not needed than to run the risk of missing material that will help him discover the issues of the proposition.

## DEFINITION OF TERMS

A third essential step in analyzing a proposition is to define its terms. Such definitions may help to uncover the issues of a dispute. In the proposition, "Resolved: That labor organizations should be placed under the jurisdiction of antitrust legislation," an understanding of "antitrust legislation" is a prerequisite to a discovery of the issues. In the controversy over the spot of shade, discussed in Chapter 7, understanding the phrase, "by rights," helped locate the issues. In any case, a definition of terms will serve the cause of clarity.

Certain principles of definition should be followed, and several methods are available. Such principles and methods apply also in evaluating any definitive claims, whether the term is included in the proposition or not.[2]

### PRINCIPLES OF DEFINITION

1. *Define only new or ambiguous terms.* Some words refer so clearly to a *single* person, object, institution, or event that further

[2] For an earlier discussion of definitive claims, see p. 102.

clarification is superfluous. "The United States," "World War II," the "1100 block on North Neil Street in Champaign," and similar terms require no definition. New and technical terms, however, must be defined, as must any familiar term that permits various interpretations. "Diplomatic recognition" could refer to *de jure* or to *de facto* recognition. "At 90 per cent of parity" could refer to base years 1910–1914 or to an average of the past five or ten years. What are to be included as components of "economic aid": technical assistance, loans, grants, defense support, military aid?

2. *Interpret the defined term to fit the context of the controversy.* No single "correct" definition of any complex term will be appropriate in every context. Indeed, if one simple explanation exists, probably no definition is needed. The purpose of a definition as part of the analysis of a proposition is to set forth *relevant* meanings of a term. Thus, in the proposition, "Resolved: That the United States should adopt a *policy* of free trade," the term "policy" in this context would mean "course of legislative and executive action," not "written contract," nor "method of gambling," nor "shrewdness in the management of affairs." To define terms within the context of a controversy, one must often define by phrases rather than by words. "Free trade," "diplomatic recognition," "economic aid," and "guaranteed annual wage" are more clearly defined as phrases.

3. *Use authoritative sources for definition.* Although a good dictionary presents the common usage of a term, debaters frequently want a more sophisticated definition. Such definitions may be found in general and specialized encyclopedias, in government documents, in textbooks and monographs, and in journal articles. Black's *Legal Dictionary* may be consulted for definitions of legal terms. The UN Charter may provide a serviceable definition of one of the functions of that organization. The validity of a definition from any authoritative source depends on the same criteria used to evaluate the support for a warrant in an authoritative proof.[3]

4. *Define terms objectively.* If deliberation is to be critical, terms must be defined objectively. When a debater defines such terms as "discrimination in employment," "the right to work law," "nuclear weapons," "free trade," and the "non-Communist world," his task is not to register his feelings and attitudes or those of other persons. Rather, he should try to understand what such terms mean to most persons and how they relate to the proposition he is analyzing. He confuses his purpose if his definitions employ question-begging language.

[3] See pp. 159–60.

## METHODS OF DEFINITION [4]

DEFINITION BY CLASSIFICATION. This method of definition, commonly used in ancient times and called *genus et differentia,* is still useful to debaters. The method consists of placing a term within a class of similar phenomena and showing how it differs from other species of the same class.[5] For example, "Socialism is an economic system that differs from capitalism in its . . . and from communism in its. . . ." By placing a term in its proper class ("economic system"), the debater understands the general nature of the term; by contrasting that term with its nearest neighbors, he distinguishes it from those other terms most likely to be mistaken for it.

Classification does not require rigid compartmentalization of ideas. When the species of a class differ only in degree, they may be distinguished by placing them on a *continuum*. One may classify a particular concept of democracy by constructing a scale that represents the degrees to which individuals participate in making public policy, by calling one extreme "pure democracy" and the other "pure totalitarianism," and by placing the particular concept to be defined along the scale between the two other concepts nearest in meaning. Definition by continuum is particularly useful when defining terms that refer to morals or values. By recognizing degrees of virtue, debaters can avoid the "two-valued orientation" which often falsifies facts by making an action or a person entirely good or bad, valuable or worthless, etc.

Sometimes, using the method of classification, a debater may make clear the meaning of a term by contrast, by explaining why it does not fall in a given species. Definition by *negation* is a variation of classification because the only kinds of terms used in such contrasts are species of the same class. "By 'diplomatic recognition,' we do not mean *de jure* recognition, which may imply approval of the recognized government. Rather, we mean *de facto* recognition, the simple act of showing an

[4] Some writers list numerous methods of definition. Most of the commonly included types are subsumed by the three methods in our exposition. For example, definition by continuum, by comparison-contrast, and by negation are part of classification; definition by function seems synonymous with the operational description; definition by example or by enumeration of detail could be considered under any of our three heads. Furthermore, authoritative definition is a principle rather than a method, because any definitional method may have authoritative sanction or lack it.

[5] Definition by classification is not to be confused with proof by classification, discussed on pp. 145–47. The purpose of the latter is to prove a designative or evaluative claim concerning *a member of a class* by reference to an assertion about *the class itself*. Definition by classification, on the other hand, distinguishes the meaning of *one class member* by reference to the meaning of *another member of the same class*.

awareness that a certain government is *in fact* in charge of the affairs of that state." If a continuum is implicit in the definition, the contrasting terms are usually closely proximate on the scale. "The gifted child is not one of merely more than average intelligence, nor is he necessarily a genius. Rather, he is. . . ."

DEFINITION BY NECESSARY CONDITIONS. A second method of definition consists of enumerating the conditions that must be met before a term is properly employed. An action may be termed a "breach of contract" from a legal point of view only if (*a*) a contract exists, (*b*) that contract has been violated, and (*c*) damages have resulted. A "federal world government" must meet certain minimum conditions: (*a*) each nation must surrender at least part of its sovereignty to the international organization; and (*b*) the international organization must have certain governmental powers delegated to it, for example, to tax, to maintain a police force, to regulate international commerce, to enforce international law. A breach of contract or a federal world government may have additional features, but the necessary conditions established by common or technical usage must be met to justify the labels.

DEFINITION BY OPERATIONAL DESCRIPTION. Definition by classification or by necessary conditions works well enough for static ideas. But if a debater wants to know what something "does" or how it "works," a more dynamic method is required. Some terms are defined meaningfully only by describing how they operate or function.

A proposed federal fair employment practices commission may be defined by explaining how an alleged act of discrimination would be handled through its machinery. Compulsory health insurance is defined operationally when the debater enumerates the essential features of the proposal and describes how these features would function in actual practice.

To select the best method of definition for any given term, the debater will do well to consider how that term may be most clearly, authoritatively, and objectively defined within the context of the proposition. Although no formula exists, definition by classification may best set the scope of the proposition, definition by necessary conditions may best establish criteria, and definition by operational description may best define the proposal embodied in the proposition.

## DETERMINING THE ISSUES

When a debater has discovered the immediate causes of a controversy, learned its historical background, and defined its ambiguous terms, he is ready to begin the most important phase of his analysis of a proposition: He must locate the issues. His task is to "locate" rather than "invent" them, because they inhere in the proposition itself and are there to be found.[6]

Unless a debater finds the actual issues and builds his entire discourse around them, he cannot hope to gain a decision from a critical observer. If the claim of a proof does not directly or indirectly help establish a debater's stand on one of the issues, the proof is irrelevant, no matter how strong.

How, then, does one determine the issues of any controversy? How to locate issues depends on whether one is analyzing a proposition of definition, fact, value, or policy. But although the method for finding issues in each type of proposition should be considered separately, the debater must understand from the outset an instructive interrelationship that exists among the kinds of issues appropriate for each type of proposition.

The structure of issues becomes increasingly complex as one moves from a study of propositions of definition to those of fact or value, and is most complex of all in propositions of policy. The issues in a proposition of definition are purely *definitive*. In propositions of fact or value, the issues may be *definitive* and *designative*. Propositions of policy yield a combination of *definitive, designative,* and *evaluative* issues.[7]

For example, before 1954 one of the leading questions in race relations considered the validity of the doctrine that separate but equal educational facilities should be provided for Negro and white students. The relationship of questions of definition, fact, and value in four kinds of propositions concerning the separate but equal doctrine may be illustrated in the chart below:

| *Proposition* | *Question* | *Issues* |
|---|---|---|
| Definition | What does "equal" in the separate but equal doctrine mean? | (1) Does "equal" mean condition *a* (definitive)?<br>(2) Does "equal" mean condition *b* (definitive)?<br>(3) Does "equal" mean condition *n* (definitive)? |
| Fact | Are separate facilities actually equal? | (1) What does "equal" in the separate but equal doctrine mean (definitive)? |

---

[6] For a more complete discussion of the nature of issues, see pp. 88–92.
[7] Our classification of propositions and issues corresponds to our earlier classification of claims. For an explanation of definitive, designative, and evaluative claims, see p. 102.

| Proposition | Question | Issues |
|---|---|---|
| Fact | | (2) Do the facilities provided for each race meet the conditions defined as part of the concept of equality (designative)? |
| Value | Is the separate but equal doctrine harmful? | (1) What do we mean by "separate but equal" (definitive)?<br>(2) By what criteria shall we define "harmful" (definitive)?<br>(3) Does the doctrine meet these criteria (designative)? |
| Policy | Should the separate but equal doctrine be made illegal? | (1) Is the doctrine harmful enough to justify the proposal (evaluative)?<br>(2) Can the doctrine be made illegal (designative)?<br>(3) Can we adopt the proposal without incurring harmful effects (evaluative)? |

All of the relationships illustrated in the above chart may not be present in every controversy. However, a debater should understand that any dispute may yield several specific propositions concerning a definition, a fact, a value, or a policy, and that analyzing one proposition may help him analyze a more complex proposition in the same subject-matter area. For example, the analysis of a proposition of fact may be a part of the analysis of some proposition of value or policy in the same problem area.

ISSUES IN A PROPOSITION OF DEFINITION

Although definitive *issues* are often vital in deciding propositions of fact, value, or policy, not often is a *proposition* of definition a matter of public controversy; that is, not often is the meaning of a term the ultimate concern in a debate.

On the other hand, propositions of definition are debated, as several examples show: "Resolved: That 'equal,' in the separate but equal doctrine, means equality in the psychological status of students as well as in the physical facilities of schools." "Resolved: That 'diplomatic recognition' need not connote a moral approval of the recognized government."

Although no pat formula exists for discovering issues in a proposition of definition, two suggestions may prove helpful. First, choosing an appropriate method of definition may reveal the issues. For example, in debating the proposition that the study of public speaking may be called a science, the issues may be located by an operational description of the study of public speaking or by enumerating the conditions a study must meet to justify the label of "science."

Second, when authoritative sources are consulted, the credibility of any source may become an issue. For example, the authoritativeness of any person who has interpreted the constitution or by-laws of an organization is an issue in a dispute over the validity of that interpretation.

## ISSUES IN A PROPOSITION OF FACT

Whereas propositions of definition are language-bound and merely inquire whether certain meanings are appropriately assigned to certain terms, propositions of fact are related to the external world and inquire whether something was, is, or will be "so." More specifically, propositions of fact designate the state of being of some person, idea, or institution, or assert the occurrence of some past, present, or future event. In addition, propositions of fact are limited to those debatable questions that require inferences. Whether or not an authority holds a certain position or title is not a matter for argument; it is not an *inferential* but an *informative* question.[8]

Propositions of fact are frequently debated. "Resolved: That Smith is medically insane." "Resolved: That Jones committed first-degree murder." "Resolved: That federal aid to the public schools will lead to federal control." "Resolved: That our direct foreign aid program antagonizes a substantial number of recipient nations." These represent only a small sample of the propositions concerned with past, present, or future events or states of being.

Propositions of fact may contain two kinds of issues, *definitive* and *designative*. An issue could grow out of a dispute over the meaning of one of the terms of the proposition. Whether "control" means auditing procedures or educational policy-making may vitally affect the decision to accept or reject the proposition that federal aid leads to federal control. Whether "antagonized" means complaints by government officials of recipient nations or actions that oppose U.S. foreign policy may vitally affect the decision to accept or reject the proposition of fact concerning foreign aid.

Although any disputed term may be an issue, it may or may not become a *contested* issue in an actual debate. The prosecuting attorney may define "first-degree murder" or "medically insane" by legal prece-

---

[8] Whether or not the authority's statement should be believed is debatable. Indeed, information about a position or title supports the warrant that the authority's statement is credible. For a further discussion of the distinction between inferential and informative questions, see pp. 14–15.

dents so well established that the defense attorney will not contest the definition. Even so, the prosecutor must define such terms initially to make out a *prima facie* case. And when legal precedent has not settled the meaning of a legal term, the definitive issue that results may be hotly contested.

When analyzing a proposition of fact, therefore, the debater must find those issues that inhere in the definition of disputed terms. He must also discover the designative issues implicit in the facts of the case.

The discovery of these issues is difficult. Like the issues of a proposition of definition, they are not found in any easy, formulary fashion. The best method, as illustrated in Chapter 7, is to study carefully the background of the controversy, particularly the immediate causes and the history. By making an inventory of data related to the controversy, by discovering what "facts" are disputed, and by deciding which among the disputed "facts" are *vital* to a decision on the proposition, the debater can locate the issues.

In the hypothetical question concerning to whom the spot of shade, by rights, belonged, such a method of study yielded two designative issues: (*a*) Did Mr. N promise Mr. A the shade in the event of A's illness? (*b*) Is A now actually ill?

## ISSUES IN A PROPOSITION OF VALUE

In a proposition of value, debaters assign opposing evaluations to a person, object, event, or idea. "Resolved: That Candidate X is better than his opponent." "Resolved: That the present administration has been beneficial to farmers." "Resolved: That unpredictable medical costs are harmful enough to require a new system of health insurance." "Resolved: That federal controls are harmful enough to justify rejecting federal aid to education." The purpose of these propositions of value is to evaluate candidates, administrations, medical costs, and federal controls.

Every proposition of value includes at least one term that implies a value dimension, such terms as "better," "beneficial," "harmful," "good," "desirable," "disadvantageous," and "detrimental." Unless such terms are defined, argument becomes *de gustibus non est disputandum* ("about matters of taste there is no disputing"). When someone asserts that Candidate X is "better" than Y, and someone else claims with equal vehemence that Candidate Y is "better" than X, the result is uncritical deliberation about an undebatable situation, until the term "better" is defined.

Value terms may be defined by formulating the conditions sufficient to justify the use of the term in the context of the controversy. Thus, a "better" candidate for the U.S. Senate might be defined as one superior to his opponent in (*a*) experience, (*b*) ability to represent his state, and (*c*) positions on current controversies. An evaluation of the two candidates can be debated critically if proofs are presented to establish that one candidate meets these three criteria better than the other.[9]

A definition of a value term may merely serve as a clarification preliminary to the discovery of the issues in a proposition of value, or such a definition may itself constitute an issue.

If an incumbent senator argues that "better" candidate means the one who is more experienced, his opponent may be forced to raise a definitive issue by arguing that other values are included in the concept of "better" candidate. If a debater argues that a "harmful" health insurance system means one that fails to permit every American family to budget every medical expense, his opponent will have to argue that such a definition is unwarranted. Otherwise, in both instances, terms have been defined so that the subsequent designative issue may well be incontestable.

Defining value terms, then, transfers the ground for decision from vague emotional abstractions to explicit designative questions that can be answered by reference to substantive and authoritative proofs.

The debater's second task is to discover the designative issues that follow a definition of the value term. In a debate on any proposition of value, the designative issues are whether the subject of the evaluation meets the criteria defined. If, for example, "beneficial to farmers" means higher and more stable incomes, the designative issue is: Has the present administration provided such values?

Designative issues in a proposition of value take two forms. In some propositions, satisfying each criterion, *as considered individually,* becomes a separate issue. If three criteria are involved, three issues result. For example, if one defines "decisive leadership" as one of the *necessary* conditions of Presidential greatness, then whether a President provided decisive leadership is a designative issue in analyzing the proposition that he was a great President. No matter how well a person or an object meets other criteria, a failure to satisfy a *necessary* standard makes mandatory a rejection of the proposition of value.

In other propositions, the single designative issue is how well the subject for evaluation meets *a group of standards considered jointly.* In such propositions, no single criterion is a necessary one. For example, a debater may fail in part of his task of proving that Candidate X is better than Y in experience, in deliberative ability, and in positions on current

---

[9] Our analysis of propositions of value has been stimulated by Paul Edwards' *Logic of Moral Discourse* (Glencoe, Ill.: Free Press, 1954). See especially pp. 105–20.

controversies, and still, by a joint consideration of all three standards, establish that X is the better candidate. One frequently must make this kind of evaluation, whether personally or as a member of a decision-making group.

## ISSUES IN A PROPOSITION OF POLICY

Whereas propositions of value merely appraise, propositions of policy call for action. The affirmative advocates and the negative opposes some specific change in policy. Some action verb combined with the auxiliary "should" is invariably present. A federal fair employment practices commission should be enacted, direct economic aid should be discontinued, a city's water supply should be fluoridated—these are the kinds of propositions in which debaters try to translate belief into action.

Propositions of policy are more complex than those of definition, fact, or value, for a critical decision to take an action or change a policy is determined by a large number of *intermediate claims* involving questions of definition, fact, and value.

THE STOCK ISSUES ANALYSIS. A generalized method for discovering intermediate claims systematically is called the stock issues analysis. This method has two important advantages: First, because its framework represents a complete system, the debater who employs it properly is assured an *exhaustive* analysis of a proposition of policy. Second, because the system applies to all propositions of policy, an ability to make a stock issues analysis is cumulative. A debater who has made six such analyses is better able to make a seventh.

But a stock issues analysis is only a *generalized* method. The ultimate task of a debater is to discover the issues of a *particular* proposition. To do so, he must recognize that some of the stock issues or some of their components do not yield an actual issue in a specific controversy, whereas other stock issues may yield several. He must also recognize that he must be thoroughly informed about the background of the dispute. The function of the stock issues analysis, *to extract the actual issues of a controversy,* must be kept clearly in mind as one studies the method and applies it to particular propositions of policy.

Although the stock issues analysis has been used by many debaters over a long period of time, the method is not altogether standardized. What follows in this chapter is an attempt to combine the best features of variations from many writers and debaters.[10]

We recognize three stock issues. (1) *Is there a need for a fundamen-*

[10] See Lee S. Hultzén, "Status in Deliberative Analysis," in *The Rhetorical Idiom*, ed. D. C. Bryant (Ithaca, N.Y.: Cornell University Press, 1958), pp. 97–123. Although our interpretation differs at several points from his, our treatment borrows from his analysis.

tal change of policy? (2) *Will the proposal remedy the problems inherent in the present policy?* (3) *Can the remedy be applied without serious disadvantages?* These stock issues and their components will help the debater discover the actual issues in a proposition of policy.

1. *Is there a need for a fundamental change of policy?* This question is the first stock issue raised in a proposition of policy. The issue usually occurs first chronologically, since, as indicated earlier in this chapter, lamentable situations constitute the immediate causes of a controversy. The issue is also first in importance because the second issue is controlled by the first. We cannot ask if unresolved problems are remediable until we know they exist.

Whether a fundamental change of policy is needed depends on four subissues: (*a*) *Do serious problems actually exist?* (*b*) *Do such problems result in enough harm to require a change of policy?* (*c*) *Is the present policy to blame for the alleged problems?* (*d*) *Is any policy short of the one proposed inherently incapable of mitigating the alleged problems?* Each of these subissues must be further analyzed and illustrated.

*a. Do serious problems actually exist?* Because of inertia, men do not ordinarily even deliberate making a policy change unless one or more serious problems are alleged. The debater must, therefore, prove *designatively* that the alleged problems actually exist.

In a debate on whether the federal government should adopt a fair employment practices law, the affirmative must first prove that discrimination in employment practices exists. In the proposition that U.S. economic aid be restricted to loans and technical assistance, the affirmative may allege the existence of such problems as antipathy toward the program by the uncommitted nations of Southeast Asia, waste and inefficiency of the aid program, and the high cost of the program.

In most propositions, however, the question is not merely whether the problem exists. Rather, the issue is whether the problem is sufficiently *extensive* to warrant any real concern. In the two examples above, debaters are likely to argue about the *extent* of discrimination, antipathy, waste, and cost.

*b. Do such problems result in enough harm to require a change of policy?* The mere existence of an extensive problem-situation does not warrant a policy change. The affirmative must also prove *evaluatively* that the alleged problems result in enough harm to justify a change of policy.

Given existing values, is extensive discrimination in employment practices sufficiently harmful to warrant a new proposal? Given existing values, is enough harm caused by the antipathy of recipient nations, the waste and inefficiency, and the cost of the program to justify a new foreign aid policy?

When more than one problem is alleged, as in the foreign aid example, the first stock issue yields actual issues in one of two ways. First, the existence and harmfulness of *each problem considered separately* may be at issue. The harmfulness of the antipathies of the uncommitted nations of Southeast Asia toward the aid program, apart from considerations of inefficiency or cost, may warrant a new program.

Second, in some propositions, the existence and harmfulness of *all alleged problems considered together* may be the issue. Here, only by proving that each problem exists and produces harm can the affirmative justify a change. Whether by alleging one or many problems, however, the affirmative must establish that enough harm is caused to demand a policy change.

  c. *Is the present policy to blame for the alleged problems?* To determine if the present policy is to blame, one inquires by the method of "agreement" whether the present policy is causally related to the existence or harmfulness of a problem—for example, discrimination in employment—and by the method of "differences" whether the absence of a federal law can be held primarily accountable for the problem of discrimination.[11] If the present policy is not to blame for the problem, that problem is not *inherent* in the present policy, and accordingly there is no need to change that policy.

Negative debaters frequently contest this issue by showing that other causes have contributed to the problem. The settlement of the issue, then, is a matter of degree: which is *primarily* responsible for the deficiencies: the existing policy or a set of other causes?

  d. *Is any policy short of the one proposed inherently incapable of mitigating the alleged problems?* That serious problems require some sort of action does not constitute a need to make a *fundamental* change of policy. Such a claim establishes only a need to do *something*. To justify the kind of change called for in the proposition, an affirmative debater must show that only this kind of *fundamental* change can reduce the seriousness of the problem.

The focal point of this issue depends on the position taken by the negative. Will trends already at work toward less discrimination in employment ultimately solve the problem? Can alteration of existing local ordinances and state laws solve the problem? Can new legislation on the local or state level solve the problem? If so, the fundamental change of a federal law is not necessary. Can reforms in administration of the present economic aid program remove the antipathy, inefficiency, and cost? If so, the fundamentally different program proposed is not

[11] See Mill's first two canons, as stated on p. 130.

needed.

In short, the issue is whether the problems are inherent in the present order, so that trends or alterations are inadequate solutions.

2. *Will the proposal remedy the problems inherent in the present policy?* One may agree that serious problems exist, cause harm, and are inherent in the present policy, and yet reject the proposition because it does not supply a satisfactory remedy. Thus, the second stock issue inquires if the affirmative proposal can remedy the alleged problems.

The affirmative usually presents a specific version of its proposal by indicating what features are to be included. The presentation of this version, customarily called the "plan," is a preliminary step in analyzing the "remedy" issue but is not itself an issue. The exposition of the plan is often an extension of the definition of the term in the proposition that points to a remedy. As indicated earlier in this chapter, a good way to define such terms as "fair employment practices law," "diplomatic recognition," or "compulsory health insurance" is to present an operational description ("plan") of such programs.

Whether the proposal would adequately remedy alleged problems depends on two subissues: (*a*) *Can the remedy be put into effect?* (*b*) *Will the remedy create a workable system to replace the allegedly unworkable one?*

a. *Can the remedy be put into effect?* A negative answer to the question always justifies rejecting the proposition. That which cannot be put into effect and enforced obviously will produce no adequate remedy for any problem. Thus, whether a remedy *could* be undertaken helps one decide critically whether it *should* be adopted.

Whether the remedy *would* be adopted, on the other hand, is irrelevant. The popularity of a proposal may point indirectly to signs of its probable effectiveness, but it does not function directly as proof. If a proposal requires the active support of important or numerous persons, however, the likelihood of such support is relevant in deciding whether the remedy can be put into effect. The co-operation of certain governments may be a necessary condition for developing a federal world government or implementing a disarmament proposal. One might critically reject a highly unpopular national bill that could not be enforced, for such a "remedy" could not be put into effect.

In short, although sufficient popular approval to enact a proposal is not vital to prove its workability, enough respect for it to make it enforceable becomes a necessary prerequisite. No unenforced proposal will remedy any problem.

b. *Will the remedy create a workable system to replace the allegedly unworkable one?* A remedy need not remove every trace of a problem, but the *seriousness* of the problem-situation must be removed. A federal fair employment practices law is an adequate remedy if it renders discrimination in employment no longer a seriously harmful problem. Thus, the issue may be formulated: Will the new law prevent most instances of discrimination by punishing those who violate the law?

To determine whether alleged problems can be remedied by restricting U.S. economic aid to loans and technical assistance, a debater must apply the remedy to each problem. Will restricting aid to loans and technical assistance deal adequately with, first, the antipathy of Southeast Asian countries, second, the waste and inefficiency of the program, and third, its high cost?

3. *Can the remedy be applied without serious disadvantages?* Solving significant problems, however, is not sufficient justification for adopting a policy. Reasonable men do not murder their enemies even when assured that such action will remedy a serious problem. They inquire if there are results to such actions more disadvantageous than the ills they hope to cure.

The discovery of serious disadvantages is not determined by the nature of the problems that seem to require that policy. Thus, the third stock issue, unlike the second, is not controlled by the first. Yet the "serious disadvantage" issue is not totally unrelated to the "need" issue. For the negative debater must do more than prove disadvantageous results of a proposal; he must prove that such results are *more seriously harmful* than the present problems alleged by his opponent. Although war entails evils, an invasion of our shores might create a problem serious enough to justify warfare, even with its disadvantages.

The "serious disadvantage" issue is also related to the proposed remedy. Whether a disarmament proposal endangers U.S. security, and to what degree, depends on what kind of disarmament is advocated.

There are two subissues in the "serious disadvantage" stock issue. (*a*) *Can the proposal be put into effect without incurring disadvantageous results?* (*b*) *Do such results fail to justify the rejection of the proposition?*

These components of the "serious disadvantage" issue function similarly to those in the "need" issue. A *designative* component asks if a serious disadvantage *will occur* if the remedy is adopted; and an *evaluative* component inquires whether the disadvantage is *harmful enough* to justify rejecting the remedy—does the harm entailed outweigh the values gained?

*a. Can the proposal be put into effect without incurring disadvantageous effects?* The negative debater must first prove that such effects will probably occur if the proposition is adopted. If he is to argue effectively that federal controls justify rejecting federal aid to the schools, he must prove that federal aid entails federal controls. To establish that disadvantages warrant rejecting a free trade policy, a negative debater must prove the probable occurrence of such disadvantages as (1) the destruction of infant industries, (2) an injurious competitive situation for marginal industries, and (3) a threat to national security.

*b. Do such results fail to justify the rejection of the proposition?* To prove that federal aid entails federal controls does not by itself provide sufficient reason for rejecting the proposition. A debater must also establish a claim that federal controls will seriously restrict local freedoms or interfere with other values.

When a group of disadvantages are designated, the analysis may follow the same two courses available in the "need" issue. Either a negative debater could argue that three disadvantages *conjunctively* justify rejecting the remedy—in which case its position on the occurrence and cumulative harmfulness of *all three* disadvantages must be maintained. Or he could contend that each disadvantage *by itself* justifies rejecting the proposition—in which case each disadvantage is an issue, and only the occurrence and harmfulness of that disadvantage must be upheld.

Thus, if all three disadvantages of free trade are required to prove enough harm to warrant rejecting the proposition, then the negative must prove the occurrence and seriousness of all three allegations, to win the issue. If, on the other hand, the threat to national security by itself is more harmful than the problems presumably remedied by free trade, by proving the existence and seriousness of such a threat the negative can win an issue and deserve the critical decision in the debate. Regardless of the number of disadvantages alleged, *the negative aims to establish that at least one of them justifies rejecting the proposition.*

## THE INTRODUCTION TO THE BRIEF

In Chapter 15, the task of building a debate case will be discussed. The debater's first step in this process is to make a complete inventory of his proofs and to assemble them systematically. Such an inventory of argument and evidence is called, ironically, a *brief*.

The introduction to a brief expresses in writing the analysis of the proposition. The introduction precedes the body of a brief just as the analysis of a proposition precedes the formulation of a case. Whereas the body of the brief is argumentative, the introduction is expository.

ANALYZING THE PROPOSITION 229

A generalized outline of an introduction to a brief should summarize the steps in analyzing a proposition.[12]

OUTLINE OF AN INTRODUCTION TO THE BRIEF

I. What are the immediate causes of the controversy?
II. What is the historical background of the dispute?
   A. What is the history of the problem?
   B. What is the history of past and present attempts to alter the problem-situation?
III. How may the terms of the proposition be defined?
IV. What are the issues of the proposition (of definition)?
   A. Does the method of definition locate the issues?
   B. Does the source of the definition locate the issues?
IV'. What are the issues of the proposition (of fact)?
   A. Are there any disputes over the meaning of a term?
   B. What are the disputed facts vital to the proposition?
IV''. What are the issues of the proposition (of value)?
   A. Do the value terms of the proposition yield any definitive issues?
   B. Does the subject of the evaluation meet the criteria included in the definition of the value term?
IV'''. What are the issues of the proposition (of policy)?[13]
   A. Is there a need for a fundamental change of policy?
     1. Do serious problems actually exist?
       a. Does problem *a* exist?
       b. Does problem *b* exist?
       c. Does problem *n* exist?
     2. Do such problems result in enough harm to require a change of policy?
       a. Is problem *a* harmful enough?
       b. Is problem *b* harmful enough?
       c. Is problem *n* harmful enough?
       d. Do problems *a* through *n* conjunctively cause enough harm?
     3. Is the present policy to blame for the alleged problems?
       a. Is it to blame for problem *a?*
       b. Is it to blame for problem *b?*
       c. Is it to blame for problem *n?*
     4. Is any policy short of the one proposed inherently incapable of mitigating the alleged problems?
       a. Can the problems be mitigated by foreseeable changes or trends of circumstances?
       b. Can the problems be mitigated by minor alterations of the present policy?

[12] For a sample introduction to a brief of a specific proposition, see the brief in Appendix C.
[13] In a proposition of policy, issues are usually phrased in question form so that the affirmative must answer "yes" and the negative "no."

c. Can the problems be mitigated by some policy change short of the one proposed?
B. Will the proposal remedy the problems inherent in the present policy?
  1. Can the remedy be put into effect?
     a. Could the proposal be undertaken?
     b. Would the policy be adequately enforced?
  2. Will the remedy create a workable system to replace the allegedly unworkable one?
     a. Will the remedy ameliorate problem *a?*
     b. Will the remedy ameliorate problem *b?*
     c. Will the remedy ameliorate problem *n?*
C. Can the remedy be applied without serious disadvantages?
  1. Can the proposal be put into effect without incurring disadvantageous results?
     a. Can it be effected without disadvantage *a?*
     b. Can it be effected without disadvantage *b?*
     c. Can it be effected without disadvantage *n?*
  2. Do such results fail to justify the rejection of the proposition?
     a. Does disadvantage *a* result in too little harm to justify rejecting the proposition?
     b. Does disadvantage *b* result in too little harm to justify rejecting the proposition?
     c. Does disadvantage *n* result in too little harm to justify rejecting the proposition?
     d. Do disadvantages *a* through *n* conjunctively cause too little harm to justify rejecting the proposition?

## QUESTIONS

A. To Check Your Comprehension and Memory
  1. What are the four types of propositions?
  2. What are the immediate causes of a controversy?
  3. Why must a debater discover the immediate causes of a controversy?
  4. How does a debater discover the immediate causes?
  5. What two kinds of historical materials must a debater find in analyzing a proposition?
  6. What kinds of terms should be defined?
  7. Why should terms be defined within the context of a controversy?
  8. How is the validity of authoritative definitions determined?
  9. Why should terms be defined objectively?
  10. What is definition by classification? by continuum? by negation? by necessary conditions? by operational description?
  11. Why must debaters determine the issues?
  12. What are the relationships among questions of definition, fact, and

value in the four kinds of propositions?

13. What are two suggestions for discovering the issues in a proposition of definition?

14. What are propositions of fact?

15. What two kinds of issues may be contained in a proposition of fact?

16. How are designative issues determined in a proposition of fact?

17. What is a proposition of value?

18. What is a value term?

19. How does a definitive issue develop in a proposition of value?

20. What questions do designative issues answer in a proposition of value?

21. If no criterion of a value term is mandatory, what is the single designative issue of a proposition of value?

22. What is a proposition of policy?

23. What are the values and limitations of the stock issues method of analyzing a proposition of policy?

24. What are the three stock issues?

25. What must the affirmative prove to establish a need for a fundamental change of policy?

26. In what ways does the analysis of the first stock issue differ when more than one problem is encountered?

27. What are the two subissues of the second stock issue?

28. What is the affirmative "plan"?

29. Which of the other two stock issues is controlled by the "need" issue?

30. How is the "serious disadvantage" issue related to the "need" issue? to the "remedy" issue?

31. What are the two subissues of the third stock issue?

32. How many seriously harmful disadvantages must the negative establish to justify rejecting the proposition?

33. What is a brief?

34. What is included in an introduction to a brief?

*B. For Class Discussion*

1. Why are the motives and emotions of debaters and judges not relevant in analyzing a proposition?

2. In what ways does the analysis of the proposition suggested in this chapter meet the requirement that debating be fact-centered?

3. Make a list of propositions of policy for which the stock issues analysis seems only partly suitable. Justify your inclusion of each proposition.

# EXERCISES

*A. Written Exercises*

1. Prepare an introduction to a brief on a proposition you are preparing to debate in class; include all four steps of analysis discussed in this chapter. A sample introduction to a brief appears in Appendix C.

2. Find the issues in the proposition of one of the debates presented in the Appendix. Which issues are contested in the debate?

*B. Oral Exercise*

Present a five-minute speech in which you analyze the issues of a controversy you are preparing to debate, and defend your claim that each is an issue.

## SUGGESTIONS FOR FURTHER READING

Paul Edwards, *The Logic of Moral Discourse* (Glencoe, Ill.: Free Press, 1954). Drawing from recent writing in logic and ethics, Edwards tries to answer three questions: (1) What is the meaning of moral judgments? (2) What kind of disagreement is moral disagreement? (3) Are moral arguments whose premises do not include any moral judgment ever valid?

Lee S. Hultzén, "Status in Deliberative Analysis," in *The Rhetorical Idiom*, ed. D. C. Bryant (Ithaca, New York: Cornell University Press, 1958), pp. 97–123. The author explains the classical analysis of *status* in legal speaking, constructs a framework for an analysis of *status* in policy-making speeches, and discusses the validity and utility of the framework.

Warren C. Shaw, *The Art of Debate* (Boston: Allyn and Bacon, 1922). Read Chapter 3, "Finding the Issues." Shaw defines the issues, states the requirements for the issues, and presents and illustrates a detailed process for finding the issues.

## Chapter 15
# BUILDING THE CASE

> *In every act alike of perception, understanding, belief, conviction, doing, performing, there are present in the propositions involved the two factors of (a) logical relevance and (b) "emotional" congruity.* CHARLES H. WOOLBERT

As EXPLAINED earlier, whereas propositions are analyzed independently of anyone's beliefs, *cases* are designed to influence belief. Furthermore, since cases are developed to alter the beliefs of a particular group of readers or listeners, every debate on the same proposition presented to a different set of decision-makers demands a different case.

Proposition analysis also differs from case construction in the degree to which debaters may exercise a freedom of choice. Analyzing a proposition is a process of *discovering* what is inherent in the proposition itself. Building a case, on the other hand, subject to certain restrictions, is a process of *selecting* whatever proofs one wants to include.

A debate case may be defined, therefore, as *a structure of proofs a debater selects to substantiate his claims on the issues of a controversy for the purpose of influencing the beliefs of a particular audience.*

Because a critical decision is based on the relative strength of two opposing cases, building a case is obviously a significant part of a debater's preparation. The strength of a case is determined by two criteria: (a) reasoning in a valid way from accurate evidence to claims relevant to the issues; and (b) identifying with the beliefs and values of those who decide the fate of the proposition.

These two principles are not separable except for purposes of analysis. A case, no matter how "logical," is not *reasonable* to the judges unless its claims are warranted by their system of values. And a case is not *believable,* no matter how pleasing, unless the best evidence and inferences are employed by the debater and understood by the judges.

The process of constructing a strong debate case includes two principal phases: (a) *assembling the proofs that may be advanced reason-*

ably; and (b) *selecting those proofs that will be most convincing to the critical reader or listener.*

The first step is carried out in essentially the same manner for those who favor and those who oppose the proposition. The second step is taken somewhat differently by affirmative and negative debaters.

## ASSEMBLING THE PROOFS

The necessary ingredient for a strong case is a substantial number of proofs. After excluding those he no longer considers relevant to the issues he has discovered, the debater should classify the remaining proofs under a comprehensive set of categories.

The instrument for organizing available proofs in a systematic way is the *brief, an inventory of relevant contentions supported by evidence.*

### THE STRUCTURE OF A BRIEF

Among the materials included in an introduction to a brief, the enumeration of issues is particularly significant because its structure becomes the organizational pattern for the body of the brief.

If a debater has correctly determined the issues and subissues of a controversy, the formulation of the structure of contentions in the body of the brief is purely a linguistic problem. Each of the questions in the pattern of issues becomes a declarative statement in the brief. "Is Mr. A ill?" becomes in the affirmative brief, "Mr. A is ill," and in the negative brief, "Mr. A is not ill." "Is there a need for compulsory health insurance?" becomes in the affirmative brief, "There is a need for compulsory health insurance," and in the negative brief, "There is no need for compulsory health insurance." [1]

### PARALLEL AND SERIES CIRCUITS

When a debater has drawn up the structure of claims based on his analysis of issues, his next step is to complete the substructure of proofs supporting these claims. Such proofs may be organized, following an analogy to electricity, in one of two ways: Electrical devices may be wired in either a *series* circuit, being connected by a single wire, so the current passes through each to reach the next one; or they may be wired in a *parallel* circuit, so the current goes back and forth from a main line to each unit.

A debater may pattern his claims accordingly. He may prove a claim

[1] See the relationship between the analysis of issues and the structure of contentions in our sample brief in Appendix C (pp. 393–412).

BUILDING THE CASE 235

by a *series* of connecting and interdependent proofs, in which the claim of the one becomes the evidence for the next.² Or he may establish a claim by a group of *parallel* and independent proofs, each of which closes the circuit and proves the same claim.³

The following diagrams illustrate the proof patterns of each circuit:

SERIES CIRCUIT

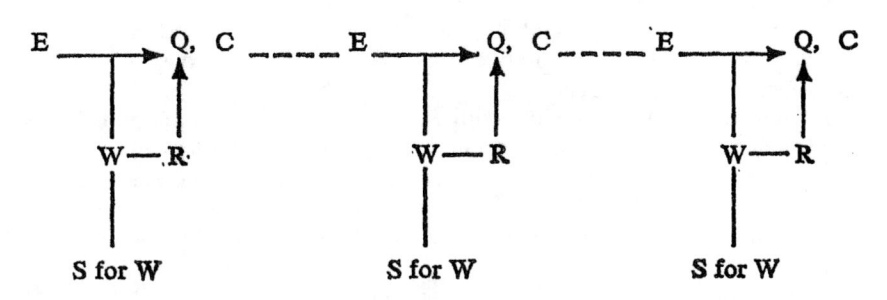

```
E ──→ Q, C ----- E ──→ Q, C ----- E ──→ Q, C
    ↑                 ↑                 ↑
    │                 │                 │
  W─R·              W─R               W─R
    │                 │                 │
  S for W           S for W           S for W
```

PARALLEL CIRCUIT

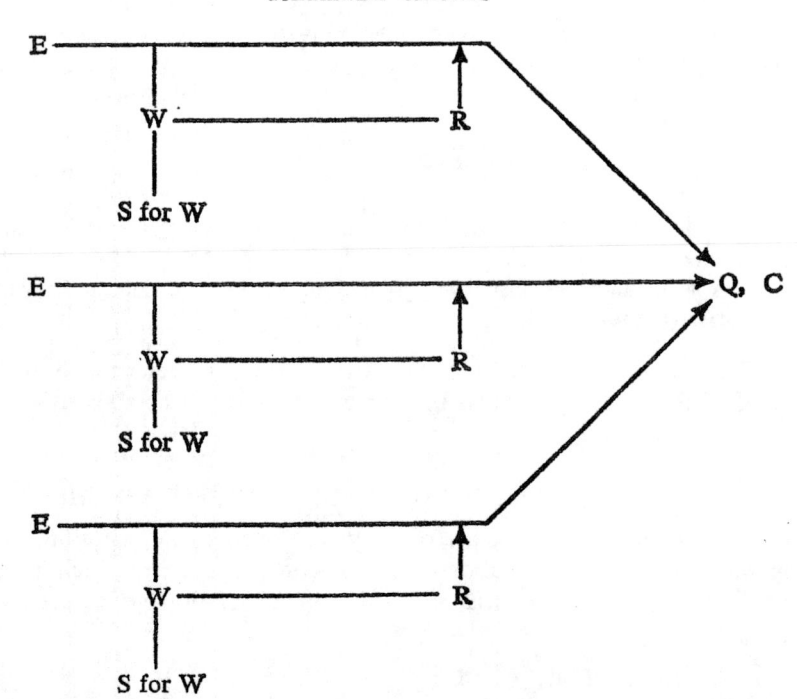

```
E ───────┐
         │        ↑
         W────────R
         │
       S for W

E ───────┐
         │        ↑                    Q, C
         W────────R
         │
       S for W

E ───────┐
         │        ↑
         W────────R
         │
       S for W
```

² The term in classical logic and rhetoric for such a proof circuit is the *sorites*.
³ George Campbell, eighteenth-century rhetorician, called this pattern a "bundle of independent proofs."

In the *series* proof circuit, the debater develops a chain of argument in which each proof is necessary to the establishment of the series. To support the contention that a policy of free trade would interfere with the U.S. national security, the following series proof circuit could be advanced:

1. If a war breaks out, the U.S. needs product A in great quantities to maintain its security.
2. Since present supplies of A would probably be cut off during a war, the only way to secure the product rapidly is to convert Industry X to the manufacture of this product.
3. Industry X can be rapidly converted to making A only if the industry remains at full productive efficiency in making its present product, B.
4. Industry X can remain at full productive efficiency in making B only if it is protected by the present tariff against foreign competitors.
5. Industry X can be protected by such a tariff by rejecting the policy of free trade.
6. Therefore, the policy of free trade interferes with the maintenance of U.S. national security.

In a *parallel* proof circuit, on the other hand, each of several proofs independently bears upon the same claim. That the price of steel products will go up may be proved by a number of parallel arguments:

1. The price of steel has gone up (cause–effect).
2. Economist X says that the price of steel products will go up (authoritative).
3. Other comparable products have increased in price under similar circumstances (parallel case).
4. A wage increase has been granted to workers of the steel products industries (cause–effect).

The relative strength of each parallel proof is determined without reference to other proofs in the circuit designed to establish the same claim.

## PUTTING PROOF CIRCUITS IN THE BRIEF

When main contentions are directly supported by one or more proofs in *parallel* circuit, no elaborate substructure is needed. Each item of evidence appears in the brief in a subordinate relationship to the claim:

I. Claim, because
   A. Evidence (proof 1), and
   B. Evidence (proof 2), and
   C. Evidence (proof 3), etc.

When a *series* of proofs is placed in a brief, each superior and its subordinate statements also represent an evidence–claim relationship. The evidence that Nurse X reports that Mr. A has a temperature of 103 degrees supports the claim that he has a fever. This claim then functions as evidence that Mr. A is ill. In turn, Mr. A's illness supports the claim that he is entitled to the spot of shade:

*Resolved:* That Mr. A by rights is entitled to the spot of shade, because
I. Mr. A is ill, because
   A. Mr. A has a fever, because
      1. Nurse X reports that Mr. A has a temperature of 103 degrees.

Although a chain of proofs sometimes has a large number of links, it must ultimately be based on an evidential statement that will be accepted without further proof.[4] Such evidence and its source must be indicated clearly and completely in the brief. Information concerning the source may be entered in parentheses and placed at the conclusion of the evidence, or the bibliographical data may be placed in the left margin of the brief.[5]

Of the six elements of proof, only evidence and claims are characteristically included in a brief. The other elements, particularly the warrant, ought to be implied strongly. An item of evidence supports a claim and thus should be placed subordinately to it *only* if one of the principles of reasoning discussed in Chapters 10 and 11 adequately warrants the evidence–claim inference.

To illustrate, consider the following excerpts from a hypothetical brief: [6]

The federal government should adopt a program of compulsory health insurance for all citizens, because
I. There is a need to prevent needless death and suffering which results when people must neglect their health by making medical decisions on economic grounds, because
   A. Neglect of health causes needless death and suffering, because
      1. The Conference on the General Welfare reported in 1959, "Due to inadequate medical care over a third of a million lives are needlessly lost each year."
   B. The neglect of health is caused primarily because many persons are led to make medical decisions on economic grounds, because

[4] Some writers limit "evidence" to such statements; we view "evidence" more broadly (see pp. 99–101).
[5] The sample brief in Appendix C illustrates the former method.
[6] Materials for this illustration are taken from Mr. Gene Clements' first affirmative constructive speech in the sample debate in Appendix A. See pp. 351–54.

1. Many persons delay or forego medical care because they cannot afford to pay medical bills, and
2. Others delay or forego care because they are uncertain as to what the ultimate cost will be, and
3. Still others delay or forego care because they may not feel sick.

C. Making medical decisions on economic grounds is inherent in the present system of paying medical bills.

Note that the items in the brief, as in any outline, are subordinate to prior items under which they are indented. Thus, "I" is subordinate to the proposition; "A," "B," and "C" are subordinate to "I"; and "1," "2," and "3" are subordinate to "B."

But the subordination is of two general types. An item in a brief may be subordinate to another as a part is to a whole. For example, the classes of persons who cannot pay medical bills, those who are uncertain about the cost, and those who may not feel sick are subordinate, *as parts,* to the statement that "many persons" (*as a whole*) are led to make medical decisions on economic grounds.

A second type of subordination is a proof relationship. The layout of two proofs included in the above portion of a brief may show the role of reasoning in briefmaking. Notice particularly in the examples on page 239 that the evidence of each proof in the brief is subordinate to the claim, and that the warrant and other proof elements are not stated in the brief but must be implied.

## CHOOSING THE CIRCUIT

Whether a series or a parallel proof circuit is better is partly a function of the proofs available for use in a particular dispute. When a genuine choice between the two circuits is possible, the parallel is to be preferred over the series circuit. Whereas each unit added to a series circuit increases the resistance and weakens the electrical current, in a parallel circuit the total resistance is actually decreased and the current strengthened when new units are added.

Since each proof is necessary to establish the final claim in a series circuit, the refutation of *any* proof in the circuit refutes the final claim. The more proofs in the series, the more proofs an opponent may refute. If Christmas tree lights are wired in series circuit, one burned-out lamp puts out every lamp in the entire strand.

In a parallel proof circuit, on the other hand, each proof is independently connected with the final claim. The refutation of one proof, therefore, leaves untouched other proofs of the circuit; and the larger number of valid proofs advanced, the more probable the final claim.

## EXAMPLE 1: MOTIVATIONAL PROOF

(E) There is a need to prevent needless death and suffering that results when many persons must neglect their health by making medical decisions on economic grounds.

Therefore, (C) the federal government should [(Q) probably] adopt a program of compulsory health insurance for all citizens.

Since (W) the federal government should be motivated by the value of preventing needless death and suffering.

Unless (R) other values such as cost, maintaining private insurance companies, etc., have greater motivational value than the prevention of needless death and suffering.

Because (S for W) the federal government is charged with the responsibility of promoting the general welfare of all citizens.

## EXAMPLE 2: AUTHORITATIVE PROOF

(E) The Conference on the General Welfare reported in 1959, "Due to inadequate medical care over a third of a million lives are needlessly lost each year."

Therefore, (C) neglect of health causes needless death and suffering.

Since (W) the Conference on the General Welfare is an authoritative source for such statements.

Unless (R) more authoritative sources say otherwise/substantive proofs of greater probative force yield a different claim/etc.

Because (S for W) the Conference is composed of competent men in this field/it is in a position to get relevant and extensive data/it is reasonably free from prejudice/etc.

If Christmas tree lights are wired in parallel circuit, one burned-out lamp decreases the total amount of light but does not create total darkness.

Whether in parallel or series circuit, every relevant and reasonable proof should be included in the brief. Each claim must be supported with a quantity of high-quality evidence, and the evidence–claim inferences should be adequately warranted. The more strong proofs assembled systematically in the brief, the more likely a strong case can be developed for a particular debate.

## DEVELOPING THE AFFIRMATIVE CASE

When an affirmative debater has assembled every relevant and reasonable proof in his brief, he is ready to select those to constitute his case for an impending debate. The selection of proofs, however, is limited in two ways: First, to earn a critical decision, an affirmative case must include enough proofs to overturn the presumption in favor of the present definition, fact, value, or policy. The case must be *prima facie*, i.e., its proofs must initially justify adopting the proposition before any negative arguments need be presented. Second, the proofs of an affirmative case must maintain convincing claims on every issue contested by the negative.[7] Within these limits, the affirmative debater selects the proofs he puts in his case.

### PROPOSITIONS OF DEFINITION, FACT, AND VALUE

In regard to three of the four types of propositions, two illustrations may clarify what part of the affirmative case is mandatory and what part is selected by the debater to fit the needs of a particular debate occasion and audience.

Turn again to the controversy over the spot of shade (pp. 81–92). You will recall that the presumption lies with Mr. N, and Mr. A has assumed the burden of proving that he, not Mr. N, has a right to the spot of shade. Mr. A's freedom to select from available proofs is restricted in two ways: First, he must include enough proofs to establish a *prima facie* case that (*a*) an agreement exists that the spot of shade belongs to him if he is ill, and (*b*) that he is now ill. Second, he must include enough proofs to maintain these claims if Mr. N elects to attack them. Only within these limits can A select the proofs most likely to convince his particular group of readers or listeners.

[7] For a more extended discussion of the theoretical basis for these two restrictions, see pp. 86–93.

Similarly, when Candidate A argues that he is better qualified than his opponent, Senator N, he must meet the same two requirements before selecting his proofs.[8] He must incorporate enough units of proof to build a *prima facie* case, and have ready those necessary to maintain his claims on all contested issues. If one issue inquires which candidate has the better points of view on current controversies, Candidate A must advance sufficient proof to establish and maintain his claim that his points of view are superior. In building this argument, however, he may select representative controversies on which to base his comparison and choose the proofs that develop it.

## PROPOSITIONS OF POLICY

Although a question of policy introduces new complexities, the same procedure should be followed and the same criteria satisfied. To prove that the further development of nuclear weapons should be discontinued by international agreement, an affirmative debater must develop a *prima facie* case and be prepared to defend any issue the negative may contest. An examination of each stock issue will reveal several important options, however.

To prove his stand on the "need" issue, as explained in Chapter 14, an affirmative debater must show that serious problems inherent in the present policy require a fundamental change of policy. Suppose the affirmative brief includes the contentions that further development of nuclear weapons (*a*) results in a serious radiation hazard to world health, (*b*) makes more probable a world nuclear war, and (*c*) increases the number of world states who have nuclear capability, thus making future control more difficult. If each contention is sufficient to justify a change of policy, the affirmative debater is completely free to decide to employ any one or any combination of these contentions. Furthermore, he may also choose any combination of proofs that support each contention.

In regard to the stock issue of "remedy," an affirmative debater must prove that his proposal can be put into effect and that it will ameliorate the alleged problems. Once again, however, he has several options. He may select the features of his plan, the proofs to show workability, and the proofs to show a remedy for each problem. For example, he may choose the kind of international organization to promote the agreement on the test ban, and determine what inspection and enforcement ma-

---

[8] Which of two candidates has the presumption and which the burden of proof depends on the status of the judges' beliefs and values before the debate. In our illustration we are assuming that Senator N, the incumbent, has the natural presumption and Candidate A the burden of proof. See pp. 82–85.

chinery to employ.

The affirmative debater has different requirements and options in developing his case on the "disadvantages" stock issue. He has no burden of proving a claim on this issue as part of making out a *prima facie* case, and the negative initiates the contention that serious disadvantages are entailed by the proposition. Because the affirmative debater is obliged to win every contested issue, however, he must be prepared to neutralize each disadvantage advanced by the negative.

Although the affirmative debater has no voice in selecting disadvantages, he has the full decision on what opposing stands to take and what proof of them should be. If the negative contends, for example, that U.S. military security would be endangered by stopping the development of nuclear weapons, the affirmative may argue that military security would not be threatened or that a threat to security is not harmful enough to warrant rejecting the proposition.

Building an affirmative case, then, is a combination of meeting requirements and exercising options. Whether the controversy is one of definition, fact, value, or policy, the affirmative must justify the proposition with a *prima facie* case designed to maintain strong claims on contested issues. Within these limits, and except for the "disadvantages" stock issue in a dispute over a question of policy, the affirmative debater may choose how to develop his stand on each issue.

## DEVELOPING THE NEGATIVE CASE

Building a negative case also involves requirements and options but differs significantly from the affirmative. Affirmative requirements become negative options, and affirmative options become negative requirements. Whereas the affirmative has the burden of proof and must initiate and maintain claims on *every* issue, the negative has only the burden of going forward with the debate and must only advance claims on at least *one* issue.

### PROPOSITIONS OF DEFINITION, FACT, AND VALUE

Consider again the same two illustrations from the perspective of the negative. Mr. N has three options: (1) He may contest either or both of the two issues. (2) He may choose one of two general methods of attack or combine the two approaches. He may argue that Mr. A has not satisfactorily proved his claims and attempt to refute A's proofs; or he may initiate constructive contentions of his own to prove that the prior agreement A describes did not take place, or that A is not now ill; or he may attempt both procedures. (3) He may also select the proofs for his constructive arguments. Only when Mr. N chooses to refute is he restricted in his selection: he obviously is limited to proofs that will counter *those specific proofs advanced by Mr. A.*

Senator N may similarly exercise three options and face one restriction: He may decide (1) what issues to contest, (2) whether to build constructive contentions, refute Candidate A's contentions, or both, and (3) what proofs he will employ to support his constructive contentions. But when he refutes Candidate A's contentions, he is restricted to proofs that neutralize *A's particular arguments.*

## PROPOSITIONS OF POLICY

In a controversy over a question of policy, the negative still has the option of deciding which issues to contest and whether to advance constructive arguments or limit the case to a refutation of affirmative arguments.[9] In addition, he has specific options and requirements in developing a case on each of the stock issues.

In regard to the "need" issue, the affirmative selects the problems that allegedly justify the proposition, and the negative decides which of three positions to take and which proofs to employ.

First, he may choose to *defend the status quo* by denying a justification for a change of policy. He may argue that no serious problems require the change, e.g., that the alleged hazard of radiation is not sufficient to demand a cessation of nuclear weapons development. Or he may claim that the present policy is now, or soon will be, adequate to deal with the alleged hazard, e.g., that nuclear weapons that emit little or no radiation will soon be developed.

Second, the negative may elect to *modify the status quo* and present a *repairs case.* Here, he concedes that serious problems exist and that the present policy *at the moment* is not solving them. He argues, however, that such inadequacies are not inherent in the present policy and that slight modifications can meet the problems. For example, the negative can admit that radiation creates a health hazard not prevented by *present* testing methods, but argue that altering such methods—for example, by testing weapons only underground—will preclude a serious radiation problem. The negative may thus argue that there is no need for a fundamental change of policy and yet escape defending the perhaps untenable position that the present system is harmless.

Third, the negative may present a *counterplan.* If he employs this

[9] The negative case that includes no constructive arguments is sometimes called a "direct refutation" or a "negative negative" case. Such a case is relatively weak psychologically because no motivational proofs are included.

kind of case, he can admit that serious problems inherent in the present policy demand a change of some sort, but argue that his counterplan would be superior to the affirmative proposal. For example, if the affirmative advances the proposition that U.S. economic aid should be restricted to loans, the negative could claim that problems resulting from the present aid program could be better solved by his counterproposal to channel all aid through the United Nations.

When a counterplan is advanced, the "need" issue drops out of the controversy, and issues are raised in the other two stock issues. Which of the two proposals is more practicable? Which of the proposals entails the fewest serious disadvantages? [10]

The negative has one major restriction in building his case on the "remedy" issue. All negative arguments must be adapted to the specific features of the particular affirmative plan. Proofs of the impracticability of the plan the negative wishes his opponent had presented are plainly beside the point. To argue that a test ban could not be properly enforced and hence could solve no problems, the negative must take into account the particular enforcement mechanism advocated by the affirmative.

The negative also has important options when he contests the "remedy" issue. He may choose whether to contest either or both of the subissues: (a) Is the proposal workable? and (b) Will the proposal solve the alleged problems? He may also select the proofs to support his claims on these subissues.

In regard to the "disadvantage" issue, the negative may select the disadvantages he wants to advance. Just as the affirmative chooses the problems to justify accepting the proposition, the negative selects from his brief the disadvantages that justify rejecting the proposition. He may also select the proofs to support his claim that disadvantageous effects will result and cause enough harm to justify a decision against the proposition.

The negative, however, is restricted in one respect, as he develops such a claim. He must argue that disadvantageous effects will be produced by the particular interpretation of the proposition presented in the affirmative plan. The argument that the USSR would gain military advantages from a test ban must be presented in full consideration of any features of the affirmative proposal designed to preclude military gains for any nation.

Thus, the negative, like the affirmative, develops his case within the context of options and requirements. Whereas the affirmative must de-

[10] For a more extended discussion of counterplans, see Roger E. Nebergall, "The Negative Counterplan," *The Speech Teacher*, 6 (Sept. 1957), 217–20.

fend every issue, the negative may choose which issue or issues to contest. In debates on questions of definition, fact, or value, the affirmative may choose his stand on each issue and the proofs to support each stand, and the negative may elect to construct counterproofs, refute affirmative arguments, or both. In debating a question of policy, the affirmative selects the ground of argument in the stock issues of "need" and "remedy," and the negative adapts his arguments to those the affirmative has initiated. Only in the "disadvantages" stock issue may the negative select the terrain by initiating the arguments; the affirmative must make the adaptation.

## CRITERIA FOR SELECTING PROOFS

Throughout this chapter, a major distinction has been made between those parts of a case required by a critical analysis of the proposition and those selected at the option of the debater. If the brief has been developed well, a debater has at his disposal more relevant and reasonable proofs than he can possibly present in any single debate. Within the limits of the requirements just discussed, the debater is free to decide which proofs to include in his case. How shall he decide?

The easy answer is that a debater should choose his strongest proofs. But by what standards does he identify them?

One standard is the *force* with which a proof establishes a claim. Some items of evidence are more reliable than others. Although no good brief includes proofs that are guilty of the gross deficiencies discussed in Chapter 12, some warrants are stronger than others in certifying the movement from evidence to claim. Some proofs may be accepted without reservation; others require reservations that may gravely weaken them. Finally, proofs require qualifiers ranging from "possibly" to "certainly" (or "almost certainly").

But proof strength also depends on *believability*. In Chapter 13, you will recall, the thesis was developed that the belief of listeners and readers is of central concern in establishing a proposition through proofs. Although a critical decision is based on the proofs presented on the issues of a proposition, ultimately such a decision represents the *belief* of the person making that decision.[11]

Furthermore, both axes of belief, objective and personal, must be considered. Along the objective axes, substantive and authoritative proofs connect the controversial item of belief with related data already

---

[11] See pp. 203–06 for a more detailed discussion of the role of belief in decision-making.

believed by listeners or readers. Along the personal axis, motivational proofs relate the item of belief to the values of the believer. Critical appraisal will demand an examination of all relevant data (objective axes), but decisions are made by individuals whose value systems influence their beliefs (personal axis). The debater who wants to influence healthy, not pathological, beliefs will not ignore either dimension.

## PROPOSITIONS OF DEFINITION, FACT, AND VALUE

Which axis should receive primary emphasis? The critical debater should try to influence *object-oriented* beliefs when the proposition is one of definition, fact, or value. Motivational proofs are irrelevant. Whether "diplomatic recognition" connotes the moral approval of the recognized government (definition), whether discrimination in employment is extensive (fact), or whether the present administration has benefited farmers (value)—these questions are best answered by substantive and authoritative proofs that connect the item of belief with knowledge, experience, or testimony concerning the objective world.

Although the motives, values, and feelings of the believer are unrelated to the proof requirements of a definitive, designative, or evaluative claim, even the most critical listener or reader cannot escape the influence of the personal belief axis. If such claims are debatable, variations in the perception and interpretation of related data are inevitable, and the alternatives are decidedly influenced by values, norms, and attitudes.[12] Because of varying experiences and values, some individuals are more receptive than others to a given item of belief. The man who considers smoking immoral is probably more receptive than a chain smoker to the proposition of fact that smoking cigarettes is the principal cause of lung cancer. Such persons will perceive and interpret differently the same information—even when both make a conscious effort to suspend final judgment until they have heard all relevant proofs on both sides of the proposition. Data concerning the definition of diplomatic recognition or the value of the present administration to farmers will similarly be perceived and interpreted differently by persons of different experience and values.

Furthermore, if the object-oriented belief of a definitive, designative, or evaluative claim is to be healthy, the believer must be able to square the belief with his own values.

Thus, although the debater should select his most *forceful* substan-

---

[12] See Solomon E. Asch, *Social Psychology* (New York: Prentice-Hall, 1952), pp. 450–501; Muzafer Sherif, "A Study of Some Social Factors in Perception," *Archives of Psychology*, 1935, No. 187; and David K. Berlo, *The Process of Communication* (New York: Holt, Rinehart & Winston, 1960), pp. 217–34.

tive and authoritative proofs in trying to influence object-oriented beliefs concerning questions of definition, fact, or value, he must also recognize *believability,* the personal dimension, as a significant second criterion.

## PROPOSITIONS OF POLICY

As the analysis of the proposition and the development of the case structure are more complex in questions of policy than those of definition, fact, or value, so the selection of proofs is also more complex in questions of policy.

As in other types of propositions, definitive and designative claims require *object-oriented* proofs, i.e., substantive and authoritative. Whether a problem exists, whether the present policy is responsible, whether the affirmative proposal would remedy the ills of the present policy, and whether disadvantageous effects would result—in selecting proofs to answer these and similar questions the debater must emphasize the objective dimension and consider the values of the believer as a secondary criterion.

Ego-oriented proofs are appropriately employed in establishing evaluative or actuative claims in propositions of policy. Whether a fear of a possible nuclear war is enough to warrant an international agreement to stop testing, or whether the aspiration to maintain military strength by continued testing is strong enough to justify rejecting the ban—these are *evaluative* questions that are answered primarily by the criterion of *believability.*[13]

*Actuative* claims are also supported by ego-oriented proofs. The affirmative must prove that the proposition should be adopted, and the negative that it should not. The proof for these opposing actuative claims is *motivational,* and hence the values of the believer become the primary standard for selecting proofs.[14]

The evidence for the motivational proof of the affirmative is derived from claims established concerning the first two stock issues of "need" and "remedy." The U.S. direct economic aid program is lowering our prestige in Southeast Asia, costing the taxpayer heavily, and is wasteful and inefficient; these problems could be solved by substantially reducing the program or eliminating it. The actuative *claim* that the U.S. should reduce or eliminate its aid program is *warranted* by such evidence only if the problems are related to judges' values sufficient to *motivate* such action.

[13] For a review of evaluative claims, see p. 102.
[14] For a review of actuative claims, see p. 102; to review motivational proofs, see pp. 162–66.

A second example: The testing of nuclear weapons increases the probability of nuclear war and subjects the world to health hazards through radioactive fallout; these problems would be solved by an agreement to prohibit further testing of nuclear weapons. That such an agreement should be made requires a motivational *warrant* to carry the above *evidence* to the *claim*. The elimination of such problems must be considered valuable enough to justify the action.

No matter how certainly one or more problems exist and how satisfactorily the affirmative proposal would remedy them, unless eliminating a problem is valuable to a believer, he has no motive to accept an actuative claim. In developing contentions on the "need" and "remedy" issues, therefore, the affirmative debater must choose proofs he can relate well to the values of his readers and listeners.

The negative debater, on the other hand, employs motivational proofs related to his stand on the "disadvantages" stock issue. The *evidence* is derived from definitive and designative claims that adopting the proposition entails serious disadvantages. The actuative *claim* is that the proposition should be rejected. The *warrant* states some value that justifies the inference from evidence to claim.

For example, whether a debater may move from evidence that federal financial assistance will produce federal controls to the claim that such assistance should be rejected depends on the values of the listeners or readers. Is local autonomy of the public schools an important value? Is federal control sufficiently disadvantageous to warrant rejection of the proposition?

Whether the claim that agricultural price supports should not be discontinued is warranted by the evidence that eliminating the supports would bankrupt marginal farmers, again, depends on one's values. Does the federal government have a responsibility to marginal farmers? Will subsidization of marginal farmers benefit the "public welfare"?

When the negative debater selects his proofs to show that disadvantages exist or are harmful, therefore, he must regard the personal beliefs of his listeners and readers as a primary criterion. Indeed, his only reason to take a stand on the "disadvantages" issue, and make that stand be viewed as an *issue,* is to motivate a rejection of the proposition, by identifying with the values of listeners or readers the debater's claim that serious disadvantages will occur if the proposition is adopted.

Affirmative and negative debaters, then, try to establish conflicting actuative claims in a controversy over a question of policy. If the evidence for such claims is equally valid, the judge must discriminate among the values that warrant these claims. Only when he does this can he make a critical decision. Is the value of solving certain financial problems of the public schools more important than the value of local control over the public schools? Is the decreased likelihood of world nuclear war more important than the value of increased military strength?

In short, when contesting a question of policy, both affirmative and negative debaters must select from their briefs only valid proofs. In developing designative and definitive claims, they should emphasize the objective-belief axes. For their evaluative and actuative claims to accept or reject the proposition, the affirmative must choose problems, and the negative, disadvantages, that provide the greatest possible motivation for the believers.

QUESTIONS

*A. To Check Your Comprehension and Memory*
 1. What is a debate case?
 2. On what two standards does the strength of a case depend?
 3. What are the steps in the process of building a case?
 4. What is a brief?
 5. What portion of the introduction to a brief determines the structure of the body of a brief?
 6. Distinguish between parallel and series proof circuits.
 7. Which type of proof circuit requires the more complex substructure?
 8. What proof elements are included in a brief?
 9. Why is the parallel circuit preferred over the series?
 10. What are the requirements for an affirmative case in a debate on any type of controversy?
 11. What are the requirements and options of the affirmative in constructing a case on a question of definition? of fact? of value? of policy?
 12. In what stock issue(s) are arguments customarily initiated by the affirmative? by the negative?
 13. What are the requirements and options of the negative in constructing a case on a question of definition? of fact? of value? of policy?
 14. What three approaches may a negative debater take in contesting the "need" issue in a question of policy?
 15. When the negative advances a counterplan, what are the issues?
 16. By what two standards does a debater determine which are his strongest proofs?
 17. Which belief axis should receive the primary emphasis in attempts to establish definitive claims? designative claims? evaluative claims? actuative claims?
 18. What kind of proof is appropriate in a question of policy that is not appropriate in other kinds of questions?

19. In relation to which stock issue(s) is (are) **motivational proofs** attempted by the affirmative? by the negative?

20. On what basis does a judge decide between two opposing actuative claims?

B.  *For Class Discussion*
1. What is the relationship between a brief and a case?
2. Relate the requirements and options of affirmative and negative cases to the theory of issues.
3. Are the standards of validity and believability separable? Why?
4. How does a judge determine which is the stronger of two opposing cases?

## EXERCISES

A.  *Written Exercises*
1. Prepare a complete brief on your side of a proposition you are preparing to debate in class. Consult the sample brief in Appendix C.
2. On the same proposition, enumerate the values and motives one must consider in building his case.
3. Prepare an outline of contentions you will advance for a particular debate on this proposition.
4. Outline one of the cases in one of the debates included in the Appendix.
5. Select a proposition of policy, and formulate the following kinds of negative cases:
    a. defense of the status quo
    b. modification of the status quo
    c. counterplan

## SUGGESTIONS FOR FURTHER READING

Glenn R. Capp, Robert Huber, and Wayne C. Eubank, "Duties of Affirmative Speakers—A Symposium," *The Speech Teacher*, 8 (March, 1959), 139–49. A series of practical suggestions on how the affirmative case is developed and defended in the four speeches of a traditional debate.

Roger E. Nebergall, "The Negative Counterplan," *The Speech Teacher*, 6 (Sept. 1957), 217–20. When a college negative debate team offers a counterplan, there are two points for decision: (*a*) Has the affirmative overturned the presumption in favor of the status quo? (*b*) Is the affirmative proposal better than the negative counterplan? Unless both questions are answered affirmatively, the judge must vote for the negative.

Robert P. Newman, "Ethical Presuppositions of Argument," *The Gavel*, 42 (May 1960), 51–54. "Before the *status quo* can be condemned, and an alternative considered, standards of value have to be invoked if only implicitly; and both the existing state of affairs and any proposed plan have to be measured against them." Newman then examines three major ethical systems and suggests how ethical issues may be discovered in a particular proposition of policy.

James L. Robinson, "Are We 'Overlegalizing' School Debate?" *The Speech Teacher*, 9 (March 1960), 109–15. Robinson answers the title question affirmatively, contends that school debating relies too heavily on the analogy to courtroom debating, and defines proof as what the audience accepts.

Charles H. Woolbert, "Persuasion: Principles and Methods," *The Quarterly Journal of Speech*, 5 (Jan. 1919), 12–25; (March 1919), 101–19; and (May 1919), 212–38. Although this three-part article formulates a general system of persuasion, its suggestions will help the debater as he develops his case.

# Chapter 16
## ATTACK AND DEFENSE

> *Complete liberty of contradicting and disproving our opinion is the very condition which justifies us in assuming its truth for purposes of action; and on no other terms can a being with human faculties have any rational assurance of being right.*
> JOHN STUART MILL

SOME OF THE criteria for determining the strength of a debate case have been discussed in preceding chapters. Although such criteria as the validity of proofs, the relevance of proofs to the issues, and the relation of proofs to the values of listeners and readers are important, they are not by themselves sufficient. They do not take into account the entire debate process, since they may be employed to evaluate a case before the actual debating starts.

Another essential criterion for gauging the strength of a case may be applied only when one debater confronts another. More than anything else, such confrontation makes debate a critical instrument for arriving at collective decisions. The debater is not only permitted to question and criticize an opposing case, he is expected to do so. The critical decision is made not after the mere presentation of the constructive arguments that compose the cases, but only after each debater has criticized the case of his opponent and replied to the criticisms of his own case.

Together, these two actions constitute the dynamic confrontation of cases called *attack and defense*. Only through such interaction do the cases prepared in the library and the study come to life during actual debates. The critical decision is determined not by the relative strength of two cases on paper before the debate, but by the effectiveness with which the two cases are attacked and defended during the debate itself.

To manage well his attack and defense of cases, a debater must be able to answer four questions: *What is the objective? What procedure should be employed? What are the methods? How may attack and defense be integrated?*

## THE OBJECTIVE OF ATTACK AND DEFENSE

The ultimate purpose of attack and defense is not to engage in sparring with " 'tis" and " 'taint"—even when such sparring is supported by proofs. *The objective is to refute or re-establish a claim on one of the issues of the controversy.*[1]

Refutation, therefore, involves more than raising objections, even valid ones, to opposing proofs. The goal of attack is not achieved until valid objections are related to an *issue*. Similarly, one has not adequately defended his case against an opposing refutation until he has re-established his stand on an *issue*.

## THE PROCEDURE OF ATTACK AND DEFENSE

To clearly and lethally refute an argument, a debater must take the following four steps:

1. *State the proof he means to refute.* Unless the listener or reader can identify the proof being attacked, he is inevitably confused and cannot critically evaluate the refutation. The first step, therefore, is a clear statement of the opposing proof, preferably in the language of the opponent.

2. *State his objection to the proof.* The debater should then explain, if possible in one clear sentence, why he objects to the proof.

3. *Support his objection.* Although a debater may on occasion justify mere questions concerning an opposing proof, the refutation is substantially strengthened if proof is offered to support the objection.

4. *Show how his refutation seriously weakens the opponent's stand on one of the issues.* This fourth step is perhaps the most important. Unless the refutation is related to an issue, a debater has not gained the maximum advantage from his attack. To discredit an authority, to criticize a causal relationship, or to indict a proof as irrelevant is of little value until the debater shows how his refutation attacks the opposing case at one of the issues. By winning a clash on an issue, the refuting debater strikes a fatal blow at the opposing case as a whole.

Some debaters complain that such a time-consuming procedure limits the amount of refutation possible. Yet a few *vital* refutations

[1] For a discussion of issues, see pp. 88–92.

254  DEVELOPING ARGUMENTATIVE DISCOURSE

communicated *clearly* are more valuable than a larger number of unrelated objections organized loosely as a sort of "grocery list."

Hurling a hodge-podge list of objections at an opponent has been termed "shotgun" refutation, and the analogy is apt. A good deal of shot may be scattered, and some of it may reach a target. But, unlike shooting into a flock of geese, bagging a few arguments by random refutation does not satisfy the objective. The debater must aim with the precision of a rifle at the issues of a controversy.

A similar four-step procedure should be employed in defending against refutation. To re-establish a unit of proof, a debater must (1) state the proof he intends to re-establish and the objection his opponent has asserted, (2) explain why the objection is not valid, (3) support his explanation, and (4) show how the explanation reaffirms his proof and re-establishes his case as unimpaired by the objection raised.

The final step, again, is a vital part of the defense. Merely to refute the refutation may not clearly rebuild one's contention on an issue and thus re-establish his case. The safest defense includes strong links between the rejuvenated proof and the entire case.

## METHODS OF ATTACK AND DEFENSE

A debater may refute an opposing case by raising one of seven kinds of objections. He can (1) find deficiencies in any of the proofs presented as part of the opposing case; (2) turn the tables on an opposing proof; (3) reduce a proof to absurdity; (4) argue that a series of opposing proofs is insufficient; (5) overwhelm an opposing proof by presenting a stronger counterproof; (6) show that two or more opposing proofs are inconsistent with one another; and (7) pose a dilemma.

### FINDING DEFICIENCIES IN A UNIT OF PROOF

Probably the most common method of attack is to raise direct objections against opposing proofs. The five classes of proof deficiency—faulty evidence, unwarranted claims, weak warrants, ignored reservations, and overstated claims—have already been considered at length.[2]

The debater should listen carefully for deficiencies in his opponent's proofs. Each proof is subject to a large number of possible weaknesses. For example, an authoritative proof can be refuted by showing the testimony to be inaccurate, quoted out of context, or without adequate authoritative warrant. The cause–effect proof that the price of automobiles will go up because the price of steel has gone up can be refuted

[2] See Chapter 12.

by discrediting the evidence, questioning the causal relationship between the two sets of prices, or by citing reservations, e.g., decreased production costs may compensate for the increased cost of steel.

In no method of attack is a systematic and thorough procedure so important. Merely to criticize opposing evidence as outdated, to indict the reasoning as fallacious, or to cite some other proof deficiency may seem to one's audience like picayune quibbling. The safe method of attack is to complete each step of the procedure: to focus on a proof, to spot the weakness, to support the objection, and to show how the deficiency weakens the opponent's stand on an issue.

A debater may defend against an attack that cites a proof deficiency in one of four ways. First, he may argue that his proof has been misunderstood and that the objection does not justly apply to his proof. He may support this defense by restating the original proof and showing how it has been misinterpreted.

Second, he may deny the alleged deficiency and support his denial. For example, if an authority's credentials are challenged, he can present proof of the dependability of his authority.

Third, he may deny that the alleged deficiency destroys his original proof. For example, he may argue that even if his information is four years old, the date is irrelevant to the point of his original claim.

Fourth, he may show a deficiency in the refutative proof with which his opponent has supported an objection to the original proof. For example, suppose proof that an increase in the price of steel entails an increase in the price of automobiles is refuted by pointing to an instance in which the one increase did not follow the other. The refutative proof could be disproved by showing that the "parallel" case is not parallel, that the evidence itself is inaccurate, or that the single contrary instance does not refuse the original causal generalization built on many proofs.

## TURNING THE TABLES

A second method of attack involves no direct criticism of a unit of proof. Rather, a debater takes either the evidence or the complete proof of an opponent, reinterprets the material, and draws a different conclusion, one damaging to the opponent's cause. Although this method of attack may be applicable relatively rarely, when it is employed the refutation is devastating.

Suppose a debater tries to prove the inadequacy of voluntary health insurance to cover large and unpredictable medical expenses, by presenting evidence that major medical policies cover less than 20 per cent of the population. His opponent could turn the tables by pointing out that major medical policies represent a new and rapidly growing development. That as many as nearly 20 per cent of the population now have such policies, he could argue, is evidence of the ability of voluntary health insurance companies to conceive and sell new ideas to meet the problem of high and unpredictable medical costs.

Since turning the tables always involves a reinterpretation of a proof, the best defense against such a method of attack is to deny the validity of the new interpretation. One may argue that after the early popularity of major medical policies, the plateau reached in the last few years signifies an inability to cope with the problem.

## REDUCING TO ABSURDITY

A third method of attack, often given the Latin name, *reductio ad absurdum,* is similar to turning the tables: in each method the debater accepts part or all of his opponent's proof. Whereas in turning the tables a debater reinterprets the proof and turns the conclusion in the opposite direction, the debater reduces an argument to absurdity by extending the significance of the conclusion.

In contending that intercollegiate football should be abolished because it is dangerous, a debater may present evidence that sixteen players received fatal injuries as a direct result of 1959 football competition. His opponent could employ *reductio ad absurdum* through a series of analogies: "In 1959 almost 40,000 persons were killed in automobile accidents. Should we abolish cars? The National Safety Council reports that a substantial number of accidents occur in the home. Should we abolish homes? Some persons die in bathtubs. Should we abolish bathing? We do not get rid of cars, homes, bathtubs, or intercollegiate football merely because they involve danger; values are also present. So let us see if the values of intercollegiate football justify the limited danger cited by my opponent. . . ."

Arguments may also be reduced to absurdity by revealing their consequences. For example: "Our opponents tell us that whether the Soviet Union violates the agreement is irrelevant, because a single violation will automatically cancel the agreement. But what are the consequences? Russia plans its new developments in the laboratory, makes a technological breakthrough in nuclear defensive weapons, and conducts a quick series of tests to validate the weapons. They then launch a surprise attack and successfully defend against our attempts to retaliate. As we are being destroyed, we call out indignantly, "We cancel the agreement! We're going to resume our nuclear testing!"

The best defense against *reductio ad absurdum* is to show that the extension of the argument is unjust. When the refutation consists of analogies, the attack can be blunted by showing dissimilarities between one's proof and the absurd situations his opponent has alleged to be analogous. Are the dangers of intercollegiate football really analogous to accidents in the home or bathtub? When *reductio ad absurdum* describes the consequences of a proposal, the consequences can be denied or their harmfulness minimized. If Russia continues laboratory research on nuclear weapons of defense, so can we; the agreement gives neither nation a military advantage.

## ARGUING INSUFFICIENCY OF A SERIES OF PROOFS

Some debaters call this method the "so what" attack. Like the two previous methods, arguing the insufficiency of a series of proofs denies no single opposing unit of proof. Instead, a certain proof is accepted and followed by the query, "So what? What have you really proved?"

For the "so what" attack relates not to one unit of proof but to a whole structure of proof. In effect, the debater who employs this method says, "Your argument is adequate as far as you have gone, but you have not gone far enough to prove satisfactorily your stand on the issue."

A debater may argue proof insufficiency against either a series or a parallel proof structure. Against a *series* proof structure, the insufficiency is an omission of one or more necessary proofs. For example, suppose a debater argues that federal aid to education will be accompanied by federal controls. His opponent may reply, "So what? The federal government has a right to certain controls, and the negative team has never proved that these controls would be harmful to anyone. Until our opponents prove that the effects of federal control are harmful enough to counterbalance the value of solving important financial problems of the public schools, the federal control bugaboo does not justify rejecting federal aid."

Against a *parallel* proof structure, the "so what" attack is developed in one of two ways: Either a group of parallel proofs is attacked as insufficient *collectively* to support a claim, or each proof in the parallel circuit is attacked *individually*. Suppose an affirmative debater contends that the U.S. needs a change of policy to solve three inherently harmful problems. The negative debater could argue either that Problems A, B, and C together are not harmful enough to require a change of policy, or the attack could be individualized. The proofs relating to Problem A could be called deficient in some way, the proofs relating to Problem B reduced to absurdity, and the proofs relating to Problem C said to be insufficient to warrant the affirmative proposal.

In general, the defense against the method of attack just described is to present motivational proofs that answer the "so what" question. Federal controls must be proved sufficiently harmful by themselves or in conjunction with other disadvantages to motivate rejecting federal financial assistance to the public schools.

An even better defense, of course, is to construct a case that does not invite the "so what" inquiry. To show sufficient harm to justify a change or sufficient disadvantages to justify rejecting a proposition is a necessary criterion of a good case.[3]

### PRESENTING COUNTERPROOFS

Counterproofs may be defined as proofs that deny the opposing claim by overpowering it with an alternative argument. If a debater can get his counterproof accepted, he has effectively refuted an opposing belief without directly attacking it.

Refutation by counterproof is possible whether one employs the same or a different type of proof. A counterproof by sign refutes a proof by less probable sign. For example, a reliable index that predicts an economic recession can refute a less reliable index that claims a recession is not approaching. An authoritative proof can be refuted by contradictory testimony from a more credible authority.

A counterproof can also take the form of a different type of proof. An analogy can be refuted by a proof by parallel case. An authoritative proof can be refuted by a generalization. A proof by classification can be refuted by a cause–effect proof. In short, any relatively weak proof can be successfully attacked by any relatively stronger counterproof.

Suppose a debater argues that unused scholarship funds signify that students do not need financial aid to go to college. His opponent may present the counterproof that surveys indicate that a substantial number of qualified and eager high school graduates are prevented from attending college for financial reasons.

Refutation by counterproof is, at its best, a deadly weapon. At its worst, it is mere quotation-counting: "My opponent has only two authorities who support his position; we have four." Effective refutation by counterproof requires the debater to show that his counterproof is more probable than his opponent's proof.

[3] The same principle applies, to some extent, in defending against any attack. In regard to the one in question, however, the attack is only possible when a case lacks an essential ingredient. If the proposition is a debatable one, other attacking methods can be employed even against good cases.

## EXPOSING AN INCONSISTENCY

In this method of attack, two or more claims of an opposing case are exposed as inconsistent. Such claims ordinarily appear in widely separated parts of a case, since most debaters can avoid inconsistencies among adjacent claims. For this reason and others, spotting inconsistencies is difficult. Debaters so intently examine individual units of proof or groups of closely related proofs that inconsistent positions among widely scattered proofs sometimes go unnoticed. The art of exposing inconsistencies demands that a debater look at an opposing case as a whole unit and consider how its ideas are interrelated.

The value of the attack, however, justifies the trouble one takes to make it. Each of the inconsistent positions is itself undermined, the case as a whole is weakened, and the confidence of the listener or reader in the critical ability of the opposing debater may be badly shaken.

One of the common inconsistencies of affirmative debaters discussing a question of policy is to allege extensive problems and present minimal proposals. Suppose, for example, the affirmative argues that a large number of American families need help in meeting their medical expenses, and then offers a federal compulsory insurance program financed by a tax increase inadequate to pay these expenses. The negative may inquire, "Which argument does the affirmative want us to believe? Do many families need a lot of help with medical expenses? If so, more money is needed than their tax proposal can yield. Or is their tax proposal adequate to provide a satisfactory insurance program? If so, then the argument concerning the need for financial assistance is grossly exaggerated."

Negative debaters are sometimes guilty of the same inconsistency in reverse. For example, consider the negative debater who argues that Congress need not be given the power to reverse decisions of the Supreme Court because, historically, few unpopular decisions have been rendered and because present methods provide adequate remedy for these few. Later, he argues that a major disadvantage of the proposal is that Congress would spend too much time reviewing court decisions. The affirmative may well contend that the two stands are inconsistent: Either few unpopular decisions have been rendered, and Congress won't be burdened in considering them; or Congress may have many unpopular decisions to review and a need is established for adjudicating them in Congress.

The best defense against the exposé of an inconsistency is to prevent the attack by constructing a consistent case. Once the attack is made, however, the debater may be able to argue that either or both of the allegedly inconsistent claims have been misunderstood, and thus an apparent inconsistency is not real. For example, suppose we have misquoted the opponent of the proposal to give Congress the power to reverse Supreme Court decisions. He may reply, "I did not argue that few unpopular decisions have been made in the Supreme Court. What I did say was that present remedies have almost always proved adequate. Such a claim is not at all inconsistent with the contention that Congress does not have time to review all of the unpopular decisions that present remedies already can handle."

## POSING A DILEMMA

The dilemma is in one important respect similar to the method of attack just discussed: Both methods assume that the opponent has taken or logically must take an untenable position. The debater guilty of an inconsistency has already asserted such a position, i.e., he has made two or more statements that, taken together, are indefensible. In posing a dilemma, a debater tries to prove that his opponent must accept one of a group of statements, and then he proves that each of the alternatives, metaphorically called "horns," damages the opposing case.[4]

One of the favorite dilemmas posed by negative debaters in arguing questions of policy employs a combination of proofs within the stock issues of remedy and disadvantages: Either the proposal will solve problems (or be enforceable, contain certain controls, etc.), and the result will be disadvantageous (in cost, loss of freedom, etc.); or the disadvantage can be avoided, but the problems remain unsolved. For example, either (a) the federal government will make certain its money is spent wisely—at the expense of harmful federal controls; or (b) the proposal will be enacted without controls—but with no assurance that the money will be spent wisely to solve financial problems.

But the dilemma is not a method of attack limited to the negative. An affirmative debater who advocates the removal of union membership as a condition of employment could argue that such legislation would have one of two effects: Either (a) union membership might decline—proving that persons remain members only under a compulsion that ought not exist, or (b) membership might not decline—refuting the common argument that such a proposal weakens organized labor by decreasing its membership.

To make the attack effective, a debater must state a dilemma succinctly enough to emphasize the either–or nature of the horns, without

---

[4] Some writers define "dilemma" as including two, and only two, options and use such terms as "trilemma" and "polylemma" when more than two alternatives are offered. In common usage, the term "dilemma" means an argumentative situation in which *two or more* indefensible choices are extended to an opponent.

oversimplifying the alternatives. In addition, the dilemma must meet two logical requirements: First, the alternatives must be all-inclusive; no possibility should be omitted. Second, each of the alternatives must be proved damaging to the opposing cause.

These two tests suggest defenses against a dilemma. One defense is to state and support a new alternative, one ignored by the opponent. For example, an advocate of federal aid to education may respond, "My opponent presents two alternatives. Either disadvantageous controls must be a part of our proposal, or else the federal aid won't get to the right place to solve the problems. But there is a third alternative. Under the plan we have suggested, the federal government audits expenditures to assure that the money is wisely spent to ameliorate financial problems of the public schools, but no controls beyond the audit are involved—and we can't see the harm of this limited control."

In a second defense, the debater accepts one of the horns of the dilemma. For example, the advocate of compulsory unionism could argue that under voluntarism union membership would decline, thus weakening the collective bargaining power of organized labor, and admit that part of the membership decline would represent the departure of dissatisfied, once-compelled members. He could deny, however, that the compulsion is unjustified, by comparing the alleged evil of compulsion with the values of a strongly organized labor movement.

## THE INTEGRATION OF ATTACK AND DEFENSE

Regardless of the specific format employed, any debate consists of, first, an initial presentation of constructive arguments, and, second, an attack on an opposing case and a defense of one's own. Only in the first speech in a debate does a speaker or writer have the relatively simple task of organizing only constructive materials. In all other presentations, he has the difficult problem of organizing both attack and defense.

How a debater solves this problem depends to some extent on (*a*) whether the question is one of definition, fact, value, or policy, and (*b*) what format is employed. But certain principles apply generally to all four types of controversies and to various formats. These general principles may best be illustrated within the context of a single college debate pattern and one kind of controversial question. Let us select the most frequently employed college debate format, the "traditional," [5]

[5] See pp. 318–20.

and the most complex kind of question, one of policy. The student who can organize constructive and refutative materials well in traditional debates on questions of policy will probably be able to adjust to new debate patterns on other kinds of questions.

Of the four constructive and four rebuttal speeches in the traditional format, only the first affirmative constructive speech is devoid of the elements of attack and defense. The other seven speeches pose two kinds of organizational problems: (*a*) integrating constructive and refutative arguments in the three other constructive speeches; and (*b*) organizing the attack and defense of cases in the four rebuttal speeches.

## THE FIRST NEGATIVE CONSTRUCTIVE SPEECH

Not having yet spoken, the first negative speaker has no prior proofs to defend. But he must combine an attack on the arguments of the first affirmative speaker with a presentation of his own constructive arguments. He may accomplish these two purposes either simultaneously or separately.

If his constructive contentions directly refute the first affirmative contentions, then the negative debater may *simultaneously* construct his own case and attack the opposing case. For example, suppose a negative debater had planned to contend (*a*) that the Supreme Court is generally able to serve as a wise final adjudicator of cases involving constitutionality, and (*b*) that we now have adequate methods of redressing the occasional unwise decisions. If the first affirmative speaker presents contentions directly opposing these, the best organizational method for the first negative speaker is probably to state his own contentions and employ his proofs to refute the opposing contentions. He must make clear, however, that he is simultaneously building his own, and attacking an opposing, case.

As a result of simultaneous construction and refutation, the first negative speaker clearly joins the issues. By clashing so directly with the affirmative contentions, he forces his opponents to supply satisfactory answers to the issues or lose the critical decision.

On the other hand, if the first negative speaker discovers that some of his constructive arguments do not refute any of the first affirmative's contentions, his recourse is to present constructive and refutative proofs *separately*.

That negative arguments are unrelated to affirmative contentions may be accounted for in several ways. First, the negative speaker may have analyzed the proposition so poorly that some of his arguments may not be relevant to any issue. If so, he must decide on the spot to discard such arguments.

Second, the affirmative speaker may have misinterpreted the proposition and hence ignored a relevant idea. If so, the first negative debater should point out the omission and present his constructive argument. For example, suppose an opponent of a federal program of compulsory health insurance was prepared to contend that a combination of individual resources, voluntary health insurance, charity, and government welfare adequately financed the nation's health care. If the first affirmative speaker contends only that voluntary health insurance inadequately finances medical care, the first negative could (*a*) attack the contention concerning voluntary health insurance, (*b*) charge his opponent with a faulty analysis of available resources, and (*c*) present his constructive contention that a combination of the four methods can adequately finance medical care.

Third, the negative contentions may be related to an issue not discussed in the first affirmative speech. If so, time permitting, such contentions should be presented after the affirmative proofs are attacked.

The first negative constructive speech is one of the hardest to organize effectively. The first negative debater must relate his constructive material to the first affirmative speech, and he must quickly decide what to do with prepared arguments that seem unrelated to that speech.

## THE SECOND AFFIRMATIVE CONSTRUCTIVE SPEECH

The second affirmative speaker has three primary tasks in organizing his speech. In most debates, such tasks can serve as main headings of his outline.

First, he must defend his colleague's contentions against attacks made on them by the first negative speaker. He will most clearly do so if he employs the same outline his colleague used—not the outline of his opponent—and if he follows the procedure suggested earlier in this chapter.[6] His methods of defense will depend on the methods of attack employed by his opponent.

Second, he must attack the negative constructive contentions not related to his colleague's arguments. If the first negative speaker has presented separately an argument that actually relates to an affirmative contention, however, the second affirmative speaker should consider it when he defends that affirmative contention.

Third, he should complete the affirmative case by presenting the remaining constructive contentions. He will do well to time carefully in advance this part of his speech, so he can pace himself and save enough time to communicate it clearly.

[6] See p. 254.

## THE SECOND NEGATIVE CONSTRUCTIVE SPEECH

Since the second negative constructive speech is followed immediately by the first negative rebuttal, the two speeches may in some respects be regarded a unit. What is not covered in the second constructive speech may be considered in the first rebuttal (with one exception).

Like the preceding speaker, the second negative may accomplish three objectives in his constructive speech. Unlike his predecessor, however, only one of these *must* be completed in his speech; the other two may be achieved either in his speech or later in his colleague's rebuttal.

He *must* present the remaining constructive contentions. This task is vital, particularly in many propositions of policy. The negative contentions concerning the stock issues of "remedy" and "disadvantages" can be presented in no other speech. The first speaker cannot present these contentions in his constructive speech because the relevant parts of the affirmative case are often not advanced until the second affirmative speech, and debating conventions prohibit the initiation of constructive contentions in rebuttal speeches. Furthermore, the contentions that an affirmative proposal is impracticable and will cause serious disadvantages are, in many controversies, the strongest arguments a negative team can advance. Consequently, the second negative speaker must allow himself enough time to complete his development of these contentions.

The other two objectives are to renew the attack on affirmative arguments and to defend the contentions of his colleague. These tasks, however, may be undertaken either in the second constructive or first rebuttal speech. Most negative teams determine in advance a division of these labors, so they can most efficiently use their time defending their contentions and attacking the opposing case.

## THE FIRST NEGATIVE REBUTTAL

Since constructive arguments may not be initiated in rebuttals, the organization of the four remaining speeches focuses solely on attack and defense. The integration of constructive and refutative materials is no longer an organizational problem.

Yet few rebuttal speeches are well organized. Many debaters have one list of arguments they want to attack and another list of arguments they want to defend, and they rapidly tick off as many items as they can.

Although the organization of rebuttal materials can be completed only when the preceding speaker sits down, and, for this reason, the debate itself must in large measure dictate how materials are presented, one simple pattern is usually effective: If a debater organizes his attack and defense around the main contested issues, he will have covered systematically the vital matters. He must also be selective. Only arguments that can materially influence a critical decision are worth attacking or defending in rebuttal speeches.

In his rebuttal, the first negative speaker tries to complete an attack on affirmative contentions not refuted in the preceding speech, and a defense of his own contentions not yet defended. In addition, since he has now heard the complete affirmative case, he should look for inconsistencies among opposing arguments.

### THE FIRST AFFIRMATIVE REBUTTAL

In his rebuttal, the first affirmative speaker has two primary tasks. First, and most important, he must defend the affirmative case against the attacks made in the two preceding speeches. His best plan is to review his original contentions and answer the most damaging attacks on each. He must resist the temptation to spend a lot of time "smashing" weak attacks; instead, he should limit himself to the ones that made him wince. He must also recognize that his ultimate objective is to show that, in spite of what may have been a strenuous negative attack, the affirmative contentions are still valid reasons for adopting the proposition.

His second task is to refute negative constructive arguments not directly related to his own case. In particular, he should reply to the allegations that his proposal is unworkable and will be disadvantageous, since the first affirmative rebuttal is usually the first opportunity of the affirmative team to refute such arguments.

The importance and difficulty of the first affirmative rebuttal are obvious. Under the standard time limits of ten-minute constructive speeches and five-minute rebuttals, the first affirmative speaker has five minutes in which to counteract fifteen minutes of negative argument. In no other speech is selectivity so crucial, since time may not permit the presentation of every relevant attack and defense.

### THE SECOND NEGATIVE REBUTTAL

The major objective of this speech is, through attack and defense, to establish strong enough claims on each contested issue to withstand the arguments of the final rebuttal speech.

The earlier advice to organize attack and defense around the issues is particularly important in this speech. By relating to one of the issues every proof defending negative and attacking affirmative contentions, the second negative speaker clarifies the position of his team, increases the probability of winning at least one of the issues, and thus justifies a decision to reject the proposition.

The "shotgun" negative debater, on the other hand, even if he wins a large number of clashes of opinion, may not have given any listener or reader a single reason strong enough to justify a vote against the proposition.

## THE SECOND AFFIRMATIVE REBUTTAL

Like the final negative speech, the second affirmative rebuttal represents a last opportunity. The goal of the second affirmative speaker is to re-establish the case for adopting the proposition.

Like all affirmative speeches, the emphasis is more on defense than attack. For this reason, some experienced debaters separate these two elements. They begin with an attack on negative contentions, follow with a defense of the affirmative case, and conclude with a plea to adopt the proposition. The attack consists of a refutation of every negative contention that could conceivably justify a vote against the proposition. The defense is a systematic review of affirmative contentions, together with a reply to every damaging negative attack. The final plea relates the affirmative case to an appealing value that motivates endorsing the proposition.

## QUESTIONS

*A. To Check Your Comprehension and Memory*

1. Why is effectiveness of attack and defense an important criterion of the strength of debate cases?
2. What is the objective of attack and defense?
3. Enumerate the four steps a debater should take in refuting an argument.
4. What is "shotgun" refutation?
5. Enumerate the four steps a debater should take in defending an argument that has been attacked.
6. What are the seven methods of attacking an opposing case?
7. How can a debater defend against the charge that one of his proofs is deficient?
8. How does a debater turn the tables?
9. Define *reductio ad absurdum*.
10. How can a debater attack the proof sufficiency of a series proof structure? of a parallel proof structure?
11. Can a counterproof attack a proof of the same type? of a different type? Discuss.
12. Why are inconsistencies among arguments sometimes difficult to spot?

ATTACK AND DEFENSE 267

13. In discussing a question of policy what is a common inconsistency of affirmative debaters? of negative debaters?
14. How can a debater defend against the charge of inconsistency?
15. What is a dilemma?
16. Name a favorite dilemma of negative debaters in arguing a question of policy.
17. What are the two requirements of a good dilemma?
18. What are two defenses against a dilemma?
19. What two organizational problems face the debater in the last seven speeches of a traditional debate on a proposition of policy?
20. Explain the difference between simultaneous and separate treatment of constructive and refutative proofs in the first negative constructive speech.
21. How can one account for situations in which the prepared negative constructive contentions seem unrelated to the first affirmative constructive speech?
22. What are the three primary duties of the second affirmative speaker in his constructive speech?
23. What *must* the second negative debater do in his constructive speech?
24. What tasks may be undertaken either in the second negative constructive speech or in the first negative rebuttal?
25. In general, how should rebuttal speeches be organized?
26. Why is the first affirmative rebuttal speech important?
27. What is the major objective of the second negative rebuttal? of the second affirmative rebuttal?

*B. For Class Discussion*
1. Which element, attack or defense, is more important to the affirmative team? to the negative team? Why?
2. To what extent can excellent cases preclude refutation? Are some kinds of attacks more easily prevented by a good case than others?
3. What is the primary reason why attack and defense are necessary parts of a justification for calling debate a critical instrument?

EXERCISES

*A. Written Exercises*
1. Construct an argument and compose at least three different methods of attacking it. Then defend against each attack.
2. Make a chart of attacks and defenses employed in the sample college debate in Appendix A. In a series of columns, paraphrase the initial argument, the attack, the defense, the re-attack, the redefense, etc., until the argument stops or the debate ends. In parentheses, label the methods of attack and defense. Include at least five such clashes.

*B. Oral Exercises*

1. Present a single proof. A classmate will be assigned to refute your proof. You will be given an opportunity to defend it.

2. Present a five-minute speech in which you insert one cleverly disguised inconsistency. Your classmates will try to spot it.

3. Present a dilemma. See if your classmates are able to offer and support an additional alternative or to accept and support one of the choices you supplied.

## SUGGESTIONS FOR FURTHER READING

Aristotle, *Rhetoric,* in *The Rhetoric and Poetics of Aristotle,* tr. W. Rhys Roberts (New York: Random House, 1954), 1402a 29–1403a 33. Divides refutation into countersyllogisms and objections, argues that the former are built along the same lines of argument as the original syllogisms, and discusses and illustrates four kinds of objections.

William T. Foster, *Argumentation and Debating,* rev. ed. (Boston: Houghton Mifflin Co., 1917), Chapter 9, "Refuting Opposing Arguments: Special Methods." Discusses the selection, the position, and the presentation of refutation; then analyzes and illustrates four special methods of refutation.

Herbert L. James, "Standards for Judging Refutation," *The Register,* 9 (Spring 1961), 21–25. Reports the opinions of fifty-seven college debate coaches on twenty-nine provocative questions concerning selected standards and procedures of refutation.

## Chapter 17
# STYLE AND DELIVERY: CLARITY

> ... clearness, force, and beauty of style are absolutely necessary to one who would draw men to his way of thinking; nay, to anyone who would induce the great mass of mankind to give so much as passing heed to what he has to say.
> WOODROW WILSON

CHAPTER 9 pointed out that if deliberation is to be critical, each fact and value entered as evidence must be given exactly the weight it deserves—neither more nor less. Further, it was suggested that just as the worth of evidence may be overstated through accident or design, so may its worth be understated through ineptitude.

To guard against the dangers of overstatement, the debater should sensitize himself to the unfair devices discussed in the section of Chapter 9 entitled "An Ethic of Evidence," and to the strategems of argument explained in Chapter 12. To insure that ideas are entered into deliberation at their full worth, two requirements must be met. The first involves the substantative skills of analysis and inference which have already been considered. The second requirement involves the communicative skills of style and delivery and remains to be considered.

Properly understood as aids to insuring that ideas are exhibited at their full worth, style and delivery are not luxuries or frills. No less than the procedures of analysis and proof, they are indispensable to producing the critical decisions at which debate aims.

Many writers and speakers have affirmed this truth. Henry James, the novelist, remarked, "What is merely stated is never really presented." Lord Chesterfield advised his son, "Vulgar, coarse, and ill-chosen words will deform the best thoughts, as much as rags and dirt will the best figure." Daniel Webster wrote in a letter to a young friend, "Depend upon it; it is with our thoughts as with our persons—their intrinsic value is mostly undervalued, unless outwardly expressed in an attractive garb."

So far as style and delivery may contribute, the worth of an idea will be made evident if that idea is stated *clearly* and *attractively* enough so that its attentive consideration does not prove painful to the reader or listener.

The twin criteria of clarity and attractiveness apply equally to style and delivery. Just as the language in which an idea is expressed must be clear and agreeable, so must its oral presentation possess these qualities.

How the debater may achieve clarity in style and delivery forms the subject of this chapter. How he may render his style and delivery attractive will be considered in the chapter that follows.

## CLARITY IN STYLE

The uninitiated sometimes suppose that while special effort or aptitude is required to produce discourse of literary merit, no problem is involved in expressing oneself clearly.

Nothing is further from the truth. Language is an intractable master rather than an obedient servant. It takes command of ideas and reshapes them. Try as he will, the debater often cannot make the most elementary concept intelligible to others, while his best efforts to produce simple, straightforward prose may result in meandering sentences full of vague terms and awkward constructions.

The surest path to clarity of expression is hard and persistent effort. As the old saw has it, "One must apply the seat of the pants to the seat of the chair." Assuming a generous measure of patience and industry, however, the following advice may prove helpful.

### CLEAR AND COMPLETE COMPREHENSION

The first step in achieving clarity of style is to make certain that one understands himself the idea he wishes to communicate to others. Each idea, therefore, must be studied from many points of view. It must be broken into its parts, and these parts brought together in various relationships. It must be fitted into the broader subject to which it belongs, and related concepts noted. If the idea is unusually complex, it may need to be reduced to outline form; if new, it may need a chance to germinate.

As aids toward understanding ideas, the processes of analysis outlined in Chapter 14 are useful. To them must be added any other method of study that promises to promote full and accurate comprehension.

## SELECTING THE PROPER WORDS

ACCURATE WORDS. Once the idea is clearly understood, the next task is to select the words that express it most precisely. This step is crucial because words are the basic units of thought. Unless accurate words are chosen, clear and exact meanings cannot be communicated.

Consider this cluster of terms: *tax, levy, assessment, duty, impost, customs, excise, toll, tariff.*

A *tax* is a compulsory contribution levied upon persons, property, or business for the support of government. . . . A *levy* implies money or supplies collected, often by force, to meet a special emergency. An *assessment* is an amount, usually based on the value of property or investments, and levied on a person by an authority or a society; as, an *assessment* on a property for an improvement shared by neighboring properties. A *duty* or *impost* is levied on imports and exports: *customs* are collected on imports at the frontiers of a country. . . . An *excise* is a tax levied on manufacture, trading, or sports. A *toll* is paid for the right to pass over a bridge, through a tunnel, etc., to defray the cost of the structure. . . . A *tariff* is a *duty* or *tax* on some particular class of goods. . . .

Or compare *law, enactment, command, edict, decree, statute, ordinance,* and *regulation.*

*Law* . . . is any legislative *enactment* to enforce justice and prescribe duty. . . . *Command* [is] personal and particular, as the *commands* of a parent. . . . An *edict* is the proclamation of a law by an absolute sovereign or other authority; we speak of the edict of an emperor, the *decree* of a court. . . . *Statute* is the recognized legal term for a specific *law; enactment* is the more vague and general expression. We speak of municipal *ordinances* [and] army *regulations.* . . .[1]

Mark Twain once said that the difference between the right word and the nearly right word may be "the difference between the lightning and the lightning bug." Certainly, it may be the difference between conveying the exact meaning intended, and some other meaning which confuses or obscures the desired thought.

SIMPLE WORDS. When more than one word or expression meets the test of accuracy, a safe rule is to prefer the shorter or simpler alternative over the longer or more difficult.

Say "darken" rather than "obfuscate," "learn" rather than "ascertain," "begin" rather than "inaugurate," "state" rather than "common-

---

[1] The two quoted passages are from *Standard Handbook of Synonyms, Antonyms, and Prepositions,* ed. James C. Fernald, rev. ed. (New York: Funk and Wagnalls, 1947). Reprinted by permission of the publisher.

wealth," "the courts" rather than "the judiciary," "movement of peoples" rather than "population migration."

Long and difficult words puzzle a listener or reader. When used in combination, they raise diction above the level of easy comprehension. Lincoln remarked, "Speak so that the most lowly can understand, and the rest will have no difficulty." This statement is sound advice for the debater.

SPECIFIC WORDS. Because general words cover a range of particulars, they diffuse meaning and allow a reader or listener to choose from among a number of possibilities.

Suppose a debater attacks "the American college" as undemocratic. To one person the phrase "American college" calls up the picture of a small agricultural school in a rural community. To another it calls up the picture of a sprawling state university; to a third, a metropolitan skyscraper institution; to a fourth, a tradition-laden Ivy League college. Or suppose a newspaper story reports that Mr. Jones has been charged with a "traffic violation." One reader assumes he was caught speeding; another, that he "ran" a red light; still another, that he parked in a restricted zone. Because the terms of the statement are general rather than specific, they allow for multiple interpretations and render precise communication difficult.

To promote clarity, always choose the most specific term available—the term that covers only the precise area of meaning intended. Say "embezzlement" rather than "corruption," "cruiser" rather than "naval vessel," "Explorer VI" rather than "rocket," "textbook" rather than "publication," "Professor William H. Jones of the Department of Economics at Amherst" rather than "a prominent eastern economist," etc. The first alternative leaves little doubt concerning the specific act, object, or person referred to; the second allows a leeway in choice and hence opens the road to misunderstanding.

CONCRETE WORDS. Concrete words denote things immediately perceptible by the senses—things we can see, hear, feel, smell, or taste.

Examine the following pairs of terms: beautiful, violet-hued; noise, clang; rough, sandpaper-like; odorous, rose-scented; appetizing, spicy. Not only is the second word in each pair more specific, but it refers to something that can be directly sensed.

Because concrete words are rooted in immediate sensory experience, a reader or listener seldom needs to reflect in order to grasp their meaning. They, above all other words, convey ideas quickly and clearly. In addition, they lend force to language because sensory experiences possess a vividness that abstract ideas lack.

An Eastern proverb says that if one wishes to win understanding he must change ears into eyes. How concrete words help accomplish this transformation may be seen by comparing these sentences:

When unemployment occurs, suffering results.

When men lose their jobs, their families are cold and hungry; their children go without books and medicine; their wives wear worn-out shoes and dresses.

WORDS WITH FAMILIAR REFERENTS. Words are not things. They are signs or symbols that stand as substitutes for events, objects, persons, experiences, or feelings.

Unless a reader or listener is acquainted with the "life fact" a word stands for—with what is technically called its "referent"—the symbol will have no meaning for him. The agricultural terms "shucking," "harrowing," and "polling" bewilder rather than enlighten the city dweller; the nautical terms "port," "starboard," "bow," and "stern" are lost on the person who knows nothing about ships; talk of "cuts" and "credit hours" is meaningless to the young man or woman who has not attended college.

If ideas are to be clear, words must call up familiar referents in the minds of listeners or readers. When strange or esoteric terms cannot be avoided, they must be translated into familiar language.

NONTECHNICAL WORDS. Every trade and profession, every field of study, develops a language of its own. The vocabulary of this language is composed in part of "manufactured" words and in part of everyday words used in strange or specialized ways. Such words are called *jargon*.

Although technical words may be meaningful to experts in a field and, indeed, essential to their activities, they are usually gibberish to the layman.

What, for example, would the average reader or listener, untrained in the vocabularies of psychology and sociology, make out of this sentence? "While societal norms invariably elicit voluntary commitments on the part of the thoroughly acculturated, to the social migrant such norms demand accommodations of the most radical nature." Or what could a person untrained in the language of the financial pages infer from this sentence? "Minor fluctuations in rails and industrials, reflecting an increased tendency toward profit taking, today drove lower a market that for the past several weeks has been definitely bullish."

The debater will probably encounter many technical words in the books and reports he studies in preparing his arguments and, for the sake of accuracy, may occasionally wish to transmit some of them to his readers or listeners. But he should always use technical words sparingly and take care to translate into more immediately understandable terms those which cannot be avoided.

In particular, the debater should not forget that this caution applies to his own specialized field of endeavor—debating itself. Many debaters sprinkle their language with the technical terms of argument—*status quo,* "burden of rebuttal," "need issue," *post hoc,* "proposition of policy," and the like. Because these terms, no less than the technical expressions in any field, confuse rather than enlighten the layman, they should generally be avoided. If, for some compelling reason, they must be used, they should be accompanied by appropriate explanations.

## ARRANGING WORDS IN SENTENCES

With accurate, simple, specific, concrete, and familiar words selected, the debater must arrange them into suitable sentences. Here three considerations apply.

SHORT SENTENCES. Other things being equal, short sentences convey ideas more clearly than do long ones. By "short" is not meant three- to five-word sentences of the "I see a cat. The cat is gray." variety. Complex ideas can seldom be communicated accurately in sentences of this length. Moreover, an unbroken string of short sentences makes for a jumpy and disconcerting style.

But long sentences, even when skillfully handled, put a strain on the attention and memory. The ideal is for each sentence to be just long enough to accommodate the idea it seeks to communicate.

Henry Ward Beecher, the famous clergyman and lecturer of the last century, gives this advice in his *Yale Lectures on Preaching:*

> Involved sentences, crooked, circuitous, and parenthetical, no matter how musically they may be balanced, are prejudicial to a facile understanding of the truth. . . . A good fireman will send the water through as short and straight a hose as he can. No man in his senses would desire to have the stream flow through coil after coil, winding about. It loses force by length and complexity. . . .
>
> Don't whip with a switch that has leaves on it, if you want to tingle.

SIMPLY STRUCTURED SENTENCES. For maximum intelligibility, a sentence should not only be as short as practicable, but the thought should move forward naturally and easily, without awkward interruptions and without distracting excursions into related ideas.

Consider the following sentence, spoken during a debate in the House of Commons, by the eighteenth-century English statesman Edmund Burke:

> I remember that the noble Lord on the floor—not in a former speech, to be sure (it would be disorderly to refer to it—I suppose I read it somewhere)

—but the noble Lord was pleased to say that he did not conceive how it could enter into the head of man to impose such taxes as those of 1767 (I mean those taxes which he voted for imposing and voted for repealing) as being taxes contrary to all principles of commerce, laid on British manufacturers.

Now compare this sentence with a passage from a speech on a similar subject, delivered in the House of Lords, November 18, 1777, by another famous British statesman, Lord Chatham:

> The desperate state of our arms abroad is in part known: no man thinks more highly of them than I do. I love and honor the English troops. I know their virtues and their valor. I know they can achieve anything except impossibilities; and I know that the conquest of English America is an impossibility. You cannot, I venture to say it, you cannot conquer America. Your armies in the last war effected everything that could be effected; and what was it? It cost a numerous army, under the command of a most able general, now a noble lord in this house, a long and laborious campaign, to expel five thousand Frenchmen from French America. My lords, you cannot conquer America.

Here, although not all the sentences are short, they are all direct and simply structured. They render the speaker's meaning instantly and unmistakably clear. Moreover, the precision of expression adds weight to the ideas.

Study, finally, these closing paragraphs of President Franklin Roosevelt's radio address to the nation on September 3, 1939, announcing America's policy of neutrality at the outbreak of World War II.

> This nation will remain a neutral nation, but I cannot ask that every American remain neutral in thought as well. Even a neutral has a right to take account of facts. Even a neutral cannot be asked to close his mind or his conscience.
>
> I have said not once but many times that I have seen war and that I hate war. I say that again and again.
>
> I hope the United States will keep out of this war. I believe that it will. And I give you assurances that every effort of your government will be directed toward that end.
>
> As long as it remains within my power to prevent it, there will be no blackout of peace in the United States.[2]

The passages from Chatham and Roosevelt represent the ideal of simple, direct statement toward which the debater should aim.

PRECISE SENTENCES. Words which themselves are clear may be so combined that the sentences they comprise are vague or ambiguous. To help insure precision of communication, avoid the following:

[2] *New York Times,* Sept. 4, 1939, p. 6.

*a.* The combination of terms into phrases or meaning clusters that lack precision. ("While the situation has certainly improved *more than was expected,* it is still *far from what we might wish.*")

*b.* Indefinite antecedents or antecedents too far removed from the terms to which they refer. ("Prominent senators, having engaged in a long and exhaustive study of the problem, calling many witnesses and taking much testimony as well as travelling to all parts of the country, it was finally decided that further delay would be unwise and wasteful.")

*c.* Improperly placed modifiers. ("The depression began just after he had been elected, introducing new problems and bringing a great deal of suffering to all.")

*d.* Improper use of negatives. ("No teacher in the state is required by law not to spank a naughty child.")

*e.* Unnecessary wordiness. ("The bill that was eventually passed after much deliberation and that I wished to quote from here, I shall be unable to quote from directly due to the fact that, unless I am mistaken, I seem, at least for the moment, to have mislaid it.")

*f.* Ambiguous statements. ("Calling the secretary of state on the phone, the senator said he had been in error in his recent speech.")

## PARAGRAPHS AND LARGER UNITS OF THOUGHT

Of great aid in promoting clarity is the proper arrangement of paragraphs and larger units of thought. Here, in addition to the rules of unity and coherence that govern all good speaking or writing, the following considerations are pertinent.

1. *Follow some systematic order of thought progression.* The pattern employed may be chronological, spatial, topical, or causal. That some pattern be clearly perceived is probably more important than the particular pattern selected.

In explaining the development of an institution or practice, proceed *chronologically* by tracing the stages through which that development passed. In describing how something is organized or arranged, use *spatial* order, associating those parts or elements that are contiguous in space or related in function. In discussing a group of related ideas or arguments, organize them *topically* and emphasize their parallel relationship. In accounting for the existence of a phenomenon, work systematically from *cause to effect* or from *effect to cause.*

In presenting constructive arguments, adhere, as a general rule, to the Aristotelian order of stating your case and proving it. In refuting a contention advanced by an opponent, retrace the pattern he followed in developing it.[3]

Just as accurate and clear words, when presented in a jumbled order, result in an unclear sentence, so do clear and accurately framed sentences, when unsystematically arranged, obscure the meaning of a paragraph or larger unit of thought.

2. *Carry forward the thought at a proper speed.* As a close student of his subject, the debater is intimately acquainted with many relevant facts and arguments. Often, however, he errs in supposing that his readers or listeners are equally well informed. He touches upon ideas so briefly or so telescopes his proofs that they cannot be grasped by the nonexpert.

Every good piece of argumentative discourse must "march"—must constantly press forward, carrying the thought to its natural conclusion. But it must not push forward so rapidly that it becomes a kaleidoscope of swiftly changing proofs, no one of which is fully understood as it is presented and all of which are soon forgotten.

If an idea is to be made clear, it must be held for a time in the mind of the reader or listener; he must have an opportunity to savor and digest it. Examples, illustrations, and comparisons, as well as reiteration and restatement, are of the greatest possible use in holding ideas in focus. An important idea should be approached from many different points of view. It should be exemplified and illustrated, compared or contrasted with related ideas, or restated in different language. Nothing is gained by "hitting an idea and bouncing off" or by striking it a glancing blow. The recipient must be able to come to grips with it fully and firmly. It must for a time fill his mind and command his undivided attention.

Many debaters mistakenly believe that the strength of a cause is to be measured by the number of arguments covered in an allotted time or space. But more important than the total number of arguments mentioned is the strength and pertinence of each. The debater does better to move more slowly and make sure that a few significant ideas are clear than to hasten over many points fleetingly. Arguments that are not understood can have little influence.

3. *Include all major elements in the development of an argument.* For the same reason that an important argument should not be passed over too quickly, no step essential to its comprehension should be omitted. Only in the rarest instances will the nonexpert reader or listener be able to supply the missing element and follow the thought to its conclusion.

Every debater should learn the difficult art of "pacing" his discourse.

[3] For further suggestions on organizing refutation, see pp. 253–54.

On the one hand, he must not bore by laboring obvious details; on the other, he must not neglect to mention the crucial links on which a proof depends. Determining the "pace" appropriate to a given subject and audience requires much practice, but the reward is worth the effort. Clarity is, in large measure, the result of sound judgment in the use of details.

4. *Supply previews, transitions, and summaries.* Previews, transitions, and summaries promote clarity by keeping the reader or listener reminded of where he has been, where he is, and where he is going. These devices are especially important in oral discourse, where such visual helps as paragraphing, subject headings, and outline symbols are unavailable. But in writing, too, they make a major contribution to intelligibility.

The principal caution is to avoid hackneyed transitional and summary phrases. "Be that as it may," "On the contrary, we would submit," "Moving on to the next point," "Therefore, in review," etc. are used by debaters much too frequently. Variety and flexibility of expression should be the aim here, as in all kinds of discourse.

5. *Flag important ideas.* The wise debater gives his leading arguments positional or spatial emphasis. Moreover, by the skillful handling of previews, transitions, and summaries, he helps his listeners or readers recognize their importance.

In addition, however, significant arguments may be signaled out by explicit "pointing" or "flagging." The debater may say, "But by far the most compelling reason, . . ." "Please pay particular attention to the following figures, . . ." "Now, what this declaration substantially means is, . . ." "Brought down to cases, . . ." "In other words, . . ." etc.

Sometimes flagging is viewed as an unnecessary laboring of the self-apparent and, therefore, as offensive to an intelligent reader or listener. When tactfully employed, however, flagging is usually welcomed by persons earnestly interested in following a discourse. Without question, it promotes the clarity of an argumentative speech or essay by indicating the relative importance of ideas.

6. *Provide abundant examples, illustrations, and comparisons.* Besides holding ideas in the focus of attention, examples and illustrations enhance clarity by making ideas concrete. Because they denote actual persons, places, events, or occurrences, they bring abstract conceptions into the realm of immediate experience and serve, as Beecher remarked, as "the windows through which light is shed on our argument."

Comparisons aid clarity and facilitate learning because they enable the recipient to connect the unfamiliar with the familiar. They provide bridges over which he may advance from the known to the unknown

## STYLE AND DELIVERY: CLARITY

and over which he may return to interpret and verify his findings. The psychologist William James in his *Talks to Teachers* laid down as one of the central tenets of all instruction that the teacher should begin a new lesson by mentioning what the student already knows; then the new material should be related to this base of previous knowledge. By following similar advice, the debater can do much to make his ideas and arguments clear.

### TWO EXAMPLES OF CLEAR ARGUMENTATIVE DISCOURSE

As notable examples of clear argumentative discourse, consider the two following passages. The first is taken from the well-known address that Lincoln made at Cooper Union on February 27, 1860. The second is from a speech by John C. Calhoun, assailing the so-called Force Bill, and was delivered in the Senate in 1833.

Judging by all they [the people of the South] say and do, and by the subject and nature of their controversy with us, let us determine, if we can, what will satisfy them.

Will they be satisfied if the Territories be unconditionally surrendered to them? We know they will not. In all their present complaints against us, the Territories are scarcely mentioned. Invasions and insurrections are the rage now. Will it satisfy them, if, in the future, we have nothing to do with invasions and insurrections? We know it will not. We so know, because we know we never had anything to do with invasions and insurrections; and yet this total abstaining does not exempt us from the charge and the denunciation.

The question recurs, What will satisfy them? Simply this: we must not only let them alone, but we must somehow convince them that we do let them alone. This, we know by experience, is no easy task. We have been so trying to convince them from the very beginning of our organization, but with no success. In all our platforms and speeches we have constantly protested our purpose to let them alone; but this has had no tendency to convince them. Alike unavailing to convince them is the fact that they have never detected a man of us in any attempt to disturb them.

These natural, and apparently adequate means all failing, what will convince them? This, and this only: cease to call slavery wrong, and join them in calling it right. And this must be done thoroughly—done in acts as well as in words. Silence will not be tolerated—we must place ourselves avowedly with them. Senator Douglas's new sedition laws must be enacted and enforced, suppressing all declarations that slavery is wrong, whether made in politics, in presses, in pulpits, or in private. We must arrest and return their fugitive slaves with greedy pleasure. We must pull down our free-State constitutions. The whole atmosphere must be disinfected from all taint of opposition to slavery, before they will cease to believe that all their troubles proceed from us.

I am quite aware they do not state their case precisely in this way. Most of them would probably say to us, "Let us alone; do nothing to us, and say what you please about slavery." But we do let them alone,—have never disturbed them,—so that, after all, it is what we say that dissatisfies them. They will continue to accuse us of doing, until we cease saying.[4]

Has Congress the right to pass this bill? There are two views of our Constitution, going back to its fundamental principles; one contained in the proclamation and the message of the President [Andrew Jackson] which has given birth to this bill [the Force Bill], and the other the ordinance and proceedings of the people of South Carolina. As one or the other of these views may be correct, the bill must be pronounced constitutional or unconstitutional. If it be true, as stated by the President, that the people of these United States are united on the principle of a social compact, as so many individuals constituting one nation; if they have transferred to the general government their allegiance; if they have parted with the right of judging, in the last resort, what powers are reserved and what delegated; then indeed the states are without sovereignty, without rights, and no other objection can be made to the bill but what might be made to its expediency. But, if on the other hand, these positions are utterly false; if, in truth, the constitution is the work of the people forming twenty-four distinct political communities; if, when adopted, it formed a union of States and not of individuals; if the states have not surrendered the right of judging in the last resort, . . . there is not the shadow of foundation in the Constitution to authorize the bill; but, on the contrary, it would be wholly repugnant to its genius, destructive of its very existence; and involve a political sin of the highest character—of the delegated acting against the sovereign power—of the creature warring against the creator.[5]

## A TEST OF CLARITY IN STYLE

To test the clarity of his style, the debater may ask these questions: Will a reasonably intelligent and attentive listener be able to understand my arguments readily? Will my opponents, as informed students of the subject, find it impossible to misunderstand them?

When the first of these tests goes unmet, the debater's point is lost upon those in whose hands the decision lies. When the second is unsatisfied, the progress of deliberation is delayed, the central issues clouded or distorted, and ill feeling rather than a dispassionate reflective attitude prevails. For these reasons, clarity of expression—such clarity as conveys meaning fully, precisely, and readily—is as much a part of good debating as are a knowledge of the subject, cogency in proof, and skill in adaptation and rebuttal.

[4] *Complete Works of Abraham Lincoln*, ed. John G. Nicolay and John Hay, 2 vols. (New York: Century Co., 1894), I, 611–12.
[5] *Register of Debates in Congress*, 22nd Cong., 2nd Sess., pp. 187–88.

## CLARITY IN DELIVERY

When debate is oral rather than written, intelligibility depends not only on the proper use of language, but also on the proper use of voice and body in communicating ideas to listeners.

### VOICE

Two aspects of vocal delivery, *rate* and *articulation,* require the debater's particular attention.

RATE. Faced with restricted time limits and stimulated by the excitement of the argument, many debaters increase their normal speaking rates and develop a "machine-gun" type of presentation. They pour out a staccato flow of two hundred or more words a minute, with few pauses or breathing spells.

Machine-gun delivery is unpleasant to listen to. Moreover, it defeats the end of critical deliberation because arguments presented in this manner are difficult for an audience to digest and evaluate. Only occasional flashes or glimpses of meaning are received. Claims, warrants, and evidence are jumbled.

Recently, mathematicians and communications engineers have developed a new science called "information theory." One of the subjects information theory studies is the efficient use of communication channels. What is the maximum amount of information that can be transmitted over a given channel in a fixed period of time, without loss of meaning through distortion or the inability of the recipient to "decode" the message as rapidly as it is being sent? Investigations have shown that for any channel there is an optimum speed at which information may be sent. Sending it at less than this optimum rate makes for an inefficient use of the channel's capacity; sending it more rapidly "overloads" the channel and results in loss of understanding.

The principle of optimum rate applies in debate. For best results, the debater must neither underload nor overload his "communication channel." Speaking too rapidly is as inefficient as speaking too slowly. The rate of utterance, while fast enough to retain interest, must be adapted to the capacity of the listener to follow and understand.

ARTICULATION. Clear vocal delivery depends, second, on clear articulation. Debaters, like other speakers, are frequently guilty of lip, tongue, and jaw laziness. They do not move the parts of their articulatory mechanism freely enough to produce sharp sounds.

No one would seriously recommend that the debater practice the affected and overly precise articulation favored by the "elocution" teachers of an earlier day. But in the interest of critical decision-making, if not common courtesy, he owes it to his audience to articulate his words clearly.

The road to improved articulation is for most speakers an easy one: Be aware of the part active tongue, lip, and jaw movements play in clear articulation. Learn to manipulate the parts of the articulatory mechanism freely. Unless one is hindered by a speech defect—in which case he should consult a trained clinician—this program will usually bring results.

### BODY

The debater who would make his meaning clear must be physically responsive to the ideas he presents.

Physical responsiveness is a blanket term and encompasses the finer changes of facial expression and muscle tension, as well as the gross movements of the arms, legs, and torso. It also includes directness or eye contact with one's listeners.

Gestures used to describe size, position, or relationship of parts, to set off one idea from another, or to reinforce contentions are indispensable aids to intelligibility. So also are changes in facial expression and muscle tone. Movement about the platform relieves tension and "paragraphs" the speech into its major divisions. Eye contact commands the listener's attention and contributes to an impression of sincerity on the part of the speaker.

The part that effective bodily delivery plays in promoting intelligibility is sometimes overlooked. Debaters forget or disregard lessons learned in their public speaking courses. The good speaker is alive physically as well as mentally. His body is as alert and responsive as his mind. He uses every resource at his command to render arguments clear.

### THE USE OF NOTES

Because he deals with complex subject matter and because his speaking must be largely unrehearsed, the debater, more than most public speakers, is dependent on notes. Nor is this fact particularly to be deplored, provided he learns to use them unobtrusively. Properly employed, notes help insure the complete and accurate statements on which a critical decision depends; improperly employed, however, they detract from the clarity of physical and vocal delivery.

Observation indicates three undesirable practices in the use of notes. First, many debaters carry to the speaker's stand large stacks of books, magazines, and newspapers. These materials do not impress the average listener as much as is sometimes supposed. Instead, they tend to impair eye contact, bodily responsiveness, and vocal presentation. Eyes buried in books cannot look at listeners; hands busy turning pages cannot aid communication with meaningful gestures; the voice that comes from behind a magazine or newspaper is muffled and dampened.

All would agree that the debater must have at hand the data necessary to prove his claims. Except in rare instances, however, these data should be recorded on cards or small slips of paper rather than read from original sources. When books and magazines are referred to directly, they should be so marked and organized that the desired passage can be found quickly.

Second, many debaters, out of habit, glance at their notes even when the idea they wish to present is clear in their minds. Like the man who continues to walk with a crutch after his leg has healed, they depend on an unnecessary and bothersome support. The ideal is to consult one's notes sparingly, using them only when proceeding without aid is impossible. Note-laden delivery is never good public speaking; hence, it can never be good debating.

Third, when debaters read verbatim statements contained in their notes, they often do so poorly. The importance of reading such statements at a reasonable rate, clearly and intelligently, of grouping the words into natural thought units, and of expressing ideas with appropriate inflection and emphasis, is obvious. If the reading is poor, meaning will be obscured or distorted and critical decision-making impaired.

The debater should strive to become a skilled oral reader, as well as an apt extemporaneous speaker. Proficiency in both modes of presentation is essential if ideas are to be entered into deliberation at their full worth.

## A TEST OF CLARITY IN DELIVERY

To evaluate the clarity of delivery, one may apply a double test: Have I avoided obscuring in any way the full and precise meaning of each idea and argument offered? Beyond this, have I enhanced the intelligibility of ideas and arguments by rendering them clearer and more meaningful than they would be if read silently or recited in a lifeless monotone?

Admittedly, the test is not an easy one. Yet it is of first importance. Just as sound argument is of no avail if presented in an unintelligible style, so a clear style is useless if delivery obscures meaning. Clear delivery completes the chain, of which correct analysis and cogent proof form the first links. If collective judgments are to be critical, thinking must not only be informed but, through the medium of delivery as well as style, the results of that thinking must be accurately transmitted to others. If one cannot be a good debater unless he analyzes correctly and reasons soundly, by the same token, he cannot be a good debater unless he writes and speaks clearly.

## QUESTIONS

*A. To Check Your Comprehension and Memory*

1. What two requirements must be met if ideas are to be entered into deliberation at their full worth?
2. What is the "surest" path to a clear style?
3. What more specific directions may aid the debater in reaching this goal?
4. Name six requirements that words must meet if they are to be clear.
5. What three considerations should govern the framing of sentences?
6. Define a "short sentence."
7. Explain some of the causes of vague or ambiguous sentences.
8. What considerations are important in arranging paragraphs and larger units of thought?
9. Name four patterns of "thought progression" that may be used in organizing a discourse.
10. What is meant by "pacing" a speech or essay? Why is pacing important?
11. Define "flagging." How does flagging help promote clarity?
12. State two reasons why examples and illustrations clarify ideas.
13. How do comparisons aid clarity?
14. State the test of a clear style.
15. What two aspects of vocal delivery require the debater's special attention? Why?
16. Define "optimum rate."
17. How may articulation usually be improved?
18. Explain the importance of physical responsiveness in good public speaking.
19. Name three common faults in the use of notes.
20. State the double test by which the clarity of delivery may be gauged.

*B. For Class Discussion*

1. Comment on this sentence from Swift's "Letter to a Young Clergyman": "When a man's thoughts are clear, the properest words will generally offer themselves first, and his own judgment will direct him in what order to place them, so as they may be best understood." Do you agree or disagree? Why?
2. In striving to be clear, may a speaker or writer sometimes oversimplify an idea? What effect does such oversimplification have on critical delibera-

tion? How may this danger be avoided?

3. Can an absolute standard of clarity be imposed on speaking and writing? Or is clarity always relative to the knowledge and intellectual level of the persons addressed?

4. If a word is clear only when its "referent" is familiar, how do we learn about new phenomena lying beyond the realm of our immediate experience?

5. Listen as a group to a recording of an argumentative speech by some well-known speaker. Decide whether the speaker's articulation, rate, inflectional patterns, etc. helped clarify his ideas. Could even greater clarity have been achieved by these means?

## EXERCISES

*A. Written Exercises*

1. Read one of the debates printed in the Appendix or another debate assigned by your instructor. Find at least three passages that strike you as admirably clear. Defend your choice in a short written statement, referring directly to the standards set forth in this chapter. Then find at least three passages which are less clear than you think they might be. Rewrite these passages so as to attain greater clarity.

2. Write a short argumentative essay on a subject of your own choosing. Exchange the essays so that each is read by at least two other members of the class, who criticize the word choice, sentence structure, etc. from the point of view of clarity. Then rewrite the essay, following the criticisms offered.

3. Prepare a paper summarizing and evaluating Quintilian's discussion of delivery, as listed in the "Suggestions for Further Reading" at the end of this chapter.

*B. Oral Exercise*

Select some relatively complex term or concept with which you are familiar as a result of special thought or study ("balance of trade," *"de jure* recognition," "States' rights," "indirect price controls," "pragmatism," or the like).

Paying particular attention to word choice, sentence arrangement, and the order and pace of thought progression, prepare a three-minute speech in which you make this concept as clear as you can to the other members of your class.

Test how successful you have been by seeing whether, as a result of your speech, your listeners can now state the meaning and significance of the concept correctly.

## SUGGESTIONS FOR FURTHER READING

Waldo W. Braden and Mary Louise Gehring, *Speech Practices: A Resource Book for the Student of Public Speaking* (New York: Harper & Bros.,

1958), Chapter 6, "The Speaker Expresses His Ideas." Excerpts from speeches—some by students—illustrate how appropriate style helps clarify ideas and distinguish related concepts.

Quintilian, *Institutio Oratoria*, 11.3. A thorough and judicious discussion of the role of delivery in effective public speaking, by a great Roman teacher of rhetoric. As pertinent and sound today as when it was written.

Herbert Spencer, "The Philosophy of Style," *Essays: Scientific, Political, and Speculative* (London: Longman, Brown, Green, Longman, and Roberts, 1858–1874). Develops the principle of "economy of attention" as the controlling consideration in style. "A reader or listener," says Spencer, "has at each moment but a limited amount of mental power available. . . . Hence, the more time and attention it takes to receive and understand each sentence, the less time and attention can be given to the contained idea; and the less vividly will that idea be conceived." Frequently reprinted. See, for example, Wilbur Samuel Howell, *Problems and Styles of Communication* (New York: F. S. Crofts, 1945), pp. 165–99.

Jonathan Swift, "A Letter to a Young Clergyman," in *Prose Works*, ed. Temple Scott (London: G. Bell, 1900–1914), III, 200–07. Swift discusses common faults of style, chief among them the use of "obscure" or "hard" words, and criticizes an author's concern with displaying his own learning rather than communicating important ideas to others. Many reprints available.

## Chapter 18

# STYLE AND DELIVERY: ATTRACTIVENESS

*True beauty is never divorced from utility.* QUINTILIAN

IF DELIBERATION is to be critical, the debater's style and delivery must be attractive as well as clear. Communication that is unattractive irritates and repels. Instead of receiving attentive consideration, ideas go unheeded.

Summarizing the habits of most listeners and readers, the sixteenth-century English rhetorician Thomas Wilson observed, "Delight them, and win them; weary them, and you lose them for ever." Every debater should remember this dictum.

To be attractive, style and delivery must, first, be free of distracting traits and mannerisms. Clichés, awkward phrases, and clumsy gestures offend the person of developed sensibilities. Worse still, they impair clarity because they take attention away from the ideas being expressed and center it upon themselves.

Attractiveness and clarity, therefore, coincide. If style and delivery are free of distractions, attention is given to matter rather than manner, and intelligibility is promoted. Conversely, if discourse is clear, reading or listening is rendered less arduous and hence more enjoyable. As the Roman teacher Quintilian remarked in the quotation placed at the head of this chapter, "True beauty is never divorced from utility."

## ATTRACTIVENESS IN STYLE

Although style cannot be attractive unless it is clear, clarity alone does not make language agreeable.

Consider the prose of the mail order catalogue or legal contract. The style is lucid, conveying meaning fully and precisely; yet it is not attractive. It informs, but does not please.

If an argumentative speech or essay is to be agreeable, the style must possess other qualities besides clarity. These qualities are individuality, freshness, vigor, ease, and figurativeness.

## INDIVIDUALITY

In his essay "On Style" the German philosopher Schopenhauer wrote:

> Style is the physiognomy of the mind, and a safer index to character than the face. To imitate another man's style is like wearing a mask, which, be it never so fine, is not long in arousing disgust and abhorrence, because it is lifeless; so that even the ugliest living face is better.

Schopenhauer states a principle of first importance: To be pleasing, a style must mirror, rather than hide, the writer's or speaker's personality and habits of mind.

Do not, in the pursuit of a model or of an abstract ideal, attempt to sound like someone else. Do not hide behind a mask of language. Every man has a personal idiom—a way of expression that distinguishes him. Employing this idiom openly marks one as honest and ingenuous. Attempting to suppress it arouses distaste and mistrust. Study good models and appreciate their excellences, but do not ape them. Instead, strive to bring your own idiom to the highest state of perfection.

Just as people react unfavorably to pretense in dress and manners, so do they find pretense in style displeasing. They like best writing and speaking that enable them to meet the author face to face.

## FRESHNESS

Closely related to individuality is freshness—the avoidance of the hackneyed and commonplace.

Words or phrases are often repeated until they lose meaning and become offensive to any but the dullest mind. Such are the adjectives "stupendous" and "colossal," so often used to extol the achievements of movie makers, and the terms "impending crisis," "hard facts," and "mounting tension," used to describe international developments. Such also are the overworked "signpost phrases" ("Be that as it may," etc.) discussed in Chapter 17.

But even when style is free of worn-out expressions, discourse may lack freshness because the ideas conveyed are old or dull. New insights and penetrating interpretations are lacking.

Debaters, no less than motion picture producers and journalists, have favorite phrases which they employ far too frequently. "The gentlemen of the opposition," "we submit," "in their next stand upon the floor," and "my colleague and I" are heard, especially in high school and college debate, to the point of irritation. Moreover, debaters, no less than other speakers and writers, are often guilty of purveying the banal —nothing fresh or stimulating is evident in their remarks. No one demands literary distinction in a workaday argumentative speech or essay. One does, however, have the right to expect that, occasionally, thought will rise above the commonplace. Moreover, the language should be reasonably free of hackneyed words and phrases.

Great pieces of argumentative discourse nearly always break the customary bonds and exhibit freshness in both conception and expression. At many points in his debates with Douglas, Lincoln's thought and style display remarkable inventiveness. So also, within a more formal framework, do the style and thought of such great Senatorial debaters as Webster, Benton, Borah, and Taft. In the courtroom, Clarence Darrow invariably exhibited a freshness that raised his speaking above the commonplace. By studying the speeches of these men, the debater may see the originality of thought and expression that animated argument permits and may come to appreciate the importance of originality in presenting ideas attractively.

## VIGOR

"Vigor" is a blanket term encompassing such qualities as alertness, energy, color, and animation—all of those characteristics that awaken language and make it vibrant rather than sluggish.

Vigor enhances the attractiveness of style for the same reason that it enhances the attractiveness of any aspect of human thought or behavior. In the visual arts, in music, in literature and drama, in physical movement, men are drawn to the colorful, the vivid, the animate, but are uninterested in the drab, the sallow, the static.

Similarly, men are attracted by speaking or writing that is infused with intellectual and emotional energy—in which force of thought and depth of conviction are everywhere evident. Perhaps energy is esteemed because the human animal is himself an animate being, endowed with the dynamic qualities of purposeful thought and action. Whatever the cause, the preference of most persons for the vigorous and energetic is undeniable—a fact that every speaker and writer must recognize.

Vigor of expression springs ultimately from vigor of thought and breadth of understanding. The debater must strive to communicate to others ideas that seem to him to be of vital importance. He must draw his arguments from an abundant storehouse of facts and express them in language at once precise and rich in connotative power. Out of the combination of earnestness and knowledge a vigorous style will emerge. Say only what is believed and believed deeply; communicate only what seems of crucial importance; speak or write always from a thorough understanding of the subject. These recommendations are the guide lines that lead to vigor of expression.

As an example of energy in argumentative discourse, examine the following sentences from a speech by the Irish statesman Henry Grattan. The speech was delivered during the course of a debate in the Irish Parliament, on February 14, 1800, and was directed against Isaac Corry, Chancellor of the Exchequer.

The right honorable gentleman says I fled from the country after exciting rebellion, and that I have returned to raise another. No such thing. The charge is false. The civil war had not commenced when I left the kingdom; and I could not have returned without taking a part. On the one side there was the camp of the rebel; on the other, the camp of the minister, a greater traitor than that rebel. The stronghold of the Constitution was nowhere to be found. . . . I could not join the rebel—I could not join the Government—I could not join torture—I could not join half-hanging—I could not join free quarter—I could take part with neither. I was therefore absent from a scene where I could not be active without self-reproach, nor indifferent with safety.[1]

## EASE

Ease is a synonym for naturalness or effortlessness of expression. In a style that is easy, each word falls into place naturally. The reader or listener feels that the ideas are expressed exactly as they should be, exactly as he himself would express them. There are no ill-fitting joints between words, no hacked-off sentences, no tortuous constructions, no gaps in rhythm. Ideas grow naturally one out of the other; arguments flow forward without interruption. Jonathan Swift once declared, "Style is proper words in proper places." This principle perfectly describes the easy style.

But an easy style is also "natural" in a second sense: It is free of artificiality and conscious straining after effect. It does not try to be "oratorical," to produce resonant phrases, striking epithets, or "purple" passages. Self-consciousness is absent; expression is simple and has the relaxed, almost casual, quality of informal conversation.

An easy style is attractive for many reasons. Awkward phrases obscure meaning; the brutal forcing of language into unnatural patterns offends taste; pompousness grows tiresome and may even give rise to discomfort; the constant struggle to be grandiloquent wearies. Soon the

[1] *The World's Best Orations,* ed. David J. Brewer, 10 vols. (St. Louis: P. Kaiser, 1899), VI, 2332.

reader or listener wishes the author would cease his exertions toward elegance and express himself naturally.

Consider this paragraph from a speech that Pierre Soule delivered in the U.S. Senate on March 22, 1852. Instead of being attracted by Soule's language, one is more likely to feel an acute embarrassment for the speaker.

> Sir, public opinion . . . scorns the presumptuous thought that you can restrain this now growing country within the narrow sphere of action originally assigned to its nascent energies, and keep it eternally bound up in swaddles. As the infant grows, it will require a more substantial nourishment, a more active exercise. The lusty appetite of its manhood would ill fare with what might satisfy the soberer demands of a younger age. Attempt not, therefore, to stop it in its onward career; for as well might you command the sun not to break through the fleecy clouds that herald its advent in the horizon, or to shroud itself in gloom and darkness, as it ascends the meridian.[2]

Contrast the foregoing paragraph with the following portion of a "fireside chat" delivered by President Franklin D. Roosevelt on December 29, 1940. Note the naturalness of Roosevelt's language. Observe, in particular, that "ease" and "vigor" are not inconsistent. In their simplicity and directness, President Roosevelt's sentences have not only grace and attractiveness but also remarkable energy.

> Tonight, in the presence of a world crisis, my mind goes back eight years to a night in the midst of a domestic crisis. It was a time when the wheels of American industry were grinding to a full stop, when the whole banking system of our country had ceased to function.
>
> I well remember that while I sat in my study in the White House preparing to talk with the people of the United States, I had before my eyes the picture of all those Americans with whom I was talking. I saw the workmen in the mills, the mines, the factories; the girl behind the counter; the small shopkeeper; the farmer doing his Spring plowing; the widows and the old men wondering about their life's savings.
>
> I tried to convey to the great mass of American people what the banking crisis meant to them in their daily lives.
>
> Tonight I want to do the same thing, with the same people, in this new crisis which faces America.[3]

## FIGURATIVENESS

As the passage from Pierre Soule in the preceding section illustrates, figurative language used for ornamentation or display impairs, rather than enhances, the attractiveness of style. But when figures grow out

[2] *Congressional Globe,* 32nd Cong., 1st sess., 1851–1852, Appendix, pp. 353–54.
[3] *New York Times,* Dec. 30, 1940, p. 6.

of thought spontaneously and are used to convey meaning forcibly, they perform a useful service in argumentative discourse.

Compare the well-known figurative expression, "Too many cooks spoil the broth," with the same idea stated in literal form: "If an excess number of persons attempt to participate in a culinary project, the results will not be good." There is little question as to which statement conveys the idea more clearly and vigorously.

Figures have served many outstanding debaters well. Lincoln epitomized the great issue facing the nation in the 1850's with the phrase, "A house divided against itself cannot stand." In 1864, he won re-election on the metaphor, "Don't change horses in the middle of a stream." William Jennings Bryan made vivid the cause for which he spoke with the sentences, "You shall not press down upon the brow of labor this crown of thorns. You shall not crucify mankind upon a cross of gold." Franklin Roosevelt compared friendly nations to "good neighbors." Woodrow Wilson declared in the campaign of 1912 that America stood at "the crossroads of freedom." Daniel Webster opened his famous speech on the Compromise of 1850 with an extended figure likening the debate-weary Senate to a storm-tossed ship. Cicero's fury against Catiline burst forth in the series of rhetorical questions high school Latin students struggle to translate, "How much longer, O Catiline. . . ."

When a figure occurs to the debater spontaneously and embodies in a clear and fresh way the idea he wishes to communicate, it should be employed without hesitation. The fault lies in forced or strained figures or in figures used to decorate discourse rather than to evoke the desired thought. Properly employed, figures serve, rather than defeat, the end of critical deliberation, by enabling a speaker or writer to give his ideas the weight they deserve.

## A TEST OF ATTRACTIVENESS IN STYLE

To test the attractiveness of his style, the debater may ask these questions: Have I so expressed myself that a reasonably intelligent and interested reader or listener can attend to my ideas with a minimum of effort? Have I so expressed myself that my ideas can be attended to without annoyance or discomfort?

# ATTRACTIVENESS IN DELIVERY

Attractiveness in delivery, like attractiveness in style, depends, first, on the absence of disturbing traits and mannerisms. Yet speaking that is free of distractions may be dull and monotonous and soon weary listeners.

To render delivery attractive, the debater must cultivate a speech pattern marked by vocal variety, bodily responsiveness, a conversational spirit, and a courteous and objective attitude.

## VOCAL VARIETY

One of the principal causes of unattractiveness in delivery is a monotonous voice. Listening to a speaker who continues minute after minute at the same pitch, volume, and rate is like driving alone down a deserted highway at night. It is a rare listener, indeed, who is not lulled by the experience.

Without consciously striving for unusual or dramatic effects, the debater must vary his vocal patterns sufficiently to give his arguments their full worth. His voice must follow the trend of ideas freely and naturally; one thought must be set off from another by changes in inflection; pauses must be introduced to emphasize important points and make transitions clear; major contentions must be underlined by an increase in volume or a decrease in rate.

No debater should introduce vocal changes arbitrarily; nor should he exaggerate them simply to display his virtuosity. But, on the other hand, he should not neglect them as unessential to promoting wise collective decisions. Vocal monotony makes such decisions difficult or impossible, by causing ideas to be valued at less than their true worth. It is one of the commonest, and most deadly, forms of understatement.

## BODILY RESPONSIVENESS

Besides enhancing intelligibility, bodily responsiveness is an important means of making a debater's delivery attractive. Just as movement and energy in language animate style, the same qualities, when present in physical behavior, animate delivery. Moreover, their attractiveness may be explained on the same ground—that man responds favorably to the vivid and animate but is unmoved by the drab and lifeless.

While speaking, the debater should move freely but purposefully. He should respond naturally to the ideas he is expressing. Arm gestures and changes in muscle tension and facial expression should accompany his remarks. If notes interfere with these responses, they should be reduced in number or complexity.

Effectiveness in delivery depends to a great extent, of course, on the voice—on what the audience hears. But to a much greater extent than is sometimes realized, it also depends on the body—on what the audience sees. Physical unresponsiveness is unnatural; awkward movements distract and annoy. Only when the speaker's mind, voice, and body work as a unit, each supporting and reinforcing the others, will maximum effectiveness in any sort of public address be achieved. To this general rule, oral debate as a mode of public address is no exception.

## A CONVERSATIONAL SPIRIT

For many decades teachers and critics have recognized that good public speaking is not "oratory." Instead, it is essentially conversational in mode and spirit. Ideas are presented simply and clearly, without the expansive phrases and vacuous diction of the "spread-eagle" style.

But "oratory" is not the only kind of speaking that violates the conversational principle. The rapid-fire machine-gun delivery condemned in the discussion of clarity, the excessively loud and forceful manner, and the memorized presentation with its regularly recurring patterns of pitch and stress, likewise are inconsistent with the doctrine that good public speaking must possess the spirit of animated conversation.

While "oratory" appears to be dying, these other violations of conversational delivery are still alive. Far too many high school and college debaters shout too much and talk much too rapidly. Far too many of their colleagues present memorized constructive speeches and, sometimes, even memorized rebuttals.

Such delivery is poor debating, not only because it is unpleasant to listen to, but because it makes reflective deliberation difficult. No listener can think systematically or make decisions critically when he is shouted at or repelled by the impersonality of the memorized speech.

Good oral debating demands thorough preparation and earnestly held convictions. But the preferences of listeners equally demand that delivery be reasonably restrained in rate and volume, and, above all, that it be extemporaneous. Only then will it exhibit the conversational quality on which successful communication largely depends.

## A COURTEOUS AND OBJECTIVE ATTITUDE

If decisions are to be arrived at critically, debaters must maintain a courteous and objective attitude toward opponents, judges, and auditors. Moreover, such an attitude helps make delivery attractive. For attractiveness of presentation demands more than a flexible voice and animated bodily action. It also requires that the speaker reveal himself as the sort of person men admire and want to know better.

Listeners find sarcasm, boorishness, and belligerence distasteful. They are attracted to delivery that displays the same friendliness, tolerance, and restraint that they admire in any area of human relationships.

In competitive college debate, success or failure is sometimes determined as much by a debater's attitude as by anything he says or fails to say. And this is only as it should be. College debating is a training ground for the important debating situations of adult life. Therefore, the student should learn early that audiences react favorably to gentlemanliness and resent rudeness—resent it so greatly, in fact, that it may result in the loss of the speaker's cause.

### A TEST OF ATTRACTIVENESS IN DELIVERY

To test the attractiveness of his delivery, the debater may ask these questions: Have I spoken so that listening to my arguments has been an enjoyable, rather than a painful, experience? Have I spoken so that attention was always centered on the ideas being expressed rather than on eccentricities of presentation? Have I maintained the courteous and objective attitude that debate as a method of critical deliberation demands?

If the debater can answer "yes" to these questions, he has spoken well.

### QUESTIONS

*A. To Check Your Comprehension and Memory*

1. How do attractive style and delivery help insure that deliberation will be critical?
2. What is the first requirement style and delivery must meet if they are to be attractive?
3. How are attractiveness and clarity of style related?
4. What qualities besides clarity must be present if style is to be attractive?
5. Why is "individuality" in expression important?
6. What is meant by "freshness" of style?
7. How may the debater come to appreciate the importance of "freshness" in effective argumentative discourse?
8. What is meant by "vigor" of style?
9. From what two sources does a vigorous style ultimately spring?
10. Describe an "easy" style.
11. Why is an easy style attractive?
12. How do figures of speech, properly employed, help promote critical choices and decisions?
13. What questions may the debater ask to test the attractiveness of his style?
14. What four elements contribute to attractiveness in delivery?
15. In what ways do debaters frequently violate the conversational spirit?
16. Why is a courteous and objective attitude important in debate?

17. What questions may the debater ask to test the attractiveness of his delivery?

*B. For Class Discussion*

1. Gauge the relative contributions style and substance make to the formation of critical judgments. Is substance more important than style? If so, by how much? If you had only a limited amount of time to spend preparing an argumentative speech or essay, how would you divide it between attention to substance and attention to expression? Defend your decision.

2. How may the debater develop a more attractive style? What part does the reading of good authors play in this process? What part is played by listening to good speakers? by practice in writing and speaking? by studying textbooks on writing and speaking? What other means of improvement should be used?

3. Attend, as a group, an argumentative speech or debate. Using the criteria set forth in this chapter, criticize the delivery of the speaker or speakers. Can you reach agreement concerning the attractiveness of their vocal and physical delivery? Can you agree concerning the presence or absence of distracting mannerisms? As a result of this experience, what do you conclude about the preferences and tastes of listeners?

## EXERCISES

*A. Written Exercises*

1. Select a short speech or essay that contains many figurative expressions. (The "Gettysburg Address" would be a good one to work with.) Rewrite the text in the plainest and most literal language possible. Eliminate all of the figures. Read aloud in class, first, the original version of the speech or essay and then your revised version of it. Let the class judge which better communicates the author's ideas, which is more agreeable to listen to, etc.

2. Turn in to your instructor a short essay, the style of which displays to a high degree the qualities of individuality, freshness, vigor, ease, and figurativeness.

*B. Oral Exercise*

Present a five-minute argumentative speech on a subject of your own choosing. Let the instructor and class criticize the attractiveness of your style and delivery.

## SUGGESTIONS FOR FURTHER READING

William Norwood Brigance, *Speech Composition*, 2d ed. (New York: Appleton-Century-Crofts, 1953), Chapter 6, "The Use of Words." See especially the discussion of vividness in word choice and sentence structure, pp. 220–68. Many excellent examples emphasize the importance of vividness in style and suggest how it may be attained.

Buffon, *Discourse on Style* (1753). The address delivered by a famous writer upon his election to the French Academy. Besides containing the celebrated epigram, "The style is the man himself," the address argues that attractiveness of expression "supposes the united exercise of all the intellectual faculties. Ideas and they alone are its foundation." Many editions and translations are available. See, for example, *The Art of the Writer,* ed. Lane Cooper (Ithaca, New York: Cornell University Press, 1952), pp. 146–55.

Cicero, *De Oratore,* III, 37–54. One of the world's great orators advises concerning the selection and arrangement of words, and speculates on the part an attractive style plays in effective persuasion.

The preferred translation is by E. W. Sutton and H. Rackham (Cambridge, Massachusetts: Harvard University Press, 1948), but any will serve.

Richard Whately, *Elements of Rhetoric* (London, 1828), Part 4, "Of Elocution or Delivery." A strong plea that the student follow the natural or "think-the-thought" method in delivery—that he concentrate on what is being said rather than on how he is saying it.

*Part V*

# ARGUMENTATIVE DISCOURSE IN PRACTICE: COLLEGE DEBATE

*Chapter 19*
# A PHILOSOPHY OF COLLEGE DEBATE

*Our purpose in debating is to learn, not to win; or rather, learning is the only way of winning that makes any sense.*
ARNOLD J. TOYNBEE

THROUGHOUT this book, debate has been treated as a method that enables citizens to make decisions critically on matters of public interest. In a college environment, students have the opportunity to apply what they learn about debate principles and to develop necessary attitudes and skills. Schools cannot often provide real-life debating—*actual* disputes involving *actual* issues, persons, and decisions. But they do the next best thing: Experiences that approximate real-life debates are provided both in the classroom and in extracurricular forensics programs.

In this and the next two chapters, we shall investigate how college debating gives students an opportunity to develop debate skills and attitudes. This chapter is devoted to the history, the objectives, and some of the philosophic problems of college debating. In Chapter 20, we discuss the types of college debate and the occasions on which such debating may be employed. In Chapter 21, problems in evaluating college debates are discussed.

## A BRIEF HISTORY OF COLLEGE DEBATE

Academic debate has a long tradition. Protagoras of Abdera (481–411 B.C.), an itinerant Greek teacher, is generally considered the "Father of Debate," since he is believed to have been the first teacher to organize argumentative contests among his pupils. From the schools of Greek and Roman philosophers, through the era of medieval scholasticism, to the schools of colonial United States, academic debate has persisted as an educational method—as part of the academic curriculum, in public academic exercises, and in extracurricular clubs and societies.

The so-called syllogistic disputation, involving the attack and defense of a stated thesis, was a popular debate form in the early colleges in the United States. Until about 1750 it was an exercise in formal logic carried on exclusively in Latin, and participation was demanded of all juniors and seniors as part of their courses of study. In the disputation, a thesis was defended by a single person who was called a *respondent,* and he was confronted by four opponents. A *moderator* maintained order, presided, summarized the proceedings, and apparently rendered some sort of verdict. After 1750, English gradually replaced Latin, and the disputation came to take on many characteristics of debate as we know it in our schools today.

Long before debate had become a part of the curriculum, the students themselves conducted debates in extracurricular groups called "literary societies." One such society, the Spy Club, was organized at Harvard in 1719 to encourage student speaking. The Pronouncing Society was formed at Brown in 1771 for "mutual improvement in the art of speaking." And about 1777, the Speaking Club was organized at Harvard to "improve in the Art of Speaking." Its discussions dealt with actual public problems, and, what was quite important at that time, were in English rather than Latin.

The literary societies strongly influenced college life from the late eighteenth century until the twentieth century. Their programs fulfilled a social, as well as an intellectual, need and included devotionals, a musical number, papers and speeches, a short reading or skit, a debate, reports of members who had been appointed to criticize the debate, a recess, group singing, and the business meeting.

But the debate was the featured attraction. It consisted of four or six prepared speeches, followed by a general debate participated in by all society members, and often concluded by a decision determined by a vote of the members.

Some local literary societies are still in existence, but they are very few in number. Gradually, they became less popular because of changes in student life and the advent of speech courses and intercollegiate debating.

Courses in debate were instituted at Harvard in 1874. By 1907, Thomas C. Trueblood, who in 1892 had established one of the early departments of speech at the University of Michigan, reported that Harvard, Cornell, Michigan, and Wisconsin, as well as many smaller institutions, had made systematic training in debate a part of the curriculum. Courses in argumentation and debate soon became generally accepted as part of the curriculum and retain that status today.

The earliest reported intercollegiate debate took place in 1873 between the Hinman Society of Northwestern University and the Tri Kappa Society of the University of Chicago. This debate was a "friendly contest" in which no decision was rendered.

The first intercollegiate decision debate seems to have occurred on May 5, 1881, between the Phi Alpha Society of Illinois College and the Adelphi Society of Knox College. The next day, another decision debate was held between the Peiehessophian Society of Kirkpatrick Chapel, New Brunswick, New Jersey, and the Philomathean Society of New York University. Among other early debates, Harvard met Yale in 1892, and Northwestern met the University of Michigan in 1894. The growth and expansion of intercollegiate debating was meteoric. By 1895, at least sixteen colleges had participated in such contests.

At this time, extracurricular forensics moved into a new phase.[1] A majority of colleges and universities sponsored intercollegiate teams, and many triangular leagues were formed. During this period, the interest of students in debate rivalled their interest in athletic contests. Three honorary forensics societies were formed—Delta Sigma Rho in 1906, Tau Kappa Alpha in 1908, and Pi Kappa Delta in 1915—and the local chapters of these organizations gradually replaced the literary societies as the focal points of debate activity on college campuses.

A third period of intercollegiate debating began shortly after the close of World War I when forum debates became popular. Forum debates had three distinctive features: (1) They were usually nondecision. (2) They included questions from the audience after the prepared speeches. (3) They were held away from the campus before a civic club or some other adult audience. Forum debating did not replace competitive intercollegiate debating entirely. Rather, the two forms existed together in many forensics programs.

The present period of extracurricular debating is characterized by the debate tournament. The first tournament was sponsored by Southwestern College, Winfield, Kansas, in 1923, and Pi Kappa Delta conducted the first national tournament at Estes Park, Colorado, in 1926. Not until the depression period of the 1930's, however, did the tournament mushroom in number, size, and popularity. The primary impetus for its growth was the economic necessity of affording a maximum amount of debate training at the lowest possible cost. The tournament provided four, six, or eight rounds of debate, for as many teams as desired to enter, and did

[1] We are organizing the development of intercollegiate debating as has W. R. Diem in his "History of Intercollegiate Debating in Ohio," *Speech Activities*, 6 (Spring 1950), 5–8. Diem recognizes four periods: (1) literary societies until 1895; (2) triangular leagues, 1895–1920; (3) forum debates, 1920–1930; and (4) debate tournaments, 1930 to date.

so in a relatively short period of time. Although the debate tournament is one of the staples of intercollegiate debating today, most forensics programs offer a variety of speech experiences.

## THE OBJECTIVES OF COLLEGE DEBATE

College debate directors recognize three general objectives for their programs: (1) to achieve competitive success; (2) to develop specific skills and attitudes; and (3) to train students to speak effectively in situations that approximate conditions of actual debates in the adult world. Whatever philosophy of debate an educator may hold today depends primarily on the relative emphasis he gives these objectives.

Some teachers look upon debating primarily as a "game" or "sport" and consequently emphasize its *competitive elements*. Under this view, the success of a forensics program is measured by the number or percentage of debates won and the number and size of the trophies and plaques collected.

Others emphasize the development of certain *skills* to be derived from debate experience. Here, the measure of success is the degree to which debaters develop skills in research, analysis, reasoning, refutation, composition, and delivery.

A third group stresses, in the words of W. H. Davis, an "approximation of actual conditions of 'real-life'" debating. Davis states: "The 'contest' feature, the 'sport' element, while still present, becomes secondary; and superiority, skill, becomes inconceivable apart from the total persuasive effect secured by the contestant."[2] The third point of view, then, emphasizes the *training* of the whole debater.

A debate program based on the third view differs from one emphasizing the mere development of skills, in three ways, as the following chart suggests:

| *Training* | *Skills* |
|---|---|
| Skills may be considered an intermediate objective developed for later use in practical debating situations. | Skills are end products, valuable in their own right. |
| Forms of college debate must develop *all* the desired skills as they interact. | Forms of college debate may develop only *some* of the desired skills *independent* of others. |

[2] "Is Debating Primarily a Game?" *The Quarterly Journal of Speech*, 2 (April 1916), 173.

| Training | Skills |
|---|---|
| Debate situations must closely resemble those in which college debaters will find themselves as adult citizens; audiences are a necessary part of the training situation. | Training situations designed to develop some of the desired skills are satisfactory even if they do not closely approximate "real-life" debating; audiences are not essential. |

## PHILOSOPHIC PROBLEMS OF COLLEGE DEBATE

Within the context of these objectives, six philosophic problems entailed in college debating should be considered: (1) What kinds of debate experience should be provided in curricular and extracurricular debate, and what emphasis should be placed on each? (2) What is the proper role of competition in college debate? (3) Should debate "handbooks" be used? (4) How many questions should be debated each year? (5) Where does the responsibility lie for enforcing ethical practices? (6) Should college debaters speak on both sides of a proposition, regardless of conviction?

### WHAT KINDS OF DEBATE ACTIVITIES SHOULD BE PROVIDED?

The teacher of sixteen or more students in a one-semester (or one-quarter) course in argumentation will not have time to offer a wide variety of debating experiences in the classroom. He will concentrate on those forms in which the fundamental principles of analysis, proof, and refutation may most easily be studied and practiced. Since his main concern is the teaching of fundamental principles, however, time limitations need not interfere seriously with his objective.

Harder to answer is the question: What types of debate should be employed in the extracurricular program? Here, one finds the answer by recalling the objectives of college debate.

Today, the bulk of extracurricular debating takes place in tournaments. The tournament efficiently gives a large number of students sustained, repeated practice in oral argument, and may, when properly planned and conducted, furnish a uniquely useful type of training.

Since practice is repeated, and the student gets an immediate chance to apply the evaluations of the critic, as well as his own self-evaluations, training in certain skills may effectively, and sometimes very rapidly, be developed. Moreover, since the skills of using evidence, analyzing, reasoning, and refuting are stressed by judges and opponents alike, these skills in particular may often be learned quickly and thoroughly in tournament debating.

Tournament debating is open to two major criticisms. First, as has often been pointed out, it tends to stress competitive elements, thus potentially impeding the achievement of sound educational objectives. The tournament itself, however, should not be blamed for excesses and indefensible practices engaged in by some colleges. Many schools have proved that tournaments, wisely planned and conducted, are excellent means for developing skills in research and reasoning, without interfering with the attainment of other goals.

A second charge is harder to answer. The directors of forensics at the Big Ten universities have put this criticism well:

> The skills developed in tournament debating do not comprise the whole of the rhetorical skills needed by a student for effective participation in the public address of American society. Most of the significant debating in our society is addressed to an audience both larger than, and oriented differently from, the "expert" judge. The student who implicitly or explicitly comes to regard the eliciting of a "decision" from an expert judge as a significant end of discourse has confused himself as to the role of debating in American society. Thus, the skills developed in tournament debating are partial skills.[3]

This statement is a serious criticism. Because of the nature of tournaments, those skills that require the interaction of the debater and his message with an audience cannot be taught. What is more, the practice of the skills that can be taught is carried on in a "hothouse" atmosphere—one which, if it does anything, makes the student proficient only in the use of those techniques in that atmosphere and not in the quite different situations of "real-life" debate.

Finally, even those skills that can be developed through tournament debating—research, reasoning, analysis, refutation, and the like—are developed as if in a vacuum, apart from the total context of debate. The tournament debater, therefore, often cannot discover the interrelationships of the skills he has "learned" with those he has not, and is likely to have distorted ideas even about these "learned" skills.

This criticism, although admittedly serious, does not argue for the abolition of tournament debating. What it suggests is that tournament debating must fit in with a total forensics program. If the director of debate (*a*) restricts the role of the tournament to the preliminary development of those skills for which tournament rigor is appropriate; (*b*) makes clear to his students that tournaments develop only some of the skills

---

[3] "A Statement on the Place of Tournament Debating in Speech Education," *The Quarterly Journal of Speech*, 40 (Dec. 1954), 436–37.

they will need for adult debating; and (c) supplements the tournament with diversified debating and speaking situations that emphasize adaptation to the audience, the tournament may play a most useful and practical role in debate training. Some of the many activities that may supplement the tournament are discussed in Chapter 20.

The inexperienced debater can usually most profitably begin his training in tournaments. After tournaments make him proficient in fundamental skills, he is ready to apply them in the "educational laboratory" of "real-life" occasions. As N. Edd Miller has put it, the tournament may best be regarded as a "practice situation, not an end product. The end product would be the effective presentation of arguments to audiences." [4]

In short, the tournament has its proper role in achieving educational objectives and, if properly conducted, may make a valuable contribution to the total development of the student.

## WHAT IS THE PROPER ROLE OF COMPETITION?

Two kinds of competition must be distinguished. Competition among *ideas* is an essential characteristic of debate, as has been indicated in the early chapters of this book. In real-life debates, a decision is made after the audience has listened critically to competing points of view and competing arguments.

The second sort of competition, a contest among debate *techniques*, is *not* an essential part of debate itself, but merely a means of teaching students some of the skills and attitudes that debate involves. This competition obtains when a critic judge decides which side did the "better debating."

About competition that is decided by a critic's vote, three views are held: (a) Competition should be employed as an essential motivation for debaters; there is no great cause for alarm. (b) Competition interferes inherently with educational objectives and should be eliminated from college debating. (c) Competition should be retained for its motivational value, but great care should be taken, since indefensible practices may grow subtly from any very great emphasis on competitive procedures.

An unlimited and unconcerned emphasis on competition conflicts with the aims of an argumentation course, which must necessarily be based on something other than a win-and-loss record. The sensitive student, in an argumentation course that helps him as an all-round debater, will be bewildered if he participates in an extracurricular forensics program

[4] "Some Modifications of Contest Debating," *The Speech Teacher*, 2 (March 1953), 140.

based only on the "game" concept. Five other pitfalls, soon to be discussed, also justify rejecting the point of view that competitive procedures may be employed without concern for the consequences.

The second view—that competition should be eliminated from college debate—must also be rejected. Students need the motivation that competition offers. Psychologists Hurlock, Bykowski, Müller, Whittemore, and Scott report the following findings: (*a*) competition stimulates increased effort; (*b*) competition has a greater influence on performance than do appeals to utility and altruism; and (*c*) the net gain in performance of groups in which rivalry exists over those in which it does not is substantial.[5] Our observation leads us to believe these findings apply to college debaters.

Nearly all students learn that competition keeps them at the hard job of mastering debate skills. In colleges that have strongly emphasized educational objectives, perhaps a gradual shift away from competitive goals may be achieved without loss of student interest in the program. But students who engage in some competitive debating seem to work harder in preparation and consequently develop fundamental skills faster than students who are not exposed to the demands of decision debating.

Because of its motivational appeal, competition should continue to influence college debaters. Such a point of view assumes, however, that competitive goals are secondary to educational objectives and that certain pitfalls, mentioned below, can be avoided.

OVEREMPHASIS ON TOURNAMENTS. Viewing debate merely as a game may result in too much emphasis on tournament debating (where most of the competitive elements are to be found), and in the neglect of other forms of college debate more closely related to real-life situations.

If the tournament is king, the advanced debater often has "no time" to prepare for audience debates and rejects invitations to speak because he is going to "another tournament" that weekend. Moreover, he reasons that going to many tournaments is the only way to get ready for the state, regional, or national championship tournaments that come at the end of "the season." The faculty director, for his part, cannot afford to spend money to provide audience debates for his experienced debaters, because he wants his "top four" to compile an impressive win-and-loss record.

EXPLOITATION OF DEBATERS. The first pitfall leads to a second danger from competition. When faculty directors overemphasize competitive aspects of college debate, they may unwittingly "exploit" their best debaters. Such exploitation takes two common forms: First, the good debater is persuaded to participate exclusively in competitive events and

[5] Reported in Clarence W. Edney, "Forensic Activities," *Southern Speech Journal,* 19 (Sept. 1953), 11.

thus is deprived of the diversified training that would make him a more effective speaker in later years. Second, for the sake of a good squad record, he may be asked to participate so often that his academic standing is impaired.

THE "STAR SYSTEM." A third competitive pitfall is the converse of the second. As the best debaters may overparticipate, less experienced debaters may have few chances to speak or may be excluded altogether from the forensics program. A competitive climate encourages the "star system," as the director concentrates his time, energies, and budget on those debaters who are most likely to "win for him."

Of course, a major function of extracurricular debating is to provide *intensive* training for interested and able students; accordingly, securing equal participation for all is inconsistent. Debaters with great ability should participate more often than less talented students. At the same time, to limit a squad to four or eight students and turn away others who lack experience is grossly unfair. When the "star system" is combined with scholarship programs and recruiting methods that guarantee the college an annual squad of hand-picked high school debaters and discourage or shut out the inexperienced student, the "game" concept has clearly usurped supremacy over educational objectives.

An educationally oriented forensics program should (*a*) provide some sort of debate training for anyone who has sufficient interest and intelligence to benefit; and (*b*) provide a more intensive program for the superior student.

HOTHOUSE STRATEGIES. An uncontrolled urge to win may also lead to an overemphasis of *strategies*. No one complains about the use of strategies for developing the most convincing case for a given group of listeners or readers. But the college debater may employ strategies of another kind, such as dodging issues, trapping opponents into wasting time, withholding information, delaying arguments until "strategic" moments when the opponent cannot answer them, and similar tactics.

Such tournament strategies are deplorable, not only because they are so obviously game-motivated or because they are useless elsewhere, but because their practice is antithetical to critical deliberation. The debater who is well informed on the proposition and well schooled in debate fundamentals does well enough competitively without resorting to the use of hothouse strategies.

OVERCOACHING. The last pitfall to be avoided in utilizing competition as a motivator is "overcoaching." The pitfall is not a new one: as early as 1896 its evils were recognized.

Overcoaching may clearly be traced to competitive influences. Few argumentation teachers are charged with helping students too much, and few directors of forensics are charged with helping too much the debater who is not speaking to "win." Many high school and college debate coaches, on the other hand, have been accused of doing work that competitive debaters should do for themselves.

Overcoaching is utterly reprehensible. Experience is the great teacher. Debaters will best learn the skills of analysis, proof, and refutation by trial and error. They learn little from delivering the ready-made arguments of the coach. If the primary objective is to train debaters for life, this pungent comment by Gladys Borchers should be heeded: "From debating the debater can take many things into life. Unfortunately, he can't take the coach."

To draw a line between the coach as logographer and the coach as guide and advisor is easy. Since he is more than an administrator or a chaperon, he must freely offer suggestions and criticisms but he does not write debate speeches. Finer distinctions, however, are difficult. Whereas case-making is clearly the primary responsibility of the student debater, the place where faculty suggestion stops and faculty case-making starts is not easy to determine. Developing lines of refutation is also a primary responsibility of the debater, but the distinction between faculty advice and faculty formulation may not be altogether clear in specific instances. At least the faculty director can always keep his educational objectives in view.

One test of his success is whether the upper-class debater, with two or three years of extracurricular experience behind him, is able to prepare for debates with little or no help from his coach. If he cannot, the probability is strong that he has been "overcoached."

In summary, then, competitive elements should be incorporated into extracurricular debate only if debater and instructor can avoid the dubious practices that competition often entails. In particular, a debate program should avoid (a) an overemphasis on tournaments to the neglect of more realistic speaking events; (b) an exploitation of experienced debaters; (c) too little use of less experienced debaters under a star system; (d) the use of hothouse strategies; and (e) overcoaching by the faculty advisor.

## WHAT IS THE PLACE OF THE DEBATE HANDBOOK?

In Chapter 5 such publications as the *Congressional Digest,* the *Reference Shelf,* and the *NUEA Discussion and Debate Manual* were recommended. There are, however, debate "handbooks," which we certainly do not recommend. These commonly consist of collections of evidence, ready-made briefs and cases, and hints on debating—with a heavy emphasis on "tricks-of-the-trade strategies." Why should such books be avoided?

First, and most important, they rob a debater of training in research and analysis. Like overcoaching, the handbooks do for a debater what he should do for himself. If a college debater derives his evidence and analysis from a handbook, and his case and lines of refutation from his coach, there is little left for him to do. Aside from composition and delivery, he becomes the parrot of the handbook and the puppet of his coach.

A second reason for avoiding the handbook is that the competitive chances of a debater are better without it. A speaker who has relied heavily or exclusively on the handbook for his evidence and arguments is not very likely, after the first tournament or two, to be a match for the debater who has dug out his own materials and has carefully read and digested what comes before and after the notes he has taken. In short, the debater whose knowledge of the question is derived from his own research is likely to have a competitive advantage over a speaker who knows only what somebody has handed him.

## HOW MANY QUESTIONS SHOULD BE DEBATED EACH YEAR?

A committee composed of representatives from the honorary forensics fraternities and other speech organizations annually help debate directors select a national intercollegiate debate proposition. With rare exceptions, this proposition is the only one debated at tournaments during that academic year.

Concentrating on one proposition during a debate season encourages careful preparation. Only at the price of considerable research and thoughtful analysis are debaters prepared for the kind of critical deliberation stressed throughout this book. Debates conducted on different propositions from different subject-matter fields each week would undoubtedly produce a superficial understanding of the controversies.

Yet repeated debates on the same topic provide minimal training in the skills of analysis and case construction. Often debaters make no significant changes in case or in their understanding of a proposition after the first few tournaments. Late-season tournaments become dry, sterile, uninteresting exercises.

Can one devise a system that encourages careful preparation and avoids repeating the same material time after time? Two suggestions are worth serious consideration.

First, all college debating need not be tournament debating. A well-diversified forensics program offers experiences in speaking before audiences and over radio and television, as well as in tournaments. New propositions can be debated on these occasions.

Second, the one-proposition system can be modified even in tournament debating. Twenty years ago, Richard Murphy proposed that the year's work be built around a single *topic* and that different specific propositions growing out of that topic be used at tournaments, as conditions warranted. He suggested: ". . . two or three propositions selected during the year . . . with a proposition at the end of the season that would combine the partial inquiries. . . . The final debates could be culminations rather than fatigued anti-climaxes." [6]

For example, if United States foreign aid were the topic for a year, the following specific propositions might be debated:

*Resolved:* That direct economic aid should be discontinued.
*Resolved:* That all economic aid should be administered through the United Nations.
*Resolved:* That United States economic aid should be restricted to loans.
*Resolved:* That the United States should substantially increase the amount of its foreign aid.
*Resolved:* That the _____ Bill on foreign aid should be adopted by Congress.

The genius of Murphy's proposal is that debaters derive the benefits gained from systematic and exhaustive research in one subject-matter area and hence develop the attitude that critical deliberation requires careful preparation. At the same time, debating each new proposition in that subject-matter area provides a new experience in analysis and case construction. The proposal is defensible educationally and should prove interesting for the students.

## WHO SHOULD ENFORCE ETHICAL PRACTICES?

One should recognize that the majority of college debaters and their instructors observe ethical standards scrupulously. A good record can, however, be made better.

Chapter 9 enumerated several kinds of ethical infractions in presenting evidence, e.g., suppressing data, quoting material out of context, failing to date information or to state its source, deliberately falsifying or emotionalizing information or delaying its presentation until so late in the debate that it cannot receive due consideration by an opponent.[7]

The misuse of evidence is only one of the unethical practices some-

---

[6] "Flexible Debate Topics," *The Quarterly Journal of Speech,* 28 (April 1942), 163.

[7] See pp. 116–18.

times found in college debating. Certain of the practices discussed earlier in this chapter—hothouse strategies, overcoaching, etc.—provide additional instances. To the growing list, one might add: personal attacks on an opponent, deliberately misquoting an opponent, participating in a debate without adequate preparation, and unethical selection and conduct of judges.

Unethical practices are policed, to some extent, by the self-regulating mechanism of the debate process itself. Chapter 2 pointed out that debate procedures have imbedded in them certain controls that help the contending parties arrive at reflective judgments critically. Two of these controls, in particular, also help to enforce ethical practices in college debate: (1) Each party is obliged to probe and criticize the beliefs of his opponents. (2) Judgment is made not by the debaters themselves, but by an impartial arbitrator.

Certainly the opposing team is one of the most effective means of insuring ethical practices. Many college debaters have learned, the hard way, the peril of misusing evidence against opposing debaters who have read up thoroughly on the proposition. One does not soon forget hearing, "Had my opponent finished the quotation. . . ."

Since the judge is often well informed on the proposition, he, too, is able to enforce ethical standards, by penalizing violators.

Faculty advisors must share a part of the responsibility for inculcating in students a lively sense of social and ethical concern. They can promote high ethical standards by making clear to students the code of ethics they should follow and by scrupulously exemplifying such standards themselves.

Neither opposing debaters nor judges nor faculty advisors, however, can guarantee ethical practices. Proper conduct ultimately depends on the debaters. Each debater is himself responsible for his own behavior; he alone makes the decisions that result in ethical or unethical practices.

## SHOULD STUDENTS DEBATE BOTH SIDES OF A PROPOSITION?

A philosophic controversy of long standing has become particularly active in recent years. The question is this: Under what circumstances, if any, should a debater be permitted, encouraged, or even compelled to debate both sides of a proposition, thereby perhaps violating his convictions on a subject? [8]

The question is sometimes justifiably avoided. Some college debaters

---

[8] See in Appendix B (pp. 376–92) a debate between Professor Murphy and Professor Cripe on this question, together with a reading list of additional comments on the controversy.

often have no strong convictions on a proposition, especially during the early stages of their preparation. Hence, when no conviction exists, no conviction can be violated. But one still needs a principle to apply when a debater *does* have a conviction on a proposition.

Three positions on the question of changing sides may be recognized. The first view, outright advocacy of debating both sides of a proposition, is supported by two arguments. Debating both sides (*a*) provides a thorough understanding of the question, and (*b*) develops a better understanding that any debatable proposition has two sides, that a debater must know the opposing view as well as his own, and that objectivity is an essential attitude for a debater.

A second view is that debating both sides is not justified under any circumstances. The principal argument here has been stated by Richard Murphy: "Debate, the argument goes, is a form of public speaking. A public statement is a public commitment. Before one takes the platform, he should study the question, he should discuss it until he knows where he stands. Then he should take that stand." [9] The advocates of this view argue that college debaters who speak against their convictions are guilty of dishonesty and pretense; that if college debate is regarded as training for life, the practice of debating both sides is liable to develop insensitive attitudes toward the role of the debater in public affairs. The college debater who courts ambivalence may well become the politician who "talks out of both sides of his mouth."

The argument is potent. If educators must choose between advantages of debating both sides—some of which may be obtained partially through preparation short of actual presentation—and the value of training debaters to become honest and responsible deliberators, then they must choose the latter course.

A third position represents an attempt to achieve some of the advantages inherent in both of the other points of view. It is this: College debaters may speak on both sides of a proposition in practice situations but not on public occasions. For example, intrasquad practice debates are pure training; no public is invited. Since no public statement is made, no public commitment is involved.

But what is a tournament? Is it a practice situation or a public occasion? To some, the tournament is an end product, a public occasion. Another view, however, is that the tournament is a pedagogical exercise designed to develop certain partial skills and attitudes; that it is a preliminary, and perhaps necessary, apprenticeship for other forms of college debate that more nearly approximate real-life debating. To those who hold this view, debating both sides in a tournament is reasonable

[9] "The Ethics of Debating Both Sides," *The Speech Teacher*, 6 (Jan. 1957), 2.

and ethical. But in debates designed for audiences in situations resembling real-life occasions, debaters should espouse their convictions as they will in later years as adult debaters.

## QUESTIONS

*A. To Check Your Comprehension and Memory*
1. Who is the "Father of Debate?"
2. Describe a syllogistic disputation.
3. Trace the history of literary societies.
4. Trace the development of intercollegiate debate in the United States.
5. List three general objectives of college debate.
6. How can one distinguish between the *skills* and the *training* approaches?
7. What are the principal values and limitations of tournament debating?
8. What is the proper role of tournament debating in a forensics program?
9. What two kinds of competition are discussed in this chapter?
10. What are three points of view on the role competition should play in college debate?
11. Describe the five pitfalls of overemphasizing competition in extracurricular forensics.
12. What are debate "handbooks"? Why should they be avoided?
13. What are the advantages and disadvantages of debating the same proposition for an entire academic year?
14. Describe Professor Murphy's proposal concerning the choice of debate propositions.
15. What unethical practices are sometimes found in college debating?
16. How best may ethical practices be insured?
17. What are the advantages of debating both sides of a proposition?
18. What is the argument against debating both sides?
19. What is the rationale for the point of view that debaters may speak on both sides of a proposition in practice situations but not on public occasions?

*B. For Class Discussion*
1. What emphasis would you give each objective of college debate in relation to the others?
2. What emphasis would you give tournaments in relation to other college debate occasions?
3. What is the proper role of competition in extracurricular debating?
4. How can extracurricular debate opportunities be best distributed among students of varying ability and experience?
5. Under what circumstances, if any, should college debaters be permitted, encouraged, or compelled to debate both sides of a proposition?

## EXERCISES

*A. Written Exercises*
1. Write a short expository paper on one of the following topics:
   a. the disputation
   b. the literary society
   c. a history of curricular argumentation and debate
   d. curricular argumentation at your college
   e. a history of intercollegiate debating
   f. extracurricular debating at your college
   g. the objectives of college debate
2. Write a short argumentative paper on one of the following topics:
   a. Should tournament debating be abolished?
   b. Should competitive elements of extracurricular debating be de-emphasized?
   c. Should extracurricular debate training be restricted to superior students?
   d. Should the current practice of debating the same proposition for the whole academic year be modified?
   e. Should students debate both sides of a proposition, regardless of conviction?
3. Write a critical evaluation of the debate between Professors Murphy and Cripe, printed in Appendix B.

*B. Oral Exercises*
1. Prepare a five-minute expository speech on one of the topics listed in Written Exercise #1.
2. Participate in a parliamentary debate on one of the controversies listed in Written Exercise #2. (See Chapter 20, pp. 326–28, for a description of the parliamentary debate format.)

## SUGGESTIONS FOR FURTHER READING

Douglas Ehninger, "Six Earmarks of a Sound Forensics Program," *The Speech Teacher,* 1 (Nov. 1952), 237–41. Discusses the "co-curricular" nature of academic debate, and argues that forensics programs should be regulated by educationally defensible principles.

James Gordon Emerson, "The Old Debating Society," *The Quarterly Journal of Speech,* 17 (June 1931), 362–75. An interesting account of the color and excitement of the debating society, expressing a hope that extracurricular debating can somehow recapture some of the enthusiasm of the early societies.

Richard Murphy, "Flexible Debate Topics," *The Quarterly Journal of Speech,* 28 (April 1942), 160–64. Presents in full the proposal sum-

## A PHILOSOPHY OF COLLEGE DEBATE 317

marized in this chapter for modifying the present one-proposition system.

Egbert Ray Nichols, "A Historical Sketch of Intercollegiate Debating," *The Quarterly Journal of Speech,* 22 (April 1936), 213–20; (Dec. 1936), 591–602; 23 (April 1937), 259–78. The title is self-explanatory, and the treatment is excellent.

Ota Thomas [Reynolds], "The Teaching of Rhetoric in the United States During the Classical Period of Education," in *A History and Criticism of American Public Address,* ed. W. Norwood Brigance, 2 vols. prep. under the auspices of the Speech Association of America (New York: McGraw-Hill Book Co., 1943; reprinted by Russell and Russell, 1960), I, 193–210.

Wayne N. Thompson, "Discussion and Debate: A Re-Examination," *The Quarterly Journal of Speech,* 30 (Oct. 1944), 288–89. Discusses several of the philosophic problems treated in this chapter.

Thomas C. Trueblood, "Forensic Training in Colleges," *Education,* 27 (March 1907), 381–92. Interesting description of the early years of curricular and extracurricular debating.

Karl R. Wallace, ed., *A History of Speech Education in America,* prep. under the auspices of the Speech Association of America (New York: Appleton-Century-Crofts, 1954). A comprehensive collection of essays on various phases of speech education. Read particularly Chapters 3, 7, 11, 12, 19, and 20.

## Chapter 20
# TYPES OF COLLEGE DEBATE

*Where there is much desire to learn, there of necessity will be much arguing, much writing, many opinions; for opinion in good men is but knowledge in the making.* JOHN MILTON

REAL-LIFE debating is conducted in various forms and in the context of such diversified situations as the courtroom, the arbitration session, and the letter-to-the-editor column. Time limitations restrict the argumentation class to a few types of debate. But although the extracurricular forensics program seldom includes written debates, it can provide as many oral forms as can real-life debating.

In this chapter we shall describe the formats of five general patterns of college debate and consider some of the major situations in which they are conducted. The five patterns are *traditional, cross-examination, direct-clash, legislative,* and *multilateral.*

The primary purpose of any of these five patterns of college debate, in whatever situations they are conducted, is to provide training for the student who will one day participate in real debates which determine actual decisions. Some college debate experiences are provided in formats and on occasions which approximate real-life debate, and hence the training is direct. Other debate patterns and situations do not very closely resemble real-life debate, and the student is trained only indirectly. Always, however, whatever the pattern or situation, the student has the opportunity to learn the nature and function of the materials of argument and to develop skills in research, reasoning, analysis of propositions, construction of cases, refutation, style, and delivery.

## TRADITIONAL DEBATE

The structure of a traditional debate has several characteristics. Two teams of speakers are always involved: an affirmative team defends a controversial proposition, and a negative team opposes it. Each team is given the same amount of speaking time. Both constructive speeches and rebuttals are included. Because the affirmative has the burden of proof, it has the privilege of presenting the first and last speech. No speaker is subject to interruption, and no provision is made for the direct questioning of speakers by opponents. The following order of speeches is customary:

First affirmative constructive speech
First negative constructive speech
Second affirmative constructive speech
Second negative constructive speech
First negative rebuttal speech
First affirmative rebuttal speech
Second negative rebuttal speech
Second affirmative rebuttal speech

Most college debates employ the traditional pattern. If training in lifelike formats is a primary objective, such an emphasis is hard to justify, but in developing certain skills traditional debating is as valuable as it is popular. It is a good pattern for teaching debaters research, analysis, reasoning, refutation, composition, and delivery.

With only minor procedural changes, traditional debates are adapted easily to most of the college debate situations discussed later in the chapter. The length of speeches may be increased or decreased from the usual ten-minute constructive speech and five-minute rebuttal. The number of speakers on each team also may vary. Although two speakers customarily constitute a team today, until the 1930's the standard number was three. For purposes of programs for civic clubs, radio, or television, each side may consist of only one speaker. To assure the affirmative the first and last word, the following format is employed:

| | |
|---|---|
| Affirmative constructive speech | 10 min. |
| Negative constructive speech and rebuttal | 15 min. |
| Affirmative rebuttal | 5 min. |

In most traditional debating, members of a debate team represent the same school. The customary practice in tournaments and elsewhere may be varied, however, by *split-team* debating. In individual split-team debates, a speaker from College A is teamed with a speaker from College B, and the team is opposed by another speaker from College A and another from College B. In tournaments, an affirmative team of speakers from Colleges A and B oppose a negative team composed of students from Colleges C and D. The newly constituted teams are given an hour or so to prepare, and the debate is judged by a faculty member from

College E. Split-team debating places a premium on solid preparation and deft negotiation of cases.

Traditional debates may be held with or without audiences. If an audience is present, the debate may be concluded with a forum period during which listeners are invited to ask questions. Sometimes a forum is substituted for the rebuttal speeches, and a speaker from each team presents a brief summary after the questions are concluded. A forum often stimulates audience interest and gives college debaters valuable training in answering questions and objections raised by listeners.

## CROSS-EXAMINATION DEBATE

Cross-examination debate resembles the traditional pattern in involving two teams that present cases attacking or defending a proposition. The essential difference is that opposing speakers are questioned as an integral part of the cross-examination pattern.

In addition to achieving many of the values derived from the traditional pattern, cross-examination debating has special advantages of its own. The fear of facing embarrassing questions often motivates debaters to prepare carefully. Asking and answering questions may help to develop a flexible extemporaneous speaking style. The ability to ask and answer questions effectively is itself valuable, particularly for those students who anticipate participation in actual debates in the courtroom. Finally, cross-examination debating usually interests an audience because the clash of arguments is cast into a dramatic form.

Special care should be devoted to learning how to ask questions effectively. Four principles are particularly important:

1. Establishing a few basic claims through organized series of questions is much more effective than jabbing at random with a disorganized array. Each series should establish a principal constructive contention, refute a major opposing argument, or expose an inconsistency among opposing proofs.

2. Each series of questions should be carefully planned in advance, so that early questions lay the foundation for later ones. All reasonable answers to the first question should be anticipated, and alternate second questions prepared. Similar alternate questions should be held in readiness throughout the series. Practice cross-examination debates will help students sharpen their questions and anticipate replies. Speakers must be flexible enough to adjust prepared series of questions to the specific cases presented by their opponents and to responses that are made to early

questions in the series.

3. The final claim growing out of each series of questions should not be a subject for questioning, nor should the significance of the answers be discussed during the questioning period. The discussion of admissions should be saved for the next constructive speech. The ability to make maximum use in a subsequent speech of the results of the questioning period is an essential part of the art of cross-examination.

4. The time allotted to questions should be used wisely. Debaters should avoid complex questions, extended statements, and questions that require or invite extended answers.

Asking questions is only half of the art of cross-examination debating. Speakers must also be prepared to defend their stands against the questions of their opponents. Three principles should be observed in answering questions:

1. Colleagues should decide in advance the positions they *must* maintain during a debate. They should anticipate series of questions they may receive, and plan answers that help them maintain their positions. Practice cross-examination debates will aid in such preparations.

2. If a question is unclear or ambiguous, the respondent may ask for clarification. To ask for clarification to waste time, however, is unfair, and listeners are likely to recognize such stalling tactics.

3. The respondent should answer each question as directly and fairly as possible. He should avoid dodging the issue or hedging his reply with so many qualifications that the answer becomes meaningless. The debater is not restricted to "yes" or "no" replies, and he may need to make brief qualifications. But the art of answering questions is to make clear and concise statements *that answer the questions* and, at the same time, defend fundamental positions in the debate. Extended explanations and qualified statements may be offered in the constructive speeches that follow.

Unlike the traditional pattern that has only one format, with minor variations, there are several distinctive cross-examination formats, five of which deserve special mention.

### THE OREGON STYLE

An early cross-examination pattern was developed at the University of Oregon. The "Oregon style" includes six parts, and the time limits for each may be varied to fit the occasion.

First affirmative constructive speech
First negative constructive speech

Second negative questions first affirmative
Second affirmative questions first negative
Third negative summary
Third affirmative summary [1]

A major value of the Oregon plan is its simplicity. The debate is divided into three distinct units—constructive speeches, questioning period, and summaries—and so it is easily followed by an audience. The main limitation of this plan is that all participants do not receive training in cross-examination skills. The two first speakers have no opportunity to ask questions; the two second speakers do not respond to questions, nor do they make speeches; and the two third speakers neither ask nor answer questions.

## THE MICHIGAN STYLE

As originally developed, the Michigan style of cross-examination debating included ten steps:

First affirmative constructive speech
First affirmative questioned by first negative
First negative constructive speech
First negative questioned by second affirmative
Second affirmative constructive speech
Second affirmative questioned by second negative
Second negative constructive speech
Second negative questioned by first affirmative
Negative rejoinder
Affirmative rejoinder

More recently, the University of Michigan has employed a new cross-examination format specifically designed to include an audience-participation period. The new format has eight parts:

Affirmative constructive speech
Negative questions affirmative
Audience questions affirmative
Negative constructive speech
Affirmative questions negative
Audience questions negative
Negative rejoinder
Affirmative rejoinder

The Michigan plan may conveniently be adapted to teams of one, two, or three debaters, and time limits are flexible.

[1] The summary may be presented by the first or second speaker if two-man teams are employed.

The Michigan and Oregon formats differ in two features: (a) In the Michigan variation the audience participates in the questioning, whereas in the Oregon style debaters are questioned only by their opponents; and (b) in the Michigan style the questioning is conducted immediately after each case has been presented, whereas in the Oregon format all questioning is delayed until both cases have been fully presented. Michigan-style debating shares with the Oregon plan the disadvantage of not giving debaters training in all cross-examination skills.

### THE MONTANA STYLE

A third distinctive cross-examination format was developed at the University of Montana. This plan has ten component parts:

First affirmative constructive speech
First affirmative questioned by second negative
First negative constructive speech
First negative questioned by first affirmative
Second affirmative constructive speech
Second affirmative questioned by first negative
Second negative constructive speech
Second negative questioned by second affirmative
Negative summary
Affirmative summary

Because the structure of the Montana plan is more complex than either the Oregon or Michigan variations, it is not often used in debates designed for audiences. Montana-style debating is admirably suited for tournaments, however, since each speaker gains experience in all cross-examination skills. Time limits vary considerably and adaptations may be made easily to fit local conditions.

### THE HECKLING DEBATE

The distinguishing characteristic of the heckling debate is that debaters are questioned during the course of their speeches and not in a separate period set aside for this purpose. In addition to stimulating audience interest, heckling debates offer students valuable experience in the atmosphere of rough-and-tumble argument when sharp questioning must be met with quick answers.

Although procedural rules vary, principles are standard. A heckle may consist of a question or brief comment, and it counts as part of the speaker's allotted time. The debate includes four constructive speeches; there are no rebuttals or summaries. Each speaker answers heckling questions or comments without help from his colleague, and then proceeds with his speech. Only the first and final few minutes are free from interruption. A chairman presides, rules on the length and appropriateness of heckling, and, in general, prevents the debate from degenerating into shouting or quibbling.

## THE MOCK TRIAL

The mock trial adapts judicial procedure to the deliberation of questions of public policy. It was developed at Western Reserve University and has been used in a variety of situations, particularly on radio and television. Warren Guthrie describes the procedure as follows:

> In opening the trial the judge in a three-minute speech, gave the background of the question . . . [and] prepared the audience for the discussion to follow. He was followed by the attorney for the plaintiff, who told the judge and the jury, and the audience, in brief form the case which he expected to establish through the examination of his witnesses. The attorney for the . . . [defense] had a similar period of three minutes in which to make the same partition of his case. . . .
> Following these partitions, the witnesses for the plaintiff were called. . . . The direct-examination was limited to four minutes, and at its close the [defense] attorney . . . was given an opportunity to ask questions in cross-examination.
> The same procedure was followed with plaintiff's witness number two and number three. Then the witnesses for the defense were called, sworn, and examined according to the same plan. At the conclusion of testimony the [defense] attorney . . . summarized his case, and addressed a final plea to the jury. . . . He was followed by the attorney for the plaintiff. . . . These speeches were also limited to three minutes each. At their conclusion the judge instructed the jury to decide the case strictly on the evidence presented, to disregard the oratory of the final plea, and to return an immediate verdict. With their verdict the formal discussion closed and the meeting was thrown open to general discussion from the floor.[2]

The witnesses questioned in a mock trial may be subject-matter experts, or they may be college debaters who have studied the opinions of certain experts well enough to answer questions as if they were the experts themselves.

## DIRECT-CLASH DEBATE

To locate the issues in a controversy and to clash on these issues in a debate is one of the most difficult skills for students to develop. The

---

[2] "The Reserve Plan for Intercollegiate Discussion," *The Quarterly Journal of Speech*, 25 (Oct. 1939), 394–95. Reprinted by permission of the editor of *The Quarterly Journal of Speech* and the Speech Association of America.

primary purpose of the direct-clash pattern of college debate is to develop this ability.

Direct-clash debate, like the traditional pattern, consists of speeches by two teams of debaters who have no opportunity to direct questions to one another. In a direct-clash debate, however, instead of treating the proposition as a single unit the speakers consider separately each of the issues or subissues that come into controversy and argue them one at a time.

The direct-clash pattern was originated at North Carolina State College and has been used successfully both for audience occasions and in tournaments. Its most effective use, however, seems to be in the classroom or in intrasquad debates.

Specific rules for direct-clash debating vary widely. The number of debaters on each team, the length and number of speeches in each clash, and the number of clashes in the debate are adaptable.

Other procedures are uniform. The issues are selected in advance. Usually, one speaker from each team presents the contentions his team is prepared to defend in supporting or opposing the proposition. The issues or subissues to be debated are then selected by the judge or negotiated by the two teams.

The first clash is initiated by the affirmative team, as are the subsequent odd-numbered clashes; the negative initiates the second and other even-numbered clashes. A clash consists of a series of speeches presented alternately by affirmative and negative debaters. Each speaker is expected to talk directly to the disputed issue or subissue and to answer the argument advanced by the immediately preceding speaker. After the first two speeches, a clash may be stopped by the judge, and a decision awarded whenever a speaker has made an ineffectual answer, dodged the issue, or shifted ground; or the clash may continue until each debater on each team has had an opportunity to speak. When a decision is desired, the first team to win a specified number of clashes, usually two or three, is declared the winner of the debate.

# LEGISLATIVE DEBATE

Two characteristics distinguish the legislative pattern of college debate. First, there is no sharp distinction between debaters and audience; each person present is a member of the assembly and enjoys speaking privileges. Second, in legislative debating no teams are formed to prepare and present consistent cases. Although those who share convictions on the question may meet in advance to exchange ideas and plan strategy, no formal cases are constructed. During the debate each speaker presents his own convictions, even if they disagree with those of other "party members."

Legislative debating is conducted under two formats, *congressional* and *parliamentary*. The purpose of congressional debate is to pass a number of bills that reflect the majority will concerning the solution of a particular problem. The motions to be debated are usually reported to the assembly by committees composed of representatives of that body. The purpose of parliamentary debate, on the other hand, is to debate a single resolution that is usually selected and phrased by the group sponsoring the debate.

## CONGRESSIONAL DEBATE

Some sort of mock legislative assembly, patterned after an actual body at the local, state, national, or international level, is the necessary setting for congressional debating.

The rules for such debates are based on parliamentary procedure but may be modified to meet the purposes of the assembly; consequently, regulations governing congressional debating vary considerably. Usually, speeches are brief, so a large number may be heard in a relatively short time. Moreover, one may ordinarily interrupt a speaker, by asking through the chairman if the speaker will yield for a question or a comment.

At any given moment, congressional debating is *bilateral*. Speakers advocate either that the immediately pending motion should be adopted or that it should be rejected. The entire debate on a main motion and its subsidiary motions, however, may become *multilateral*. For example, amendments introduce other points of view that delegates may attack or defend.

## PARLIAMENTARY DEBATE

Since 1921, debaters from the United States have met teams representing British universities. Since World War II, exchange visits between debaters from these countries have become an annual activity sponsored by the Institute of International Education and the Speech Association of America.

As one result of a developing interest in British debating as exemplified by the Oxford and Cambridge unions, a parliamentary debate format has been developed and widely used by colleges in the United States. This format involves relatively minor modifications of the procedures followed in the British debating unions.

As generally practiced in American colleges, the parliamentary debate includes four assigned speeches of perhaps eight to ten minutes in length, followed by many shorter speeches by members of the assembly. The debate, therefore, provides an interesting audience situation for the principal speakers and an opportunity for many less-experienced students to participate in the ensuing argument.

A parliamentary debate may be conducted on a strictly on-campus basis, with local students as principal speakers. An intercollegiate debate may be arranged by inviting two debaters from another school to join two local debaters as principal speakers. A parliamentary debate may become one session at a conference or tournament. For example, since 1956 the final session of the annual conference of the Western Conference (Big Ten) Debate League has been a parliamentary debate. Audience interest may be stimulated by inviting two prominent public figures and two college debaters to present the principal speeches on a split-team basis. A modification of the format makes an interesting program for civic clubs, with members of the club forming the assembly after the principal speeches have been concluded.

The special rules used for a series of intercollegiate parliamentary debates at the University of Illinois seem to be typical of parliamentary debating as practiced in the United States:

1. It is a parliamentary custom for the affirmative members of the audience to sit on the chairman's right (as the chairman faces the audience) and the opposition to seat themselves to his left. If at any time during the debate the sentiment of any member should change, he should move to the other side of the aisle.

2. There will be two principal speakers for and two against the resolution, and they will not be subject to interruptions during their principal speeches.

3. Members may speak for three minutes from the floor, by rising and addressing the chairman. The chairman will recognize speakers on both sides of the aisle, alternately, and preference will be given to members who have not spoken.

4. Members wishing to interrupt a speaker to insert a comment or ask a question should use the following procedure:

"Mr. Chairman, will the speaker yield for a comment (or question)?"

The speaker by option may or may not allow himself to be interrupted, by stating: "Mr. Chairman, the speaker will (not) yield for a comment (or question)."

5. If a speaker yields to a member of the opposition, the interruption will not be included in his three minutes. If a speaker yields to a concurring member, the interruption will be included in his time.

6. Debate may be ended by general consent or by a motion to end debate. The proper form is: "Mr. Chairman, I move to end debate." The motion

requires a two-thirds vote.

7. The motion to adjourn may not be offered until there has been a vote on the resolution.

8. Any question not covered by these special rules will be decided in accordance with *Robert's Rules of Order* (revised).

## MULTILATERAL DEBATE

The four debate patterns just described are *bilateral:* one proposition is supported or opposed. The college pattern we are calling *multilateral* either permits or requires the presentation of more than two points of view.

Multilateral debating is a useful experience for college debaters because many adult occasions entail more than two fundamental positions. Campaign speeches by a number of candidates and the advocacy of several legislative bills at a committee hearing by representatives of special-interest groups are examples.

To prepare for such occasions, college debaters must develop special skills in analyzing issues and organizing materials. Several formats of multilateral college debate are designed to help students develop these skills.

### PROBLEM-SOLVING DEBATE

The problem-solving debate was designed at the University of Washington to merge some of the characteristics of group discussion with those of debate. The format usually includes six speeches:

Analysis Speech, team A
Analysis Speech, team B
Solution Speech, team A
Solution Speech, team B
Evaluation Speech, team B
Evaluation Speech, team A

The first two speakers present the background of the problem delineated by the question; analyze its nature, extent, and causes; and discuss the criteria that ought to be considered when proposing solutions.

The second pair of speakers may accept the analysis offered by either of the preceding speakers, combine elements of both, or present new ideas. The primary task of solution speakers, however, is to advance a proposal or a combination of proposals that solve the problem.

The two final speakers evaluate the ideas and recommendations set forth by the first four. They may choose between the two analysis speeches or present an analysis that includes elements of each. Similarly, they may accept the proposals of either solution speaker or combine the best features of each speech. The evaluation speakers are also free to add any important ideas on analysis or solution that they feel have been omitted from the debate.

Problem-solving debate differs from other patterns in several ways. First, the debate is limited to six constructive speeches; there are no rebuttals, question periods, or summaries. Although each speaker may comment on preceding speeches, his primary task is to set forth his own point of view.

Second, although most problem-solving debates involve two teams, speakers do not function as teams in the usual sense. Debaters may freely criticize and refute their colleagues. When decisions are declared, the basis for judging is not which team, *as team,* did the more effective debating. Rather, the better of the two analysis speakers, solution speakers, and evaluation speakers are selected by paired comparisons, and the team that has two (or three) "superior" speakers is declared the winner.

Third, in problem-solving debate the topic is phrased as a question, not as a proposition or resolution. Instead of debating whether federal financial assistance should be given colleges and universities, problem-solving debaters might inquire what should be done to solve financial problems of higher education. The four solution and evaluation speakers may advocate four different combinations of proposals.

## SYMPOSIUM DEBATE

A *symposium* is a series of speeches on the same subject, which, taken together, form a coherent pattern. When a series of informative speeches are presented, the symposium is not a debate but an information-sharing public discussion. The symposium becomes a debate when a series of speakers present views on how a public controversy should be resolved, and the listener is to decide which resolution is best.

The question in a symposium, as in problem-solving debate, is phrased in multilateral form. A first speech usually analyzes the background of a disputed problem, and the remaining speeches, three to five in number, offer different approaches for solving it. A forum period is often included to permit an exchange of ideas between debaters and audience. Time limits vary to fit the occasions.

An interesting variation of the symposium format is the "Portland style" of debating, employed in an annual tournament sponsored by Portland State College, Portland, Oregon. Each of three speakers supports his own answer to the tournament question. The debate is held before an audience and includes constructive speeches, a cross-examination period, a forum, and summaries. The decision is rendered by the audience rather than by "expert" judges. A unique feature of the tournament is that student moderators, assigned to preside over the debates, compete among themselves.

The Portland-style tournament is difficult to administer, since the tournament director must secure varied audiences and assign participants so that each debate includes speakers with fundamentally different proposals. But the format is interesting to audiences and is educationally valuable to debaters, who receive training in many skills.

### CONFERENCE DEBATE

Like other multilateral debate formats, conference debate combines elements of discussion and debate. Halbert E. Gulley developed this plan in 1945 for use at Shrivenham University, a school for American servicemen in England.

In conference debate, a group meets to draft a policy proposal on a specific question. Each member makes a preliminary statement of his position on the controversy. The group then tries to reach a decision through discussion. Each time a clash develops, the chairman opens the floor to formal debate. After speechmaking on the issue is over, the question is decided by majority vote. In the same way the conference takes up another aspect of the policy.

Conference debate not only provides training in both discussion and debate, but also illustrates their complementary functions.

## COLLEGE DEBATE SITUATIONS

Just as forensic educators have developed diversified patterns of college debate, so have they made use of a wide variety of situations in which to practice these patterns. We shall group the situations into five categories, describe some of the variations of each, and indicate which patterns are best for each occasion.

### THE TOURNAMENT

Most college debates take place in tournaments. The purpose of tournaments is to provide many practice situations in a short time. Tournaments vary considerably, however, in the kinds of training included.

DEBATE TOURNAMENTS. Some tournaments are devoted exclusively to debate. Each team is provided a specified number of debates, usually varying from three to eight, against teams from other schools.

Sometimes each college is required to enter the same number of affirmative and negative teams in units of four debaters; other tournaments require each team to debate both sides of the proposition, alternating round by round. Some tournaments limit a school's entry to one two-man team or one four-man unit; others permit unlimited entries.

In some tournaments, no decisions are rendered; others require judges to award decisions but declare no tournament "winner," as such; still others not only declare winners in first, second, and third place, but award trophies or plaques symbolizing the achievement. The basis for determining winners in some tournaments is the number of decisions won and the numerical ratings assigned by the judges; in other tournament settings, the teams with the best records at the end of a certain number of preliminary rounds compete in a series of elimination rounds until only one "champion" remains.

In some tournaments, opposing teams are matched by drawing lots; other tournaments are round-robin affairs, each team competing against every other team. Some tournaments involve the participation of hundreds of teams; others are much smaller. The smallest is the round-robin triangular tournament: three four-man units participate in two rounds of debate.

Although the traditional pattern is the most popular in tournaments, the cross-examination pattern (particularly the Montana Plan), direct-clash debating, and several of the multilateral formats may be employed with good results.

SPEECH TOURNAMENTS. Speech tournaments, as distinguished from strictly debate tournaments, feature performance in many speech activities other than debate. Discussion, extemporaneous speaking, oratory, and parliamentary assemblies are the events most often included.[3] Contests in after-dinner speaking, poetry reading, prose reading, folk-tale telling, and listening are also sometimes held.

FORENSIC EXPERIENCE PROGRESSION. The forensic experience progression is a popular kind of speech tournament. It combines training in a variety of speech activities—extemporaneous speaking, discussion, debate, and so on—into one conference occasion and focuses attention on a single subject-matter area. The University of Denver pioneered the use of this format, and other colleges have since adopted similar programs.

The Western Conference Debate League annually sponsors a conference similar to a forensic experience progression. Although specific details vary from year to year, the conference always includes several

---

[3] Some forensics educators, including the authors, deplore the use of contest discussion as a medium for training students in techniques of group discussion. The case against contest discussion and the proposal of a substitute format is presented in Wayne E. Brockriede and Kim Giffin, "Discussion Contests Versus Group Action Tournaments," *The Quarterly Journal of Speech*, 45 (Jan. 1959), 59–64.

speech activities. In 1959, for example, expository speeches, group discussions, advocacy speeches, and parliamentary debates were included.

## ON-CAMPUS DEBATES

As noted earlier, the public debate between teams representing two colleges was popular during the early years of the twentieth century. Although tournaments have since come to dominate intercollegiate debating, single debates have by no means disappeared.

Some on-campus debates are designed to provide audience experience for more advanced debaters. Many colleges and some conferences schedule home-and-home debates for campus audiences, i.e., each college alternately serves as host. Other teams engage in audience debates by making extended tours throughout the country. Many American colleges annually feature an international debate in which visiting teams from Oxford or Cambridge participate. The patterns most often used in audience debates are the traditional, cross-examination, and parliamentary formats. An audience forum is frequently included.

Advanced debaters may also participate in debate clinics that demonstrate procedure and technique to argumentation classes and forensics groups in high schools and colleges.

Many colleges operate intramural debating programs for those students who lack the time or ability required for extensive participation in intercollegiate events.

## THE SPEAKERS' BUREAU

Since 1924, when Wabash College inaugurated one of the early student speakers' bureaus, the idea has spread to many colleges and universities. Faced with the virtual absence of audiences in tournaments and the difficulty of providing varied audiences on the campus itself, many directors of forensics take their speakers and debaters to clubs and organizations in the local community and surrounding area.

Speakers' bureaus usually send a letter or brochure announcing the availability of specified programs to clubs and organizations within a prescribed area. Some bureaus list only speeches; others include a variety of offerings—debates, discussions, book reviews, readings, and even skits and plays. Debate programs often match one-man teams and last only thirty minutes. Several kinds of debate patterns interest audiences, but one of the cross-examination formats is probably most frequently employed.

Although speakers' bureaus provide valuable audience experiences for advanced speakers and debaters and, at the same time, serve the surrounding area, many forensic educators feel strongly that the proper role of a speakers' bureau is to supplement rather than replace other college debate situations.

## THE MOCK ASSEMBLY

Unlike other college debate situations for which all or most debate patterns may be employed, mock assemblies utilize only legislative debating. As the name implies, mock assemblies are policy-making groups artificially formed to provide training for college debaters.

Although each mock assembly has its own purpose, scope, and parliamentary rules, general procedures are standard. A steering committee designs the assembly before it convenes, and the delegates are notified of the plans. Preliminary plans may include formulating procedural rules, selecting a topic for deliberation, and assigning delegates to various committees that will explore separate areas of the topic.

The assembly is called to order by a temporary chairman who calls for a report of the credentials committee and presides over the election of a permanent chairman. Other officers are then elected. The group divides into committees to formulate bills and resolutions and decide whether to recommend their passage. After a committee has framed its majority report, a dissatisfied minority, if there is one, may meet to write a report of its own. The assembly as a whole finally meets to hear each committee's report, to debate bills and resolutions presented, and ultimately to pass or defeat such measures.

As a vehicle for legislative debating, the student mock assembly creates an occasion bearing a "close approximation to a life setting and in a situation redolent with the spirit of democracy itself." [4]

One of the early student deliberative assemblies was the Model League of Nations Assembly sponsored in 1927 by the School of Citizenship and Public Affairs at Syracuse University. The movement has spread rapidly since then. Fifteen student legislatures had been permanently established by 1939, the year of the first national student congress sponsored by Delta Sigma Rho, national forensics honorary fraternity.

Most mock assemblies have been intercollegiate in character, but the format is also adaptable to the local campus scene.

## RADIO AND TELEVISION DEBATE

Although some college debates have been broadcast, relatively little has been written concerning the problems of adapting debate to radio, nor has radio debating ever become very popular.

[4] Joseph F. O'Brien, "An Appraisal of Contemporary Forms and Phases of Forensics in Pennsylvania," *Bulletin of the Debating Association of Pennsylvania Colleges*, 15 (Dec. 1948), 44.

College debates, however, have been presented extensively on television. Since the first college debate was televised in 1940—between teams representing Bucknell College and Columbia University—many forensics programs have experimented with the new medium.

The Sinclair Oil Company has sponsored a biweekly televised intercollegiate tournament among colleges in Texas; and in 1962 NBC initiated a weekly series, "Championship Debate," and gave it nationwide coverage. Traditional debates have been presented by Northwestern University; cross-examination debates by Wayne State University and the University of Illinois; mock trial debates by Western Reserve University, Michigan State University, and the University of Michigan; and parliamentary debates by the University of Illinois.[5]

Other formats have been suggested—among them the committee hearing, the direct-clash debate, and the use of a dramatic vignette or film clip to begin the debate and crystallize the issues. As N. Edd Miller has pointed out, "The only limiting factor to the multitude of possible debate formats for television is the imagination of the debate director." With such imagination, any of the existing debate patterns, and new ones as well, can be adapted for use on television.

In adapting college debating to radio or television, debaters face rigid time limits (the program is usually thirty minutes long) and must adapt to an unseen audience. The central problem of conducting radio or television debates, however, is stated by Edward Stasheff and N. Edd Miller: "The format must be varied so as to emphasize the dramatic conflict inherent in most debates and to suggest emotional as well as intellectual opposition. . . . The home audience must be made to feel a part of the program if maximum interest is to be maintained." [6]

QUESTIONS

*A. To Check Your Comprehension and Memory*
1. Enumerate five general patterns of college debate.
2. What are the distinguishing characteristics of each?
3. What principles underlie the structure of traditional debate?
4. What is split-team debating?
5. What is the technique of asking questions in a cross-examination debate? of answering questions?

---

[5] Other colleges have televised these and other debate patterns; our list includes only those reported in N. Edd Miller, "Possible Formats for Presenting Debate to TV Audiences," *The Gavel*, 40 (Jan. 1958), 25–26; and Wayne E. Brockriede and David B. Strother, "Televised Forensics," *The Speech Teacher*, 6 (Jan. 1957), 30–35.

[6] "Televising a Debate in a Courtroom Setting," *The Speech Teacher*, 3 (Sept. 1954), 215.

6. What are the differences among Oregon, Michigan, and Montana styles of cross-examination debating?
7. Describe a heckling debate.
8. Under what college debate pattern may the mock trial be classified?
9. What is the primary purpose of a direct-clash debate?
10. How may parliamentary and congressional debating be distinguished?
11. What are the aims of each of the three pairs of speakers in a problem-solving debate?
12. Under what conditions does a symposium become a debate rather than a form of public discussion?
13. How is a Portland-style tournament conducted?
14. Describe a conference debate.
15. What is the primary purpose of a forensics experience progression?
16. What are some of the values of speakers' bureaus?
17. What debate pattern is most frequently employed in speakers' bureau programs?
18. Describe the procedure followed in a typical mock assembly.
19. What types of debate have successfully been televised?
20. What is the central problem of adapting debate to radio and television audiences?

*B. For Class Discussion*
1. Which college debate patterns provide training in most of the skills that college debating should develop?
2. Assuming that one pattern is superior to others in training college debaters, should that pattern be used exclusively, or should a variety of types of debate be employed? Why?
3. Assume that you are a director of forensics. What debate situations would you try to provide? What part would each play in your total program? Answer these two questions in the light of each of the following three assumptions:
    a. You are primarily motivated by the "game" concept.
    b. You are primarily motivated by the "skills" approach.
    c. You are primarily motivated by an effort to train debaters.

EXERCISES

*A. Written Exercises*
1. Indicate which debate format would be most appropriate for each of the following situations, and write a short paper explaining why:
    a. a practice debate tournament for novice debaters.
    b. a forty-minute program for a civic club.
    c. a mock United Nations Assembly.
    d. a one-hour television program.
    e. a public debate between your college and Oxford University.

# 336   ARGUMENTATIVE DISCOURSE: COLLEGE DEBATE

2. Write a short paper in which you describe and criticize the *pattern* of a debate you attended outside of class and the *situation* in which the debate was presented.

**B. Oral Exercises**

1. Make a short speech in which you explain a college debate pattern. Refer to the sources listed at the end of this chapter and in footnotes.
2. Participate in at least two different types of debate in the classroom.

## SUGGESTIONS FOR FURTHER READING

William Norwood Brigance, "Letter to the Editor," *The Quarterly Journal of Speech*, 23 (Feb. 1937), 127–31. Outlines the rationale and procedure of the Wabash College Speakers Bureau.

Wayne E. Brockriede and David B. Strother, "Televised Forensics," *The Speech Teacher*, 6 (Jan. 1957), 30–35. A description of some of the problems faced in producing a series of television discussions and debates at the University of Illinois.

Milton Dickens, "Newer Types of Debate and Debate-Discussion," *The Gavel*, 23 (March 1941), 52–54. A good brief description of nineteen different types of debate and discussion; also includes references to fuller treatments of these types.

Douglas Ehninger, "Outline of Procedure for the English Style of Debate," *The Gavel*, 30 (March 1948), 5–13. A description of a series of parliamentary debates conducted at Ohio State University, together with a statement of the rules by which they were governed.

Lloyd H. Fuge and Robert P. Newman, "Cross-Examination in Academic Debating," *The Speech Teacher*, 5 (Jan. 1956), 66–70. Summarizes the aims, principles, and techniques of cross-examination debating.

J. Stanley Gray, "The Oregon Plan of Debating," *The Quarterly Journal of Speech*, 12 (April 1926), 175–80. A description of Oregon-style cross-examination debating.

Warren Guthrie, "The Reserve Plan for Intercollegiate Discussion," *The Quarterly Journal of Speech*, 25 (Oct. 1939), 392–96. A description of the mock trial.

Charles H. McReynolds, "A New System of Debate," *The Quarterly Journal of Speech*, 26 (Feb. 1940), 6–11. A description of the aims and procedures of heckling debates.

Joseph F. O'Brien, "An Appraisal of Contemporary Forms and Phases of Forensics in Pennsylvania," *Bulletin of the Debating Association of Pennsylvania Colleges*, 15 (Dec. 1948), 32–45. A comprehensive discussion of many types of academic debate.

————, "The Historical Development of Student Assemblies," in *The Student Congress Movement*, Lyman S. Judson, ed. (New York: H. H. Wilson, 1940), pp. 9–23. The title is self-explanatory; the treatment is excellent.

Frederick W. Orr and Albert L. Franzke, "The University of Washington Plan of Problem Solving Debate," *The Bulletin of the University of Washington*, Extension Series No. 8, Jan. 1938. Describes the rationale, principles, procedures, and uses of the problem-solving debate format.

Edwin H. Paget, "Letter to the Editor," *The Quarterly Journal of Speech*, 27 (Feb. 1941), 125–28. Outlines the procedure and gives detailed regulations governing direct-clash debating.

Darrel R. Porter, "The Use of Cross-Examination in Debate," *The Quarterly Journal of Speech*, 18 (Feb. 1932), 97–102. Discusses the values of cross-examination debating and describes the Montana Plan.

"A Statement on the Place of Tournament Debating in Speech Education," *The Quarterly Journal of Speech*, 40 (Dec. 1954), 435–39. The directors of forensics at Big Ten universities present a case for diversified forensic activities and discuss what they are doing toward achieving this objective at their own schools.

## Chapter 21
# EVALUATING COLLEGE DEBATE

*He who decides a case without hearing the other side . . . though he decide justly, cannot be considered just.* SENECA

THE OUTCOME of a real-life debate is a decision that judges make after determining the issues of a controversy and weighing the relevant arguments and evidence advanced by both sides. Judges, however, neither rate nor criticize the argumentation skills of the debaters.

Although decisions in college debates have no real effect in the adjudicating of actual disputes, they are usually awarded to stimulate better preparation. College debate judges also function as critics; they rate the argumentation ability of debaters and present oral and written critiques of the debate. They do so to provide a general index of how well students are developing certain skills in argument and to point the way toward further development.

Three kinds of evaluation, then, are provided in college debate training: (1) *decisions;* (2) *quality ratings;* and (3) *critiques.*

## THE DECISION

### ON WHAT BASIS IS THE DECISION MADE?

This question has been argued for over forty years. The principal disputants in the early controversy were James M. O'Neill, who contended that the judge should function as an argumentation expert and award the decision to the team that did the more skillful debating, and Hugh M. Wells, who maintained that the judge should be a "juryman" and decide in favor of the team that presented the preponderance of evidence on the issues.

O'Neill asserted that judging the ability of the debaters was the fairer method. He argued that if the proposition were not balanced, if it were absurdly worded, or if the burden of proof were placed on the wrong side, the judge would be forced to vote for the team that drew the "fortunate" side of the resolution.

Wells, on the other hand, replied that debate coaches should be expected to phrase debatable propositions properly. He argued that the debate judge, like the juryman in a trial, should decide the dispute on the merits of the cases made by the opposing parties. The debating skills should serve no function other than to "drive the thought home." To give skills greater weight is really to "accredit them twice" and to call too much attention to "the mechanics of debate," making them ends in themselves. This procedure, he claimed, would lead to abuses and misuses of debating techniques.

If college debating is viewed primarily as a game, the O'Neill position is appropriate. By instructing judges to determine which team is more skillful, one more nearly assures a fair contest.

When the principal objective is to train students to become effective adult debaters, however, the juryman method becomes more realistic. As in the real world, decisions are then based on issues, cases, and evidence. Debating skills play their role in preparation and presentation, but participants know that their skills are not to be exhibited as end products. Rather, they are to function as handmaidens to the clarity and forcefulness of their cases.

How can judges decide which is the stronger case? They decide either debates to determine actual policy or those to train college debaters, by asking two questions: (1) Has the affirmative side established a *prima facie* case on the issues of the controversy? Unless the affirmative discovers the issues and constructs an adequate initial case relevant to them, the negative should be declared the winner. (2) Has the affirmative satisfactorily established its stand on each contested issue? The affirmative is not obliged to win every clash of opinion in the debate; it does not even have the burden of gaining an edge on every contention. It must, however, *gain assent on every issue*.[1]

## WHO SHOULD SERVE AS JUDGES?

Early in the history of intercollegiate debating, decisions were rendered by a board of three public speakers, such as judges, attorneys, politicians, or ministers. Although boards of three, five, seven, or nine judges are still occasionally employed today, more often a single judge decides which team has won the debate.

Usually the single judge is a debate coach from a neutral college. When the number of available coaches is insufficient, tournament direc-

---

[1] Review Chapter 7 for the theory that underlies the process of arriving at debate decisions.

tors call on speech teachers who are not debate specialists, on faculty members from other departments, or on public speakers who were former debaters.

When the judge is to fill the role of the expert who evaluates debating skills, the debate coach is very probably the most satisfactory judge. If the judge is to function as a juryman, an informed layman is adequate.

Indeed, to insure that debating techniques are not stressed too much, the use of laymen, at least part of the time, may be desired. In presenting a case for the use of lay judges, Joseph Wigley draws an interesting analogy between college debaters and salesmen. He suggests that just as the budding car salesman should not practice exclusively on other salesmen or on the sales manager but should also try out his arguments on automobile mechanics, so should the college debater supplement his experience in speaking to debate instructors by addressing arguments to subject-matter experts or, at least, to informed laymen. Wigley concludes that the "art of persuasion is not confined to persuading other rhetoricians." [2]

Since in college debating the judge, in addition to rendering a decision, evaluates debaters and presents a critique of the debate, one should keep all these functions in mind when selecting judges. Because they are particularly equipped to evaluate argumentative skills and to assess cases as they are attacked and defended, debate instructors, as judges, can help students develop the knowledge and skills necessary for effective debating.

Perhaps the best answer to the question of who should be tournament debate judges is that students will profit most if they are sometimes judged by debate coaches and sometimes by laymen.

In certain types of college debating, the decision is expressed by an audience vote. In legislative debating, for example, each member of the assembly casts his vote to decide whether the resolution or bill is passed or defeated. Some writers distinguish between the critical judgment of an expert and the vote of an assemblyman on the "merits of the question." And yet an assemblyman should decide through the same process of analyzing issues and weighing proofs as the experienced tournament judge. In short, the distinction is merely one of the degree of ability and experience of the decision-maker. To the value of training speakers, a mock assembly adds the bonus of helping students to develop their critical decision-making powers.

For some audience debates, decisions are determined by a shift-of-opinion ballot. This ballot, introduced by Professor Howard Woodward, has been employed as a measure in experimental research; [3] it is also

[2] "The Art of Persuading *Whom?*" *The Gavel*, 43 (May 1961), 67–68.
[3] As an experimental measure, the Woodward ballot has been found reasonably

useful in deciding debates in which the proposition gives a decided advantage to one side. Whereas the result of a simple vote for or against such a resolution may be predetermined, the shift-of-opinion ballot makes for a genuine contest that stimulates both sides to influence opinion.

The shift-of-opinion ballot asks listeners before the debate starts to record opinions on the proposition as favorable, undecided, or opposed. After the debate, they are again asked to record opinions. A common variation of the Woodward Ballot follows:

*Before the Debate*

_____ I favor the proposition
_____ I am undecided or neutral
_____ I oppose the proposition

*After the Debate*

_____ I more strongly favor the proposition
_____ I favor the proposition
_____ I am undecided or neutral
_____ I oppose the proposition
_____ I more strongly oppose the proposition

The ballot is scored by ignoring those ballots that indicate no shift of opinion, counting the ballots that represent shifting opinions, and awarding the decision to the side toward which a majority of the shifts are made.

## WHAT QUALITIES SHOULD THE JUDGE POSSESS?

Whether the college debate judge is a subject-matter expert, an informed layman, a specialist in argumentation, a student member of a mock assembly, or a member of an audience who fills out a shift-of-opinion ballot, he should have two important characteristics: Like those who judge actual debates, he must participate *actively* in the debate, and he should be *objective*.

A debate judge is not an inert vessel or an automatic computing machine. Rather, he is an *active* participant in the debate. He brings his own knowledge and experience into play as he asks himself if the affirmative has accurately identified the actual issues of the controversy; if the affirmative proofs adequately support initial stands on those issues; if the negative attack is adequate; and if the affirmative satisfactorily reestablishes its stands. Although he should not penalize a team that does

---

valid and reliable when the votes of an audience of thirty or more are considered. See Alan Monroe, "The Statistical Reliability and Validity of the Shift-of-Opinion Ballot," *The Quarterly Journal of Speech*, 23 (Dec. 1937), 577–85.

not employ the arguments and evidence he would have selected had he been speaking, the judge requires both teams to talk to the issues, and he evaluates critically the proofs they do present. Such standards are not always achieved in either academic or real-life debating. But the conscientious judge actively tries to respect the highest tradition of realistic argument.

In what senses are judges, and indeed all critical listeners, said to be *objective?* Although the judge takes his knowledge and experience to the debate, he tries not to let his prior convictions influence him unduly. He is willing to suspend final judgment until both sides have had a fair opportunity to influence his decision. Among other things, a debate judge is a person who has trained himself to recognize his own convictions and biases and to set them aside when he becomes a decision-maker.

Most college debate judges are objective in this sense. A study of 158 decisions given by forty-four judges at an annual University of Nebraska Debate and Discussion Conference in 1951 reported that the opinion of the judges on the "merits of the question" debated had no significant effect upon their decisions.[4]

## QUALITY RATINGS

Decisions serve useful functions in learning situations by motivating debaters to prepare thoroughly and by encouraging debaters to analyze the issues and speak to them in the debate. A mere win-and-loss record, however, should not comprise the total evaluation of the debater. Debate coaches and experienced debaters recognize that the value of a given percentage of wins depends considerably on the excellence of opposing teams and on one's luck in winning those debates "that could have gone either way." A very good or a very poor record at any given tournament might be quite misleading. In fact, the win-and-loss record, even at the end of a whole season, is seldom by itself a very reliable index of the progress the debater is making.

Judges also evaluate students by assigning *quality ratings* to each debater. The quality rating system is by no means a precise measure of the debater's ability, since an "excellent" rating does not signify the same caliber of debating to all judges. In one tournament, for example, judges applied a fifteen-point scale to sixteen teams. Each judge could have awarded as many as 240 points during the tournament. The total ratings assigned by each judge ranged from 124 to 197 points. The differ-

[4] Robert L. Scott, "The Objectivity of Debate Judges," *The Gavel*, 37 (Nov. 1954), 14–15.

ence of seventy-three points between the most generous and the least generous judge represents a difference of about four and a half points in average team ratings on the fifteen-point scale.[5]

Fortunately, the reliability of quality ratings seems to increase as the number of ratings in rounds of debate accumulate. Eccentric ratings tend to cancel one another out. Even so, a better index of the development of a student's ability is probably obtained by combining win-and-loss records with quality ratings.

Two quality-rating methods are employed in college debating. One method involves a *single* judgment on a scale—usually a five-point or fifteen-point scale. Judges are merely asked to evaluate the "general debating ability" of each debater. The sample ballot on page 344 illustrates the "single-score" rating.

The other method requires the judge to evaluate separately *a number of debating skills* and to assign a score for each skill. Seven categories of skills are commonly considered: case, evidence, refutation, analysis, delivery, organization, and language.[6] In using either of the quality-rating methods, a judge may be asked to indicate a team rating in addition to evaluating individual debaters. The team rating may represent a simple sum of the scores of the debaters on the team or may allow for the added influence of "team work."

The "itemized" quality rating method has become more popular in recent years. Many tournament directors utilize a ballot employing this method, prepared by the American Forensic Association, a professional organization composed of forensics educators. Below is the AFA ballot. Unlike the ballot on page 344, which is torn in half to provide each team a half-page copy of the ratings and decision, the AFA ballot is prepared in triplicate, so that each team and the tournament director will have a copy.

Both the "single-score" and the "itemized" quality-rating methods have their advantages. The primary advantage of the itemized rating of debate skills should be obvious: The judge is able to communicate to students his evaluation of specific debating skills. Surely this information is worth having if the primary purpose of quality ratings is to afford the student an index of his progress.

[5] Richard F. Krueger, "The Reliability of Debate Judges," *The Gavel*, 32 (Nov. 1949), 7–9.

[6] Giffin reports that "average" judges assign the following relative values to these seven skills: case, 19.1 per cent; evidence, 17.18 per cent; refutation, 17.00 per cent; analysis, 14.78 per cent; delivery, 14.65 per cent; organization, 8.88 per cent; and language, 5.29 per cent. See Kim Giffin, "A Study of the Criteria Employed by Tournament Debate Judges," *Speech Monographs*, 26 (March 1959), 69–71.

## DEBATE BALLOT

Round ___ Room ___ Judge _____
Affirmative _____ Negative _____

Rate the effectiveness of each debater on the following point scale: Superior, 14–15; Excellent, 11–13; Good, 8–10; Fair, 4–7; and Poor, 1–3.

*Rating*

1st aff. _____ _____
2nd aff. _____ _____
1st neg. _____ _____
2nd neg. _____ _____
I award the decision to the _____ team.
        signed _____
                            JUDGE

Place any comments concerning the affirmative team on the reverse side of this half of the ballot.

---

Round ___ Room ___ Judge _____
Affirmative _____ Negative _____

Rate the effectiveness of each debater on the following point scale: Superior, 14–15; Excellent, 11–13; Good, 8–10; Fair, 4–7; and Poor 1–3.

*Rating*

1st aff. _____ _____
2nd aff. _____ _____
1st neg. _____ _____
2nd neg. _____ _____
I award the decision to the _____ team.
        signed _____
                            JUDGE

Place any comments concerning the negative team on the reverse side of this half of the ballot.

---

    The single rating of general debating ability is, of course, easier to complete. Furthermore, the judge who must rate debaters on a number of skills may concentrate on the evaluation of skills and award the decision on that basis. The judge who only assigns a single rating, on the other hand, may more conveniently arrive at his decision by critical

## American Forensic Association Debate Ballot

FORM **A**

ROUND_____ ROOM_____ DATE_____ JUDGE_____

AFFIRMATIVE_____ NEGATIVE_____

### Individual Ratings

Check the column on each item which, according to the following scale, best describes your evaluation of the speaker's effectiveness:

1—poor   2—fair   3—adequate   4—good   5—superior

1st Affirmative_____(NAME)           1st Negative_____(NAME)

| | 1 | 2 | 3 | 4 | 5 |
|---|---|---|---|---|---|
| Analysis | | | | | |
| Evidence | | | | | |
| Argument | | | | | |
| Refutation | | | | | |
| Delivery | | | | | |

Total_____

| | 1 | 2 | 3 | 4 | 5 |
|---|---|---|---|---|---|
| Analysis | | | | | |
| Evidence | | | | | |
| Argument | | | | | |
| Refutation | | | | | |
| Delivery | | | | | |

Total_____

2nd Affirmative_____(NAME)          2nd Negative_____(NAME)

| | 1 | 2 | 3 | 4 | 5 |
|---|---|---|---|---|---|
| Analysis | | | | | |
| Evidence | | | | | |
| Argument | | | | | |
| Refutation | | | | | |
| Delivery | | | | | |

Total_____

| | 1 | 2 | 3 | 4 | 5 |
|---|---|---|---|---|---|
| Analysis | | | | | |
| Evidence | | | | | |
| Argument | | | | | |
| Refutation | | | | | |
| Delivery | | | | | |

Total_____

### Team Ratings

Assign to each team the rating which best describes your judgment of its performance:

1—poor   2—fair   3—adequate   4—good   5—superior

Affirmative_____ Negative_____

### Decision

In my judgment, the better debating was done by the_____
(AFFIRMATIVE OR NEGATIVE)

_____
(JUDGE'S SIGNATURE AND SCHOOL)

Comments:

Reprinted by permission of the American Forensic Association.

deliberation of issues and proofs. Finally, since one may not safely assume that each of the four or five skills on a rating scale command equal importance in any given debate, the sum of the ratings may not very accurately reflect the general debating ability displayed.

One observation about quality ratings should be carefully noted: Quality ratings are not "speaker" ratings, but "debater" ratings. Specifically, they are not designed merely to evaluate delivery. Delivery is only one of the skills on an itemized scale and should be regarded as only part of the general debating ability evaluated on the single-score rating.

Whether the judge is a critic or a juryman, and whether he employs a single-score or itemized rating scale, *the decision and the quality ratings should agree.* The critic-judge, in the O'Neill tradition, who gives higher ratings to one team and awards the decision to the other contradicts himself flatly. If the team receiving the decision really did the "better" debating, surely the superiority ought to be reflected in the quality ratings.

The juryman-judge, following Wells, will award his decision on the basis of issues, cases, and evidence. His ratings, therefore, ought to reflect his judgment of the abilities of debaters to analyze issues and construct cases. Only with difficulty may the juryman-judge employ an itemized rating scale while he is concentrating on the issues. But at the end of the debate he should be able to make a reasonably accurate estimate of how the various skills functioned in the presentation of cases. If he does so, his ratings will be consistent with his decision.

Such consistency is important. To say that one team won the debate and the other team was "more skillful" places a strange interpretation on debate skills.

## CRITIQUES

The value of critiques depends primarily on the objective of debate training. If debating is merely a game, and the win-and-loss record the primary goal, debate-coach judges will not be anxious to help their teams' future opponents to improve. Nor will coaches want judges to make suggestions that "might confuse the debaters." If, on the other hand, educational objectives are paramount, if the goal is to train students in the skills that make effective adult debaters, then oral and written critiques are necessary.

The oral critique, coming immediately after the debate, has considerable value. The judge can help debaters in several ways. He can identify the contested issues, trace them through the debate, and explain the basis for his decision. He can praise well-constructed cases, clear and forceful arguments, and sharp refutation; and he can criticize weaknesses and suggest improvements. In short, the critic judge is a *teacher,* and, particularly in the tournament, the debater has a ready opportunity to put the critic's advice to use.

Written critiques are valuable for two reasons. In the first place, for those situations in which oral critiques are not feasible the written critique is the judge's only method of communicating his praise, criticism, and suggestions to the debater. Unfortunately, some tournaments do not provide enough time for oral critiques after each round of debate. At other tournaments, directors discourage them by refusing to allow the judge to reveal his decision.[7] Still other tournaments employ more than one judge for each round of debate, and so oral critiques may not be practicable.

A second reason for encouraging written critiques is to help the coach do a more effective job of teaching his debaters. This argument, valid even when oral critiques are presented, is advanced by Thomas Hopkins:

> The one person who should know how well a team debated is the debater's coach. The debaters, of course, try to satisfy this need, but, unfortunately, the judge's spoken words quite naturally tend to become more obscure with succeeding rounds. When the debaters, on the way home, relate the words of the various judges they show evidence of the wear of time and the tear of unintentional but natural partiality. The coach, in short, can not hope to obtain an accurate account of the oral critiques given the debaters by all the judges.[8]

Like quality ratings, the written critique may be a single unstructured criticism of the debate, or the critique blank may ask the judge to make specific comments on particular debating skills. The unstructured critique blank is illustrated by the sample ballot on page 344. The structured critique may follow several possible forms, one of which is exemplified by the ballot used in a tournament sponsored by Wayne State University, as shown on page 348.

# COLLEGE DEBATE EVALUATION AND CRITICAL DELIBERATION

Decisions, ratings, and critiques should reflect the concept that debate is a critical instrument of deliberation. Throughout this book, we have emphasized that the process of debate is designed to assist people in arriving at collective decisions through critical method rather than snap

---

[7] A judge is frequently severely limited in making an oral critique if he is not allowed to disclose his decision during the critique. We believe, in general, the value of the oral critique justifies revealing decisions after each round.

[8] "A Case for Written Critiques at Major Debate Tournaments," *The Gavel*, 39 (Jan. 1957), 47–48. Reprinted by permission of the editor of *The Gavel*.

348   ARGUMENTATIVE DISCOURSE: COLLEGE DEBATE

```
                    "DEBATE  DAY  IN  DETROIT"
                    WAYNE  STATE  UNIVERSITY
   ROUND _____        AFFIRMATIVE _____      NEGATIVE _____
   DECISION: In my opinion the better debating was done by the _____
             side representing school _____
                                         _____ Judge
   -------------------------------------------------------------------
                    AFFIRMATIVE CRITIQUE SHEET
                   Average   Above Average    Good     Excellent   Superior
   Affirmative team:  6 7 8      9 10 11    12 13 14   15 16 17   18 19 20
   1st Affirmative:   6 7 8      9 10 11    12 13 14.  15 16 17   18 19 20
   2nd Affirmative:   6 7 8      9 10 11    12 13 14   15 16 17   18 19 20

   1st Aff. _____    2nd Aff. _____
   Case and Analysis                Case and Analysis




   Support of Issues (Evidence & Reasoning)   Support of Issues (Evidence & Reasoning).




   Attack and Defense               Attack and Defense




   Delivery                         Delivery




   Audience Adaptation              Audience Adaptation.
```

Reprinted by permission of Professor Marvin Esch, Director of Forensics, Wayne State University.

judgment. College debaters, no less than those who participate in actual controversies, should recognize the essence of the critical method in debate.

The judges of college debates should exemplify the critical attitude themselves. They should make decisions after determining the issues and weighing the proofs; they should award quality ratings, whether by single-rating or itemized scale, that evaluate those skills exhibited by debaters in analyzing issues and advancing proofs; and they should present oral and written critiques to help debaters learn as youths what they must practice as adults.

## QUESTIONS

*A. To Check Your Comprehension and Memory*
1. What three types of evaluation are provided in college debate training?
2. What is O'Neill's point of view on the basis for awarding decisions in college debates?
3. What is Wells's point of view on the basis for awarding decisions in college debates?
4. What questions should a judge answer in deciding which is the stronger case in a debate?
5. What is the case for assigning informed laymen to serve as tournament debate judges?
6. What is the case for assigning college debate coaches to serve as tournament debate judges?
7. How is the decision expressed in a legislative debate?
8. What is a shift-of-opinion ballot?
9. What does it mean to say that the judge should be an active participant in the debate?
10. In what sense should debate judges be objective?
11. What is a single-score rating? an itemized rating scale? What are the advantages of each?
12. What kind of rating scale is included on the American Forensic Association ballot?
13. Why should the quality ratings agree with the decision?
14. What is the value of an oral critique? of a written critique?
15. What is the difference between a structured and an unstructured written critique form?
16. In what ways can college debate judges reflect a critical attitude?

*B. For Class Discussion*
1. Which point of view, O'Neill's or Wells's, is more consistent with the idea that debate is a critical decision-making process? Why?
2. In the sample college debate in Appendix A, four judges voted for the affirmative and three for the negative. Why do judges not always agree in deciding who wins a college debate?
3. Which method of assigning quality ratings, the single score or the itemized rating, is preferable? Why?

## EXERCISES

*A. Written Exercises*

1. Decide who won the sample college debate in Appendix A. Justify your decision in a short paper from the point of view either of a critic judge or a juryman.

2. Rate the general effectiveness, on a fifteen-point scale, of each of the four speakers who participated in the college debate printed in Appendix A. Also, on a five-point scale, rate them on analysis, evidence, argument, refutation, and language.

*B. Oral Exercise*

Prepare to debate the controversy concerning the critic judge versus the juryman method of deciding college debates.

## SUGGESTIONS FOR FURTHER READING

James Milton O'Neill, "The Juryman's Vote in Debate," *The Quarterly Journal of Speech*, 3 (Oct. 1917), 346–55.

Hugh Neal Wells, "Judging Debates," *The Quarterly Journal of Speech*, 3 (Oct. 1917), 336–45.

────── and James M. O'Neill, "Judging Debates," *The Quarterly Journal of Speech*, 4 (Jan. 1918), 76–92.

────── and ──────, "Juryman or Critic—A Final Reply," *The Quarterly Journal of Speech*, 4 (Oct. 1918), 398–433.

This series of articles represents a debate on the question of who should judge college debates—the critic judge or the juryman. The debate, interesting in its own right, stimulates thinking about central problems in judging debates and illuminates the process and theory of debate itself.

# Appendix A

# A SAMPLE COLLEGE DEBATE

*Resolved:* That the United States should adopt a program of compulsory health insurance for all citizens.

*This debate is the championship round in the 1961 West Point National Invitational Debate Tournament between Harvard University and Kings College. The affirmative team, representing Harvard, was adjudged the winner by a vote of four to three. The following text, except for a few alterations designed to clarify meaning, is a verbatim transcript of the debate.*

### FIRST AFFIRMATIVE CONSTRUCTIVE SPEECH
#### MR. GENE CLEMENTS, HARVARD UNIVERSITY

LADIES AND GENTLEMEN, because Larry and I feel that the dollar sign has no place in medicine, we are resolved that the United States should adopt a program of compulsory health insurance for all citizens: a program of spreading the risk of medical expense throughout society, compulsory in the sense that it would be financed through federal taxes. Now, in this first speech we'd like to show you that there's a compelling need for a change, that a program of compulsory health insurance could meet that need, and that such a program would be beneficial to the American people.

Starting first with a need for a change, Larry and I will present three contentions: number one, the neglect of health is today causing needless death and suffering; number two, the primary reason for this neglect of health is that people are led to make medical decisions on economic grounds; number three, this problem is inherent in the present system.

First, then, we contend that the neglect of health is today causing needless death and suffering. The Conference on the General Welfare reported in 1959, "Due to inadequate medical care over a third of a million lives are needlessly lost each year." Frankly, Larry and I are appalled by such a tragic waste of human life. But, of course, the problem extends far beyond those who die to the many more who suffer without the care they need. U.S. Public Health Service reported, "Last year 49.9 per cent of all acute disabling medical conditions received no medical attention whatsoever." And that this neglect endangers the health of every one of us was pointed out by the *Public Health Reports* last February, when they said, "Eight hundred thousand Americans with serious contagious diseases need medical supervision to protect the health of the general public, but four hundred thousand of these—that's one-half—are receiving no medical supervision of any kind." The Conference on the General Welfare pretty well sums up the situation when they say, "The health needs of the nation are grossly neglected."

The question, then, is, Why? And that's our second main contention. The primary reason for this neglect of health is that people are led to make medical decisions on economic grounds. In other words, in seeking medical care, all of us have to ask ourselves, "How will the bill be paid?" Our first point here is that many people just can't pay. Professor A. F. Weston of Washington University wrote last December, "Families are often forced to decide against seeking care that they desperately need because of the high cost of necessary medical services." Professor B. J. Stern of Columbia was a little bit more explicit when he wrote in the *Sociology of Medicine,* 1960, "For the vast majority of the people, adequate medical care has grown increasingly beyond reach because of its cost." And Professor Strauss of Columbia wrote last July, "The result of such high cost is that many health needs are neglected."

Our second point is that for still more people, even if they can pay some medical bills, uncertainty as to what the ultimate cost will be leads them to postpone the care or to forego it entirely. This point's substantiated by Professor of Sociology E. L. Kuhs, when he said, "The possible cost of treatment before serious disease is later discovered must remain an unknown factor, and this uncertainty often determines whether to seek care in the first place."

Our third point is that for all of us—even if we can pay all the medical bills—the economic deterrent remains, because although we know that diagnosis and early treatment are necessary, we just may not feel sick. So we decide to economize by avoiding care. As Jerome Rothenberg said in *The American Economic Review,* "Consumers tend to economize by seeking medical attention only when they feel very ill, discouraging early diagnosis and treatment." In other words, because we must all make economic decisions in seeking medical care, we often postpone in the hopes that our symptoms will just go away. Sometimes they don't. We conclude, then, that the primary reason for the neglect of health is that people are led to make medical decisions on economic grounds. We must always ask, "How will the bill be paid?" No matter what mechanism of the present system we try to rely on, this question still remains.

And that's our third main contention. This problem is inherent in the present system. Because as Professor of Economics B. A. Weisbrod pointed out last June, "No voluntary system can remove the need to make economic decisions in seeking medical care." In self-financing where the cost of care is directly a factor, of course, this defect is obvious. But even voluntary insurance suffers from the same inherent factor. First, as Professor Ernest Haverman wrote last month, "Nobody can afford all the insurance he needs, and in deciding which of life's risks to brave, most individuals decide to take a chance on the family's health." And that's not too difficult to understand when you realize, as did Professor Stern of Columbia, "Even the better voluntary prepayment plans offer too little and cost too much to be included in the budget of the majority of the population." In short, you still have to ask, "How will the bill be paid?"

As *Public Health Reports* observed in June 1959, "Even when people decide to pay the premiums for some kind of insurance policy, the economic factor remains because the amount of coverage they can buy depends, of course, on how much money they have." That's why we say that the problem is inherent in any voluntary system of medical financing. There's thus a compelling need to combat unnecessary death and suffering in the United States.

The program we adopt must be universal, since everyone is faced by economic decisions in seeking medical care. And it must be compulsory because no voluntary method of financing removes the need to make those economic decisions.

The plan we advocate is basically pretty simple. All medical bills would be sent to local boards composed of doctors and representatives of the public. These boards would set the fees, control abuses, and send cumulative bills to the Department of Health, Education, and Welfare, which would then pay them out of an insurance fund, financed through compulsory taxes. It would be run just like any other insurance program, except that the premium would be based on the ability to pay, and the benefits would be comprehensive, covering the diagnosis, cure, medication, treatment, or prevention of disease. Unlike the present system, the affirmative plan, by making insurance compulsory for all citizens, eliminates the need to make economic decisions in seeking medical care, for a compulsory tax based on financial ability has prepaid it. Our plan thus meets the need by freeing the American people to decide whether to get medical care on the basis of whether or not they need it.

Finally, Larry and I think that our plan could accomplish something really constructive in addition to meeting the need. And we'd like to present the major advantages of our plan right now, so that the negative team will be able to consider them right from the beginning of the debate.

Our first advantage is that compulsory health insurance would prevent medical cost from causing severe economic hardship. Now the logical way to prevent any expense from causing financial hardship is, of course, to distribute that expense on the basis of financial ability. And that's exactly what compulsory health insurance would do through a progressive tax mechanism. Under the present system any one of us might some day be struck by a financially crippling illness. In fact, Professor J. H. Richardson of the University of Leeds wrote last year, "There is conclusive quantitative evidence that a major cause of financial hardship and even poverty in the United States is heavy expenditures for medical care." Compulsory health insurance has a very real advantage here. If we remove the dollar sign from medicine, the cost of illness will no longer be allowed to transform medical tragedy into financial disaster.

Our second advantage is that compulsory health insurance would relieve the financial drain on our hospitals. Edward T. Chase pointed out in last May's *Reporter*, "The indigent often do without the care they need, to avoid receiving medical charity." But when they do accept that charity it often happens that nobody pays the bill, and then the hospitals are in serious trouble. Dr. J. P. Dixon testified in Congress in July 1959, "Unpaid bills have become such a drain on resources that the quality and availability of hospital services are seriously threatened. Many of our hospitals are on the brink of financial disaster." By paying those bills through compulsory health insurance, we could eliminate this crisis before it cripples our hospitals.

Our third advantage is that compulsory health insurance would provide adequate medical care to many who must now rely on inadequate welfare services. In fact, our plan would completely eliminate second-class citizenship from medicine by providing care on an equal basis to all as a matter of right. But reviewing the present system, the Advisory Council on Public Assistance disclosed last February, "There are glaring defects in the way the medical needs of the indigent are being met. Less than half the states fully meet welfare needs by even their own minimal standards." For those millions who must now rely on "poor man's medicine," then, compulsory health insurance provides something which the present system has failed to provide—medical equality.

The affirmative plan, then, would relieve economic insecurity; it would prevent hospital insolvency; it would remove medical inequality. In every one of these areas there's a pressing need for action. Some suggestions have been made; perhaps the negative team may even make some here today. That's why we don't claim that these are needs, in the debate sense, for the affirmative resolution. But the advantage of that affirmative program is that it strikes at the heart of each one of these problems by removing economic considerations from medicine. And you remember why we must adopt such a program. We must adopt it because a third of a million lives are needlessly lost each year, because half of all the disabling acute illnesses remain untreated, because four hundred thousand contagious disease carriers receive no medical supervision. And all of it primarily because people must ask themselves, "How will we pay the bill?"—a question that neither they nor the present system can answer. Compulsory health insurance answers that question by removing the dollar sign from medicine.

## FIRST NEGATIVE CONSTRUCTIVE SPEECH
### MR. FRANK HARRISON, KINGS COLLEGE

Mr. Chairman, distinguished guests, and gentlemen. I'd like to start by paraphrasing Winston Churchill: "Never have so many things been found so wrong with so little in so short a time." Keeping that in mind, I'd like to analyze the proposition presented to you by the gentleman of the affirmative in a somewhat reverse order. That is, I'd like to turn first to the question of these additional advantages. Now, I think it's very interesting that the first affirmative speaker told you these are not "needs," they're just additional advantages, sort of bonus points to come along with the affirmative resolution. We're going to suggest that each one of them when looked at in a more realistic light becomes a distinct disadvantage which the affirmative will have to cope with before it can substantiate the desirability of this plan.

Well, first you were told it's going to prevent hardship on the part of the individual. Now we're going to ask the gentlemen of the affirmative since when it became the duty of the federal government to make sure that no person in the United States undergoes financial hardship. If a person's home burns down, this is a tragedy; if his city is flooded, this is regrettable; but the federal government does not have the obligation to make sure that no one ever undergoes any economic hardship. We suggest, then, that the governmental theory of paternalism—the government is going to take care of everybody for every reason—we suggest that it has the disadvantage of tending to make people too dependent on the state.

All right, second we were told that the indigent often go without care rather than seek charity. Well, now, that was an interesting assertion, ladies and gentlemen. I'm going to ask you to search your memories and see if you ever found any evidence presented on it. And after we have evidence, I'd like the gentlemen of the affirmative to qualify their problem: how many people don't seek what care for what reason? Well, we were told, however, some of them do, you see; and this puts hospitals in trouble because the government doesn't pay sufficiently for the free patients which the hospitals accept. Now, we're going to agree that the hospitals are in trouble, and we're going to suggest that the major fault belongs to the hospitals because, you see, they're inefficiently administered. James Brindle, the Director of the Social Security Department of the United Auto Workers, said in the *Social Welfare Forum* for 1959, "Rapidly rising premiums are caused not only by justifiable improvements in hospital wage levels and working conditions and better technical facilities, but also by inadequate concern for the operating efficiency of hospitals, unwillingness to enforce legitimate controls, and the reluctance to experiment with new ideas."

What is our point here, ladies and gentlemen? Simply this: the gentlemen of the affirmative say quite rightly that hospitals are in trouble; and then, instead of proposing to correct the problem, they propose to have the federal government step in and subsidize inefficiency and bad administration. Indeed, Dr. Herman M. Summers, who is Chairman of the Department of Political Science at Haverford College, told the National Council of Social Workers, in May 1959, that the advocates of the affirmative resolution "assume that if the government moved in, they could continue present expenses and wasteful practices with assured payments, whereas now the countervailing pressure of organized consumers calling for more rigorous cost accounting and quality control appears to be growing steadily." Not only are the gentlemen of the affirmative subsidizing inefficiency, they are retarding the trends in the present system which will stop this inefficiency.

All right, advantage number three: we're going to eliminate second-class citizenship. How? Well, we're going to make sure that the states no longer discriminate. It seems today that in some states people get good welfare care; in other states they get bad welfare care; and this is a distinct problem. All right, gentlemen, we agree with you: it's a problem. And we suggest, as the first affirmative perhaps anticipated we would, that there is a far more simple answer to the problem than he's discussed with you. We simply pass a federal law, you see, standardizing state requirements for public assistance in medical care. It was done in social security; it was done in unemployment compensation; I see no reason why it couldn't be done under the present system.

What's the disadvantage? Well, the gentlemen, by saying that the states are doing it today, admit that it is within the potential of the state to take care of the problem. They say, "Yes, the state can take care of the medically indigent; they're doing it today." The gentlemen of the affirmative just don't like the way they're doing it. Well, then, what you're suggesting is having the federal government assume a burden that the states can and are handling. We suggest that's further centralization of our government, a further breakdown in the responsibility of the states, a further disadvantage of that resolution.

All right, having viewed the advantages claimed for it, let's turn to the resolution itself. Well, you'll recall, we were told that in the first place a neglect of health today is causing death and suffering. I don't think anyone can dispute that the medical care of the American people is not what it should be. Nor do I think anyone can dispute that there has never been in the history of the world a nation whose medical standards were as high as they could be. In short, ladies and gentlemen, the medical needs of a people are always met less fully than they could be. What the gentlemen of the affirmative have to do in this debate is show you that the reason that these needs are not being met is economic, and that their plan will take care of the need. Let's see whether this is true.

Well, first we should ask ourselves, How many people are there in the country affected by the need described by the gentlemen of the affirmative? In other words, gentlemen, and we ask you directly, What percentage of the American people are not getting adequate medical care today because they can't afford to pay for it? Now, we think this is a very fair question. The entire need described by the gentlemen is that people are not getting care for financial reasons. Gentlemen, how many? How great is your need for a universal program?

Now let's ask ourselves some additional questions. Well, first of all, if there is anyone in this country who seeks medical care, is he prevented from getting it? Dr. Leonard Larson, who was then president of the American Medical Association, who was later chairman of the Medical Care Subcommittee of the White House Conference on the Aging, told the Senate Finance Committee in 1960, "We have proved again and again that no person in the United States need go without medical care because he is unable to pay for it." After an extensive study of the subject, the *Texas State Journal of Medicine* concluded in January 1959, "Evidence is lacking that any American, aged or otherwise, who has needed and actually sought health care has been denied it." All right, point one: no one is being denied care for financial reasons.

But the gentlemen have told you people aren't getting adequate care, and the negative agrees. Why is this? Well, we suggest the reasons are subjective in nature, and they're not going to be cured by the resolution. For our authority we'll turn to the most recent government statement on the problem, the background paper on health and medical care, from the White House Conference on the Aging, January 1961: "The reasons why people do or do not seek needed medical care are many. These, in turn, are often interrelated and complex, but they include such important factors as fear, habit, tradition, mores, religious beliefs, social dicta, degree of general education, degree of health education, and convenience of the service or the facility for medical care." And in that whole long list—the most recent government statement on the problem—ladies and gentlemen, in that whole long list I didn't hear the word "cost."

Let's ask ourselves more specifically: Is cost a significant factor? George Bugbee, president of the Health Information Foundation, in the *Bulletin*, April 1959: "Economic factors seem to be a relatively minor element in this reluctance to see a physician." A national survey of old-age and survivor's insurance beneficiaries, conducted again by the Department of Health, Education, and Welfare, 1957: "On the whole there appears but little systematic relationship between the amount of medical care incurred by an elderly person and the amount of case income, or if he is married, the combined income of the couple." All right, we suggest, then, three things. First, no one is denied care because he can't afford it. Second, people are detrimenting their health primarily for subjective reasons that this resolution will not take care of. Third, the economic factor is not determining in the question of medical care.

Well, the gentlemen said, "Yes, but you see the problem, the problem which we deny, is inherent." Why? Well, first, because no one can afford all the necessary insurance. Again, an assertion of the gentlemen introduced without evidence. Let's turn to Michael M. Davis, who was a member of various medical care commissions set up by the government, who in 1956 wrote the book, *National Health Insurance:* "Though the population covered by comprehensive plans is as yet only a few million, these plans have demonstrated that comprehensive, high-quality medical care can be made available through health insurance at an annual cost of $150 to $200 for a family." This is between 4 and 5 per cent of a family income of $4000. Perhaps this is the reason that Dr. Jerome B. Cohen, of the City College of New York, concluded in his 1958 book, *Decade of Decision:* "As comprehensive is now written under group plan, it is within the financial reach of even the most modest income employee."

Well, we were told, "Yes, you see, but even after these people get insurance, it simply isn't enough." Why? Well, it doesn't cover all the cost. Now, gentlemen, we're going to accuse you of inadequate analysis here. We suggest that everyone in this room after debating the topic or listening to it this year knows there are five ways of paying medical care. You can take the money out of your pocket, you can borrow it from a bank, you can get it from private charity, you can get it from public charity, you can get it from voluntary insurance. Gentlemen, you have to show us that these five means taken *in toto,* taken together, taken as a unit, taken as a whole, if you will, are insufficient. Not just that one part is insufficient. Maybe that's why Marion Folsom, the former Secretary of Health, Education, and Welfare, wrote in his pamphlet, *Voluntary Health Insurance and Medical Care,* February 1958: "Of course, no one expects voluntary insurance arrangements to meet medical costs completely."

All right, the last question the negative will ask you in this debate: To what extent are these voluntary companies meeting their need? Well, three surveys have been taken: Odin Anderson, 1957; Cornell University, 1956; Columbia University, 1959. They all reach the same conclusions. I'd like to quote from Dr. Anderson: "Studies which relate health insurance benefits to the medical expenses of insured persons indicate that some 75 to 94 per cent of all hospital expenses, and 62 to 76 per cent of all surgical costs, are covered." Our conclusion: Those people who have insurance have their hospital bill covered up to 92 per cent, have their surgical bill covered up to 76 per cent; insurance isn't supposed to do everything. You have to tell us that all the means taken *in toto* are inadequate, gentlemen, not just a fragmentary analysis presented for affirmative reasoning.

We suggest, then, the rejection of the resolution stated.

## SECOND AFFIRMATIVE CONSTRUCTIVE SPEECH
### MR. LAURENCE TRIBE, HARVARD UNIVERSITY

Ladies and gentlemen, I felt a little strange clapping for what Frank had said, because I'm afraid I can't agree with very much of it. I don't think that Frank really denies the basic contentions that Gene made in his first speech. Let's go back, then, to that first speech and see what we tried to establish.

We suggested to you that the neglect of health is today causing needless deaths and suffering in the United States. And it's important to note that the negative team admits that contention. We've got a third of a million unnecessary deaths every year; we have four hundred thousand contagious disease carriers receiving no medical treatment; we have half of all acute disabling medical conditions going untreated.

All right, we suggested to you next that the primary reason for this neglect of health is that people are led to make medical decisions on economic grounds. And what did Frank say? Well, he said, number one: "No one is denied needed medical care, according to a very objective source, Dr. Larson, of the American Medical Association." We're going to suggest that that's not responsive to our contention, that whether or not anyone is denied care has nothing to do with whether people do not seek it for financial reasons; and we're going to suggest that, in addition to being irrelevant, Frank's statement is false. *The American Journal of Public Health* in May of 1960 says, "Incredible as it may seem in this enlightened century, we know only too well how tragically true and how increasingly frequent are the cases in which people are denied access to prescribed care because of their inability to pay." So we're going to suggest to you, in other words, that here's an additional advantage of the affirmative team. People under the present system are indeed denied care because they can't pay for it; under compulsory health insurance they wouldn't be.

All right, the second point Frank made was that there are many reasons for the neglect of health. They include fear, education, attitude, and so on. And he seemed to make a great deal out of the fact that the one publication that he has very judiciously collected doesn't happen to mention cost. But, unfortunately, we think that the problem cannot be dismissed in terms of lethargy, or lack of education, or improper health attitude. The former Assistant Secretary to the Department of Health, Education, and Welfare, E. L. Richardson, wrote in August of 1959, "We now have in America a citizenry that is keenly interested in health, and that is generally aware of what is necessary and available in medical care." The problem is not basically one of attitude or education, but one of economics. If the gentlemen are not going to discuss the authorities that we presented so far, let's look further. Let's look to Professor J. Henry Richardson, writing in *Economic and Financial Aspects of Social Security*, 1960. He says, "Illnesses are often neglected in their early stages primarily because of the expenses involved in medical care." The *New York Times*, December 7, 1959: "Millions of Americans defer needed medical treatment primarily because of the fear of cost." Professsor Hazel Kyrk, *The Family in the American Economy*, 1953: "Field studies have shown quantitatively that diagnosis and treatments are postponed or even foregone for economic reasons." That's why we concur with the University of Michigan report to the Senate Finance Committee in June of 1960, when they say that "income is the overwhelming determinant of the ability to get needed medical care." That's why we agree with the Conference of the General Welfare, December 1959, when they say that the problem of health neglect in the United States is essentially economic. We're not denying the existence of those other factors. We should move to solve other problems, too. But the primary problem is one of cost, and nothing that Frank said denies that.

All right, third of all, he turned to George Bugbee—again the president of a voluntary agency, another objective source—telling us that there's no correlation between care and income and therefore that the economic factor is not determinant. We're going to challenge Mr. Bugbee's standards here. The *Social Security Bulletin* of February 1961, says, "The latest national health survey found that the amount of medical care received by a family was significantly related to the family's income." We think that Mr. Bugbee is just plain wrong. And furthermore we don't think that any of the statements that either Mr. Bugbee or Mr. Harrison made really refute any one of our three points.

You recall, number one, we said, "Many people just can't pay the bills." Frank's response: How many people? Let's look again. Professor B. J. Stern in *The Sociology of Medicine*, 1960. He says, "For the vast majority of the people," (and Gene read this in his first speech) "adequate medical care is simply beyond reach." We turn to Professor Stern, saying that this affects the vast majority of the people. We turn to Professor Strauss, saying that the result is the neglect of health. That wasn't really denied by the opposition.

All right, then, we suggested that even more people fear the ultimate cost, even if they can pay some of the bills. Frank had nothing to say on that point.

And the negative team refused to discuss with you our third point here, and that is that even if you can pay all the bills, all of us just tend to economize. We tend to economize because we may not feel sick enough to get care. And we think this constitutes in itself a very important reason for removing that dollar sign from medicine. Because until we do, we've got a very important national problem of health neglect that we'd like to solve, and that the negative team will do nothing about.

All right, the question then is: Is this problem of health neglect inherent in the present system? And Frank went through a rather rapid enumeration of the mechanisms of the present system. There were five of them through which, somehow, you could pay for medical care. But you recall that we suggested to you that the reason the problem is inherent in the present system was, as Professor of Economics B. A. Weisbrod pointed out, that none of these mechanisms of the present system can remove the need to make economic decisions in seeking medical care. Most of those things that Frank said could be lumped under "self-financing," and here, of course, cost is directly a factor.

What about voluntary health insurance? We suggested to you that no one can afford all the insurance he needs. And this wasn't just a matter of assertion; we cited Professor Haverman, saying that most people, as a result, decide to curtail their health insurance expenditure. The negative team couldn't deny that.

What about the next point, that even if you decide to buy some kind of insurance, the amount you can buy depends on how much money you have? The negative team distorted that to mean that insurance doesn't cover all the cost. That wasn't what we said at all, but now that the negative team has brought it up, what did Frank actually tell us? He said you could get comprehensive care for $200 a family. Now, a little quick arithmetic shows you that if you multiply that by the number of families in the country, that means that this mystical company that's offering this policy would be collecting ten billion dollars worth of premiums for twenty and a half billion dollars worth of medical care. I think it would go out of business pretty fast. I'd like to see that policy. We don't think it's really comprehensive, and Professor Dickerson in his text on health insurance, 1960, corroborates that view. He says that the Federal Trade Commission objects to the term "comprehensive" in health insurance advertising; there simply is no comprehensive policy offered. And, you know, we showed you that if you don't cover certain expenses, the economic decision in that area remains. So we've got to have coverage. The negative team can't provide us that coverage; they can't even argue about the inherent defects of voluntary insurance.

And finally they suggest, "Well, the problem isn't inherent because, well, perhaps some people can get welfare." Now, we suggested to you, number one, that welfare really isn't universal. You'll remember Gene said that the need was for a universal program because everyone is faced by economic decisions in seeking medical care. And, frankly, we don't see why the gentlemen from Kings would restrict compulsory-financed medical care only to the indigent.

Number two, you'll recall that under that second advantage Gene cited Edward Chase—and again it wasn't an assertion—cited Edward Chase to the effect that a great many people are deterred from getting welfare by the stigma of the means test. And here Frank said that there just isn't any evidence available on the subject. Well, the April 1961 report of the Iowa Department on Social Welfare seems to think there is. They say there is no questioning the fact that a great many people have gone without needed medical care because they couldn't bring themselves to apply for this type of assistance through a welfare office. The report of the House Commerce Committee, on March 10, 1954, concluded, "Economic means tests are in many areas serious barriers to hospital admission, threatening the public health through the perpetuation of serious infectious disease." So we think public welfare just isn't the adequate solution to our problem; we think it isn't universal; we think it's inadequate; we think there's a means test which deters people from getting care.

All right, what about the question of inadequate public welfare? This, you'll recall, was part of our third advantage. And Frank tried to relate that to the need by saying that perhaps by improving welfare we might be able to meet that need. Well, you remember that welfare doesn't allow people to decide whether or not to get medical care on the grounds of whether or not they need it. They've got to decide, first of all, whether or not they want to be degraded. But we'd like to suggest to you that Frank hasn't given us a workable counterplan for expanding welfare to the point where we could rely on it. In the Senate Finance Committee on June 29, 1960, Governor Nelson Rockefeller—and I'd suspect he knows something about financial matters—said that "the financing of state plans for expanded welfare would present serious financial strains on the state. It's likely that even under federal participation, a number of states couldn't participate at all." So we think that the negative's nebulous counterplan wouldn't meet the need. We don't think it's even related to the need, because welfare doesn't remove the need to make decisions of economic origin in seeking medical care, and we're still left with the problem that the present system cannot meet, that can be met by removing the question of how the bill will be paid, through a program of prepayment.

Now, what about those three advantages that would result from such a program? Number one, we suggested it would relieve economic insecurity. And Frank said, "Why is it the duty of the federal government?" We're not suggesting that it's the duty of the federal government; we're simply suggesting that it would be advantageous for the federal government to prevent medical tragedy from leading to financial disaster. And, frankly, I think the gentlemen from Kings are being a little inconsistent here. They advocate welfare to take care of people when they've already been forced into that position, but they're not willing to prevent anyone from being pushed into that welfare program.

All right, what about the second advantage—that we'd prevent hospital insolvency? I think Frank misinterpreted this point and said we were saying something about higher premiums, and then suggested that we'd be subsidizing inefficiency. I think that's a distortion. The fact is that more efficient administration of our hospitals is independent of the affirmative plan. We could accomplish it with or without the affirmative plan. The problem is those unpaid bills that are putting our hospitals out of business, and as a matter of fact Frank hasn't suggested any other way in which we could solve this very important need for some kind of action.

In that third area—that we'd remove medical inequality, that we'd provide adequate care to states that have inadequate care now for welfare services—well, Frank said, "Here, there is a problem." What he'd have us do is standardize welfare levels. Presumably, since we showed you there aren't more funds in the states, he'll have to standardize them at the low levels of the present time. We don't think that's a solution. We think that again there's an undenied advantage to the affirmative plan here.

For these brief reasons, then, we still believe that we should remove the dollar sign from medicine, that we should adopt a program of compulsory health insurance for all citizens.

## SECOND NEGATIVE CONSTRUCTIVE SPEECH
### MR. PETER SMITH, KINGS COLLEGE

Ladies and gentlemen, as second speaker for the negative in this debate, I'd like to go over the objections which we might have, which we do have, to the affirmative plan as suggested in the first affirmative speech, and then attempt to re-analyze some of the so-called affirmative advantages and attempt to look at them in light a little bit more realistic than the gentlemen from Harvard have done.

First of all, in regard to that affirmative plan, we'd like to point out that although we were given some very, very general details as to the cost and method of financing, we weren't told by the members of the affirmative team anything at all as to the general cost of their proposal. Now, this, we think, is most interesting, because the members of the affirmative team, on one hand, are contending that the American people have the barrier of money between them and medical care which they need. And the whole philosophic basis of the affirmative case is this very interesting thesis: If we take the dollar sign out of medicine, we can solve the problem.

And how are they going to take the dollar sign out of medicine? By that very old, utopian method—they're going to let the government pay for the program and let the people take advantage of it, based upon their need. This is all very interesting. But I think, as even the gentlemen on my right must realize, that the government gets the money from someone. The government is going to collect this money from the very means which they suggested, some kind of a compulsory tax. Now, I'd like the members of this affirmative team to justify the fact that, on one hand, the American people don't have enough finances to pay for this system through the present method, no matter what it might be, and yet, on the other hand, somebody, somewhere, is going to have enough money so the federal government can get it in compulsory taxation, and give it back to the hospitals and doctors, and provide the American people with free medical care. The illusion that one can remove the dollar sign from medicine is just that—an illusion—and the members of the affirmative team realize it. The only way in which that could be done were if doctors, hospitals, and all aspects of our medical facilities were to go completely without pay and give free service.

The dollar sign isn't being removed; it's being transferred. We're going to have a middleman. And the members of the affirmative team cannot, at least they haven't so far and I don't think they can, say that it's going to be done at any greatly reduced cost. First of all, according to the *Source Book of Health Insurance Data* for 1960, the total cost of medical care for the American people last year was approximately eighteen billion dollars. Now we'd like the members of the affirmative team to show us where the affirmative and where the federal government under their program is going to get this fund to finance the program.

Secondly, we'd like the members of the affirmative team to justify one very important thing for us. We've been told in very general terms that the federal government is going to take over the entire system of financing medical care. By this, we would presume that the federal government is going to pay everyone's medical bills for all of his medical expenses.

And yet throughout this debate, though we have been given some general philosophic needs and some general arguments as to some people who don't get medical care, there's nothing specific at all in this affirmative proposal. What do I mean by specific? Well, the members of the affirmative team not once have ever given us any reason why the federal government should pay the total medical bill. They haven't shown us that the American people experience any difficulty paying their dental expenses. They haven't shown us that we experience any difficulty paying our nonprescribed drug expenses. They haven't shown us that we experience any difficulty paying for sunglasses that doctors might prescribe. They haven't even shown us any particular reason why the need exists in the field of hospital care, surgical care, or personal physician care. They've given us some general statements as to people who don't get the care.

We'd like the members of the affirmative team to justify this particularly so they can prove to us we should allow the federal government to take over the entire system. Granted, and we'll grant this just for about ten seconds, there may be a need in some specific area, but we'd like the members of the affirmative team to show us that it exists in every facet of our medical system today. Because this is the only grounds upon which they can justify a plan which supposedly pays everyone's medical bills. The plan, it seems, is about "x" times larger than the affirmative need. I had to say "x" because I don't know exactly how big the affirmative need is, but again the members of the affirmative team should show us exactly why there's a need for the federal government to pay the full amount of everyone's medical bill.

Well, then the members of the affirmative team went a little bit further. They told us that they're going to have local boards to regulate any abuses which might creep into the system. This is all well and good; the affirmative team is suspecting that there are going to be some abuses. But we contend that local boards aren't a satisfactory means of solving the problem. My colleague pointed out that the hospitals are in a financial mess due to the present system. I can read some quotations here, pointing out that in many cases there are abuses on the local level. Either some doctors who don't live up to the code they're supposed to live up to, or too many patients who want to take advantage of a free system, or too many hospital administrators and persons in hospitals, who are either too negligent or too crooked, will take advantage of such a type of proposal. Now the members of the affirmative team have provided for some type of regulation, but it's on a local, and not a federal or even state, level. In other words, the very persons who under the present system and under their proposal, also, may perpetrate the violations are going to be judges in their own case under the affirmative proposal. This, too, will add to the general cost, the "x" cost of that affirmative proposal—a significant disadvantage of the affirmative team.

Well, in regard to the so-called over-all points given to us by the members of the affirmative team in this debate, in regard to advantages, we were told there are three things wrong with the present system. Now these things aren't "needs" in the debaters' sense; they're needs as far as the United States is concerned. And the affirmative proposal, it just happens, is going to solve these needs.

Now, it is the contention of the members of the negative team that, first of all, the affirmative proposal won't solve these problems. Secondly, it's going to make some of them a great deal worse than they are under the present system. You'll recall one of them is the contention by the members of the affirmative team that we're going to remove the financial drain of free care on the hospitals. Well, my colleague pointed out that they weren't giving you the whole story there, that a great part of the reason why hospitals were in financial difficulty is through their own inefficiency, through practices—bad practices—which occur in the hospital. What was the answer of the second affirmative speaker to this point? He told you, "Well, first of all, we're going to get rid of free care which hospitals have to give." And secondly, he argued that we didn't propose any alternatives. Now, we don't think it's the obligation of the members of the negative team to provide a counterplan. We'd only like to point out that, first of all, this affirmative proposal won't specifically be solving the whole problem since a great part of the problem is hospital inefficiency, and they are taking no federal or state means to solve the problem of hospital inefficiency.

Secondly, the members of the affirmative team have more or less, by asking us to provide a solution, admitted that the problem exists within the present system. Well, let's carry it one step further. We don't think it's just a problem of hospitals being run wrong, or hospitals having to give a lot of free care to people who can't afford to pay their bills. We think it's something that goes much deeper. For there is a general shortage of hospital and general medical facilities throughout the United States. And it's the contention of the members of the negative team that the affirmative proposal won't come anywhere near to solving this problem. Now, why is this so? Well, I made a big point out of the lack of substantial and adequate regulation before. Why did I do this? Well, I did this because it's one of the things that comes about when you have a complete—and nothing could be more complete than this affirmative proposal—a complete system of prepayment for medical expenses. F. J. Snyder, a research analyst for the Public Affairs Institute, *Health Insurance for the Aged*, 1960: "An unfortunate by-product of the increased use of hospitalization insurance is the overutilization of hospital facilities. The abuse of medical insurance results in further packing already overloaded hospitals." And Mr. Snyder concludes his statement by saying, "Any successful government-sponsored health insurance will have to meet the problem of unnecessary use of hospitals and unnecessary surgery."

I stress the word "unnecessary" because I realize the affirmative are quite willing to come up here and say that this increased use of hospitals will be by people who aren't getting the care now. I say "unnecessary" because it will be persons who don't need medical care who will yet flock to these hospitals and to these doctors, overutilizing these facilities.

And there is very definitely a shortage. I don't think I have to prove it, but I'd like to point out exactly how seriously it exists and where it exists. *U. S. News and World Report,* May 9, 1958: "Because of the short supply of doctors, hospitals often cannot obtain the physicians they need even when they seek to hire them." Now, the members of the affirmative team may well try to point out that their program, their program of "x" amount of compulsory health insurance, is going to solve this problem—this problem of hospitals being abused, this problem of an overutilization of facilities or a shortage of doctors. But it just isn't so. Professors Baisden and Hutchinson, the University of California, *Health Insurance,* 1958: "The mere act of providing more money for medical care does not necessarily result in an increase in either the quantity or quality of services." And Mr. F. J. Follman, Jr., Director of the Research and Information Bureau of the Health Insurance Association of America, *Voluntary Health Insurance and Medical Care,* 1958: "The existence of a broadly established insurance mechanism, no matter how effective, does not nor can not increase the medical personnel or facilities available."

What conclusion can we reach here? Well, one of the advantages that we're supposedly going to have when we adopt this affirmative proposal is that medical care is going to be made more adequate. Everyone's going to have the wonderful advantages of adequate medical care, just due to the adoption of this affirmative proposal. But we pointed out that we do have a problem of a shortage of facilities and doctors. The affirmative have no adequate measures in its plan for providing against unnecessary overutilization of these facilities, and compulsory health insurance, *per se,* won't solve this problem.

And what's going to be the result? Well, Mr. Seely Greenberg, a medical reporter for the *Providence Journal,* says in *Harper's,* 1960, "The frequent instances of careless medical care by overworked doctors is among the most frequent complaint of patients today." In other words, we can see that overworked doctors, overstrained facilities, give inadequate medical care. And the affirmative proposal is going to worsen this situation, leading to a greater amount of inadequacy in medical care given to the American people. Their proposal isn't achieving an advantage; they're creating an even greater disadvantage through the adoption of the affirmative proposal.

For these reasons and the objections to the need which my colleague brought up before, which he will continue in the first negative rebuttal, we beg that the affirmative proposal be rejected. Thank you.

## FIRST NEGATIVE REBUTTAL SPEECH
### MR. FRANK HARRISON, KINGS COLLEGE

Ladies and gentlemen, as first speaker for the negative returning to this podium, I'd like to discuss with you again the question of whether or not there's a need for the affirmative resolution, and I'd like to discuss with you some of the refutations of arguments which the second affirmative speaker wishes I'd made.

Now the first thing, you'll recall, that I asked the affirmative team was specifically, gentlemen, how many people in the United States are not getting adequate medical care because they can't afford to pay for it? I said, "Gentlemen, give us the statistics." And that was a very clever answer we heard. We were told, according to some authorities, that the vast majority of the American people can't afford out of their own resources to pay for medical care. And that simply does not answer the question. The question, gentlemen, to repeat, is: how many people aren't getting care because they can't afford to pay for it? Perhaps the vast majority can't afford it from their own resources. You'll recall there are five ways in which they can pay for medical care, only one of which is straight out of their own resources. They can borrow, they can go to charity, they can have insurance. Simply, the answer given does not reply to the question.

Well, then we were told, you see, the people are making medical decisions on economic grounds. I came to the rostrum and I quoted Dr. Larson, who was not very objective. I'm sorry; he was testifying under oath at the time, however. Some authority, however—and I think this is cute—some authority knows the circumstances in which people are denied care because they can't afford it. I wish that authority would tell the American Hospital Association, because their president appeared before the House Ways and Means Committee in July of 1959 and he said, "I am not aware of cases where people have been refused hospital or medical service because of their inability to pay for it." And furthermore, a representative of the AFL-CIO, Mr. Cruikshank, was asked a now-famous debaters' question by Congressman Alger of Texas—to please give examples of the circumstances, give specific cases in which people have been denied care. And I think the gentlemen can search the record of the House Committee on Ways and Means and will find that Mr. Cruikshank notably did not reply.

All right, we went on a little further. You'll recall I quoted from the most recent source I could get hold of, the White House Conference in January of 1961. They said there were many reasons why people aren't getting care. The gentlemen of the affirmative said, "Well, it was nice of the negative team to pick out the one source that would go along with them." It was also nice for the negative team that that source happened to be the most recent and the most authoritative. But they said, "Well, you see, there are a lot of other problems involved here, we admit this. The problem is that economics is the main problem." Now, gentlemen, even if we concede that for a minute, you're missing the point. The point is your need isn't going to meet your plan, because you've admitted that there are other barriers beside economic barriers. So even assuming this grand hypothesis, even assuming that we're going to be able to strike down the financial barrier, the other barriers still remain. The other barriers are still effective. People still aren't going to doctors. And that very lovely need isn't met by that comprehensive plan.

Well, we were told, "Yes, you see, but income is the overwhelming determinant." All right, ladies and gentlemen, I'd like to take a look at what happens when that overwhelming determinant is taken away. Drs. Odin Anderson and Paul Shipley, in *Comprehensive Medical Insurance,* 1959. They begin by discussing the fact that there are three plans—the General Health Insurance Plan, the Health Insurance Plan of New York, and the Windsor Plan—which prepay the patient's visits to the doctor's office in the first place. They pay for the patient every time he goes to the doctor's office. Obviously, no cost to him. Now, according to the theory of this affirmative team, wouldn't you think that people would be going to doctors far more frequently than they are when they don't have such insurance? Let's look at the conclusion. A recent release of the National Health Survey showed that 37 per cent of the population had not seen a physician within a year. Under the most favorable financial circumstances—the absence of any such barriers to physicians' services in GHI, HIP, and Windsor—25 to 32 per cent of the enrollees will not seek physicians' services within a year. Thirty-seven per cent don't go when they don't have insurance; 32 per cent don't go when they *do* have insurance. Gentlemen, we suggest your economic determinant isn't determining too much.

Well, then, we were told, "You see that all the negative sources in this debate simply don't stand because Mr. Bugbee is the president of an insurance company." Now, I'm a little tired of hearing Mr. Bugbee assailed for bias in this debate. He happens to be president of the Health Information Foundation, and is not employed by the insurance companies. And even if he is, we suggest that the Department of Health, Education, and Welfare have not yet come under the pay of the insurance companies. I cited them, too, and the gentlemen never replied.

Well, then, you'll recall, I said there are five ways of paying for medical care. I said the gentlemen had to indict each one of them, and I ask you to search your memories to see if they have. They haven't indicted government payment, they haven't indicted private charity, they haven't indicted ability to borrow. They said, "No, gentlemen, you don't get the point. The point is that these don't remove the necessity for economic decisions." Gentlemen, you haven't shown us what evils are following from these economic decisions; you haven't even shown us that they are leading to concrete harm.

But there are three advantages to the affirmative resolution. The first one, you see, is it's going to prevent hardship. Now, I suggested to the gentlemen that it's not the duty of the government to prevent people from going into debt to any degree. The gentlemen said, "Oh, that isn't the problem. They're going to become destitute under the present system." Gentlemen, would you present some statistics to prove that a significant number of people are becoming destitute? Also, we suggested that it's going to create a paternalistic welfare state. No comment from the gentlemen.

Well, then we were told that the indigent go without care. I said, "Very interesting, in fact. The indigent go without care rather than seek it." And, according to the second affirmative speaker, I said there was no evidence available. No, I said the second affirmative had to tell us how many people in the indigent group don't get care because they can't afford it. And we still haven't heard that answer. But we were told, you see, that more efficient administration of hospitals will occur independent of the resolution. I read an authority in this debate, Dr. Summers, who said it wouldn't, that it would occur under the present system, and not under the resolution.

I think we can conclude that the resolution still deserves to be rejected. Thank you.

## FIRST AFFIRMATIVE REBUTTAL SPEECH
### MR. LAURENCE TRIBE, HARVARD UNIVERSITY

After fifteen minutes of negative optimistic discussion about what the gentlemen of the opposition consider a very lovely need, we're led to believe that perhaps there is no real problem at all, that perhaps it's just some wild rumor started by four hundred thousand contagious disease carriers. But we're going to resist the temptation to reach that conclusion, because there are a couple of objections that we've got to cover before we can go back and see why that conclusion is fallacious.

Now, the gentlemen asked us, "How much will the plan cost?" And we're very concerned about that fact. We turn to Dr. Alan Gregg, in *Challenge to Contemporary Medicine*, 1957. He says that by spending only 6 per cent more than we currently spend on medical care, the government, through compulsory national health insurance, could provide completely comprehensive medical services for everyone. Now, using the gentlemen's own figure of 18 billion dollars, that means that we spend about 1.08 billion dollars more than we currently spend on medical care. Frankly, we think that the needless death and suffering in the present system really is worth about one billion dollars, at least.

Now, the gentlemen say that, "Actually, there's some quite big problem here, because we couldn't get enough money under the affirmative plan, because we haven't got enough money now." Well, number one, we weren't talking only about the inadequacy of funds. We were talking about decisions. Number two, people pay taxes progressively; they don't pay medical bills progressively.

Then the gentlemen said, "Where's the money going to come from?" Well, it's going to come from income taxes. And in *Public Finance*, 1960, Professor Troy Cauley points out, "Because of the interrelationship between government spending and the economy, far higher tax levels would in no way impair our economy's growth."

Then the gentlemen suggested that there were all kinds of things like dental expenditures and drug expenses and sun glasses, I suppose, that we ought to have discussed very specifically. Well, frankly, I thought Gene covered quite a bit in that first ten minutes without trying to apply all of his arguments to every one of these areas. We think the area of dental care is perhaps typical. *Public Health Reports,* March 1959, says, "Only 31 per cent of the American people who seriously need dental work are getting it at the present time, primarily because of the high cost involved."

Now, frankly, we think that our need really does apply to all of these areas. They told us that local boards are unsatisfactory because 430 of them were working pretty satisfactorily now. They said overutilization would result. Well, number one, that contradicts their idea that there's no cost barrier. Number two, overutilization can be effectively controlled. The *Evaluation of Medical Care Programs,* 1961, points out, "It's been shown empirically that unnecessary or wasteful use of medical services can be effectively controlled with no adverse consequences." They suggested that doctors would be setting their own fees. They forget that doctors and laymen sit on those boards. They told us that there were going to be abuses, and yet James Brindle, in the *American Journal of Public Health,* April 1957, said, "Services must be completely prepaid if the economic barrier to needed care is to be removed, and if unnecessary surgery or hospitalization is to be discouraged." That shows the necessity for comprehensive care, doesn't it, not the reason for rejecting the affirmative plan?

Finally, they suggested we've got too few facilities now. Number one, we say that even if we've got less facilities than we would like to have, that's no reason to determine who gets to use those facilities on the basis of who is the highest bidder. Number two, we say we don't really have a serious facility problem. The *New York State Medical Journal* on May 15, 1959, said, "If the public fully utilized the preventive, diagnostic, and treatment services and facilities already available, a great many of the illnesses now fatal could be effectively treated."

So let's look back at some of those illnesses. Let's see what the primary reason for the neglect of health is in the United States today. Well, number one, it was suggested that no one is denied care. We were told finally that it's really true because Dr. Larson was under oath. Well, frankly, we still think that the *American Journal of Public Health* really wasn't speaking purely out of its imagination when it suggested that people are denied care. The issue is peripheral to the debate, and we still think it constitutes an advantage of the affirmative proposal.

But the question wasn't really denied. The question is: Why don't people seek that care? And we presented Professor Richardson, Professor Kyrk, the University of Michigan reports, the Conference on the General Welfare, all saying that the primary reason they didn't seek that care was economic. The gentlemen come back and tell us that the economic factor isn't determining because there's no real correlation between money and medicine in the United States. And they say the Department of Health, Education, and Welfare agrees with them. Yet the Department of Health, Education, and Welfare national health survey for last year concluded that utilization rates soared 23 per cent as income went down 25 per cent.

So we're going to suggest to you that there really is a very basic problem in all of these areas, that when the negative team asks us, "What happens when the economic factors are removed?" they know we've already shown you. And that is that when these economic factors are removed, as they were removed in the case of Georgia, for instance, according to the American Medical Association in 1954, millions of people get that care who hadn't gotten it before. In that particular instance, one million, three hundred and eighty thousand people, when screening surveys were offered on an experimental basis, received free medical care that they hadn't gotten before the cost barrier had been removed. That's what happens. Cost is a major factor, not education.

Well, what about the question of the inherency within the present system? The gentlemen first suggested that comprehensive policies could be given to all of us for two hundred dollars. When they saw the absurdity of that suggestion, they dropped it completely in this debate. They no longer contend that they can provide that kind of policy.

They have nothing left here really, because they're not denying, number one, that the economic decision remains when you've got to decide whether or not to buy voluntary health insurance. They're not denying, number two, that the amount you can buy depends on how much money you have. They're not denying that in welfare or in any free program people are deterred by the means test; so it doesn't free people to make medical decisions on medical grounds. Yet they're not denying, finally, that if we adopted that affirmative plan, we could prevent a great deal of economic hardship, we could improve our welfare program, we could prevent our hospitals from going broke as a result of unpaid bills. All they say is that there still will be other problems that your program may not solve. We don't think that's a reason to reject our plan; we think we still should remove the dollar sign from medicine.

## SECOND NEGATIVE REBUTTAL SPEECH

### MR. PETER SMITH, KINGS COLLEGE

Ladies and gentlemen, as last speaker for the negative, I'd like to summarize the debate for the final time this week-end. First of all, the objections which I raised to the affirmative plan were answered rather hastily by the first affirmative rebuttalist. We were told that some expert says that we could finance the entire program at a cost of only 6 per cent greater than that of the present system, and this is something that our great economy can bear, so therefore there's no real problem.

Well, gentlemen, I think anyone associated with this debate topic knows that I could bring up ten sources saying your administrative cost would be six, eight, twelve, fifteen, eighteen per cent, just as you brought up one saying it was six per cent. But you are supposedly going to remove the dollar sign from an area of financing medical care; at least that was the basic affirmative thesis in this debate. Yet I pointed out in my second negative speech that you aren't really doing this at all. All you're doing is transferring it so that the federal government takes the money from the citizens of America to provide their medical care, instead of the people paying it directly, or directly through various facets of the present system. You aren't really removing the dollar sign; it is still going to be a cost for the American people to bear, of financing their medical care. Now, according to your statement, the present system is too much for the American people to bear. I asked you to break it down and consider it separately so I wouldn't have to do what I'm about to do, but you wouldn't do it so far, so I will.

The only estimate we have so far of just what the affirmative proposal is going to entail is the fact that it's going to pay everyone's expenses for every type of medical care. This is fine. The present system—everything—costs eighteen billion dollars. Theirs is going to cost 6 per cent more. And yet the American people, according to the entire affirmative stand upon this floor, can't afford the present system in its totality. So, therefore, we think the members of the affirmative team have pulled one of the greatest illogical conclusions of all time. They are contending the American people can't afford a system, and in order to help them pay their way out of this problem, we're going to provide them with a system which is going to take more money from them, remove the dollar sign from the area of medical economics, and make everybody happy. Gentlemen, this is utopia, this is utopia carried to its furthest extreme—again, an example of where the affirmative proposal does not show too much of a demonstration of its correlation to the affirmative need.

Well, then, we pointed out that regulation by local boards would be deficient. They said that doctors and laymen will sit on the board. This doesn't prove, again, that you're going to stop all kinds of abuses which exist at various levels. My colleague pointed out that the reason our hospitals are in trouble is because hospitals have inefficient practices. No real answer was here given by the members of the affirmative team. The affirmative proposal of compulsory health insurance is going to make this problem worse.

As far as overutilization of facilities is concerned, the affirmative team whitewashed it. I pointed out that one of the needs they're supposed to solve is the inadequacy of American medical care. And a result of this unnecessary overutilization of facilities is going to be a decrease in the adequacy of medical care made available to the American people. The members of the affirmative team had no answer here—an advantage turned into a distinct disadvantage.

Now, in regard to the affirmative need, I have no intention of running herd through every single quote fired at you by the first affirmative speaker, and fired right back by my colleague, and then refired by the members of the affirmative team. But I think one thing stands clear. First of all, despite the fact that a great many people die in the United States every year, it hasn't been established by the members of the affirmative team that these people died because they couldn't get needed medical care, because they couldn't afford treatment. And this is the only logical basis on which we should adopt the affirmative proposal. And the reason why is very simple. Because my colleague has contended throughout this debate that there are other factors besides purely economic ones which keep people from seeking needed medical care—everything from negligence to pure ignorance.

The members of the affirmative team have first flirted with the idea of completely refuting our contention. When we came to the first affirmative rebuttal, they were accepting it. They were saying that the primary reason is economic. Primary or not, my colleague matched the first affirmative speaker source for source, saying that you won't solve the problem by giving the people money to go to the doctor. And he gave them a specific example of where it's been done: the utilization of services didn't increase one bit. In other words, we can see that the affirmative proposal won't get at the heart of the problem—making the American people get adequate medical care when they have the means available to them.

Well, the members of the affirmative team moved a little bit further. They indict the so-called present system by considering voluntary health insurance, and they tell us that just because the amount of voluntary health insurance you have depends upon the amount of money you have, there's something wrong with voluntary health insurance. Well, my colleague pointed out the other facets of the present system. Most of them were completely ignored by the members of the affirmative team.

They go back constantly to their basic thesis that we've got to take financial problems out of the area of medicine in the United States today. Now, this we don't think is the obligation of the federal government. It certainly isn't being very well handled by the members of the affirmative team, for this very simple reason: the federal government, or the United States as a political body, has no obligation to make sure that everyone in the United States gets lavish, special care or has all his economic problems solved—this would be quite a job for the federal government. But the federal government does have some kind of an obligation to make sure that the American people get medical care when they need it. And this has no bearing upon the affirmative team's contention or the fact that the American people—some of them—die when they don't get adequate medical care. The affirmative in this debate hasn't established an essential specific reason for adopting this resolution.

And the second affirmative speaker in his rebuttal must show you that, first of all, their specific plan, *per se,* will solve the evil that they say exists in its totality. Or else the affirmative proposal won't meet that need; the need can be solved by other means, and we need not adopt that resolution. Thank you.

## SECOND AFFIRMATIVE REBUTTAL SPEECH
### MR. GENE CLEMENTS, HARVARD UNIVERSITY

Before we return to the need, let's look again at the few objections which the negative managed to sustain after Larry refuted them. They brought back the idea that we were just transferring the dollar sign. Now, granted we are transferring a dollar sign, but the crucial thing is that we're transferring it from the individual, where it deters care, to the government. Where the government pays it from a progressive tax, the individual no longer has to make an individual economic decision every time he wants care. And we've shown you, I believe, that that individual economic decision is the main cause for health neglect. That, we contend, is wherein we are transferring the dollar sign.

And the gentlemen asked us, "How in the world can we possibly pay for it if we contend we can't pay for it now?" Again, they neglect the fact that we're now doing it on an individual basis. We say there are many who can't pay for care. All of us are deterred. However, through a progressive tax, we can let everyone's care be paid for because, of course, the individual no longer has to meet all of his expenses if he is low income—if, indeed, he can't pay for his care. We certainly wouldn't think that the gentlemen of the negative are contending that this nation is too poor, too cheap, to provide adequate care to all its citizens. So we think that these objections to the affirmative proposal certainly don't stand.

Let's go back to the need itself. In the first area, we said that there was a neglect of health which led to needless death and suffering. For a while this was admitted; then the gentlemen wanted to know if these people died because they couldn't afford care. Well, my colleague directly related the one-third of a million who died needlessly—that's one out of every five deaths each year—to essentially economic problems.

In the area of, for instance, one half of all disabling acute illnesses, we sort of assumed that it was apparent that if these people are flat on their backs they know they need care. There has to be a pretty good reason why they're not getting that care. We suggested that that factor was the economic factor. And I think we proved it when we gave you Professor Richardson, the *New York Times*, Professor Kyrk, the University of Michigan survey—all of which concluded that income was the overwhelming determinant. But the gentlemen say, "No, there are other factors." Certainly, there are other factors, gentlemen. We never contended there weren't. We gave you testimony that these factors were relatively insignificant, which as yet has gone undenied. We showed you surveys in Georgia, for instance, where over a million people came out to get free preventive examinations; 85 per cent of those people had not been diagnosed previously.

Let's go a little bit farther, however. Let's go to Philadelphia, where the AFL Medical Center provides preventive examinations for certain union members at no cost. A survey recently conducted revealed that were it not for this free center 92 per cent of the members receiving preventive care would never have sought diagnosis. It suggests to us that indeed there may be a cost barrier to medical care, a cost barrier which in fact transcends those who simply can't afford care, and encompasses all of us. And this is the point which the negative has never refuted—the idea that it's not the cost of care alone, but the fact that we must make an economic decision in seeking that care, which extends the need to every one of us in this room. Every one of us—every time we put off a physical examination because we want to economize, because we want to save the ten, fifteen, twenty dollars it costs for a physical examination—has made an economic decision which may have harmed our health. We contend that compulsory health insurance can remove the need to make those economic decisions. *Public Medical Care* by Dr. Franz Goldmann pointed out, "By providing easy access to early diagnosis and thorough treatment, compulsory health insurance would greatly reduce the frequency of serious stages of illness." Compulsory health insurance can certainly meet the need in this particular area.

The gentlemen introduced a peripheral idea that people aren't denied care. Well, of course, this isn't particularly relevant to our case. We're worried about the people who never seek care in the first place. But, indeed, people are denied care. From hearings of the House Ways and Means Committee: "There's ample evidence documented by studies in Michigan, in Boston, in California, and throughout the nation, that because of inability to pay for it, literally millions of Americans go without needed medical care." So very definitely there is a problem in this area, and certainly we feel that the removal of the need to make those economic decisions can solve the problem.

We showed you in the area of inherency that voluntary insurance—and, basically, all these so-called other five factors could be lumped as either voluntary insurance, welfare, or self-financing—voluntary insurance could not remove the need to make economic decisions. In fact, it is dependent upon the income of the individual purchasing the insurance. And the negative never responded to either of these ideas. They presented a comprehensive policy which proposed for ten billion dollars to give twenty billion dollars worth of care. When we pointed out the absurdity of that, they dropped the point. We showed you in welfare that the means test deterred care—in fact, that welfare was inadequate. We shouldn't expand welfare. And in this particular area, again, the negative has dropped the point.

Ladies and gentlemen, the opposition, and indeed all of us here: the gentlemen have made cost a primary consideration. They asked us how we'll pay the bill. We've shown you we can pay the cost of the affirmative proposal in dollars and cents. The negative proposal is today being paid for through human death and suffering. How, gentlemen, will you pay the bill?

# Appendix B

# A SAMPLE PUBLIC DEBATE

### IS DEBATING BOTH SIDES OF A PROPOSITION IN TOURNAMENTS ETHICAL?

*The three articles which comprise this debate are reprinted by permission of the editor of* The Speech Teacher *and the Speech Association of America. The student who is interested in reading more discussion of the controversy should read Wayne N. Thompson, "Discussion and Debate,"* The Quarterly Journal of Speech, *30 (Oct. 1944), 296–97; Brooks Quimby, "But Is It Educational?" Speech Activities, 9 (Summer 1953), 30–31; Donald K. Smith, "Letter to the Editor,"* The Speech Teacher, *6 (Nov. 1957), 336; George W. Dell, "In Defense of Debating Both Sides,"* The Speech Teacher, *7 (Jan. 1958), 31–34; and Douglas Ehninger, "The Debate about Debating,"* The Quarterly Journal of Speech, *44 (April 1958), 128–36.*

### THE ETHICS OF DEBATING BOTH SIDES *
#### RICHARD MURPHY

"Is it not risky to ignore the ethical?" wrote Albert J. Beveridge in 1924. "The practice in high schools and colleges of appointing debate teams to support or oppose propositions, regardless of what the debaters believe, is questionable—indeed, bad," [1] he declared. Senator Beveridge's comment is only one of many that one might cull on the merits of debating in disregard of conviction. The contemporary controversy dates from Theodore Roosevelt's declaration in his *Autobiography* in 1913 that he was "exceedingly glad" that as a student at Harvard he never "practiced debating." He had "not the

---

* From *The Speech Teacher*, 6 (Jan. 1957), 1–9. Professor Murphy has served as director of forensics at several institutions. He is now Professor of Speech at the University of Illinois and past editor of *The Quarterly Journal of Speech*.

[1] *The Art of Public Speaking* (Boston: Houghton Mifflin Company, 1924), pp. 23–24.

slightest sympathy with debating contests in which each side is arbitrarily assigned a given proposition and told to maintain it without the least reference to whether those maintaining it believe in it or not." [2]

The controversy has had its worthy partisans on both sides, and feelings run deep. Opponents of debating against conviction are adamant in their position, and, so far as I am aware, partisans of the debate-both-sides practice are equally one-sided in their belief. There are, of course, variations in individual practice. Woodrow Wilson as a senior in college refused to participate in a prize debate when drawing lots put him on the side opposite his belief. But as a debate counsellor at Princeton, he once advised a debater not to worry about opposing his own conviction, but to center on his opposition to Harvard.[3] And there have been vogues in the practice. By 1917, O'Neill, Laycock, and Scales, although defending debating against conviction, noted that since colleges then had both affirmative and negative teams, ". . . it probably very rarely happens that a student who has ardent convictions talks against them in an intercollegiate contest." [4] In 1930, Dayton McKean, writing about Woodrow Wilson's attitude on the matter, explained that "debating both sides" is "a method now generally abandoned." [5] As recently as 1951, Ewbank and Auer, defending debating against conviction under certain conditions, observed that "There seems no good reason for assuming that debaters are commonly forced to debate against their convictions." [6]

But with the firm establishment of the tournament system, which received its greatest impetus in the thirties, there has been a growing tendency not only to ignore conviction and side, but also to incorporate debating both sides as a part of the structure. For example, the West Point National Invitational Tournament requires that "Teams debate opposite sides of question an equal number of times." [7] Whereas in the older systems policy was largely a matter of individual schools and coaches, now one either debates both sides or he does not debate at all, or at least not in tournaments such as the West Point. An ethic has now been imposed.

In a rather objective review of what has happened to debate, a well-known political scientist, James McGregor Burns, describes "modern debating" as primarily a system of contests. "Student debaters ordinarily do not choose their own sides." He asks, "What would Roosevelt say today if he could see the nationally chosen debate topics, with debating teams shifting

[2] *Theodore Roosevelt: An Autobiography* (New York: The Macmillan Company, 1913), p. 28.
[3] Dayton D. McKean, "Woodrow Wilson as a Debate Coach," *The Quarterly Journal of Speech*, XVI (November, 1930), 460.
[4] James Milton O'Neill, Craven Laycock, and Robert Leighton Scales, *Argumentation and Debate* (New York: The Macmillan Company, 1917), p. 376.
[5] *Loc. cit.*
[6] Henry Lee Ewbank and J. Jeffery Auer, *Discussion and Debate: Tools of a Democracy* (New York: Appleton-Century-Crofts, Inc., 1951), p. 389.
[7] *Tenth West Point National Invitational Debate Tournament* (West Point: United States Military Academy, 1956), p. 20.

from side to side with hardly a change in pace?"[8] One answer has come from a veteran debate coach, Brooks Quimby of Bates College, who asks abandonment of the debate-both-sides policy.[9]

When there is such a sharp disagreement among worthy men, whose individual systems of ethics are presumably equally impeccable, there must be some misunderstanding, some difference in purpose, or some failure to focus on the essence of the matter. It is with the thought that a close analysis may help to clarify the dispute, rather than to add to the literature of the controversy, that I write. For years I have listened to the arguments for debating both sides, and I have read all I could find on the question. But consistent with the position I have always held, that debating both sides is of doubtful virtue, I must in all honesty set down the case against it.

The argument against debating both sides is very simple and consistent. Debate, the argument goes, is a form of public speaking. A public statement is a public commitment. Before one takes the platform, he should study the question, he should discuss it until he knows where he stands. Then he should take that stand. If, in the course of the long-term debate, one finds that he has changed his conviction, he is free to cross the floor, to change his party, to do what seems consistent with his honest conviction. As Beveridge put it, public speaking "means, of course, utter sincerity. Never under any circumstances or for any reward tell an audience what you, yourself, do not believe or are even indifferent about. To do so is immoral and worse—it is to be a public liar."[10] Or, as Brooks Quimby puts the matter, "Our democracy" needs "men and women of principle, who will weigh the arguments and evidence carefully before they become advocates," rather than "men and women trained to take either side at the flip of a coin."[11] As Theodore Roosevelt stated it, "What we need is to turn out of our colleges young men with ardent convictions on the side of the right, not young men who can make a good argument for either right or wrong as their interest bids them."[12]

In reply to these simple arguments, the debate-both-sides proponents have many answers. One of the sets of answers can be classified as philosophical. The most frequent of these arguments is the necessity of a free and open platform, with no silencing of unpopular sides. There may be applications of John Stuart Mill's essay, "Of the Liberty of Thought and Discussion." As Mill argued, ". . . the peculiar evil of silencing the expression of an opinion is, that it is robbing the human race." Or the argument may be put thus, ". . . on every subject on which difference of opinion is possible, the truth depends on a balance to be struck between two sets of conflicting reasons." There is no contesting the usefulness of the debate form, in which unpopular

---

[8] "Debate Over Collegiate Debate," *New York Times Magazine*, 5 December, 1954, 30.
[9] "But Is It Educational?" *Speech Activities*, IX (Summer, 1953), 30–31.
[10] *Op. cit.*, p. 20.
[11] *Loc. cit.*
[12] *Loc. cit.*

sides may be presented because the popular side is presented to counterbalance and correct. Any valid action to keep inquiry free, to assert the essential debatability of disputed questions, is a contribution to our freedom of expression. But it is not clear that one team's debating both sides has any connection with such a policy. If one follows Mill's full recommendation, it means a policy of tolerating, attempting to understand the utterance of views one does not hold, rather than one of expressing them oneself. Mill recommended ". . . acting . . . on conscientious conviction." The "real morality of public discussion," Mill thought, consists in avoiding sophistic argument, or suppressing facts or arguments, or misstating elements in the case, or misrepresenting opposite opinion. The moral discusser, on the other hand, is tolerant, frank, and fair. It is difficult to see how one can debate both sides and avoid Mill's list of malpractices or attain to his set of moral practices.

Since debate questions are purposely framed to provide a division of opinion, there should be available speakers on either side of the matter, speakers who really believe their own arguments. To do justice to arguments, Mill thought, and to bring them into real contact with our own minds, we "must be able to hear them from persons who actually believe them, who defend them in earnest, and do their very utmost for them." If for some reason a position has to be taken that no one present believes, there are devices for indicating the position taken is not of personal conviction. Socrates, when pressed to present a case he did not believe, spoke with his face covered that he might not offend the gods. But when he spoke his conviction, he spoke with his head bare, no longer muffled for shame.[13] Since 1587, the Sacred Congregation of Rites has used a Devil's Advocate as a means of testing arguments in the process of canonization. The various devices of the *advocatus diaboli* are, of course, only a substitute for the devil himself, who, however pervasive, is not always available for a specific appearance. But these devices do permit making a case in its strongest form without the violation of any ethical principles.

A second philosophical argument is that it is necessary to understand both sides of an argument, and debating both sides helps one to understand both sides. On this point Robert Louis Stevenson is sometimes quoted:

The best means of all towards catholicity is that wholesome rule which some folk are most inclined to condemn,—I mean the law of *obliged speeches*. Your senior member commands; and you must take the affirmative or the negative, just as suits his best convenience. . . . As the rule stands, you are saddled with the side you disapprove, and so you are forced . . . to argue out, to feel with, to elaborate completely the case as it stands against yourself.[14]

Such a practice, Stevenson thought, would teach cocksure young students some humility. No doubt the practice is a useful device for the purpose. But Stevenson was speaking of procedure in "a private club," as opposed to

[13] *Phaedrus*, 237, 243.
[14] "Debating Societies," in *College Papers*.

speaking in "a public place," and with fond memories of his days in The Speculative Society at Edinburgh. And he was not recommending a method of systematically debating both sides. Certainly a blind, intolerant partisanship is a horrible quality, and if there were no other way of seeing many views than debating for them, the practice might have to be tolerated on this count alone. But there are so many ways of seeing other views. The debater can brief the other side. He can explore the other side, and read about it. In actual debate, one can listen to the other side if he will but open his ears and mind. The position of the other side can be accurately stated for purposes of refutation where it seems to be in error, or for purposes of admission where it seems to be correct. To argue that the way to discover an idea is to get up on the platform and advocate it is rather unusual pedagogy. To argue that if one does not talk against his conviction he will be ignorant of opposing views is to ignore a basic rhetorical principle that the speaker should read, and discuss, and inquire, and test his position before he takes the platform to present it. As Mill put it, "He who knows only his own side of the case, knows little of that." And he commended Cicero's practice, as a "means of forensic success," of studying "his adversary's case with as great, if not still greater, intensity than even his own."

A third philosophical argument is that it is never clear on which side the truth lies; hence all positions can be maintained with equal intensity. Addison's Sir Roger de Coverley is quoted to the effect that "much might be said on both sides." Sir Roger, of course, was dodging a judgment on a personal dispute about fishing, but even in this trivial matter he showed his usual sage judgment. That is why we argue a matter: there is a case on each side. But this is only the beginning. The end is to discover where the truth lies. A variation of this argument is the definition of truth as what can gain acceptance, regardless of what the advocates may believe. Boswell asked Dr. Johnson, ". . . whether, as a moralist, he did not think that the practice of the law, in some degree, hurt the fine feeling of honesty." Pressing the point, Boswell asked, "What do you think of supporting a cause which you know to be bad?" Johnson replied that one does "not know it to be good or bad until the judge determines it." Boswell asked whether "dissimulation" did not "impair one's honesty." Dr. Johnson was in his best form: "Sir, a man will no more carry the artifice of the bar into the common intercourse of society, than a man who is paid for tumbling upon his hands will continue to tumble up on his hands when he should walk on his feet." [15] Dr. Johnson was, of course, applying a kind of eighteenth-century laissez-faire ethic to legal disputation, and a method he himself seldom followed, since he rarely had difficulty discovering for himself what the universal and eternal truth of any matter was. But to argue in contemporary times that a public speaker who has read and discussed his question shall not bring to the deliberation any personal conviction, but shall leave it to an audience which may never have heard the matter deliberated before, is to resign the moral responsibility of the speaker.

[15] James Boswell. *The Life of Samuel Johnson*, Chap. XIX.

A fourth philosophical argument is that debaters themselves do not know what they believe. "My debaters," says one coach, "didn't know at the end of the season what side they were on." Their uncertainty is understandable. If one argues at nine o'clock that he and his colleague are firmly convinced of one side of an issue, and at ten that he is convinced of its opposite, and keeps up this shifting of advocacy for a season, it would be remarkable indeed if he really knew what to believe.

A fifth philosophical argument is that the debaters are too young to take a position on questions of public affairs. "How can an immature high school student know what our policy should be on parity prices?" a defender of both-sides debating asks. If students are debating questions over their heads, then the subjects should be simplified. But if the student is incompetent to take one position, he is certainly all the more incompetent to take two. However, we should not underestimate the intellectual capacity of our debaters, nor should we overlook the growing tendency to reduce the voting age. Debaters are either voters, or about to be, and as such will have to take positions on complex social and economic problems.

A sixth philosophical argument is that it is the function of neither the school nor the debate coach to turn out persons "with ardent convictions on the side of the right." It is sufficient to train them to think logically, and to see both sides. But the school and the teacher must have some responsibility for inducing conviction on such matters as freedom of speech, democracy, and integrity of ideas. True, we do not instruct the student how to vote for dogcatcher, but should we not give him a methodology for finding an answer in a disputed matter? The person who does nothing to determine the ballot before election day, and then enters the polling booth able only to see both sides, is not a completely useful citizen.

A seventh philosophical argument is that debating both sides, through dissociating a student from belief, teaches him the essentials of rigorous, logical thinking. It gives him skill in using facts and inferences, and in thinking accurately. If he waives belief, he may be able to think purely, his mind unclouded by prejudice and predisposition. And if he demonstrates that he is so well informed and so superior to conviction that he can debate either side on the call of a chairman, he has reached the nirvana of scientific method. Now, training in logical methods is not to be disparaged, but is not the end result the discovery of what truth the logical inferences seem to illuminate, and what position one can most validly maintain under the circumstances? Why stop the logical process before the final goal has been reached?

An eighth philosophical argument is that "lawyers do it." Even Theodore Roosevelt allowed that lawyers may have to take an assigned proposition and argue it without relation to conviction. The debaters are advocates, the explanation goes, presenting arguments now for, now against, a proposition, that an audience may see the truth. It is not quite clear, in this argument, why an audience would gain more from hearing a question debated by persons not necessarily believing their sides, than by hearing debaters of deep conviction. However, the right of a lawyer to take an unpopular case, to be permitted to make it as strongly as he can, and to suffer no social ostracism for his action, is a very precious development in social tolerance, and should not be impinged in any way. But the connection between this virtue and debating both sides is not very close. By "advocate" is meant ordinarily one who represents another in his view, or pleads his own belief. There seems to be some confusion concerning what lawyers actually do. One view is that lawyers must argue for or against a given proposition whether they want to or not. But Canon 31 of the *Canons of Professional Ethics* of the American Bar Association specifies that the lawyer "has the right to decline employment." [16] Canon 30 states that "the lawyer must decline to conduct a civil case or to make a defense when convinced that it is intended merely to harass or to injure the opposite party." [17] In other words, the lawyer is supposed to show personal judgment in taking a case, and he is not to take one merely for the sake of a suit or an argument. The Canon continues, "His appearance in Court should be deemed equivalent to an assertion on his honor that in his opinion his client's case is one proper for judicial determination." [18] By analogy one could maintain that since debate questions are debatable, anyone could with honor uphold either side. But this contention would be a distortion of the theory. In a debatable matter, a case may honorably be made on both sides, but not usually by the same person. Clarence Darrow could with honor maintain that his clients should be sentenced to life imprisonment rather than to death. He could not, with honor, argue on a following day that they should be electrocuted. Applying this principle to debating, cases may honorably be made on both sides, but not ordinarily by the same person.

Another form of the argument that debating both sides is justifiable because it conforms to legal practice is that lawyers must represent both sides. Now, if anything is certain in the legal-forensic system, it is that an advocate shall not represent conflicting interests. "It is unprofessional," reads Canon 6, "to represent conflicting interests, except by express consent of all concerned after a full disclosure of the facts." The lawyer, according to the Canon, must "represent the client with undivided fidelity." [19] Nor may the lawyer, under the *Canons,* pose as an objective seeker of truth if he represents an interest: "It is unprofessional for a lawyer so engaged [in advocacy] to conceal his attorneyship" [Canon 26].[20] These principles in the forensic system should not be confused, of course, with methods in conciliation and mediation in which a person without interest attempts to resolve conflict. The conflict of interest principle is a practical matter, not merely an abstract canon. When in 1955 it was revealed in the hundred-million-dollar Dixon-Yates

---

[16] *Canons of Professional Ethics* (Chicago: American Bar Association, 1948), p. 18.
[17] *Loc. cit.*
[18] *Loc. cit.*
[19] *Loc. cit.*, p. 9.
[20] *Loc. cit.*, p. 12.

contract that one person had been representing both interests without clear declaration, that element became a major issue in the President's cancellation of the whole contract.

A ninth philosophical argument is that debating is not public speaking, and hence not subject to the ethics of the platform, but is "educational forensics." This terminology has led to many quips, such as "It may be forensic, but is it educational?" But to state the argument fairly, it goes something like this: The method of disputing a question on both sides is an old educational device, used in ancient, medieval, and modern times. No man can say that he is equipped to defend a position until he has demonstrated he can defend the opposite. Furthermore, in life one frequently has to present a case for, or at other times, a case against, a proposition. So practice in disputation makes the ready man.

Exercises which train a student to analyze, study lines of argument, or to comprehend and resolve or decide disputed matters may have their place in the educational process. Kenneth Burke has recently suggested an exercise in which the student writes "two debates, upholding first one position and then the other." He then writes "a third piece" to analyze what he has done and to develop "a distrustful admiration of all symbolism." [21] The methods used in a closed debating society or in a classroom may be judged by pedagogical, rather than ethical, standards. But since the development of Whately's "natural method," that one learns to talk best by saying what one means and by meaning what one says, there has been a decline in the use of artificial devices. The tendency has been to make the club and classroom speaking situation an actual one, rather than make-believe.

But modern debating is something other than a medieval exercise in dialectic. It is geared to the public platform and to rhetorical, rather than dialectical, principles. The questions are not speculative or universal, but specific and timely, concerning practical public policy. The debater relies heavily on the use of authority and opinion, whereas in logical disputation an argument has to be taken on its merits. The debater uses *ethos*, a rhetorical element: "So my colleague and I ask you to agree with us." And the modern debater makes an appeal for judgment by his audience or his critic. The contemporary debater is often ill-equipped to carry on a logical disputation; he may not know one mood of the syllogism from another; but he does know certain forms of rhetoric.

Besides, much has happened since the days of medieval and Renaissance disputation. The role of the citizen in public affairs has been greatly expanded, and public discussion has become an instrument of public policy. The debater, presumably, in addition to disputing at tournaments, speaks before school assemblies, at the student council, to service clubs, and at a number of organizations of which he is a member. He is judged there, not on his ability to present both sides, but upon his honest conviction. If at such

[21] "The Linguistic Approach to Problems of Education," *Fifty-Fourth Yearbook of the National Society for the Study of Education* (Chicago: The University of Chicago Press, 1955), I, 287.

meetings it were revealed that the day before he took an opposite view, he would lose his audience.

In addition to the philosophical arguments I have considered, there are in defense of debating both sides many claims for the device in terms of administrative procedure. One argument is that if actual debates are not held until students have decided their beliefs, the program of practice will be delayed. But one may point out that many forms of speaking other than debating are available for early season work. Panels, reports, symposiums, questioning of visiting experts can be used to open a subject and to supply the motivation which comes from having to speak. A second argument is that an early debate helps to open a question, reveal the issues, and give a touch of realism to the program. If this be so, there could be little objection to an early scrub debate to feel out the question. The objection is not that on an occasion or so someone debates just for the fun of it; the objection is to systematizing debating both sides as a forensic method. A third argument is that having a two-, rather than a four-man, debate team means less cost in travel and wider school participation in tournaments. A fourth argument is that a two-man both-sides arrangement permits a school to groom its two best debaters to represent it. A fifth is that regional and national championship debaters can be selected in the method, rather than mere school or side champions. These and other arguments of convenience in programming are obvious advantages in a competitive tournament system, if one cares for such a system. Whether or not they are to be used will depend on one's views of the philosophical and ethical matters.

Before summarizing the view I present here, it might be useful to clear away a matter which seems to cause some confusion. That is whether or not arguing both sides is an essential element in debating. Many people seem to feel that it is. One director of debating, in a balance sheet of good and bad in the method of debate, lists "arguments on both sides of the proposition" as one of the "most important aspects of debate." He then lists on the liability side of debate "a certain professionalism which leads students to argue either side of any question without regard to the intrinsic merits of the ideas." This practice, he thinks, leads "either to sheer hypocrisy or to a certain paralysis of decision which prevents a person from ever making up his mind." [22] Another writer thinks "much good is to be derived from having students debate both sides," but laments that the practice causes poor public relations. She gives the example of the debater who made such an eloquent case for federal world government in a radio speech that he was invited to join the movement by a local group. They were somewhat puzzled when, a week later, he made an equally moving speech on the other side. She recommends early-season practice tournaments on both sides with sessions "closed to all persons outside forensic circles." After the secret sessions, the debaters

---

[22] Wilder W. Crane, Jr., "The Function of Debate," *The Central States Speech Journal*, V (Fall, 1953), 16–17.

come out and debate their convictions before the public, free from reproach.[23]

Actually, the both-sides methodology is not now and never has been an essential element in debate, although it may have been in certain systems of disputation. The form of debate most generally practiced, parliamentary, never has used the method. Nor has the practice been used in debate as a form of public address. Lincoln and Douglas did not shift from side to side as they journeyed through Illinois. Nor has it been an essential even in debating societies. The Oxford Union and the Cambridge Union have managed through two centuries to do without the practice. In my own experience in debating from grade school through graduate college I never had a coach who followed, or would even tolerate, the system. To believe that to debate one must debate both sides is to ignore what actual practice is.

But what are the ethics of debating both sides? If one conceives of debating as a closed club activity in which a rhetorical-dialectical exercise is used for some purpose, then perhaps the method can be judged in terms of pedagogy, rather than of ethics. But insofar as debating is public speaking, insofar as debating is a method of the platform, it will have to submit to the contemporary ethic, which is that a public utterance is a public commitment. Nor, if the view presented in this survey is correct, can the practice be justified as realistic training for the practice of the law. Debate would be in a stronger position if it were freed from the anachronistic practice of multiple positions. And those who believe in the essential processes of democratic debate, and wish to extend them, would no longer be held liable for a dubious practice, if the debate-both-sides policy were abandoned.

Now, in harmony with one established practice, let one of the men who opened, close. Said Theodore Roosevelt, "To admire the gift of oratory without regard to the moral quality behind the gift is to do wrong to the republic." [24]

## DEBATING BOTH SIDES IN TOURNAMENTS IS ETHICAL *
### NICHOLAS M. CRIPE

Richard Murphy, writing in *The Speech Teacher* for January, 1957,[1] has pointed a finger at a considerable segment of the debate coaches of America and said, "Shame on you!" Oh, he did not use those exact words, but the implication was there for every coach who allows a debater to speak publicly on both sides of a debate topic. Mr. Murphy's contention is that it is not

[23] Evelyn Kenesson de Voros, "The Purpose of College Debate," *Western Speech*, XVIII (May, 1954), 191, 194.
[24] Address at the Sorbonne, 23 April, 1910.
* From *The Speech Teacher*, 6 (Sept. 1957), 209–12. Professor Cripe is Head of the Department of Speech and Director of Forensics at Butler University.
[1] "The Ethics of Debating Both Sides," VI, 1–9.

ethical. In fact, to cite his approving quotation of Albert J. Beveridge in the article, "To do so is immoral and worse—it is to be a public liar." [2] This is a serious charge to bring against any debater or his coach. Yet this is the conclusion I draw from the contents of the Murphy article.

Any writer attempting to reply to Murphy would have to answer certain questions, such as, Is it of "doubtful virtue" [3] to debate both sides in a tournament? Is it "questionable—indeed bad"? [4] It will be my purpose in this article to try to answer those questions, and, in doing so, to contend that it is ethical to debate both sides.

The whole problem seems to be one of definition, of defining what "debate" is, and what "ethical" means. "Debate," writes Professor Murphy, "is a form of public speaking. A public statement is a public commitment. Before one takes the platform, he should study the question, he should discuss it until he knows where he stands. Then he should take that stand." [5] Such a definition applies to argument in the pulpit, in the legislative halls, in the courtroom, and in the market place, when the speaker is trying to convince an audience of the "rightness" of his stand, but does it apply to the type of tournament debating practiced today? Professor Murphy seems to imply that it does. It is my contention that such a definition is too narrow, and cannot be so applied unless one favors the discontinuance of interscholastic debate of a national proposition. In fact, if the proponents of "ethical" debate are correct, and it is immoral for a team to debate both sides, then many schools would have to discontinue debate as we practice it today. This is because there seem to be frequent recurrences of the situation where for one reason or another a predominant number of members of a debate squad favor strongly one side of the proposition. This usually results from the wording of the proposition, but, whatever the cause, debate squads are all too often most unevenly divided on their attitude toward a question. For instance, the University of Vermont could not have had a debate team in 1950 when it won the West Point Tournament if the Murphy suggestion of debating only the side believed to be right had been followed. This would have resulted from the fact that at the beginning of the year only one member of a squad of forty-two believed in the nationalization of basic industries, and he changed his mind about halfway through the season. Likewise, Grinnell College would have been unable to have a team in 1953 because every member of the squad believed that Congress should pass an FEPC law. For that matter, how many debaters this year are really against the principle of direct economic aid to foreign countries?

When the real implication of this contention against debating both sides of a proposition is considered, it becomes evident that this question involves more than some philosophical hairsplitting; it involves the future of intercollegiate debating. For if it is not ethical, then so-called "two-man debating"

[2] *Ibid.*, p. 2.
[3] *Ibid.*
[4] *Ibid.*, p. 1.
[5] *Ibid.*, p. 2.

should be stopped, and when the topic is one such as was used this past year, a great many schools could not debate unless some means could be found so that the few ethical affirmative or negative teams in the country would not be overworked. It seems to me that Murphy never attempts to solve this problem in his article. Rather, he confines himself to supporting the argument that it is not ethical for any debater to speak on the side of the proposition he believes to be the "wrong" side. Nor is any distinction made between school debaters and those in public life.

And that is probably the basic error in the reasoning of those who condemn speaking on both sides in school debate tournaments, that is, their failure to make a distinction between tournament debating and other forms of public argumentative speaking. It is my contention that interscholastic debating is a different form of public speaking from debate that we hear the legislator or the lawyer use. Various authors of textbooks in debate support this contention. For instance, McBurney, O'Neill, and Mills write, "the student should keep in mind the differences between actual life situations, such as legislature, court, or campaign, and the situations in school or contest debates." [6] W. Charles Redding writes in "Presentation of the Debate Speech," "The *form* of debate may be used for *both* expository and persuasive speaking." Later in the same essay he writes that in a debate tournament the purpose of the debating would probably be classified as educational, rather than persuasive, and that the ". . . educational type of debate, therefore, can be considered a special case of *exposition*." [7] Ewbank and Auer seem to be aware of a difference in the forms of debate when they write, "The critics often seem not to understand the purposes and procedures in school debates." [8] If we assume that when a debater at the West Point Tournament stands up to speak he has the same purposes in mind as a speaker in a public meeting or a Senator in the halls of Congress speaking on the same subject, then we would have to agree that the same code of ethics should apply. But the aim is not the same. The public speaker and the Senator want to win converts to their beliefs, probably win such strong belief that their listeners will do something about it. This is not the purpose of our debater at West Point or at any other tournament. He is not trying to convince the judges, or his opponents, or any of the debate "buffs" in his audience that his side of the proposition is the "right" side, or the only side; rather, his purpose is to convince the judges that he and his partner are the better debaters. (This should not be construed to mean that the purpose of any school debate program is only the winning of debates. It is merely that winning debates is just one of the best methods yet devised to get busy students to do the

---

[6] James H. McBurney, James M. O'Neill, and Glen E. Mills, *Argumentation and Debate: Techniques of a Free Society* (New York: The Macmillan Company, 1951), p. 4.

[7] In David Potter (ed.), *Argumentation and Debate: Principles and Practices* (New York: The Dryden Press, 1951), pp. 220–221. Italics in the original.

[8] Henry Lee Ewbank and J. Jeffery Auer, *Discussion and Debate: Tools of a Democracy* (2nd ed.; New York: Appleton-Century-Crofts, Inc., 1951), p. 388.

research of materials, the analysis, the mastering of the modes of reasoning and the principles of refutation, the developing of good speaking styles and delivery necessary to make them into effective, intelligent, and responsible debaters.)

However, the fact that interschool debating (and thus debating both sides of a proposition) differs in purpose from other forms of debate does not by itself mean that it is more or less ethical than these other types. To determine that, it would seem we must define what "ethical" means. This Professor Murphy does only by implication. His implication is that debating both sides is bad and of doubtful virtue, therefore, immoral, not ethical. That such a definition of the non-ethical is correct is pointed out in a college textbook:

... The term "moral" is essentially equivalent to the term "ethical." Etymologically, these terms are identical, the former being derived from the Latin word *"mores,"* the latter from the Greek word *"ethos,"* both words referring to customary behavior. ... Ordinarily, the opposite of "moral" is taken to be "immoral," so that we mean by a "moral man" one who is good and does what is right, and by an "immoral man" one who is bad and does what is wrong. ...[9]

So now we come to the heart of the controversy. Is it "immoral" for a school debater to debate both sides? Richard Murphy, supported by testimony from Theodore Roosevelt, Brooks Quimby, and Albert J. Beveridge, says that it is. On the other hand, men who have been long connected with college debaters and debating say it is not. For instance, O'Neill, Laycock, and Scales, speaking directly to this subject of a student's debating both sides, say ". . . it would not undermine his moral character if he did."[10] Ewbank and Auer write, "Even if debaters are assigned to the side of the question in which they do not believe, it does not necessarily follow that the experience is harmful; . . ."[11] This point of view is also taken by Wayne N. Thompson, a long-time coach of debate, now Director of Forensics at the Chicago Undergraduate Division of the University of Illinois, who writes,

Debating both sides of a proposition is neither morally wrong nor hypocritical. Some writers have charged that debating both sides results in various evils, such as insincerity, shallowness, and the presentation of arguments known to be poorly founded or fallacious. These malpractices, which also occur among speakers who debate only one side, are the result of other causes—weakness in the character of the offender or a misunderstanding of the proper function of debate.[12]

It would seem for every authority quoted by the opposition, proponents of debating both sides can also quote somebody of equal merit to uphold

[9] Ethel M. Albert, Theodore C. Denise, and Sheldon P. Peterfreund, *Great Traditions in Ethics: An Introduction* (New York: American Book Company, 1953), p. 7, footnote 1.
[10] James Milton O'Neill, Craven Laycock and Robert Leighton Scales, *Argumentation and Debate* (New York: The Macmillan Company, 1917), p. 376.
[11] *Op. cit.*, p. 389.
[12] "Discussion and Debate: A Re-Examination," *The Quarterly Journal of Speech,* XXX (October, 1944), 296.

their contention. This being the case, who is right? There are many who feel that McBurney, O'Neill, and Mills stated clearly the moral responsibility of a debater when they wrote,

> Once a cause has been undertaken, the advocate has a responsibility to present *the best possible case for his proposition within the limits of the facts as he knows them or believes them to be*. He should not deliberately do less nor does he have any moral right to attempt more. No man has a moral right to lie, cheat, or intentionally distort, much less a responsibility to do so. . . .[13]

Therefore, they believe, if a debater at any tournament presents the arguments he honestly believes to be the best possible arguments that can be presented in behalf of his side of the proposition, it would seem to be ethical debating, and that to condemn him is either to misunderstand or to misconstrue his purpose in speaking. Where only honesty and sincerity are present, where any intent to betray or deceive is absent, it is hard to find reason to condemn such public speaking as unethical.

Upon this argument, then, rests the case for debating both sides of a proposition, that the purpose of the speaker determines the ethics by which he is to be judged, that the school debater cannot correctly be judged unethical by the same rule of thumb that might be used to evaluate the ethics of the pulpit or campaign speaker. The purpose in speaking differs; therefore, what might be "right" for the one may very well be "wrong" for the other, though they both say the same words. It seems impossible to most debate coaches that anyone should condemn as a "public liar" the school debater who presents the best possible case for his proposition within the limits of the facts as he knows or believes them to be. Yet those who condemn college debaters' speaking on both sides of a proposition do just that. They are wrong.

## DEBATING BOTH SIDES *
### RICHARD MURPHY

Your invitation to make a rejoinder to "Debating Both Sides in Tournaments Is Ethical" in this issue is too enticing for an old debater to refuse. In my essay, "The Ethics of Debating Both Sides," in the January issue, I gave the various arguments that are made for a debater's taking alternate sides of a proposition. I stated those arguments as fairly as I could, and then questioned their validity. I concluded, "insofar as debating is public speaking, insofar as debating is a method of the platform, it will have to submit to the contemporary ethic, which is that a public utterance is a public commitment." I also concluded that debating both sides by one person is a "dubious practice," and that "the essential processes of democratic debate" would be strengthened "if the debate-both-sides policy were abandoned."

[13] *Op. cit.*, p. 9. Italics in the original.
* From *The Speech Teacher*, 6 (Sept., 1957), 255–56.

The immediate cause of my essay was the increase in the practice of debating both sides—a practice that comes and goes, but which was so obsolete two decades ago that one author in referring to it had to explain what it is; it is "a method now generally abandoned," wrote Dean McKean in 1930. More imperative, the practice is not only being revived on a grand scale, but also debaters are being required to conform to it. What right, I asked, have the dual-side partisans to impose their own particular ethic upon us all, and to say that one either debates both sides, or he does not debate at all? What right, I asked, have these partisans to require a student not only to debate against his convictions, but also to violate his conviction that he should not speak against his beliefs, or advocate something he does not believe?

The reply to my essay (in this issue) is addressed to none of the major issues I presented. Rather, I am taken personally to task for bringing charges, and for failing to draw upon counter authorities. The rest of the argument concerns the difficulties of applying ethics to tournament debating because of its unique system.

First of all, let me disclaim any attempt to be uncivil or impolite. I did not call anyone a liar, nor did I call upon Senator Beveridge to do so for me. "The controversy has had its worthy partisans on both sides," I wrote. The disagreement is "among worthy men," I said. True, I quoted the distinguished Senator and debater from Indiana as using the word "liar" in a reference to the ethics of debating both sides. But let me review the context. "Never," said Beveridge, "under any circumstances or for any reward tell an audience what you, yourself, do not believe or are even indifferent about. To do so is immoral and worse—it is to be a public liar." Now, is there something wrong with this statement? Does the author of the reply advocate a different principle? Evidently not, for he accepts this standard for "the pulpit," "legislative halls," "courtroom," and "market place." But he cannot accept it for debate, because, as he says, "if the proponents of 'ethical' debate are correct . . . then many schools would have to discontinue debate as we practice it today." That may be. The fundamental question in this regard is whether we shall fashion our ethics to suit our practice, or design our practice to meet our ethical standards.

As for the argument that "authorities" differ on the matter, let me explain that I at no time brought authority to bear on the *quid probandum;* such a process I should consider invalid. I did not attempt to line up saints and sinners. The great names I used were for purposes of pegging minor points, but mostly for interest and perspective. As I observed, Woodrow Wilson was inconsistent on the matter, and even Theodore Roosevelt deviated on one aspect of it. To add a tone of righteousness and certainty, I threw in Dr. Johnson on the side of the dualists. The argument was purely from principle, and it will have to be answered on principle.

The author presents several difficulties in operating a tournament on "ethical" principles. There is the situation at Vermont in 1950. They would not have been able to field a team on conviction: the squad was split 46 to 1.

But under the dual system they were victorious at West Point. Such events do happen. They recall 1936, when Vermont lined up 46 to 2 in the Landon-Roosevelt debate. But presumably some proposition is debatable in that bastion of independence, and the old Vermont principle, "Better be right than triumphant," still reigns. But to return to the point. One of the elementary principles of phrasing a debate proposition is that it be justiciable, debatable. Persons competent to operate a national tournament should be able to phrase the question so that it *is* debatable, and does not penalize regional opinions.

Shall we yield a major point in ethics because it violates a minimum essential in procedure? I admitted that in using a dualist system there are many "arguments of convenience in programming . . . in a competitive tournament system." But, I argued, "whether or not they are used will depend on one's views of the philosophical and ethical" implications. It is sometimes inconvenient to be ethical.

As for the argument that tournament debating is a special kind of discourse, and not amenable to the disciplines of platform speaking, let me review my point. I granted that "disputing a question on both sides is an old educational device used in ancient, medieval, and modern times." If such methods are used simply as pedagogical devices in a classroom or a closed club, then they may be judged according to pedagogical, rather than ethical, principles. But, I maintained, modern debate is not dialectical; it is rhetorical; it appeals for judgment, for acceptance. And audiences, even if sparse at times, are present. If one wishes to defend the method of both sides by arguing that the form is not public speaking, then he raises rather serious questions. What is the purpose of this shifting from side to side? How can one justify years of emphasis on the value of being able to argue any position, with complete indifference to where the truth may lie? Is not this better training in sophistry than in reaching honest conviction and transmitting it to audiences? Further, modern pedagogy tends to use methods of training which have some applicability to life situations. As this principle is phrased in the "Code for Contests in Public Speaking," adopted by the Speech Association of the Eastern States, and endorsed by the Legislative Assembly of the Speech Association of America, "In an educationally defensible contest a student should prepare for life by employing a method which normally he will need to use in life." Is there any reason for not applying this criterion to debate?

As I pointed out, "to believe that to debate one must debate both sides is to ignore what actual practice is." When Douglas accused Lincoln of talking one doctrine in the north and another in the south of Illinois, Lincoln resented the charge. At Charleston he declared, "I dare him to point out any difference between my speeches north and south." And at Quincy, Lincoln said, "I am altogether unconscious of having attempted any double-dealing anywhere." (Our folk phrases reflect distrust of the person who can conveniently shift from side to side: "talking out of the other side of his mouth," "wearing two hats," "working both sides of the street." And there is the very real legal phrase, "conflict of interest.")

Debate, as distinguished from dialectical exercises, has always been associated with conviction. To write of speakers who shift from side to side as having "only honesty and sincerity," as having no "intent to betray or deceive," is to use language I cannot comprehend. And to argue that a two-sides debater is analogous to a lawyer who, having undertaken a cause consistently remains faithful to it, is to confuse advocacy with shifting positions. The two-sided tournament debater has no *cause;* he has only a *purpose:* to win a debate.

These three essays: the original, the reply, this rejoinder, reveal a public stand on a disputed matter. Presumably the authors have drawn upon their training as debaters to inquire into the question, to analyze the various arguments, and to arrive at what they take to be the truth of the matter. To do so would seem to be the normal purpose of a debate. Presumably neither of us will prepare for the next issue of *The Speech Teacher* essays in which we espouse the other side, equally abounding in righteousness—unless we change our opinions. I would hold Professor Cripe's debaters and mine to the same standard.

# Appendix C

# THE BRIEF

By definition, a brief is "a storehouse of information" on a debatable proposition. In its complete or "full" form, therefore, a brief includes (1) an analysis of the proposition, (2) the representative affirmative and negative claims, (3) the data upon which those claims rest, and (4) the sources from which the data are derived.

Many debaters, however, find it sufficient to construct what is known as a "skeleton brief"—a brief which records only the steps in the analysis of the proposition and lists the representative claims. Data and their sources, instead of being entered into the brief, are kept on evidence cards.

Below are a skeleton brief and excerpts from a full brief on the proposition, Resolved: That the federal government should substantially increase its regulation of labor unions. The sections of the two briefs are numbered uniformly so they may be compared.

Material for these briefs was gathered by high school students participating in a forensics workshop at the University of Illinois during the summer of 1959.

## A SKELETON BRIEF ON THE PROPOSITION

*Resolved:* That the Federal Government Should Substantially Increase Its Regulation of Labor Unions.

### INTRODUCTION

I. Immediate causes for the discussion of this proposition are:
   A. Corruption among labor leaders has been revealed by the McClellan Committee.
   B. A controversy over state and federal right-to-work legislation has emerged.
   C. Legislation regulating labor unions is pending in Congress and the various states.
   D. The growing size and power of labor unions is viewed with concern by many persons.

II. The historical background of the proposition is as follows:
   A. The historical development of the labor union movement is as follows:
   B. The history of state regulation of labor unions is as follows:
   C. The history of federal regulation of labor relations is as follows:
   D. The history of court decisions involving labor relations is as follows:
   E. The present extent of regulation by the various state governments and by the federal government may be described as follows:
III. The terms of the proposition may be defined as follows:
   A. The "federal government" means. . . .
   B. To "substantially increase" would mean. . . .
   C. "Regulation" means. . . .
   D. "Labor unions" are. . . .
IV. The main issues in this controversy are as follows:
   A. Is there a need for the federal government to substantially increase its regulation of labor unions?
      1. Are there serious problems in labor union activities?
         a. Are there serious internal problems?
            (1) in compulsory membership?
            (2) in rights of members to vote?
            (3) in rights of members to protest?
            (4) in the administration of union funds?
            (5) in the trusteeship system?
         b. Are there serious problems which go beyond internal affairs?
            (1) in secondary boycotts?
            (2) in administering welfare and pension funds?
            (3) in political action?
            (4) in collusion between union and management leaders?
            (5) in excessive influence upon the national economy?
      2. Are these alleged problems national in scope?
      3. Are these problems inherent in existing federal regulation?
         a. Will the problems remain even if unions try to regulate themselves?
         b. Will the problems remain even if the states increase their regulation of labor unions?
         c. Will the problems remain even if the federal government "slightly" increases its regulation of labor unions?
   B. What possible federal action could be attempted which would meet the criterion of a "substantial increase" in regulation?
      1. Would exclusive federal jurisdiction be a substantial increase in federal regulation?
      2. Would a federal right-to-work law be a substantial increase in federal legislation?
      3. Would placing unions under the provisions of existing antitrust legislation be a substantial increase in federal regulation?

4. Would provisions for checking the administration of union funds be a substantial increase in federal regulation?
5. Would increased power of federal executive agencies be a substantial increase in federal regulation?
6. Would stricter enforcement of present legislation by executive agencies be a substantial increase in federal regulation?
7. Would stricter interpretation of present regulations by the courts be a substantial increase in federal regulation?
8. Would compulsory arbitration of labor disputes be a substantial increase in federal regulation?
9. Would provisions limiting the union's right to organize, strike, boycott, etc. be a substantial increase in federal regulation?

C. Will a substantial increase in federal regulation of labor unions be a practicable solution of alleged problems in the activities of labor unions?
1. Will such a policy solve various alleged internal problems in labor unions?
2. Will such a policy solve various alleged problems which go beyond internal affairs?
3. Will such a policy be enforceable?

D. Can a substantial increase in federal regulation of labor unions be instituted without incurring serious disadvantages?
1. Can such a policy be adopted without weakening the power of the states to regulate unions?
2. Can such a policy be adopted without weakening the power of labor unions?
   a. Can such a policy be adopted without weakening the strength and stability of union membership?
   b. Can such a policy be adopted without weakening the power of the unions to bargain effectively?
3. Can such a policy be adopted without endangering the maintenance of stable industrial relations?
4. Can such a policy be adopted without creating economic dislocation and competition among the various states?

### THE POSITION OF THE AFFIRMATIVE

I. There is a need for the federal government to substantially increase its regulation of labor unions, because
   A. There are serious problems in labor union activities, because
      1. There are serious internal problems, because
         a. There are serious problems arising from compulsory membership.
         b. There are serious problems concerning the voting rights of members.

c. There are serious problems concerning the rights of members to protest against corrupt and ineffective leadership.
d. There are serious problems in the administration of union funds.
e. There are serious problems in the trusteeship system.
2. There are serious problems which go beyond internal affairs, because
   a. The use of the secondary boycott by some unions is a serious problem.
   b. The mishandling of welfare and pension funds by some unions is a serious problem.
   c. Political activities of labor unions create a serious problem.
   d. Collusion between union and management leaders is a serious problem.
   e. The excessive influence of labor unions on the national economy is a serious problem.
B. Problems in the internal and external affairs of labor unions are national in scope, because
   1. Important leaders of nation-wide unions have been guilty of malpractices.
   2. Local unions in all parts of the country have been involved.
C. Problems in the internal and external affairs of labor unions are inherent in existing federal regulation, because
   1. Such problems will remain even if unions undertake self-regulation.
   2. Such problems will remain even if the states attempt to increase their regulation of labor unions.
   3. Such problems will remain even if the federal government "slightly" increases its regulation of labor unions.
II. Various kinds of federal action would meet the criterion of a "substantial increase" in regulation, because
A. Exclusive federal jurisdiction would be a substantial increase in federal regulation.
B. A federal right-to-work law would be a substantial increase in federal regulation.
C. Placing unions under the provisions of existing antitrust legislation would be a substantial increase in federal regulation.
D. Provisions for checking the administration of union funds would be a substantial increase in federal regulation.
E. Increasing the power of federal executive agencies would be a substantial increase in federal regulation.
F. Stricter interpretation of present regulations by executive agencies would be a substantial increase in federal regulation.
G. Stricter interpretation of present regulations by the courts would be a substantial increase in federal regulation.
H. Compulsory arbitration of labor disputes would be a substantial in-

crease in federal regulation.
  I. Provisions limiting the union's right to organize, strike, boycott, etc. would be a substantial increase in federal regulation.
III. A substantial increase in federal regulation of labor unions would be a practicable solution of problems in the internal and external activities of labor unions, because
   A. Such a policy would solve alleged internal problems of unions.
   B. Such a policy would solve problems which go beyond internal union affairs.
   C. Such a policy would be enforceable.
IV. A substantial increase in federal regulation of labor unions can be instituted without incurring serious disadvantages, because
   A. Such a policy can be adopted without weakening the power of the states to regulate unions.
   A'. Even if the power of the states to regulate unions were weakened, this would not constitute a serious disadvantage.
   B. Such a policy can be adopted without weakening the power of labor unions, because
      1. Such a policy can be adopted without weakening the strength and stability of union membership.
      1'. Even if the strength and stability of union membership were weakened, this would not constitute a serious disadvantage.
      2. Such a policy can be adopted without weakening the power of the unions to bargain effectively.
      2'. Even if the power of the unions to bargain effectively were weakened, this would not constitute a serious disadvantage.
   C. Such a policy can be adopted without endangering the maintenance of stable industrial relations.
   C'. Even if stable industrial relations were not maintained, this would not constitute a serious disadvantage.
   D. Such a policy can be adopted without creating economic dislocation and competition among the various states.
   D'. Even if economic dislocation and competition among the various states were created, this would not constitute a serious disadvantage.

THE POSITION OF THE NEGATIVE

  I. There is no need for the federal government to substantially increase its regulation of labor unions, because
   A. There are no serious problems in labor union activities, because
      1. There are no serious internal problems, because
         a. There are no serious problems arising from compulsory membership.
         b. There are no serious problems concerning the voting rights of members.
         c. There are no serious problems concerning the rights of mem-

bers to protest against corrupt and ineffective leadership.
            d. There are no serious problems in the administration of union funds.
            e. There are no serious problems in the trusteeship system.
        2. There are no serious problems which go beyond internal affairs, because
            a. There are no serious problems concerning the use of secondary boycotts.
            b. There are no serious problems in the administration of welfare and pension funds.
            c. Union political activities create no serious problems.
            d. Alleged collusion between union and management leaders is not a serious problem.
            e. There are no serious problems in the influence of labor unions on the national economy.
    B. The alleged problems are not national in scope, because
        1. Many of the most important and influential national leaders of labor have spotless records of service.
        2. The abuses about which so much is said involve only a small fraction of all unions.
    C. The alleged problems in the internal and external affairs of labor unions are not inherent in existing federal regulation, because
        1. The alleged problems can be dealt with adequately by union self-regulation.
        2. The alleged problems can be dealt with adequately by state regulations.
        3. The alleged problems can be dealt with adequately by a "slight" increase in federal regulation of labor unions.
II. The negative admits that certain proposed measures would constitute a "substantial increase" in federal regulation of labor unions, i.e.,
    A. A federal right-to-work law would be a substantial increase in federal regulation.
    B. Placing unions under antitrust laws would be a substantial increase in federal regulation.
    C. Compulsory arbitration of labor disputes would be a substantial increase in federal regulation.
    D. Provisions for checking the administration of union funds would, in some cases, be a substantial increase in federal regulation.
    E. Provisions limiting the unions' right to organize, strike, boycott, etc. would, in some cases, be a substantial increase in federal regulation.
II'. The negative denies that certain proposals would constitute a "substantial increase" in federal regulation of labor unions, because
    A. Exclusive federal jurisdiction would not be a substantial increase in federal regulation, because
        1. Such a policy would grant only the power to regulate, and could not guarantee the exercise of such power.

## APPENDIX C 399

      2. The federal government would be less likely to exercise such power than would the state governments.
  B. Increased power of federal executive agencies would not be a substantial increase in federal regulation, because
      1. There is no guarantee that the increased power would be used.
      2. The executive agencies do not exercise all of the power they presently possess.
  C. Stricter enforcement by executive agencies of existing legislation would not be a substantial increase in federal regulation, because
      1. Existing legislation is too narrow in scope.
      2. Existing legislation lacks the "teeth" which make enforcement possible.

III. A substantial increase in federal regulation of labor unions would not be a practicable solution of the alleged problems in the activities of labor unions, because
  A. Such a policy would not solve various alleged internal problems of unions.
  B. Such a policy would not solve alleged problems which go beyond internal union affairs.
  C. Such a policy is not enforceable.

IV. A substantial increase in federal regulation of labor unions cannot be instituted without incurring serious disadvantages, because
  A. Such a policy would weaken the power of the states to regulate labor unions.
  A'. Weakening the power of the states to regulate labor unions constitutes a serious disadvantage.
  B. Such a policy would weaken the power of labor unions, because
      1. Such a policy would weaken the strength and stability of union membership.
      1'. Weakening the strength and stability of union membership constitutes a serious disadvantage.
      2. Such a policy would weaken the power of the unions to bargain effectively.
      2'. Weakening the power of the unions to bargain effectively constitutes a serious disadvantage.
  C. Such a policy would endanger the maintenance of stable industrial relations.
  C'. Endangering the maintenance of stable industrial relations constitutes a serious disadvantage.
  D. Such a policy would create economic dislocation and competition among the various states.
  D'. Creating economic dislocation and competition among the various states constitutes a serious disadvantage.

## EXCERPTS FROM A FULL BRIEF ON THE PROPOSITION

*Resolved:* That the Federal Government Should Substantially Increase Its Regulation of Labor Unions.

### INTRODUCTION

. . . . .

II. The historical background of the proposition is as follows:
   A. The historical development of the labor union movement is as follows:
   1. Before 1930 employers often resorted to lockouts, yellow-dog contracts, labor spy blacklists, armed guards, and company unions in their attempts to combat labor's legitimate demands. (Nathan P. Feinsinger, "Labor Legislation and the Role of the Government," *Monthly Labor Review,* July 1950, p. 51.)
   2. In postwar years the problem of corruption in unions was serious enough for both the AFL and the CIO to take special precautions against it. (J. F. Bell, "Corruption and Union Racketeering," *Current History,* June 1959, p. 345.)
   3. "The codes of ethical practices have made articulate the conscience of the labor movement, and the expulsion of corrupt unions has demonstrated a courageous determination to match words with action." (Clyde W. Summers, "Role of Legislation in Internal Union Affairs," *Labor Law Journal,* March 1959, p. 158.)
   4. A chronology of the development of the trade union movement would include the following:
   1820—beginning of the labor movement
   1834—effort made to form a national trade union center
   1837—national trade union movement wiped out after depression of 1837
   1866—National Labor Union formed; campaigned for eight-hour day, producers' co-operation, and labor political action
   1869—The Knights of Labor, a secret organization, formed
   1872—ILU sponsored a political party; it failed to survive
   1880—The Knights of Labor openly announced that it is a union in which all workers are welcome
   1886—The Knights of Labor has 1,000,000 members; the Haymarket bombing marks the beginning of the decline of the Knights
   1886—The American Federation of Labor, under Samuel Gompers, makes its first appearance; grew out of the Federation of Organized Trades and Labor Unions (1881)
   1900–1914—AFL membership increases from 791,000 to 2,647,000

1915–1920—new fields organized; AFL membership rises to 5,034,000

1923—AFL membership falls to 1,400,000 because of depression

1933—AFL membership rises to 3,000,000; New Deal revives unionism through protective legislation

1935—Committee for Industrial Organization formed

1936—CIO is suspended from AFL

1938—Congress of Industrial Organizations is formed

1941—Labor union membership totals 16,000,000

1955—AFL and CIO merge into AFL-CIO

B. The history of state regulation of labor unions is as follows:
1. Under the philosophy of constitutional interpretation prevailing prior to 1937, for all practical purposes industrial relations were governed by the states alone. (Archibald Cox, "Federalism in the Law of Labor Relations," *Harvard Law Review,* June 1954, pp. 1297–1348.)
2. More than three-fourths of the states have passed laws regulating labor in one way or another. Thirty-four states acted in the legislative sessions of 1947 alone. (John H. Leek, *Government and Labor in the United States,* 1953, p. 92.)
3. Protective labor legislation has been enacted or modified in nearly every session of every state legislature during this century. (Nathan P. Feinsinger, "Labor Legislation and the Role of Government," *Monthly Labor Review,* July 1950, p. 49.)
4. In 1955 New Hampshire and Wisconsin banned political contributions by both labor and management. Only Texas prohibits contributions from labor alone. New York and Wisconsin make illegal a political contribution from an employee welfare fund. (Sar A. Levitan, *Government Regulation of Internal Union Affairs Affecting the Rights of Members,* U.S. Congress Legislative Reference Service, 1958, p. 217.)
5. "Washington, New York, California, Nevada, Alaska, and Oregon have passed laws regulating union welfare funds." (*Ibid.,* p. 219.)
6. Florida requires that union officials have lived in the state for ten years and that they not be convicted felons. (*Ibid.,* p. 215.)
7. "The right of union members to elect their officers by secret ballot is guaranteed in four states." (*Ibid.,* p. 44.)
8. Five states require unions to file detailed annual financial statements. Two make the state's copy of such statements available to any member; one makes it available to select officers; one makes it public; and one does not specify. (*Ibid.,* p. 214.)
9. Six states make breach of contract by a labor union an unfair labor practice, and all states except Kansas make the same restriction on management. (*Ibid.,* p. 217.)

10. Twenty-three jurisdictions of states now explicitly permit unions to sue or be sued. (*Ibid.*, p. 216.)

C. The history of federal regulation of labor relations is as follows:
1. "The first step in the reappraisal of federal responsibilities in labor relations was taken by Congress in 1932 when, through the Norris-LaGuardia Act, it imposed drastic limitations on the power of federal courts to restrain labor union activities. The law confirmed the rights of workers to organize, to strike, and to engage in any peaceful method of self-advancement." (A. Howard Myers, "Evaluating the Proposed Labor Law Changes," *Harvard Business Review*, May–June 1954, p. 125.)
2. "Business was largely opposed to collective bargaining at first. Any enforcement of the Wagner Act met powerful resistance from industry. But by 1945 business had adjusted to the act with considerable flexibility and realism, in spite of charges that plant efficiency had been impaired by interference with managerial authority." (*Ibid.*, p. 125.)
3. Unions raised two principal arguments against the Taft-Hartley Act: (1) the potential liabilities and restrictions that unions faced under its provisions could stimulate aggressive employer action against organized groups, through damage suits, injunctions, and criminal prosecutions; and (2) the unfair labor practices provisions to which unions were now subject and the greater freedom allowed employers to express their opinions about organizations of workers could interfere with the organizational activities of unions. (*Ibid.*, p. 126.)
4. The four purposes of the Taft-Hartley Act were union-management equality, protection of individual rights, protection of third parties not directly concerned in the disagreement, and the stabilization of labor relations. (Clyde W. Summers, "Evaluation of the Taft-Hartley Act," *Industrial and Labor Relations Review*, April 1958, p. 406.)
5. Section 14b of the Taft-Hartley Act gives the states the right to have right-to-work laws. (Byrne Horton, *Dictionary of Labor Economics*, Public Affairs Press, 1947, p. 18.)
6. A chronology of federal legislation dealing with labor relations would include:
   1906—Erdman Act establishes liability of interstate railroad carriers for injuries to employees; Section 10 of Act declared unconstitutional
   1908—Employer's Liability Act establishes recovery for industrial accidents to railroad workers
   1913—Newlands Act sets up board of mediation and conciliation to handle railroad disputes
   1914—Clayton Act provides for limited use of injunctions in labor disputes and for picketing and other union activities;

## APPENDIX C 403

        exempts labor unions from Sherman Antitrust Act

1915—LaFollette Seaman's Act regulates conditions of employment

1916—Child Labor Act (declared unconstitutional in 1918)

1916—Adamson Act sets up eight-hour day for railroad workers

1920—Transportation Act provides for railroad labor board and ends federal control of railroads

1926—Railway Labor Act provides for national mediation board and prohibits interference or coercion in choice of bargaining representative

1933—Norris-LaGuardia Act prohibits federal injunctions in labor disputes and outlaws "yellow-dog" contracts

1933—National Industrial Recovery Act guarantees employees collective bargaining rights

1935—National Labor Relations Act (Wagner Act) makes the protection of workers' right to organize a national policy and encourages collective bargaining

1938—Fair Labor Standards Act provides minimum wages and time and a half for overtime (more than forty hours a week); later amended to increase minimum hourly wage

1947—Labor-Management Relations Act (Taft-Hartley Act) is passed over veto

D. The history of court decisions involving labor relations is as follows:
1. Commonwealth v. Hunt (1842). The Supreme Court declared it a criminal offense for unions to use economic or social pressures.
2. U.S. v. Adair (1908). The Supreme Court declared unconstitutional Section 10 of the Erdman Act applying to railroad employees, whereby the yellow-dog contract was outlawed, and an employer was forbidden to discharge a worker for union membership.
3. Danbury Case (1908). The Supreme Court declared that the Sherman Act pertained to unions.
4. U.S. v. Hutcheson (1941). The Supreme Court removed unions from the Sherman Act in nonviolent and nonfraudulent economic practices.
5. Allen Bradley Case (1947). The Supreme Court further increased the unions' exemption under the Sherman Act.
6. Lincoln Federal Labor Union v. N. W. Iron Company (1949). The Supreme Court upheld Section 14b of the Taft-Hartley Act.
7. Leonard v. NLRB (1953). A Circuit Court of Appeals interpreted the Taft-Hartley Act as intended to create equality between employer and employee.
8. Immunities of labor unions rest upon a few established features of American labor law as it has developed through legislation and court decisions within a generation: (1) the substantial elimination of what in practical effect is the assured method of enforcing the

law applicable to everyone else; (2) refusal of labor organizations to be treated as legally responsible organizations; (3) not distinguishing unlawful actions by labor organizations, their leaders, and their members, taken outside of the employer-employee relationship from actions taken in that relationship; and (4) committing all matters affecting labor organizations to an administrative agency instead of confining jurisdiction to matters involved in employer-employee relationships. (Roscoe Pound, *Legal Immunities of Labor Unions* [1957], p. 43.)

E. The present extent of regulation by the various state governments and by the federal government may be described as follows:
1. Federal executive agencies which have jurisdiction over questions of labor-management relations are as follows:
    a. The Department of Labor
        (1) The National Labor Relations Board
        (2) The National Railway Labor Board
        (3) The Federal Mediation Service
    b. The Department of Commerce
        (1) The Interstate Commerce Commission
        (2) The Federal Trade Commission
2. "The National Labor-Management Relations Act (1947) leaves much to the states though Congress has refrained from telling us how much. We must spell out from conflicting indications of congressional will the area in which state action is still permissible." (Harold A. Katz, "Two Decades of State Labor Legislation: 1937–1957," *Labor Law Journal*, November 1957, p. 83.)
3. "In the United States the allocation of control over labor relations under the constitutional power of Congress 'to regulate commerce with foreign nations, and among the several states' may be looked upon as the continuing process of adjustment of the federal relation. The power to regulate may be left to the states, or prohibited to the states from time to time as occasion for change arises." (P. R. Hays, "Federalism and Labor Relations in the United States," *University of Pennsylvania Law Review*, June 1954, p. 163.)
4. A more general explanation of the Congressional concept of preemption is found in Taft-Hartley Section 10a which says that the Board's power "shall not be affected by any other means of adjustment or prevention." The Wagner Act provided that this power was exclusive, but this provision was omitted when the act was amended. The Supreme Court observed that the Labor-Management Relations Act "leaves much to the states though Congress has refrained from telling us how much." The function of the pre-emption doctrine is to prevent states from attempting to occupy fields properly within the jurisdiction of the federal government by virtue of its power to promulgate the federal union, as opposed

to a federation of states. (Lloyd Scurlock, "Pre-Emption in Labor Relations," *Texas Law Review,* April 1957, p. 556.)

. . . . .

THE POSITION OF THE AFFIRMATIVE

I. **There** is a need for the federal government to substantially increase its regulation of labor unions, because
   A. There are serious problems in labor union activities, because
      1. There are serious internal problems, because
         a. There are serious problems arising from compulsory membership, because
            (1) "From the democratic standpoint, the important problems arising from compulsory union membership are: (1) the right and opportunity for employees to discard both the union shop and the union if they so desire; (2) the opportunity for union members to exercise their membership rights." (Dallas Jones, "Implications of the 'Right to Work Laws,'" *Institute of Labor Relations,* November 1957, pp. 2–3.)
            (2) "Compulsory membership deprives workers of the freedom to refuse to join an organization that cannot persuade them of the advantages of membership." (*The Union Shop Issue Today,* Industrial Relations Counselors, Inc., Memorandum 127, May 16, 1952, p. 5.)
            (3) "Compulsory membership compels a minority of rank-and-file members at least, to contribute financial support to an organization they may not like or to the policies of which they may be basically opposed." (*Ibid.,* p. 6.)
            (4) "If union officials acquire power by compulsion, rather than by consent of those over whom it is exercised they are freed from the necessity of winning support on the merits of their policies and programs. In such circumstances there does not exist for the membership a genuine and full freedom to withdraw their support from these policies and programs if they should prove harmful to the members. The result of compulsory unionism is that the personal power of union officials is increased, since the membership is a captive membership and one from which allegiance does not have to be won; the financial and economic strength of the organization is assured and increased, despite the good or bad stewardship of the officials." (*The Case for Voluntary Unionism,* United States Chamber of Commerce, 1955, p. 9.)
         b. There are serious problems concerning the voting rights of mem-

bers, because

(1) There has been a significant lack of democratic procedures in unions. ("Conclusions of McClellan Committee," *United States News and World Report*, March 28, 1958, p. 99.)

(2) The McClellan Committee recommended legislation in five areas of union operation, including legislation to insure union democracy. ("Congress Moves to Curb Labor Union Corruption," *Congressional Digest*, November 1958, p. 260.)

(3) "The election of James Hoffa as international president of the Teamsters Union was on the basis of votes of delegates selected in direct violation of the international constitution of the Teamsters Union. A survey by the committee showed that 55 per cent of the delegates to the Miami convention were illegally selected." (*Ibid.*, p. 259.)

(4) "Teamster officials have crushed democracy within the union's ranks. They have rigged elections, hoodwinked and abused their own membership, and lied to them about the conduct of their own affairs. They have advanced the cause of union dictatorship and have perverted or ignored their own constitution and bylaws." ("Senators Report on Two Big Unions," *United States News and World Report*, April 4, 1958, p. 86.)

(5) In the International Union of Operating Engineers, Local 138, William DeKoning, Sr. and Jr., maintained a dictatorship over 4000 members by allowing 800 of the more amenable members to vote, if they "voted right." In the same union, Local 3, officials took 2000 ballots to a mountain hideaway, counted 500 of them, and then awarded 1700 votes to their favored candidate. (John L. McClellan, "What We Learned about Labor Gangsters," *Saturday Evening Post*, May 3, 1958, p. 66.)

(6) "In three unions (the Teamsters, the Bricklayers, and the Street Railway Workers) there were no contests for national office in three years." (Sumner H. Slichter, "New Goals for Unions," *Atlantic Monthly*, December 1958, p. 57.)

(7) "Through fear, intimidation, and violence, the rank and file member has been shorn of a voice in his own union affairs; use of the secret ballot has been denied in many cases." (*Interim Report to U.S. Senate of the Select Committee on Improper Activities in Labor-Management Field*, 85th Congress, 2nd session, 1958, p. 4.)

(8) "The committee finds that in the Bakery and Confectionery Workers International Union actions and statements by Cross at the convention nakedly exposed an authoritarian philosophy abhorrent to legitimate American unionism.

Under his callous direction use of the secret ballot to elect international officers was abandoned, thus further intimidating possible dissenters; the use of parliamentary procedure at the convention was jettisoned after a haughty pronouncement by Cross that it was not made for bakers and confectioners." (*Ibid.*, p. 130.)

c. There are serious problems concerning the rights of members to protest against corrupt and ineffective leadership, because
   (1) "The committee finds that in the Bakery and Confectionery Workers International Union Cross sanctioned the use of violence to discourage dissents within the union and alleged obstructions without, including the beating of a fourteen-year-old son of a bakery owner during a Los Angeles strike. Cross himself was charged by two witnesses with having taken part in the slugging of union critics at the time of the union convention in San Francisco in October, 1956." (*Ibid.*, p. 106.)
   (2) "The committee finds deplorable and arrogant the behavior of the Scranton teamster officials in that rigged elections and multiple voting were numerous. Members who dared to question the leadership were beaten up and threatened." (*Ibid.*, p. 129.)
   (3) "Free speech is still an unrecognized principle in too many unions. In many unions, the right of a minority to even limited access to the union's publication for the purpose of airing alternative views and policies is severely restricted or not recognized at all." ("American Labor Today," *Nation*, December 10, 1955, p. 500.)

d. There are serious problems in the administration of union funds, because
   (1) "With these incredibly loose practices, the misuse of union funds, including outright thefts and borrowings for personal profit, has totaled upwards of $10 million in union funds—dues money—an average of $5 out of the pocket of every member of the unions covered in this report." (*Interim Report to U.S. Senate of the Select Committee on Improper Activities in Labor-Management Field*, 85th Congress, 2nd session, 1958, p. 5.)
   (2) "As an over-all finding from the testimony produced at our hearings, the committee has uncovered the shocking fact that union funds in the excess of $10 million were either stolen, embezzled, or misused by union officials over a period of 15 years, for their own financial gain or for the gain of their friends and associates." (*Ibid.*, p. 1.)
   (3) "The committee finds that Cross, president of the international, played fast and loose with union funds by failing to

provide bills to back up vouchers for some $30,000 in expenditures during 1956 alone, including $25,000 for entertainment, dinners, birthday parties, gratuities, and 'personal expenses.' " (*Ibid.*, p. 129.)

(4) "Dave Beck, former president of the Teamsters, took, not borrowed, more than $370,000 in union funds from the Western Conference of Teamsters Joint Council No. 28 Building Fund and the public relations division of the Joint Council No. 2. The money taken by Beck was used for the construction of his home, swimming pool, and the homes of four of his associates who live near him in the fashionable Sheridan Beach section of Seattle." (*Ibid.*, p. 85.)

(5) "Angelo Inciso, President, Local 286, UAW, took a $3,400 tour of Europe and other trips to South America, Jamaica, Mexico, Puerto Rico, Europe, and California. He also sought relaxation in a $45-a-day hotel in Las Vegas. Inciso has loaned a friend $40,000. He believes he gave one $1,200 diamond ring and a $1,100 diamond ring to friends. Inciso bought $360 diamond money clips from union funds to give to a teamster friend and an attorney." (Senator Paul Douglas, cited in Fletcher Knebel and Clark Mollenhoff, "Can Big Labor Clean House?" *Look,* March 6, 1956, p. 30.)

(6) "Harry Bridges in 1957 (in an unauthorized use of union funds) sent a gift of $3,000 to aid in the formation of an independent union of pier hiring bosses in the port of New York. Bridges was then president of ILWU. During the 1953 and 1954 winter when the Longshoremen were on strike in New York, Jeff Kibre was a go-between for financial aid from the ILWU for the ILA. The rackets subcommittee is in possession of photostats of checks of some of these payments." ("Racketeers and Communist-Dominated Unions," *American Mercury,* April 1959, p. 83.)

e. There are serious problems in the trusteeship system, because

(1) "When misused, trusteeship becomes a form of martial law imposed by a union over its locals. . . . Under such union martial law, the dues payer becomes a second-class union citizen shorn of all rights. He can't assemble with fellow members, or elect officers, or say how his dues money is spent, or what wages he'll work for." (Leslie Velie, "How to Steal a Union," *Readers Digest,* September 1957, p. 131.)

(2) "Two years ago, the Bakers and Confectionery Workers named George Stuart, ex-Bakers vice president, trustee, with orders to clean up a Chicago local. The cleanup became a cleanout of union funds. First, Stuart went on a car-buying binge, spending $17,000 on a Cadillac and a

sports car for himself and a Cadillac for the International president, James Cross. He listed this sum on the union books as 'organization expense.' Cleaning up further, trustee Stuart used various amounts of money exceeding $1,500 for such items as a cocktail set, a hi-fi set, pearl necklace and earrings, etc. This was set down on the books as a 'strike donation.'" (*Ibid.*, pp. 132–133.)

(3) "In the Teamsters Union 108 locals (12 per cent) are held in trusteeship, and the number rises from year to year. In the International Union of Operating Engineers about 16 locals are held under a trusteeship; no one knows for sure how many are held because the officials refuse to report." (*Ibid.*, p. 132.)

(4) "For 28 years, 6,000 members of the Operating Engineers biggest local (Chicago Local 150) have had no elections, no say over pay or working conditions—no nothing. The union is under the thumb of William Maloney, Operating Engineer's president who formed and held the local with the help of Chicago Capone gangsters." (*Ibid.*, p. 132.)

(5) "This union here has been in trusteeship for many years. We have never had the minutes of the meetings given to us. At the end of the year we never know how we stand financially. Our dues are $5 a month, among the highest in the U.S. We can't get out of the trusteeship, though. Union leaders give us one excuse after another. Some of our boys tried to do something about this by getting up a petition. The union heads found out and fined these men a couple of hundred dollars apiece." (Statement by union member in a small eastern city, cited in "Why Union Men are Complaining," *United States News and World Report*, March 29, 1957, p. 31.)

(6) "The international unions surveyed by this committee have flagrantly abused their power to place local unions under trusteeship or supervision." (Conclusions of McClellan Committee, cited in "10 Million Dollars in Union Dues Missed," *United States News and World Report*, March 28, 1958, p. 51.)

. . . . .

THE POSITION OF THE NEGATIVE

. . . . .

IV. A substantial increase in federal regulation of labor unions cannot be instituted without incurring serious disadvantages, because

A. Such a policy would weaken the power of the states to regulate labor unions, because
   1. "Federal legislation may discourage some states from acting because of their reliance upon the federal government to prevent abuse through its disclosure legislation. The effect of the disclosure act, therefore, may be to deter states from acting on their own." (Sar A. Levitan, "Welfare and Pension Plans Disclosure Act," *Labor Law Journal*, November 1958, p. 830.)
   2. The Supreme Court reversed the decision in the case of La Crosse Telephone Corporation v. Wisconsin Labor Board: "Any difference in a state's procedure and timing of the election could easily bring a different result, and the Court's holding avoids this by disallowing state action in all representation cases within the Board's jurisdiction." (Lloyd Scurlock, "Pre-Emption in Labor Relations," *Texas Law Review*, April, 1957, p. 557.)
A'. Weakening the power of the states to regulate labor unions constitutes a serious disadvantage, because
   1. "Federalism is based on the principle of reducing the dangers of governmental power by keeping it widely distributed. States serve as centers of power to prevent its concentration in the national government which might otherwise become uncontrollable and a threat to freedom." (Clyde W. Summers, "The Role of Legislation in Internal Union Affairs," *Labor Law Journal*, March 1959, p. 160.)
   2. "Multiform state legislation could test various proposals, provide experiments to guide us in evolving sound solutions, and limit the impact of our miscalculations. A mistaken remedy at the federal level could have drastic repercussions on the whole labor movement." (*Ibid.*, pp. 160–161.)
B. Such a policy would weaken the power of labor unions, because
   1. Such a policy would weaken the strength and stability of union membership, because
      a. Federal legislation might wipe out some of the union member's protection without providing an adequate substitute. (*Ibid.*, p. 161.)
      b. "Perhaps the biggest effect of right-to-work laws has been to hamper organizing by weak unions. In Iowa, says Federation of Labor president Ray Mills, 'It has become almost impossible to organize areas where workers are in an especially weak position.' In Utah, which has probably the only right-to-work law with real teeth in it, unionists complain that it is hard to organize workers at all. In fact, there has not been an organized strike or picket line for the last three years." (Editorial, *Time*, November 28, 1958, p. 88.)
      c. Secretary of Labor Mitchell stated that right-to-work laws restrict union security and undermine the basic strength of

labor organizations. ("Whose Right to Work?" *Senior Scholastic,* April 5, 1957, p. 8.)
  d. Senator John F. Kennedy has worried that "legislators with good intentions will file legislation in a shotgun fashion . . . which will permanently injure honest labor union members and officials." (Sar A. Levitan, "A Federal Assist to Insure the Rights of Union Members," *Labor Law Journal,* February, 1959, p. 80.)
1′. Weakening the strength and stability of union membership constitutes a serious disadvantage, because
  a. "The bill would provide governmental hands that would constantly probe into the viscera of every labor union. If anyone had proposed legislation of a similar nature with respect to the internal operations of corporations, employer associations, etc., there would have been universal editorial condemnation upon the ground that this would be a step toward fascism." (Comment by Henry Mayer on a bill proposed by Senator McClellan, "Public Regulation of Internal Union Affairs," *Ibid.,* February 1959, p. 90.)
  b. The real purpose of the right-to-work law is union busting. ("Whose Right to Work?" *Senior Scholastic,* April 5, 1957, p. 8.)
2. Such a policy would weaken the power of the unions to bargain effectively, because
  a. Secretary of Labor Mitchell pointed out that right-to-work laws result in undesirable and unnecessary limitations upon the freedom of workers and their employers to bargain collectively. (*Ibid.,* p. 8.)
  b. "Centralized collective bargaining calls for authority by the national officers to enforce their commitments in labor-management negotiations without hindrance by governmental interference." (Sar A. Levitan, "A Federal Assist to Insure the Rights of Union Members," *Labor Law Journal,* February 1959, p. 84.)
2′. Weakening the power of the unions to bargain effectively constitutes a serious disadvantage, because
  a. "Labor unions must have power—economic, social, and political power—if they are to carry out the social responsibilities that the very form of modern society places upon them." (William J. Smith, "Labor's Wrongs and Rights," *The Commonweal,* March 13, 1959, p. 620.)
  b. "Unless a union is strong it has little bargaining power with management. And without strong bargaining power, it could not achieve favorable working conditions." ("Whose Right to Work?" *Senior Scholastic,* April 5, 1957, p. 8.)
C. Such a policy would endanger the maintenance of stable industrial

relations, because
1. Without a union shop agreement, many businesses could not enjoy stable labor relations, which permit prosperity. (*Ibid.*, p. 8.)
2. John W. McConnell of the United States Mediation and Conciliation Service said that right-to-work laws do not improve the organization and responsibility of labor. ("Right to Work Laws," *Time*, November 24, 1958, p. 88.)
3. The union shop eliminates the "free rider" who enjoys the benefits of union representation without sharing the cost. (*The Union Shop Issue Today*, Industrial Relations Counselors, Inc., Memorandum 127, May 16, 1952, p. 4.)

C'. Endangering the maintenance of stable industrial relations constitutes a serious disadvantage, because
1. The union shop permits possible tempering of union demands and practices. (*Ibid.*, p. 4.)
2. The union shop increases the possibility of more constructive relations with labor leaders who can afford to be less militant, with their interests thus secured. (*Ibid.*)
3. The union shop reduces the probability of organizing campaigns by rival unions, with consequent disruption in the work force. (*Ibid.*)
4. "Mr. Meyers did find that one effect of the ban on union security measures, 'and perhaps its most important one,' has been to place elected union leaders much more at the mercy of members who insist that impossible demands be made on the employer as the price of their continued support." (Professor Frederic Meyers, University of California, cited in "Report on Right-to-Work," *The Commonweal*, February 27, 1959, p. 557.)

# Index

Addison, Joseph, 33
Adelphi Society, 303
Adler, Mortimer, 13, 17, 77
Affirmative; *see* Attack and defense, Case, Dispute
American Forensic Association, 343
   debate ballot of, 345
Analogy
   claim in, 143
   claims established by, 144
   diagramed, 143
   distinguished from parallel case, 142-43
   evidence in, 143, 144
   inadequate, 179
   qualifier in, 144
   reservations in, 144
   support for warrant in, 143
   warrant in, 143
Analyzing the proposition
   and the brief, 228-29
   definition of terms
      methods of definition, 215-17
      principles of definition, 214-15
   determining issues, 217-28
      in propositions of definition, 219-20
      in propositions of fact, 220-21
      in propositions of policy, 223-28
      in propositions of value, 221-23
   historical background, 213-14
   immediate causes, 212-13
   stock issues, 223
      need for change, 224-26
      disadvantages, 227-28
      practicability, 226-27
Appeals
   direction of, 10-11
   irrelevant
      to emotion, 173
      to humor, 173
      to ignorance of opposite, 174
      to popular prejudice, 173-74
      to tradition, 173
Approach, formulating the, 66-67
Argumentation
   and logic, 28
   and psychology, 28
   and rhetoric, 28
Arguments, persuasive, 34; *see also* Evidence

Aristotle, 19, 20, 125, 157, 167, 268
Asch, Solomon E., 246
Attack and defense
   integration of
      affirmative constructive, 263
      affirmative rebuttal, 265, 266
      negative constructive, 262-63, 264
      negative rebuttal, 264-65, 265-66
   methods of
      counterproofs, 258
      deficiencies in proof, 254-55
      dilemma, 260-61
      exposing inconsistency, 259-60
      insufficiency of a series, 257-58
      reducing to absurdity, 256-57
      turning the tables, 255-56
   objective of, 253
   procedure in, 253-54
Auer, J. Jeffery, 24
Authoritative proofs, 158-62
   claim in, 159
   claims established by, 161-62
   criteria for witnesses, 159-60
   in college debating, 160
   defined, 125
   diagramed, 159, 239
   distinguished from substantive proofs, 158
   evidence in, 159
   purpose of, 159
   qualifier in, 161
   reservations in, 161
   speaker as witness, 161
   support for warrant in, 159-60
   warrant in, 159
      inadequate warrant in, 181-82

Bagehot, Walter, 5, 30
Baird, A. Craig, 21, 25
Ballots, 344, 345, 348
Beecher, Henry Ward, 274
Belief
   as apprehension and feeling, 191
   as compulsory, 197-98
   and the debater's task, 203-06
   definition of, 190-93
   distinguished from doubt, 191-93
   ego- and object-oriented, 198-200, 205-06
   evaluation of
      health dimension, 200-02

413

## 414  INDEX

Belief (*continued*)
    validity dimension, 202-03
    existing beliefs, 203-04
    pathological, 200-02
    and proof deficiencies, 186
    sources of, 194-96, 204-05
        authority, 194-95
        experience, 194
        other beliefs, 195-96
    structure of, 196-203
        axes of, 196-97
        components of, 196-97
    why men believe, 193
Bentham, Jeremy, 168, 188
Benton, Thomas Hart, 289
Berlo, David K., 246
Bibliography notes; *see* Notes
Bingham, Walter Van Dyke, 41
Biographical dictionaries; *see* Libraries
Black, Max, 189
Blair, Hugh, 30
Books; *see* Libraries
Borah, William E., 289
Braden, Waldo W., 24, 285
Brandenburg, Earnest, 24
Brembeck, Winston L., 157
Brentano, F., 191
Brewer, David J., 290
Brief, the
    defined, 234
    introduction to, 228-30
    model, 237-38, 393-412
    structure of, 234
        parallel and series circuits, 234-36
Brigance, William Norwood, 296, 336
Brockriede, Wayne, 108, 157, 331, 334, 336
Brown University, 302
Bryan, William Jennings, 292
Bucknell College, 334
Buffon, 297
Burden of going forward; *see* Dispute
Burden of proof; *see* Dispute
    does not shift, 87
Burke, Edmund, 21, 274-75

Calhoun, John C., 279-80
Cambridge University, 332
Campbell, George, 235
Capp, Glenn R., 250
Case
    building the, 234-44
    circuits; *see* Proof-circuits
    criteria for selecting proofs, 245-49
    criteria of strength, 233
    defined, 233
    developing the affirmative, 240-42
    propositions of definition, fact, and value, 240-41, 246-47
    propositions of policy, 241-42, 247-49
    developing the negative, 242-45
        counterplan, 243-44

    propositions of definition, fact, and value, 242-43, 246-47
    propositions of policy, 243-44, 247-49
    *status quo*, 243
    phases of, 233-34
        assembling the proofs, 234-42
        selecting the proofs, 245-49
    *prima facie*, 86, 90, 240, 242
Castell, Alburey, 108
Cause
    argument from, 126-31
        claim in, 127-29
        claims established by, 131
        diagramed, 129
        evidence in, 127, 129
        reliability of, 128-29
        reservations in, 128, 130
        support for warrant in, 127, 130
        warrant in, 127, 129
    cause to effect, 126-29
    counteracting cause, 128
    effect to cause, 129-30
    insufficient cause, 177-78
    intervening cause, 128
    methods of John Stuart Mill for detecting, 130-31
Cause to effect; *see* Cause
Central tendencies, 153-54
    qualifier in, 154
        standard deviation, 154
    reservations in, 154
Chatham, Lord, 275
Chesterfield, Lord, 269
Chicago, University of, 303
Churchill, Winston, 39
Cicero, Marcus Tullius, 30, 97, 292, 297
Claims; *see also* Proof, Proof deficiencies
    actuative, 102, 247-48
    defined, 102
    definitive, 102
    designative, 102
    evaluative, 102, 247
Clarke, Edwin Leavitt, 123
Classification
    assumptions underlying, 146
    claim in, 145
    claims established by, 147
    defined, 145
    diagramed, 145
    evidence in, 145
    inadequate, 179-80
    qualifiers in, 145, 147
    reservations in, 146-47
    support for warrant in, 146
    warrant in, 145, 146
Clevenger, Theodore, Jr., 23
Clifford, W. K., 34
Cohen, Morris, 14, 16, 192
College debate
    competition in, 304, 307-10

debating both sides of a proposition, 313-15
and development of skills, 304
enforcement of ethical practices, 312-13
handbooks, 38, 310-11
history of, 301-04
  courses in, 302
  development of the tournament, 303-04
  forum debates, 303
  honorary forensic societies, 303
  intercollegiate, 302-03
  literary societies, 302
  syllogistic disputation, 302
  triangular leagues, 303
judging; *see* Evaluating college debate
kinds of activities, 305-07
objectives of, 304-05
philosophic problems in, 305-14
pitfalls of, 308-10
questions per year, 311-12
situations, 330-34
  debate tournaments, 330-31
  forensic experience progression, 331-32
  mock assembly, 333
  on-campus debates, 332
  radio and television debate, 333-34
  speakers' bureau, 332-33
tournaments (debate), 303-04, 308
  advantages of, 305-06
  criticisms of, 306
types of, 318-30
  cross-examination, 320-21
  direct clash, 324-25
  legislative, 325-28
  multilateral, 328-30
  traditional, 318-20
Columbia University, 334
Competition; *see* College debate
Compromise; *see* Internal method
Conference style of debate, 330
Conflict
  attitudes and procedures of, 19
  role in debate, 20
Congressional style of debate, 326
Cooper, Lane, 29
Cornell University, 302
Corry, Isaac, 290
Counterplan, 243-44
Cripe, Nicholas M., 313, 385
Critical deliberation, 16-17
  and evaluation of college debate, 347-48
Critical instruments, 6-7
  diagramed, 11
Critiques; *see* Evaluating college debate
Cross-examination debate; *see* College debate
Current affairs
  keeping up with, 45
  summaries of, 53-54

Darrow, Clarence, 289
Davis, William H., 304
Debate
  ballots, 344-45
  conflict in, 19-22
  controls in, 16-17
  as a cooperative enterprise, 19-22
  as a critical instrument, 16-17, 19
  criticisms of, 16
  decisions in, 92
  defined, 10
  function of, 14-15
  learning to, 26-28
  and a liberal education, 25-26
  as a mode of investigation, 18-19
  purpose of, 21, 66
  rationale of, 15
  and scientist's hypothesis, 21
  as self-regulative, 17
  types of; *see* College debate
Debater, the
  attitude of, 294-95
  and belief, 203-06
  in a democracy, 25
  distinguished from persuader, 18
  duties of, 261-66
  exploitation of, 308-09
  moral obligation of, 65
  personal knowledge of, 36-37
  as research worker, 34-36
  and star system, 309
Decision, points for, 92
Decisions
  collective 6, 9
    methods for making, 7
  in college debate, 338-42
  critical
    in a democracy, 25
    as fact-centered, 33
  flexibility of, 4
  as the ideal, 5
  instruments of, 5-6
  methods for making, 7-11
  reliability of, 3
  Stevenson on, 5
  worthy of man, 4-5
Defense; *see* Attack and defense
Definition; *see* Analyzing the proposition
Definitive claims; *see* Claims
Delivery; *see also* style
  absence of distractions, 292-93
  attractiveness in, 292-95
    bodily responsiveness, 293-94
    conversational spirit, 294
    courteous and objective attitude, 294-95
    vocal variety, 293
  clarity in
    bodily responsiveness, 282
    test of, 283-284
    voice, 281-82
  criteria of effectiveness, 270

Delivery (*continued*)
  in debate ratings, 345-46
  importance of, 269-70
  use of notes, 282-83
Delta Sigma Rho, 303, 333
Denver, University of, 331
Designative claims; *see* Claims
Dewey, John, 3, 16, 77, 192, 197
Dialectic, 8-9
Dickens, Milton, 336
Dictionaries; *see* Biographical dictionaries
Diem, W. R., 303
Direct evidence; *see* Evidence
Discussion, 9
  distinguished from dialectic, 9
Dispute
  concepts in
    affirmative, 93
    burden of going forward, 85-86
    burden of proof, 84-85
    issues, 88-92
      actual and contested, 90
      defined, 89
      as discovered, 92
      and evaluation, 339
      inherent in question, 90-92
    negative, 93
    points for decision, 92-93, 339
    position, 94
    presumption, 82-84
    *prima facie* case, 86, 240-41
    question, 88
    side, 93-94
  hypothetical example of, 81 ff.
  observations on, 82
  illustrative diagram, 95
Diversionary proofs, 174-76
Documents; *see* Libraries
Doubt; *see* Belief
Douglas, Stephen A., 289
Drum, Dale D., 23
Dyslogistic statements; *see* Emotional language

Edney, Clarence W., 308
Edwards, Paul, 222, 232
Effect to cause; *see* Cause
Ehninger, Douglas, 108, 157, 316, 336
Elliott, Harrison S., 16
Emerson, James G., 316
Emotional mode; *see* Motivational proofs
Encyclopedias; *see* Libraries
Enthymeme; *see* Classification
Esch, Marvin, 347
Ethic of evidence; *see* Evidence
*Ethos; see* Authoritative proofs
Eubank, Wayne C., 250
Eulogistic statements; *see* Emotional language
Evaluating college debate
  and critical deliberation, 347

critiques
  oral, 346
  written, 347-48
decisions, 338-42
  audience vote, 340
  basis for, 338-39
  shift of opinion, 340-41
judges
  and critical attitude, 347-48
  juryman vote, 338, 346
  qualities of, 341-42
  role of, 16-17, 341
  who should serve as, 340
quality ratings
  consistency, 346
  itemized ratings, 343
  sample ballots, 344-45
  single score method, 343
reason for, 338
Evaluative claims; *see* Claims
Evidence
  classified as
    direct or circumstantial, 112-13
    eager or reluctant, 115
    original or hearsay, 111-12
    positive or negative, 114-15
    pre-appointed or casual, 113-14
    real or personal, 110-11
    written or unwritten, 114
  deficient, 169
  defined, 100, 110
  presentation of, 101, 116-21
    ethic of, 116-18
    rhetoric of, 118-21
  range of, 100
  relation of ethic and rhetoric of evidence, 121
  role of fact and opinion in, 100
  verifiability continuum, 100
Ewbank, Henry Lee, 24
Example, argument from; *see* Parallel case
Examples, 278-79
Experience
  and belief; *see* Belief
  as source of knowledge, 36-37
Experimental methods; *see* Mill, John Stuart
Experts, 65
  consultation with, 37, 65
  correspondence with, 38
  interviews with, 37
  principles of, 37
External method of decision making, 9-11
  diagramed, 11

Fallacies; *see* Proof deficiencies
Fearnside, W. Ward, 189
Fernald, James C., 271
Flesch, Rudolf, 124
Forensic experience progression; *see* College debate

Forum debates; *see* College debate
Foster, William T., 41, 268
Franzke, Albert, 337
Freeman, Roger, 181
Frye, Albert Myrton, 13
Fuge, Lloyd H., 336

Gehring, Mary Louise, 285
Generalization, 134-38
  claim in, 134
  claims established by, 138
  criteria for support, 135-37
  defined, 134
  designative claim, 138
  diagramed, 135, 142
  evaluative claim, 138
  evidence in, 134
  evidence sample, 134-37
    inadequate, 178-79
  qualifier in, 138
  reservations in, 137-38
    counter-generalization, 137
    negative instances, 137-38
  support for warrant, 135
  warrant in, 134
Genung, John, 158
*Genus et differentia; see* Definition
Giffin, Kim, 331, 343
Gladstone, William Ewart, 119
Grattan, Henry, 290
Gray, Stanley J., 336
Griswold, A. Whitney, 5
Gulley, Halbert E., 23, 330
Guthrie, Warren, 324, 336

Haiman, Franklyn S., 8
Hance, Kenneth G., 16, 21, 24
Handbooks; *see* College debate
Harvard University, 302, 303
Hearsay evidence; *see* Evidence
Heckling debate, 323-24
Henry, Patrick, 142
Hillway, Tyrus, 63
Hinman Society, 303
Hitler, 5, 20
Hockett, Homer Carey, 77
Holther, William B., 189
Hopkins, Thomas, 347
Howell, Wilbur Samuel, 286
Howell, William S., 157
Huber, Robert, 250
Hudson, Hoyt, 26
Huff, Darrel, 152, 189
Hultzén, Lee S., 223, 232
Hume, David, 191, 198
Huxley, Aldous, 211

Illinois College, 303
Illinois, University of, 327, 334
Indexes to newspapers and periodicals; *see* Libraries
Information
  obtaining, 42, 45
  from correspondence, 38-39
  from interviews, 37-38
  from printed sources; *see* Libraries
Information theory, 281
Internal method of decision making
  and capitulation, 7
  and compromise, 7
  and consensus, 7
  diagramed, 11
  as dialectic, 8
  as discussion, 9
International debating, 332
Interviews, 37-38
Intramural debating, 332
Issues, 74, 88-92, 217-28, 248, 253; *see also* Analyzing the proposition, Dispute

James, Henry, 269
James, Herbert L., 268
James, William, 17, 191, 192, 193, 194, 207, 279
Jefferson, Thomas, 141
Johnson, Samuel, 42
Judging college debate; *see* Evaluating college debate
Judgment, 8, 16, 35
Juryman vote; *see* Evaluating college debate

Kirkpatrick Chapel, 303
Knox College, 303
Krueger, Richard F., 343

Larrabee, Harold A., 207
Laycock, Craven, 86, 97, 157
Lee, Irving J., 13
Legislative debate; *see* College debate
Levi, Albert William, 13
Libraries, 42
  card catalogue, 56-58
  documents
    federal, 46-48
    foreign, 48
    municipal, county, and state, 46
  fugitive materials, 49
  general books, 42-43
  newspapers and periodicals, 43-45
    authoritativeness and objectivity of, 45
    types of, 44
  reference works, 49-55
    biographical dictionaries, 51-52
    books of facts and figures, 52-53
    encyclopedias, 50-51
    indexes to newspapers, periodicals, and books, 54-55
    special publications for debate, 55-56
    summaries of current affairs, 53-54
Lincoln, Abraham, 34, 279-80, 289, 292
Lippmann, Walter, 30, 81
*Literary Digest,* 150

## 418  INDEX

Literary societies; *see* College debate
Logic, 8; *see also* Argumentation
*Logos; see* Substantive proof

Mander, A. E., 190, 207
Marjarum, E. Wayne, 77
Martin, Everett Dean, 30
McBurney, James H., 16, 21, 24
McDougall, William, 192, 197, 198
McReynolds, Charles, 336
Median; *see* Central tendencies
Meyer, Martin, 13
Michigan, University of, 302, 303, 334
Michigan State University, 334
Michigan style of debate, 322-23
Mill, James, 191
Mill, John Stuart, 130, 131, 157, 191, 252
  experimental methods of, 130-31
Miller, Clyde R., 13
Miller, N. Edd, 307, 334
Milton, John, 318
Mock assembly style of debate, 326
Mock trial style of debate, 324
Monroe, Alan, 341
Montague, W. P., 193, 208
Montana style of debate, 323
Moore, Bruce Victor, 41
Motivational proofs, 162-66, 239, 247
  claim in, 163
  claims established by, 165-66
  defined, 126
  diagramed, 163, 165, 239
  distinguished from substantive proofs, 158
  emotional mode, 162
  evidence in, 163
  inadequate, 182-83
  limitations of, 162-63
  qualifier in, 164-66
  reservations in, 164
  support for warrant in, 164
  warrant in, 163, 164
Multilateral debate; *see* College debate
Multiple fallacy principle, 169
Murphy, Richard, 312, 313, 314, 316, 376, 389

Nagel, Ernest, 16
Nebergall, Roger, 100, 244, 250
Need; *see* Stock issues
Negative evidence; *see* Evidence
Negative instances; *see* Generalization
Negative side; *see* Case, Dispute
Neiswanger, William A., 157
Newman, John Henry, 25
Newman, Robert P., 250, 336
Newspapers; *see* Libraries
New York University, 303
Nichols, Egbert Ray, 317
*Non sequitur*, 170
North Carolina State College, 325
Northwestern University, 303, 334

Note-taking
  accuracy and completeness, **68**
  how to, 67-68
  suggestions for, 63-66
Notes
  filing of, 74
  issue label on, 74
  types of
    bibliography, 69-70
    biography, 70-71
    subject-matter, 71-72
  use of; *see* Delivery

O'Brien, Joseph F., 333, 336
Oldfield, R. C., 41
O'Neill, James M., 86, 97, 157, 338, 346, 350
Ong, Walter J., S.J., 8
Oregon style of debate, 321-22
Orr, Frederick, 337
Oxford University, 332

Packard, Vance, 13
Paget, Edwin H., 337
Parallel case
  claim in, 139
  claims established by, 141
  defined, 139
  diagramed, 139, 142
  distinguished from generalization, 142
  estimating strength of claim in, 140-41
  evidence in, 139
  inadequate, 179
  invented parallels, 141-42
  proof by a collection of parallel cases, 142
  qualifier in, 141
  real parallels, 141-42
  reservations in, 140-41
  support for warrant in, 140
  warrant in, 139
Parallel circuits; *see* Proof, circuits
Parliamentary style of debate, 326-28
Pathological beliefs; *see* Belief
*Pathos; see* Motivational proofs
Peiehessophian Society, 303
Pericles, 3
Periodicals; *see* Libraries
Perry, Ralph Barton, 193
Persuasion, 18
Persuasive prefaces, 171
Phi Alpha Society, 303
Phillips, A. E., 194
Philomathean Society, 303
Pi Kappa Delta, 303
Pillsbury, W. P., 193
Plato, 8, 25, 119
Porter, Darrel R., 337
Portland style of debate, 329-30
*Post hoc* fallacy, 177
Presumption; *see* Dispute
Previews, 278

*Prima facie* case; *see* Dispute
Problem-solving debate, 328-29
Pronouncing Society, 302
Proof; *see also* Authoritative proofs, Motivational proofs, Substantive proofs
  circuits, 234-40
    and the brief, 236-38
    choosing, 238-40
    diagramed, 235
    insufficiency of, 257-58
  criteria for selecting, 245-49
  defined, 99
  detecting deficiencies in; *see* Proof deficiencies
  elements of, 99-107
    claim, 102
    evidence; *see* Evidence
    qualifier, 106-07
    relationships among, 103-05, 107
    reservations, 106
    support for warrant, 105-06
    warrant, 101, 125
  main proof line, 103
  parallel, 235, 257
  series, 235, 257
  Toulmin's analysis of, 98-99
Proof deficiencies
  and belief, 186
  deficient evidence, 169
  deficient warrants, 177-83
  ignored reservations, 183-85
  overstated claims, 184-85
  unwarranted claims, 170-76
    begging the question, 171-72
    ignoring the question, 172-76
    missing links, 170-71
Propositions
  debating both sides of, 313-15
  of definition, 218, 219-20, 240-41, 242-43, 246-47
  of fact, 218, 220-21, 240-41, 242-43, 246-47
  of policy, 219, 223, 241-42, 243-45, 247-49
  of value, 219, 221-23, 240-41, 242-43, 246-47
Protagoras of Abdera, 301
Psychology; *see* Argumentation

Questions, 88, 311-12
  asking and answering, 320-21
  inferential, 15
  informative, 15
  subsidiary, 92
Quintilian, 286, 287

Radio and television debate, 333-34
Ratings; *see* Evaluating college debate
Rationalization, 200-01
Rebuttal; *see* Attack and defense
Reference works; *see* Libraries

Refutation; *see also* Attack and defense and conflict, 20
  shotgun, 254
Reid, Loren, 119
Research, 34-36
  keeping up to date, 45
  processes of, 36-39
Reservations; *see* Proof, Proof deficiencies
Reynolds, Ota Thomas, 317
Rhetoric; *see* Argumentation
Rhetoric of evidence; *see* Evidence
Robinson, James L., 251
Roosevelt, Franklin D., 39, 275, 291, 292
Russell, Bertrand, 121, 193, 197

Sarett, Alma Johnson, 41
Sarett, Lew, 41
Saunders, T. Bailey, 175
Scales, Robert L., 86, 97, 157
Schiller, F. S. C., 108
Schmitz, R. Morel, 77
Schopenhauer, Arthur, 175, 189, 288
Schramm, Wilbur, 13
Schulter, W. C., 62
Scott, Robert L., 97, 342
Sears, Donald A., 62
Selective reporting; *see* Ethic of evidence
Seneca, 338
Series circuits; *see* Proof, circuits
Shaw, Warren C., 232
Sherif, Muzafer, 246
Shift of opinion; *see* Evaluating college debate
Shrivenham University, 330
Sign
  claim in, 132
  claims established by, 134
  diagramed, 132
  distinguished from cause, 131-32
  evidence in, 132
  inadequate, 178
  infallible, 134
  qualifier in, 133-34
  reservations in, 133
  support for warrant in, 133
  warrant in, 132
Sinclair Oil Company, 334
Sorites, 235
Soule, Pierre, 291
Southwestern College, 303
Speakers Bureau, 332-33
Speaking Club, 302
Spencer, Herbert, 286
Split-team debating, 319-20
Spy Club, 302
Stasheff, Edward, 334
Statistics
  claims established by, 154
  comparisons, 151-53
  defined, 148
  evidence in, 148

420    INDEX

Statistics (*continued*)
  inadequate, 180-81
  method of interpreting, 148
  methods of managing, 149-54
    counting and measuring, 149-51
    determining central tendencies, 153-54
    making comparisons, 151-53
  qualifier in, 150, 153, 154
  presentation of, 120
  reservations in, 150, 153, 154
  and samples, 149-50
  source of, 148
  warrant in, 149
*Status quo,* 243
Stevenson, Adlai, 5
Stevenson, Allan H., 62, 78
Stock issues, 223-28, 241-42
Stout, G. F., 198
Stratagems; *see* Proof deficiencies
Strother, David B., 334, 336
Style; *see also* Delivery
  attractiveness in, 287-92
  clarity in, 270-80
  criteria of effectiveness, 270
  importance of in debate, 269-70
  paragraphs and longer units, 276-79
  sentences, 274-76
Subject-matter background
  building a, 63-66
  importance of, 33-36
  sources of, 36-39
Subsidiary questions, 92
Substantive proofs
  characteristics of, 126
  claims established by, 155
  defined, 125
  patterns of, 126-54; *see also* Analogy, Cause, Classification, Generalization, Parallel case, Sign, Statistics
Summaries, 278
Support for warrant; *see* Proof
Swift, Jonathan, 286, 290
Syllogism; *see* Classification
Syllogistic disputation; *see* College debate
Symposium style of debate, 329-30
Syracuse University, 333

Taft, Robert, 289
Tau Kappa Alpha, 303

Television debate; *see* Radio and television debate
Thompson, Wayne N., 24, 317
Thouless, Robert H., 189
Toulmin, Stephen, 6, 98, 109, 125
Tournaments; *see* College debate
Toynbee, Arnold J., 301
Tri Kappa Society, 303
Trueblood, David Elton, 110
Trueblood, Thomas C., 302, 317
Twain, Mark, 271

Unethical practices; *see* Ethic of evidence, College debate
Unwarranted claims; *see* Proof deficiencies
Unwritten evidence; *see* Evidence

Visual aids, 111, 120
Vocal variety; *see* Delivery

Wabash College, 332
Wallace, Karl, 317
Warrant; *see* Proof, Proof deficiencies
Washington, University of, 328
Wayne State University, 334, 347
  debate ballot, 348
Webster, Daniel, 269, 289, 292
Wells, Hugh M., 338, 346, 350
Western Conference Debate League, 327, 331
Western Reserve University, 334
Whately, Richard, 84, 97, 131, 141, 157, 167, 297
Wigley, Joseph, 340
Wigmore, John Henry, 97
Williams, Cecil B., 62, 78
Wilson, Thomas, 287
Wilson, Woodrow, 141, 269, 292
Winans, James A., 158, 163
Wisconsin, University of, 302
Witnesses; *see* Authoritative proofs
Woodward ballot; *see* Shift of opinion
Woodward, Howard, 340
Woolbert, Charles H., 167, 233, 251
Written evidence; *see* Evidence

Yale University, 303
Yeager, Willard Hayes, 41

Zeisel, Hans, 157